CAREERSMARTS

Jobs with a Future

CAREER SMARTS

JOBS WITH A FUTURE

Martin Yate

BALLANTINE BOOKS · NEW YORK

Copyright © 1997 by Martin Yate

All rights reserved under International and Pan-American Copyright Conventions. Published in the United States by Ballantine Books, a division of Random House, Inc., New York, and simultaneously in Canada by Random House of Canada Limited, Toronto.

http://www.randomhouse.com

Library of Congress Catalog Card Number: 96-95205

ISBN: 0-345-39595-6

Cover design by Michele Brinson

Manufactured in the United States of America
First Edition: February 1997
10 9 8 7 6 5 4 3 2

This book is dedicated to
your
sense of direction

CONTENTS

ACKNOWLEDGMENTS

I couldn't have done this book without the help and immense effort expended by David Caruso, Ph.D., Stacey Miller, and Jill Yate. Their contributions were invaluable and made this book what it is.

This book was also an education in ways I never anticipated. My thanks to the following for their role in that education: Robert Levine, Esq., David Newman, Krishna Joshi, Joëlle Delbourgo, Elizabeth Zack, and Beth Bortz. Also, for their research work: Joann Bruening, Marcie Fraulo, Anna Gray Anderson, John Vergara, and Inga Weimer. Special thanks to copyeditor Janet Fletcher.

CAREERSMARTS

Jobs with a Future

PART ONE

ABOUT THE JOBS AND YOUR CAREER FUTURE

INTRODUCTION

How to Find a
Sensible Career Direction

This book is about finding work: work you can do, and work you will enjoy. This book is about building a profession in jobs that are going to be in demand *tomorrow*. So even if you cannot rely on any single employer to guarantee your employment, you can guarantee your own employability by choosing a profession and work experience that will be in demand by many other employers. In the uncertainties of today's new world of work, ensuring your ongoing employability is critical to your economic survival.

CareerSmarts: Jobs with a Future gives you a comprehensive view of over 175 professional jobs, all of which, according to federal statistics, offer steady growth over the coming years.

I'll carefully describe the responsibilities of each job, what it pays, what the workday is like, and the educational background and professional skill sets needed to land that job. I'll tell you how a job's growth compares with that of other jobs, and share what insiders (company presidents, professional association executives, and headhunters) believe the future holds for the profession tomorrow.

This book will not only give you a good idea of how much you will enjoy the day-to-day work life that goes with each particular job, but help you get a clear understanding of your ability to perform any of the jobs.

Finding the Job That Fits
Your Unique Personal Preferences

Will you *like* the work? You have unique needs that, when you choose the wrong job, can make your working hours a living hell. Conversely, when you match your preferences to the realities of a job, your work life can become more meaningful and fulfilling.

For example, some people don't like surprises and a pressure cooker atmosphere at work; they don't enjoy a job, or a profession, that creates stress in their lives. For these people, being able to predict what the workday is going to be like, and rarely having those predictions fail, is important for their happiness at work. But for others, having a job like this spells monotony and boredom. In *CareerSmarts: Jobs with a Future*, I have developed a way—through something called an *Affinity Profile*—that you can measure your personal preferences in each of these six critical areas:

- the degree of stress and challenge you like in your life
- the degree of autonomy you enjoy
- the amount of variety you need
- the opportunity for creativity a job offers
- your need to make a difference with your work
- your preferred social environment

Once you've done this self-analysis, you'll find you can match your personal preferences with a chart that rates the workplace realities of each job. The result? You'll know instantly if a job will be heaven or hell for you, or what the trade-offs will be that put it somewhere in between.

Do You Have the Professional
Competencies to Succeed?

It is one thing to discover that you might enjoy a particular kind of work; it is another thing entirely to recognize whether or not you can land a job in that field, and continue to prosper once you are working in the profession. This is why I have carefully evaluated each job in the book against an array of *professional competencies*[1] required in varying degrees in all modern jobs. Each job has been evaluated to measure its demands for:

1. Explanations of terms appear in Chapter 2.

- *abstraction skills*, or proficiency at analyzing patterns of information
- *system-thinking skills*, or the ability to understand the big picture
- *experimentation*
- *reasoning, math, and language proficiency*
- *ability to focus on a goal*
- *positive outlook*
- *ability to influence others*
- *smart decisions*
- *intellectual flexibility*
- *open-mindedness*
- *organization skills*
- *sense of informed risk*
- *leadership*
- *emotional intelligence*

Then (in the same way that you will discover your personal preferences for the workplace), I'll show you how—through a *Mobility Profile*—to rate yourself in each of these sought-after professional competencies, and subsequently how to compare your ratings with professional competencies required for each different job.

This process will not only help you instantly to match your professional skills against the needs of any particular job, but it will also help you to evaluate your professional mobility in an insecure world of work: the more developed each of your professional skill sets, the wider your professional horizons will be.

Your Career Future

Now, for the first time, you can have an intelligent look at what is likely to happen to your economic future given a specific career choice. You can see (by matching your personal Mobility Profile with the corresponding Professional Competencies chart that accompanies each job) if you have what it takes to do that job, or which skills you'll need to develop to get there, and you can judge (by matching your Affinity Profile with the corresponding Workplace Realities chart that accompanies each job) whether or not you will like the work once the excitement of a new job has been replaced by daily routine.

You can also use your personal Mobility Profile to evaluate just what your real-world options might be in the event of your being caught in a downsizing at your place of work. In this "what if" scenario, you can page through the book to *instantly* match your professional competencies with the in-demand jobs of today and tomorrow. At the same time you can use your Affinity Profile (which helps you measure your personal preferences) to separate the jobs you could and would enjoy doing from those you could do but would dislike because of your personal preferences.

Unhappy at work? You can combine the information from your Mobility and Affinity Profiles to help pinpoint your feelings of unhappiness or insecurity in your current job. With this knowledge you become empowered to make changes in your life: you might choose to develop needed skills to make your job more secure, or to initiate a search for a job that will give you a more supportive working environment.

Taken together, these tools allow you to set professional career courses that are rewarding and practical. They allow you to stack the odds just a little more in your favor as you plan your career—and they can afford you a sense of direction when a previously secure career comes crashing down around your ears.

This doesn't mean you will find endless numbers of jobs that match your Mobility and Affinity Profiles exactly. There are bound to be trade-offs. However, knowing what some of those trade-offs are will help clarify your judgments, and perhaps make those sacrifices that every successful career demands a little easier to bear.

CareerSmarts: Jobs with a Future will show you where you stand today, help you focus on where you want to be tomorrow, and give you a pretty good idea of the adjustments you will have to make to get there.

WHERE THE FACTS AND THE STATS CAME FROM

To identify reliable, objective measures of which industries and which job titles truly reflect the jobs of the future, my team conducted an extensive review of general and specialized business directories, government statistics and reports, magazines, newspapers and periodicals, on-line services, and reports of research organizations, professional associations, think tanks, and academic institutions.

Our federal government shines in the compilation of labor and employment statistics in on-line databases and job descriptions found in the *Dictionary of Occupational Titles, Occupational Outlook Handbook,* and the *Guide for Occupational Exploration.* We culled some material from these sources, and also consulted numerous Department of Commerce publications and databases. Additionally we conducted literature searches through such respected business periodicals as *Fortune, Forbes, Business Week, Industry Week, Barron's, The Wall Street Journal,* and *Harvard Business Review.*

As a result of this research, we not only found hard evidence of the growth industries, but recognized patterns, categories, and trends that we used in assembling the information in *CareerSmarts: Jobs for the Future*.

WHERE THE "PROFESSIONAL COMPETENCIES" AND "PERSONAL PREFERENCES" CAME FROM

To make an intelligent career choice you must consider what you enjoy, what is important to you, and what you are good at. To this end I have been working with psychologist David Caruso, Ph.D., for some years now. (His practice focuses exclusively on career and management development.) He and I come at career development from different professional directions but with a common goal: to make the complexities of modern career management more controllable.

One important aspect of career control is effective career match. Our goal of making a contribution to improve career match led to a unique facet of *CareerSmarts: Jobs for the Future*: the means to make an intelligent career choice by correlating both your professional competencies and your personal workplace preferences with a job's particular demands.

To help you make the most informed career decision possible, we accessed all the available data on professional competencies and growth jobs in order to determine what skills these jobs required. Some of the information we needed was readily available in the existing career databases (including the extensive federal research databases and publications mentioned earlier), but much of it was not. Some of the existing information was old, and, we felt, probably out of date, so we used data only when it was recent and accurate in the light of current professional thought in the field.

We also matched established beliefs about intelligent career choice against the latest thinking, most notably Rodney Lowman's work (see *The Clinical Practice of Career Assessment*, Washington, D.C.: American Psychological Association, 1991). The rest of the detailed information on career match came out of our original research, conducted over a period of three years.

The result is a comprehensive inventory of professional competencies and personal workplace preferences. This formidable task resulted in the identification of sixteen professional competencies required for entry into, and success with, today's modern careers, and a further six personal workplace preferences that define a person's affinity for a particular job or career.

Our final task was to rate each of the jobs in the book against these sixteen professional competencies and six personal workplace preferences. You will learn more about each of these career match considerations, and how to apply them to your career, in the text and graphics on the following pages.

CHAPTER ONE

Which Jobs—and Why

Now, more than ever before, you need to take an active role in the management of your career, because the one person who truly cares about your economic survival is you, and you alone.

The jobs you will discover in this book are a comprehensive selection of those that will be in the most demand because of the changing nature of our society. What does this changing world of work look like? The same, and different. Everywhere we look, we see it. It's the local hospital that employs an abundance of doctors, nurse practitioners, technicians, physical therapists, nurses, maintenance workers, and employees of almost every description; the travel agency down the street that arranges trips around the world for local businesspeople, retirees with time and cash on their hands, and others; the law firm downtown that handles malpractice suits, bankruptcies, divorces, and corporate acquisitions; and the fast-food restaurant just off the highway that feeds (and employs) just about everybody in the community at one time or another.

The work world may look the same, but jobs today are no longer lifelong appointments. You have to see the big picture—not only *which* jobs are growing, but also *why* they're growing, and *how* they are changing. If you understand the trends that are changing the world of work, you have a foundation on which to base career decisions and job searches.

Today's Trends

Two big trends will drive our economy over the next twenty years. They have to do with our aging population and the globalization of the workplace through technology. Together, these influences will continue to revolutionize the world of work.

As a society we're growing older—and richer. With two-income households, longer life spans, and baby boomers now reaching the height of their earning potential, our society is positioned to spend more money than ever before on medical care, business and personal services, recreation, and child care. Other industries that will benefit from the aging population are law, travel, retail, education, and social services.

The second trend, technology and the globalization of work, is a Pandora's box. On one hand, technology will increase productivity and simplify many jobs; this means the elimination of millions of jobs at all levels. On the other hand, automation will create new work opportunities—although *only* for those with the skills of the new workplace. Technology also will allow jobs to be executed anywhere in the world where a workforce can be trained the most cheaply.

Any prudent professional's goal should be to understand how these trends are positively affecting the growth of some jobs, what these jobs are going to be, and what it takes to get them.

The Healthiest Jobs

A major challenge in creating this book was determining which jobs to include and which to deep-six. After all, what could be a great job for me could be a living hell for you. Your professional floor could be another person's ceiling, and vice versa. If I restricted this book to just the jobs that pay $100,000 a year, that fact might look good in the title, but it would exclude the vast majority of the workforce. If I went to the other extreme and just chose jobs on the basis of government growth projections for them, I would be including job descriptions for long-distance truck drivers and the like. However, the focus of the book is to enlighten you about *career* opportunities—jobs that have potential career paths within the professional or white-collar world. Every job in this book, even if it does not represent the dream career for you, is either a place to start or a stepping-stone job along the way to your ultimate career goals.

So this book won't tell you about just the best-paying jobs, or just the most exciting jobs; instead it will give you a comprehensive review of the *healthiest* jobs. By this I mean jobs that, because of their growth, will have the greatest stability and opportunity for professional advancement over the coming years. These include not only the jobs that are growing by large percentages, but those which account for millions of workers where the growth rate might be quite slight but the scale so huge that there will be ample professional opportunities to start and develop a successful career.

So yes, you will find the exciting, the prestigious, and the high-paying jobs in the following pages, but perhaps more important, you also will find the stepping-stone jobs you have to graduate to, and from, on the way to your professional success.

DISPELLING THE CONFUSIONS

In researching each of these growth jobs, some confusing dichotomies and revelations became evident. One thing that came out is that many of the growth jobs are very similar in their basic skill requirements—which is welcome news for our professional mobility. However, it can be difficult to decipher the facts and statistics when one job may carry many titles. The more I looked into the jobs with sexy titles, the more I realized there were lots of ways to name similar jobs.

An Ecologist, as listed in one source, might be called a Biological Scientist in another, while a third source might use the job title of Life Scientist. Scientists who specialize in earth studies can be called Earth Scientists, or Geoscientists. The computer industry has numerous titles for Systems Analysts: Computer Systems Analysts, Information Systems Analysts, or Information Systems Specialists. People with these computer job titles perform very similar, if not identical, tasks.

This is not a case of one authority being right and another wrong. It reflects the confusion of our times and the realities of the workplace—that different companies call similar jobs by different names. In *CareerSmarts: Jobs for the Future*, we mention a job's other titles whenever we are aware of them. (If you are aware of titles that we have overlooked, please let me know and I'll include them in the next edition.)

There are also many jobs that fall into several categories and cross industry lines. An Urban Planner may be a Civil Engineer with a specialty. An Air Quality Specialist may be an Environmental Engineer working in the public sector. So be aware, as you pursue professional opportunities in any field, that job titles in the real world will be defined by their context.

Lastly, while new industries are being born every day, a more important change is being wrought on all existing jobs in traditional industries. Yes, computers, the Internet, and on-line global communications will create new jobs, but electronic technology will have an even greater effect on the way we all conduct business in every other job in the new American workplace. In some ways, it's a case of "the more things change, the more they stay the same."

We are being misinformed when we hear about hot opportunities for "new" jobs like "cyberwriters" or "electronic editors." Let's look at these terms, each culled from press stories. First of all, a cyberwriter's work is published electronically. But that is simply a change in the means of *distribution*; the writing job itself hasn't changed. The same holds true for an "electronic editor"; this is not a job for some new superdigital breed of editor, but a job for editors who become technologically adapted. An electronic editor is, simply, someone who becomes, as part of his or her professional skill development, competent with the editing opportunities of the new distribution system.

What we have here then is newspaper hype, with some poor journalist desperate to fill up column inches by deadline. In reality what we have more of are writers and other professionals who understand the possibilities of electronic technology and who create products and services that take advantage of its possibilities.

Technology is changing the face of every *existing* job far more than it is generating entirely *new* occupations. This changing face of every existing profession is something you need to get a fix on, and you must adapt your professional skills accordingly.

It is no longer realistic to think of your career in terms of finding a single hot job, with a stable company in a growth industry. It is no longer realistic because, while some jobs have better prospects than others, no company and no industry is immune to the changes technology has brought. What you must do is adapt to the realities of the new workplace, and that means understanding what the employment picture looks like.

THE EMPLOYMENT PICTURE

The current employment picture reveals that Health Care (especially for the elderly) and Information Technology (computers and information systems) are by far the most dramatically growing industries in America for the next decade. In the Bureau of Labor Statistics (BLS) studies on job growth projections between 1992 and 2005, six of the top ten growing industries are in health care representing 1,141,469 new positions, and two are in information technology, representing 682,000 new positions.

Technology itself has created a global economy that is going to impact all industries. Suddenly, knowledge of a foreign language becomes an important plus for employability in all areas of professional life, from medicine to science, to sales, to engineering, to teaching.

The only thing that can seemingly stagnate the growth in Health Care and Technology as well as in other growth industries will be the demise of the planet. And, the health of the planet, in itself, is a big growth industry—and yet it is not an industry unto itself. There are Environmental Lawyers, Environmental Accountants, Environmental Educators, Environmental Scientists, and Environmental Engineers. Yet as often as not, these jobs are found as an area of specialization within another profession. Another example would be the grade school teacher who takes on the additional responsibilities of Environmental Educator for the school.

Environmental jobs are indeed increasing within all these fields, and specialized education and training in these areas is to be encouraged, but there are no statistics saying that Environmental Scientists, for example, hold X amount of jobs and earn Y amount of money. The numbers fall into the Biological Scientist or Geoscientist category, but the percentage of these specialists within the category is definitely increasing as public awareness and concern for the welfare of the planet expands.

The Growth Industries

I have broken the growth jobs, and the industries in which they appear, down into four broad groupings:

HEALTH CARE

You will get an overview of how both the changes in technology and our aging society are affecting the way Americans receive their health care. I'll explain in detail the growth-oriented goals of not only medical practitioners, but administration and laboratory staff. The overview includes an insider's view of the future, from the headhunters, company presidents, and professional association executives who have their fingers on the pulse of the Health Care industry. All indicators point to growth in the following areas: Administration, Nursing, Physical Health, Dentistry, and Mental Health.

THE TECHNOLOGIES

I'll show you how the Technologies are affecting the world of work and generating excellent career opportunities. I'll also share with you what insiders think about the professional future in Biotechnology and Environmental Technology, Engineering, and Information Technology. The section provides an in-depth review of the growth jobs in these industries.

BUSINESS AND PROFESSIONAL SERVICES

Our aging American society—the richest in the world for all its problems—is developing new appetites for services and products made possible by technology. In this part of the book you will gain a new awareness of how these growth industries and their professions are adapting to the new world of work: Financial Services, Human Resources, Law, Media/Communications/Public Relations, Sales, Marketing, Food Service, and Support Services. Again you'll read what company presidents, headhunters, and industry association executives see as the professional future in each of these fields, and receive the same extensive, in-depth reviews of each of the growth jobs.

PUBLIC SERVICE

This fourth and final segment covers all the work that is done in service to us as members of the public. This covers Social Services and Education, as well as many of the jobs in State and Local Government. I'll share with you the significant changes happening in these professions and what the insiders feel the future holds. And of course, you'll get in-depth analysis of each growth job.

What's in the Job Descriptions

Not only will you get an evaluation of exactly what is driving employment in the growth industries, you will receive a close look at the high-growth jobs. Each job, or job group, has an analysis of what that specific job entails, followed by information on what it pays, the educational requirements, the experience of an actual work day, and the growth potential.

Within each of the industries, I group those jobs that have similar characteristics and educational requirements. Some of the jobs have a built-in career path; you graduate as a physician and years later you'll retire as a physician, having made a good living and provided for a comfortable retirement in the process.

With other jobs, the career paths aren't always so clear; you must look at them as a means of entry to a profession, or as a stepping-stone job, one which allows you to segue between industries or to build experience that you might later parlay into more compatible, better-paying, more prestigious work.

We are living in a professional climate where job security is worse than it has been since humans had employers. Most people working today are going to go through a number of different careers in a lifetime of work. Not just different jobs—different *careers*. This can mean starting at the bottom again more than once in your life—and if you have ever had to do it, you know that it is tough, although it can be done. The more common sense and knowledge you bring to the pursuit of any given career, the more smoothly that career will progress, and the easier the transition will be to other careers, should the need arise.

When jobs are hard to come by, it's important to remember that the bigger the job pool for your skills at any given point in time, the more likely you are to maintain your employability, and by extension, your economic survival. *So in evaluating possible career paths, always look for the way doing one job will prepare you to do other jobs.* You should note that a job's appearing in a job group (I group jobs with similar responsibilities, professional skills, and educational background) will often mean that you can, with only moderate transitional discomfort, move into other jobs within that job group, thus expanding your job-hunting horizons and improving your employability. Remember, *job groups can signal mobility within a particular industry; be a sensible starting point for a new career; or provide core skills to fall back on.*

EARNING POTENTIAL

Under this heading you will find out what the job pays *on average* to start, and what the financial future holds for experienced professionals. I used government figures whenever possible, although sometimes I added information from industry surveys to the mix if it would update the figures in any meaningful way. Always remember that these are *averages*; professionals in the field make both much more and sometimes much less than the salaries mentioned. The salaries will also vary depending on where you live; expect to make much more doing any job in a metropolitan area (because it costs so much more to live there) than you would in a smaller community.

You'll find that if you become an orthodontist, your career and earnings are laid out along pretty clear lines. But this won't be the case if you are sharp, but with an education that stopped somewhere around secretarial school. If you fall into the latter category, you don't have to view those jobs that are open to someone with your current credentials as all that a professional career has to offer; you can use what you can do today as the launching pad for where you want to get to tomorrow. And your earning potential might well improve markedly over the life of your career.

Maybe you'll enter the workplace as a secretary or administrative assistant, but perhaps you'll use the job differently from your colleagues: for on-the-job training or for learning how to manage your own staff one day. Maybe you'll make sure you work for large and small companies, and that you gain experience in human resources, sales, and finance, the three basic building blocks of any successful company; this way you can give yourself a business education for the day when you might open your own business.

In a half-century work life, there is *plenty* of time to reach your financial career horizons, no matter how distant. Where you are today is not nearly so important as where you want to be tomorrow, especially when what you are learning is part of a greater plan for the long-term success of your career. It's possible to succeed in your career aspirations, no matter where you start or where you want to go, just so long as you don't confuse today's earning capabilities with your career's potential.

EDUCATIONAL REQUIREMENTS

To succeed in the new jobs, education is more important than ever. Many companies insist on higher levels of education just to get in the door; many more offer employees assistance in furthering their education, in order to increase their employees' productivity and value. Under the "Educational Requirements" subheading for each job, you will learn about the level of education employers look for in this area, and the accreditations, certifications, and specializations that are recognized as career enhancers.

Specialization is a very important consideration in terms of your education. For instance, getting a place in medical school is very competitive, despite the fact that the health industry is booming. But there has been a decrease in enrollment in dentistry programs in recent years, even though that field is projected to have steady growth over the next decade. This could create a shortage of qualified applicants—spelling "opportunity" for those who had the foresight to pursue training in dentistry.

A DAY IN THE LIFE

"A Day in the Life" takes you beyond the job title and shows you how a typical day is spent by someone doing that job. You will also learn about the working environment and the kinds of work-related challenges you might be faced with on the job, such as stress or overtime.

JOB GROWTH

When it comes to job growth most sources consider the jobs with the highest-projected growth rate as the most promising areas for employment. But in addition to these, I also considered areas where the sheer numbers of jobs projected to be available were worthy of note, even if the job itself was not showing a high rate of growth. Secretarial positions are an example of this: while the profession is projected to grow by only a small amount, the profession overall is so huge that a small percentage in growth adds up to a huge number of additional positions by the year 2005.

The job growth figures also do not factor in replacement numbers: positions opening up due to turnover, retirement, or other factors. In professions such as sales or social services, the turnover is generally high; this will increase the number of job openings above and beyond the Bureau of Labor Statistics projected growth figures. In other areas, such as education, there are a good many positions predicted to open up (in addition to industry growth) as a result of retirement. Conversely, there are some professions, such as law and research science, where turnover is very low and where job openings will result from an increase in the growth of the industry.

Remember that the job growth predictions are exactly what they claim to be: *predictions*! The forecasts are based on government data and industry experts' vision, but they are not written in stone. An unexpected turn in the economy, a global disaster or war, or a fantastic new technology could have a dramatic effect on the future employment picture of any job. The job growth we talk about here is our best bet, taking into account all the projections available.

Long-Term Employability

Traditionally, you would choose a career, start at the bottom, and work your way up the ladder earning more money with each step. Over the years, in return for your loyalty and good efforts, you would achieve financial security and, ultimately, a comfortable retirement. Lately, this social contract between American business and working people has been broken.

Today, the social contract between employers and employees is that the employer will keep you until you can be replaced with someone cheaper. This new contract has important ramifications when you put it in the context of a half-century work life. Essentially it means that while the more experience you get the more money you will earn, there comes a point when every employer will replace you with someone, or some piece of technology, that comes cheaper than your experience and loyalty.

So in a world where you are unlikely to retire in the job you hold today, or the one you land tomorrow, it is much more important than ever before to look at the long-term ramifications of your career decisions. You will want to research viable employment in a job and an industry that's healthy now and looks like it's going to stay healthy. You will need to become more attuned to how the changing morals of the American business world affect your career stability. You will then build the foundation for future career growth and stability in a job where the odds are best that you'll be valued and needed.

Another way to achieve this maximum employability is to consider career paths that promise both *vertical mobility*—the opportunity to move upward within a company and industry—and *horizontal mobility*—the potential for moving laterally within this and other industries. Job security, even in the hottest jobs in the fastest-expanding industries, has been severely curtailed; a magazine article about a rapid-growth industry—such as computers or finance—is often followed by one talking about thousands of layoffs by some computer manufacturer or some bank that has merged. This is why considerations of vertical and horizontal mobility are so important.

VERTICAL MOBILITY

If your job title is in demand and expanding numerically, and if you are in a healthy company in a growth industry, you increase your opportunities for climbing the professional ladder. This is what is known as vertical mobility. However, considering only careers that seem to offer opportunity for vertical growth no longer guarantees your employability; you need vertical mobility harnessed with *something else*, and that is . . .

HORIZONTAL MOBILITY

You find horizontal mobility when your job title is growing in absolute numbers, and when your job title shares professional competencies with other in-demand jobs. Develop and hone these skills, and your employability increases within your profession and the industry in which you ply it—you can get similar jobs in similar companies.

You will notice, as you leaf through the jobs in Part 2 of the book, that *successful people in each of the jobs in all of the industries share differing degrees of the* same *professional competencies*. The message is simple: develop the required professional competencies, and should you have to change careers, your in-demand skills will ease the pains of transition.

However, horizontal mobility needn't stop there for people who are in the planning and evaluation stages of a new career. It is valuable for anyone in this position to consider jobs in the "Additional Opportunities" boxes that appear throughout Part 2: they contain those jobs that exist in almost every company, in every industry. In other words, they cross industry lines and professional cultures. Related jobs are also mentioned in the analyses of specific jobs and job groups. When you consider a growth job that is growing not in one industry but in five or in twelve industries, you increase your professional mobility and your chances of maintaining your employability by the same factor.

But there is good news and bad news about these "additional opportunities" jobs. The bad news is that *less than half of them can make you wealthy in and of themselves*. So you need to look at many of these jobs as starting places, or as stepping-stone jobs, that help you develop critical skills, or allow you entry or exposure to a desired industry.

The good news is that *all these jobs are going to be super plentiful*. You will find them in every company, in every industry, and in every town across the nation. So an accountant who is downsized in Albany, New York, while working for a bank not only has opportunities within banking in Albany and the rest of the country, but also the opportunity to leave banking and New York's snowy winters for, say, Phoenix and a job in health care.

However, I am not saying that if you consider one of the "additional opportunities" jobs you will never find yourself looking for work. What I am saying is that, with one of these jobs, you will have far more opportunities to remain employed and to successfully pursue your personal career goals, whatever they might be, and you will be able to move more readily between industries as your needs dictate.

CHAPTER TWO

Two Paths to Success and Satisfaction: Employing Both Halves of Your Career Brain

The facts of life say: You have to put a roof over your head. Common sense says: It would be best if your work offered a sense of meaning and fulfillment in your life. So how do people choose a career? Some people focus on their skills, looking at what they *can* do. Other people look at their interests, thinking about what they *like* to do. Unfortunately, many people forget to use *either* of these approaches, let alone both. With this book I want to help you select a career that gives you the best odds of being both successful and satisfied with your work.

I believe that there are two ways of examining your career options, each of which is complementary to the other. The best career decision you can make uses both sides of your "career brain." The best career decision uses logic *and* emotion, thinking *and* feeling, facts *and* intuition. The best career decision considers your professional competencies (those skills you can bring to a job) and your personal workplace preferences (those values that determine your work life happiness).

The worst career decision uses only one of these dimensions, or emphasizes one of them and gives the other short shrift. Let's take a closer look at what each of these dimensions is, along with its corresponding Workplace Profile.

Your Personal Preferences, or Affinity, Profile Matched Against the Workplace Realities Profile

Chances are that there's a job you've done, somewhere along the line, that you enjoyed about as much as the mumps. What's it like working at your desk every day? Well, suffice it to say that finding a job that reflects the majority of your personal preferences can be the difference between dreading Monday morning and whistling while you work. The better the match is between your personal preferences and the workplace realities of a job, the more motivated, content, and committed to your profession you will be. It's this match between your personal preferences and the workplace realities of a particular job that is what *affinity* is all about.

Affinity, in the context of your career, means what you enjoy, what you value, and what you need in order to feel happy and fulfilled in your work life. What kind of place do you want to work in? How do you want to be treated? What do you want from your job?

Many psychologists adamantly believe that the best long-term career plans consider career interests and preferences. Your affinity for what are the workplace realities of a particular profession is key to your career satisfaction and happiness. If you pursue a career in which your personal preferences do not match the workplace realities, you may be quite successful, but you may also be quite unhappy, experiencing dissatisfaction with your work life and feeling that there must be something better out there.

I've developed something called an *Affinity Profile* so you can objectively evaluate your personal preferences. Developing an Affinity Profile that reflects your personal preferences is a way of looking at your career interests, what you enjoy doing at work, and what types of activities give you pleasure. This can help you to discover new opportunities to pursue in your work life and open doors of inquiry you never knew existed. Here's the sample template:

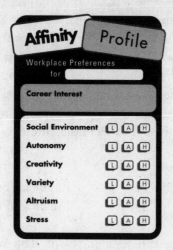

Then, every job detailed in this book has been appraised to define its major Workplace Realities, such as the Social Environment and the amount of Stress, Autonomy, Variety, Creativity, and Altruism it provides. So once you have completed your individual Affinity Profile, you will instantly be able to match it against the Workplace Realities Profiles created for each job in this book—and find which jobs are best suited to your emotional needs and preferences.

Now let's look carefully at the categories you see on the template.

CAREER INTERESTS

Jobs in this book tap one or more of these Job Interest areas:

- *Invention*—developing new ideas and expressing yourself
- *Problem Solving*—using analytical thinking to solve problems
- *Financial*—investing and managing money
- *Technology*—using complex equipment and the latest technology
- *Development*—helping, training, or teaching people
- *Project*—organizing people, information, and activities
- *Persuasion*—influencing, persuading, leading

For example, jobs such as Loan Officer, Broker, Insurance Agent, and Accountant require the performance of similar activities.[1] In these jobs, you

---

1. I have combined the Workplace Realities of those careers which are very similar. For instance, the Workplace Realities for Loan Officer and Loan Counselor are combined into a single profile.

work with clients on financial data and analyze the information. Thus they are jobs in which the focus is *financial*. For those jobs that have more than one interest area associated with it, I've offered the most important interest area first, then followed it with the interest area next in importance.

Once you've determined your personal interest areas, you can use this category to help you prioritize which careers to explore, and to think about career possibilities and alternatives. For example, these two jobs have the same interest areas:

Loan Officer   Financial/Project

Insurance Agent   Financial/Project

Although the jobs are different and your days would be different, the daily activities and needed skills are similar, so if you enjoy life as a Loan Officer, you might also enjoy the job of an Insurance Agent. (*Note:* You will figure out your Career Interests through taking the Affinity Self-Test in the next chapter.)

PERSONAL PREFERENCES

Career Interests refer to specific areas you enjoy; Personal Preferences refer to the general goals you have in terms of your work life, its social environment, and the degree of stress you experience on the job.

What kind of place do you want to work in, and how do you want to be treated?

The better the match between your personal preferences and the workplace realities of a job, the more content and fulfilled you will be in your profession. The corresponding workplace realities evaluated for every job are:

- Social Environment
- Autonomy
- Creativity
- Variety
- Altruism
- Stress

Each job is rated for Low, Average, and High levels of the workplace realities.

As I explain the six areas of personal preference, begin to think about which are important to you, and to what degree.

SOCIAL ENVIRONMENT

What It Is and Why It Is Important in Evaluating Career Choice

The Social Environment or atmosphere differs from job to job. It's the place or environment in which you work—specifically, whether you work by yourself or with others. Before you decide on a particular career, you should recognize what you would prefer: working alone behind closed doors, or surrounded by others and working closely with colleagues.

When you see that a job is rated Low on Social Environment, that means that you are often working on your own, have few meetings, and don't have a lot of direct contact with others to get your work done. A job where you are surrounded by others, but not actually working *with* them, would also be Low on Social Environment.

Jobs High on Social Environment put you into group situations, where there are many meetings and you are interacting with others. Getting your work done depends on working with others, and for some jobs, compensation is actually tied to the performance of the group. Work teams and quality circles have this type of social environment.

Low Social Environment means:
Often work alone
Few meetings
Independent contributor

High Social Environment means:
Usually work with others
Many meetings
Work projects require the involvement of others

An Occupational Therapist (page 125) is a job rated High on Social Environment, because it's a job that puts you in constant contact with clients. But then there is the Geoscientist (page 195), a job rated Low on Social Environment, in which you work alone for most of the day.

AUTONOMY

What It Is and Why It Is Important in Evaluating Career Choice

Autonomy means having a say in how your work is done. It means having a degree of independence in what you do and how it's done.

A job is Low on Autonomy when someone is telling you what to do and, sometimes, how and when to do it. If you cringe at the thought of working in a directed and controlling environment, do your best to avoid jobs that are rated Low on Autonomy. If this is not possible immediately because you lack certain skills in your profession, you can work toward developing the competencies that will allow entry into jobs with more autonomy. If you are joining the workforce for the first time, you should understand that few entry-level jobs have much autonomy; even in the professions that offer autonomy, you have to earn it.

Of course, you may want the structure of a Low Autonomy job in your work life. You may feel more comfortable working in an environment where the expectations are clear. It doesn't matter which way you feel: what's important is understanding and matching your preferences against the Workplace Realities of a particular job.

A High Autonomy score doesn't mean that you are your own boss, but it's closer to it. You are on your own, doing your job the way you want to, without someone looking over your shoulder and telling you how to do it.

In Low Autonomy jobs:
Someone else tells you what to do
You have a set schedule
You can get help and feedback
    on the job

In High Autonomy jobs:
You figure out what to do
You set your own schedule, agenda, etc.
You receive little direct supervision

For some people, one of the advantages of a career as say, a Dentist (page 147) is that no one is looking over your shoulder telling you what to do. This job is rated High on Autonomy. A job rated Low on Autonomy is that of Medical Secretary (page 98). Medical Secretaries are supervised by office managers or physicians, and typically they don't have a great deal of leeway in how they do their job.

CREATIVITY

What It Is and Why It Is Important in Evaluating Career Choice

Creativity means coming up with new ideas for, approaches to, and ways of looking at the world.

Low Creativity jobs do not offer much chance to invent things, or to produce something new and different. If Creativity is important to you on the job, then you might find a Low Creativity job boring or limiting. A job that is High in Creativity means you use your brain to come up with original solutions to dilemmas, approaches to take, or ways to market your product or services. The opportunity to reveal your sense of creativity comes in all kinds of flavors, from the inventiveness of the advertising copywriter to the ingenious ideas of the computer scientist.

With Low Creativity jobs you:	*With High Creativity jobs you:*
Work on existing products, ideas, and services	Discover, develop, or design products, services, or ideas
Use what others create	Are inventive on the job
Experience little pressure to come up with new ideas or methods	Are expected to come up with new ideas, products, or services as part of the job

Writers (page 341) earn their living by coming up with new ideas and by creating and telling stories. As you might imagine, the job of Writer is High on Creativity. On the other hand, Accountants (page 273) work with complex calculations, but aren't constantly asked to come up with new ideas, products, or services. The job of Accountant is rated Low on Creativity opportunities.

Recognize that this doesn't mean you cannot be a successful accountant if you have high creativity needs; if this is the case for you, find another creative outlet for your needs through an entrepreneurial or dream career that may help you feel more fulfilled in your work life.

VARIETY

What It Is and Why It Is Important in Evaluating Career Choice

Knowing what's happening at work on Monday morning, or having a surprise waiting to greet you, is what the rating of Variety is about. Variety spells the difference between those who need excitement in their lives and are bored with routine, and those who like security in their lives and staying in the comfort zone. Both preferences are valid; again, all that's important are *your* preferences in the matter.

Jobs that are a bit more routine, with each day pretty much like the last one, are rated Low on Variety. In these jobs you might interact with different people, and the problems might change a bit, but you are really doing the same general kinds of tasks.

Jobs rated High on Variety can mean that with them, you never know what to expect, or what the day will bring. There is also a steady stream of new challenges to be faced, new problems to be solved.

With jobs Low on Variety:

Each day generally involves the same kinds
   of tasks and interactions

Standard routine

Many predictable tasks

With jobs High on Variety:

Every day is different

No steady routine

Few predictable tasks

As a Geriatric Care Nurse (page 103 in the Home Health Care Nurses group), you know what to expect from day to day. Your patients may change, or they may be in different moods and require modifications to their programs, but the basic tasks you work on are pretty much the same. That's why this is a career rated Low on Variety when compared with other jobs. But Management Consultants (page 323) face a hectic day. They may be making a client presentation first thing in the morning, doing research on another project afterwards, and making a sales call in the afternoon. The problems they are asked to solve vary, and the people they work with differ from project to project. This job is rated High on Variety compared to other jobs.

ALTRUISM

What It Is and Why It Is Important in Evaluating Career Choice

Altruism as part of your work looks at how your job—and the services and products it delivers—helps other people or your community. Work can be a way of giving back to the community.

If Altruism is Low on your list, then you aren't especially interested in repairing the world through your work. It doesn't necessarily mean that you don't give a damn; it just means that the Altruism rating of a job has less importance to you in your career evaluation process. On the other hand, if Altruism is High on your personal preference agenda, then you will be sensitive to careers that offer the opportunity to make a difference with your work.

Here is how jobs rated Low and High on Altruism are often described:

With jobs Low in Altruism:

Work doesn't positively affect society

Job doesn't directly improve
   the community

Work doesn't impact people's lives

With jobs High in Altruism:

Work makes society a better place

Job directly improves the
   welfare of the community

Work improves people's lives

Social Workers (page 400) improve the quality of people's lives. As a Social Worker, you have a very powerful and very visible impact when you help others who truly need care. Social work jobs are High on the Altruism scale. Computer Software Engineers (page 212) work on tasks that do not directly assist in repairing the world or directly touch the lives of others, so these jobs are rated Low on Altruism.

STRESS

What It Is and Why It Is Important in Evaluating Career Choice

Some people enjoy stimulation on the job just as they enjoy a cup of coffee in the morning to jolt them into action. The dark side of this stimulation is *stress*, where the demands of work wear you down and you suffer mentally and physically as a result. Stress refers to the degree of excitement, energy, and pace you like in your work life.

You have to be tough to endure a High Stress job. The tensions are many, demands pile up, and you are pulled in several directions at the same time, often *all* the time. If this scenario makes you reach for the Pepto-Bismol, then choose another job.

For High Stress positions, you have to be in good psychological shape. If you get nervous easily or lose sleep worrying about unfinished business, then you should consider jobs rated Low on the Stress scale. If you choose to go the High Stress route, you have to work at staying psychologically fit if you expect to survive over the long haul.

A job rated Low on Stress has an easier-going pace, where you aren't always rushing to beat deadlines and bearing the responsibility for juggling multiple demands. You can focus on one thing at a time in a Low Stress job, and while you may work hard you can stay calm.

In Low Stress jobs:	In High Stress jobs:
Few demands are placed on you	Many demands are placed on you
Easygoing environment	Fast-paced environment
Projects worked on one at a time	Multiple projects and tight deadlines

You want stimulation? Try working as a Police Officer (page 444). In this profession, you literally place your life on the line every time you punch in for your shift. This is a job rated High on the Stress factor. A Librarian (page 426), whose job is a lot more focused and doesn't have the multiple, urgent, and life-threatening demands of a job such as Police Officer, is rated Low on the Stress scale.

AN IN-DEPTH LOOK AT A SAMPLE WORKPLACE REALITY PROFILE

The work of a Writer does not require close interaction with others (Low on Social Environment) and has a lot of leeway in how the work is done (High on Autonomy). The job demands consistent creativity (High on Creativity), and there's a demand for different activities (High on Variety). The job offers some opportunity to give back to the community (Average on Altruism). Writers do not get terribly stressed out (Low on Stress), except of course around deadline time.

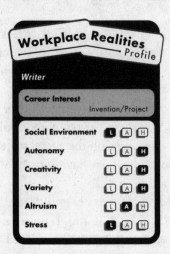

Your Personal Mobility Profile Matched Against the Professional Competencies Profile

Can you *do* the job? Do you have what it takes? Your employability depends on a specific set of skills that will get your foot in the door and your tush in the chair behind the desk.

GOING DEEPER INTO YOUR PSYCHE

If you want to consider your Personal Preferences briefly now, try these three exercises:

• *Ideal Day*: Imagine waking up one Monday morning and looking forward to going to work. Where would you go, and who would you work with? What would you do on the job? Try and develop a sense as to the type of place and the type of work you would be engaged in.

• *Best Jobs*: What have been the most interesting and exciting jobs or projects for you? Think about *why* you enjoyed these assignments or positions, and about the activities they represented. What was it about the work and the people that you enjoyed so much?

• *Obituary*: One way to generate a list of what is truly important to your work satisfaction is to write your own ideal obituary. What would it say about your work life, your career, your accomplishments?

When you have to work for a living, and you are searching around for a sense of direction, one of the most pressing questions becomes, "What can I do?" Perhaps your best friend is a lawyer and you can easily picture yourself leading the glamorous life she describes to you. But before you dash off your résumé to Sue, Grabbit & Runne, you need to do one little exercise: Read one of the Lawyers' job descriptions (page 327) and ask yourself these questions: "Can I do this job? Do I have the skills it requires? Would somebody be happy enough with my work to hand me a paycheck at the end of the week?"

Professional Competencies are the skills and experiences required to do a job. The right competencies land you jobs and get you promotions; without them, you will likely be without employment in the new corporate America. These competencies are acquired through education, formal training, and work experience. Your professional security and the overall success of your entire work life lie with building these Professional Competencies.

A career built on a firm foundation demands that you really understand all the different skills you need for professional success in a modern career, and that you have a clear understanding of the extent of your competency in each of these areas. Objectivity about which skills you possess, and the extent to which you possess them, is important. Knowing where your current abilities place you professionally will help you make practical career choices, identify areas for professional growth, and build good job interview skills.

We each have these different skills in different degrees, and as this chapter proceeds I will show you how to profile your personal set of Professional Competencies. We will refer to the results of your evaluation as your *Mobility Profile*, because it is your competencies that keep you professionally mobile, able to move up the professional ladder from one job to another because your skills are in demand.

Then, every job in this book has been appraised by Dr. David Caruso and his team of researchers to evaluate the necessary competencies required for entry.

Once you have completed your own Mobility Profile, you will instantly be able to match it against the required Professional Competencies of any of the growth jobs in the book, so you can find the best fit for *your* skills.

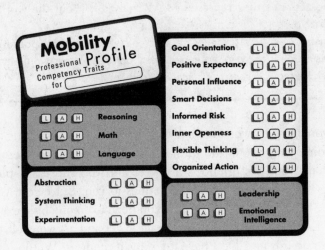

The Professional Competencies required in each of the jobs of the future fall into four main categories:

- Basic Functional Skills
- Thinking Skills
- Career Buoyancy Behaviors
- People Skills

These four categories comprise your Professional Competencies, and the degree to which you possess those competencies will determine how easily you can enter a particular new profession, and prosper once there. The better the fit between a job's Professional Competency requirements and your Professional Competencies, the more successful you will be in your career. And the more highly developed your skills become, the better your shot at performing work that is more challenging, higher paying, and more secure.

If you plan to succeed in life, you owe it to yourself to do a candid self-analysis (which you can take in the following chapter) and find which of these competencies you have in abundance, which will require determined and systematic self-development, and which may never be a strong suit, no matter how hard you try. I believe that when you know where you want to go, you can get there if you first find out where you stand today, because then you will know the path and the stepping-stones that will take you from here to there.

But first, let's explore one by one each of these professional competencies and why it is important to your career. I'll then describe careers that require different levels of each of these skills.

BASIC FUNCTIONAL SKILLS

The three Basic Functional Skills[2] for work in the modern world are:

- Reasoning
- Math
- Language

Functional Skills help you to do any job, to handle on-the-job training, and to prosper in your career. Functional Skills are so elemental to the new jobs of today that they are often unstated in a job description or a job interview. Employers expect that you come prepared with the basic Functional Skills of modern professionals. Here they are, explained in detail.

REASONING

What It Is and Why It Is Important to Your Career

At its most basic level, Reasoning means that you can carry out detailed written or verbal instructions. You can deal with problems that are routine, are obvious, and don't require you to figure out the bigger picture.

Possessing an average amount of Reasoning skills allows you to solve practical problems and deal with situations where the problems are changing, and you're never sure what the next problem is going to be. No one is there to tell you what the problem is, either; you have to figure that out for yourself. You also have to be able to follow instructions that are in written, verbal, or diagram form, or laid out as a schedule.

Higher levels of Reasoning involve applying logical and scientific thinking to a wide range of theoretical problems, as well as more practical challenges. You are able to deal with symbols, formulas, graphs, and the like.

2. These knowledge areas are defined by the Department of Labor.

Jobs requiring Low or High Reasoning skills can be described in these terms:

Jobs that require Low Reasoning skills:	*Jobs that require High Reasoning skills:*
Use commonsense solutions	Use logic to solve problems
Offer easily understood instructions	Employ symbols and complex graphs
You solve a problem someone gives to you	You must identify the problem to be solved

Law is one professional field that uses complex language and documents on a daily basis. That's why Tax Attorneys (page 328) must have High Reasoning skills to do their jobs. An Air Quality Specialist (page 438) must read and understand documents and diagrams, and so is rated Average on Reasoning skills.

I can't give you an example of a career with a future that needs only a Low level of Reasoning skills. That's because *all* of the jobs with a future require at least an Average level! That is an important bit of information to tuck away, because it tells you that working hard and developing Basic Functional Skills is critical to your pursuit of any modern professional career.

MATH

What It Is and Why It Is Important to Your Career

Performing basic mathematical operations, using decimal fractions, and computing ratios and percentages is what is needed at the Low level of Math skills. You also have to be able to understand bar graphs and do math on currency units.

The Average level of Math skills challenges you to solve problems using linear, quadratic, and logarithmic functions. You have to be able to compute probabilities and use statistical inferences.

Advanced Math skills involve advanced calculus, differential equations, and experimental research design and statistics.

Jobs with Low Math requirements:	*Jobs with High Math requirements:*
Basic math skills	Advanced formulas and computations
Understanding of simple graphs	Complex statistical diagrams

| Little statistical understanding | Ability to compute and comprehend complex statistics |

Botanists (page 185, in the Biological scientists group) don't just pick weeds and flowers: they analyze them, categorize them, and do tests and experiments. They need well-developed Math skills. Therefore, this career is rated High in this area.

Working with patients and implementing treatment programs does not tap Math skills to a great degree. Therefore, the job of Psychiatric Aide (page 163) is rated Low on Math skill requirements.

LANGUAGE

What It Is and Why It Is Important to Your Career

A job with a Low level of Language skill requirements requires a very basic reading vocabulary, the ability to communicate orally, and limited writing skills. Only a handful of careers in this book require a Low level of Language skill. Take note—or learn to!

The Average level of Language skill jumps you up to reading novels, poems, periodicals, journals, and manuals. You have to be able to write business letters and reports using standard, accepted formats. Oral communication skills are polished, allowing you to hold your own in group discussions and debate.

Advanced Language skill requires you to comprehend and explain financial reports, technical journals, and legal and other documents clearly. You could try your hand at writing manuals or speeches—or plays, novels, or poetry.

Jobs with Low Language Requirements:	Jobs with High Language Requirements:
Basic reading and writing	Understanding and creating complex technical documents
Limited vocabulary	Rich language and advanced vocabulary
Get basic points across	Speak well and convincingly

The work of an Internist (page 116, in the Family Practitioner group) requires understanding a never-ending stream of complex documents and being able to explain them to others. This job is rated High in Language requirements. But helping others who are sick is a direct, hands-on experience that does not require vast knowledge of language; consequently, a Nursing Aide (page 112) is rated Low in this area.

THINKING SKILLS

Strong Thinking Skills will enhance your long-term employability, no doubt about it. Successfully switching careers, or just changing jobs, is more likely if you have developed the skills that the hottest jobs of the next decade require.[3]

There are three Thinking Skills:

- Abstraction
- System Thinking
- Experimentation

ABSTRACTION

What It Is and Why It Is Important to Your Career

Abstraction is the ability that lets you lie on your back, look up at the clouds floating by, and say to yourself, "That cloud looks just like an elephant balancing on a ball, and that other one looks like the family dog." Abstraction takes random bits of information and gives them meaning and pattern. Another way of looking at it is to say that Abstraction allows you to take information from different sources, evaluate it all, and then tell a story. Abstraction assumes that you already know how to find and access information; it's how well you *use* that information that defines your Abstraction skills.

Abstraction skills allow you to analyze the commonplace in a fresh light, and to take the new and apply it in different contexts. Abstraction allows you to see new solutions to problems, and just as important, to discover new problems to solve. Abstraction skills allow you to take all of your life's knowledge and experience and apply it to the benefit of your job and your career to create a masterful computer program, a fearsome marketing plan, a superb invention, or the next great American novel.

Jobs that require Low Abstraction:
Focus on concrete facts and figures

Jobs that require High Abstraction:
Focus on possibilities

3. These are the skills of the Symbolic Analyst, described by Robert Reich in *The Work of Nations*. Symbolic Analysts are knowledge workers; they are problem finders and problem solvers.

Accept information as it is given	Create new patterns and meaning from existing information
Use information from a few sources	Combine information from multiple sources

A Family Practitioner (page 116) has to come up with a diagnosis based on her observation of many facts; that's why this career requires a High level of Abstraction skills. But a Billing Clerk (page 378) processes information as it is presented and does not need to figure out what it means. So, Billing Clerk is a job that places a Low demand on Abstraction skills.

SYSTEM THINKING

What It Is and Why It Is Important to Your Career

System Thinking is looking at the big picture and knowing that the head bone is connected to the neck bone, the neck bone is connected to the shoulder-bone, and so on. System Thinking looks at *relationships*. It helps you understand the *real* cause of a problem, not just what looks obvious. System Thinking lets you get beyond the surface issues to discover what lies buried deep beneath.

The Systems Analyst (page 213) who is hired to improve the performance of a computer network knows that she can increase the speed of one component in the system—the printer, for instance—but that the other components may keep the performance of the entire system slow. She is using a High level of System Thinking skills and applying them to the practical challenges of her job.

A Low level of System Thinking skills involves handling one event, one idea, or one variable at a time. Facts are disconnected from one another, and the problem you are asked to solve is already identified for you. The process is also identified for you, and it is likely to be a steady routine. There is no need for you to connect the minutiae of your job to the overall mission of your employer.

In your career, System Thinking helps you to figure out what is really going on. When you apply System Thinking at work, you develop a reputation as someone who understands causes and consequences, who can recognize and solve pivotal problems.

Jobs with Low System Thinking requirements:	*Jobs with High System Thinking requirements:*
Look at issues one at a time	Consider multiple problems simultaneously

| Examine components of a problem as independent problems to solve | Investigate relationship of one component of a problem to another |
| Solve simple problems | Solve complex problems |

When you are in charge of designing and maintaining complex computer systems, with their intricate connections, you'd better look at the big picture and understand how one component works with another. To be performed well, the job of Information Systems Manager (page 221) requires a High level of System Thinking.

Taking it one fact at a time, so to speak, is what Medical Assistants (page 94) do. They can do their job well while applying a Low level of System Thinking skills. Of course the Medical Assistant who can nevertheless apply these skills to an employer's needs is the one most suitable for raises, plum assignments, and promotions.

EXPERIMENTATION

What It Is and Why It Is Important to Your Career

When some people think of Experimentation, they get an image of a scientist pouring blue liquid from one test tube into another, watching as the liquid changes color and bubbles out of the test tube, and the scientist yelling, "Eureka! Tomorrow I take over the world!"

But many professionals who don't wear white lab coats also engage in Experimentation in their work. They come up with ideas, and then systematically test those ideas to see which works most effectively. A sales director may not be a biochemist, but he has to vary the proportions of pricing, positioning, and distribution strategies constantly to get the product mix just right—only this time, the mix is not a liquid: it's maximum return on investment.

Jobs with Low Experimentation skills:	*Jobs with High Experimentation skills:*
Accept solutions and problems at face value	Test potential solutions to problems
Implement, not experiment	Use controlled, scientific problem-solving methods
Test others' ideas	Develop own hypotheses to test

Scientists like Biochemists (page 186) spend much of their professional lives conducting experiments. In fact, even entering this profession depends on possessing developed Experimentation skills. Consequently, this career requires a High level of Experimentation skills.

On the other hand, explaining how insurance policies work and why they are valuable takes many skills, but not that of Experimentation, so Insurance Agent (page 289) is a job that requires Low levels of Experimentation competency.

PEOPLE SKILLS

In the new corporation employers are paying increasing attention to these People skills:

- Emotional Intelligence[4]
- Leadership

The higher up the ladder you climb, the more attention others will pay to your possession of these competencies. When candidates for a promotion or contenders in a competitive bid have all other Professional Competency skills in place, it is the skills of Leadership and Emotional Intelligence, working hand in hand, that will win the day for whoever possesses them in the greatest degree.

EMOTIONAL INTELLIGENCE

What It Is and Why It Is Important to Your Career

Emotional Intelligence is a form of intelligence whereby your feelings help you think better, more clearly, and more creatively. This is where your emotions—your passions and your heart—meet your thinking—your reasoning and your head. To be emotionally intelligent means that you possess the ability to:

- identify emotions in yourself and in others
- use emotions to make better decisions
- understand emotions and what causes them
- control emotions to think more clearly

4. The theory of Emotional Intelligence was developed by two psychology professors: Jack Mayer and Peter Salovey. I am using their work to define Emotional Intelligence. Jack Mayer also provided academic oversight for the work done by David Caruso in *Beat the Odds* and in this book.

Identifying emotions in yourself, and in others, is the basic building block of Emotional Intelligence. By identifying your own feelings, you are better able to express yourself with others. By identifying others' feelings, you become sensitive to faked emotions; you can see beyond the phony smile and realize that a colleague is actually annoyed. The ability to identify feelings is also applied to words, actions, sounds, faces, designs, colors, art, and drama. Emotionally intelligent people can correctly identify the feelings in a piece of music, a play, or someone's face.

Using emotions appropriately helps you to direct your thinking and your attention to what is important, and to be able to shift perspectives on a problem. When you are feeling anxious, having a vague feeling of being ill-at-ease, your Emotional Intelligence is what takes that vague sense and makes you realize that you haven't prepared enough for that big sales call tomorrow, so you should turn off the tube and polish your presentation. The result is that the meeting goes better than it would have otherwise.

You can also better understand others' points of view, and how other people are feeling, by actually creating emotions in yourself. The result is that you can say to yourself, "I know how she feels about what is going on." You have empathy and understanding for others, and this allows you to be more effective in your professional interactions. Understanding the causes of particular emotions prepares you to make better judgments, and to better understand yourself and others.

Another aspect of Emotional Intelligence is your ability to monitor and control emotions in yourself, and in others, without changing the feelings or forgetting about them. Regulating emotions starts with staying open to your feelings (an aspect of Inner Openness, page 48). Rather than ignoring an emotion, you think about it, and you feel it. That's important, since our emotions carry important messages for our brains, and ignoring these messages can play havoc with our lives. Regulating emotions allows you to feel the emotion, and allows your brain to regulate or use it as the situation demands: "I'm in a red-line rage right now, so I should calm down before making a decision." Just as you can stay open to your feelings, understand how they impact your thinking, and then control those emotions to make better decisions, so you can do this for other people.

Careers vary widely in the level of Emotional Intelligence they require.

In jobs requiring Little Emotional Intelligence you:	*In jobs requiring High Emotional Intelligence you:*
Take behavior at face value	Accurately perceive emotions in self and others
Make only rational, objective decisions	Regulate emotions and use them as the situation demands

| Accept emotions as they occur | Understand relations between emotions |
| Feel emotions as they arise | Manage your own and others' emotions |

Psychologists (page 159) pay their mortgage by understanding emotions, both their own and those of their clients. They generate strong emotions in their clients but still are able to reason with them, channeling the emotions and using them to help others make better, smarter decisions. Therefore, Psychologists require a High level of Emotional Intelligence. The work of an Accountant (page 273) requires many skills and considerable intelligence, but not Emotional Intelligence, so this career is Low on Emotional Intelligence requirements in terms of entry into the profession. Would it help for an Accountant to have High Emotional Intelligence? Absolutely: such a dimension is exactly the kind of professional competency that one day turns an accountant into a VP of Finance.

LEADERSHIP

What It Is and Why It Is Important to Your Career

We have all heard a lot of talk about leadership, but in spite of that, I don't think any two people would agree on exactly what it is. Here is how Leadership was defined for our rating purposes in the book:

Leadership involves:

- getting people to achieve a goal
- delegating tasks to others
- supervising the work of others
- empowering others
- setting the direction and tone for a team
- making decisions for others
- developing the skills of others

Leadership-oriented careers put you in an authority position, where you are supervising and directing the work of others. While there is a difference between the daily chores of a supervisor and the big-picture thinking of a president, many of the skills required for effective leadership are common to both jobs.

However, in the new world of work, there are plenty of great professions that don't demand traditional leadership skills, yet offer the same monetary rewards. Careers that are Low on the Leadership factor do not require that you lead teams, supervise others, or make decisions for others. Such careers may be found among professionals who work on a peer level with other professionals. Or they may work as independent contributors, where they do not lead (Low Leadership rating), and often, do not want to follow (High Autonomy rating). You can be a highly competent professional, doing complex and highly regarded work, without having to tell others what to do, running meetings, and setting the tone for a team or an entire organization.

Low Leadership jobs:	High Leadership jobs:
Don't supervise others	Supervise others
No group responsibility	In charge of a group, team, or department
Don't make decisions for others	Make decisions for others

Social Service Administrators (page 397) live and die by their leadership skills. They work with people and schedules and have to get a diverse group of professionals to pull together. In order to get people to work effectively as a team, a talented Social Service Administrator may have to become part corporate manager and part team coach. That's why Social Service Administrator is rated High on the need for Leadership competencies.

Highly developed leadership skills are not required by a Geophysicist (page 196, in the Geoscientist group). As a Geophysicist, you work with others but you do not decide for them or direct them in their jobs. This career is rated Low on its Leadership requirements. Of course, a Geophysicist who shows, among other things, Leadership skills may elect to run a research lab, head up an organization, or found a new company.

CAREER BUOYANCY BEHAVIORS

There is another set of skills, or competencies, that are required for overall career success with any job.

Over the last few years I have worked with psychologist David Caruso to examine which learnable workplace skills successful people share. In this research we identified a handful of developable behaviors that were common to successful corporate professionals. We found that the greater the degree to which people developed these skills, the more consistently successful their professional lives became. These are professional survival skills, or what I call Career Buoyancy Behaviors. There are eight of these behaviors,[5] and they are defined as follows:

5. These are discussed in detail in my previous book, *Beat the Odds*.

- Goal Orientation: working hard to achieve your goals
- Positive Expectancy: believing in your ability to overcome and ultimately to succeed
- Personal Influence: displaying influence and persuasion in your dealings
- Smart Decisions: using reason, savvy, and common sense to reach conclusions you feel confident to act on
- Informed Risk: taking informed chances while looking ahead
- Inner Openness: having the self awareness, emotional adaptability, and open-mindedness needed to recognize and build on personal strengths, tolerate change, and relate flexibly and constructively with others
- Flexible Thinking: creatively solving problems
- Organized Action: getting things done efficiently for a specific outcome

Every job discussed later in the book has been rated for the degree to which it utilizes each of the behaviors.

GOAL ORIENTATION: WORKING HARD TO ACHIEVE YOUR GOALS

What It Is and Why It Is Important to Your Career
"She knows what she wants and does what it takes to get it."
"He devotes tremendous time and energy to his craft."
"When you know what you want from your job, it's easier to make commitments."

Goal Orientation has two important aspects: a goal and hard work. Goal Orientation gives direction to your career needs and work projects. It helps you say "yes" to the right projects, and "no" to other projects that might be easier and more appealing, but aren't so important to the success of your job. It also encourages the hard work necessary to achieve that ultimate goal.

Goal Orientation is knowing where you want to go with your career, or the work project at hand, and having the motivation to get there. Having a goal without the drive to achieve that goal gets you nowhere. So Goal Orientation means that you are motivated and driven to achieve your goals. Dedication and hard work are necessary for career buoyancy, but without this hard work focused on specific goals and objectives, it is just so much wasted effort.

Here is how jobs both Low and High on Goal Orientation needs might be described:

Low Goal Orientation	*High Goal Orientation*
Goals clearly defined	Must develop your own objectives
Easy workload	Challenging workload
Others motivate you	You motivate yourself

A corporate Director of Training (page 313 in the Human Resources group) is responsible for identifying a company's training needs, designing and implementing the appropriate programs in response to those needs, and continually assessing the programs' effectiveness. The profession demands people who can follow complex projects, some lasting years, through to completion. Consequently, this career requires a High level of Goal Orientation. By contrast, the work of a Radiological Technologist (page 141 in the Medical Technologists group) requires much less in the way of Goal Orientation, so this career is rated Low on Goal Orientation.

POSITIVE EXPECTANCY: BELIEVING IN YOUR ABILITY TO OVERCOME, AND ULTIMATELY TO SUCCEED

What It Is and Why It Is Important to Your Career

"He is the master of his destiny and believes in his own abilities."
"She turns criticism into feedback, and failures into learning experiences, and uses both to get stronger."
"It takes years to establish career buoyancy, and sometimes all you have is a belief in yourself."

A High Positive Expectancy rating means that, when you fail, you recognize that *you* are not a failure. Failures are seen as setbacks, and setbacks are seen as temporary; all problems are seen as having resolutions. This viewpoint on your career means that you are persistent, and that you keep trying to succeed by doing more of what you are doing right, analyzing the causes of your setbacks, remedying those problems, and turning weaknesses into strengths. Naturally, when you take such a logical approach to professional challenges, you deserve to face the future with enhanced Positive Expectancy.

If you pursue a career as an Actuary (page 294), your Positive Expectancy profile won't loom large in the selection process. On the other hand, Positive Expectancy is far more important when a Sales Representative (page 351) is getting hired. In Sales, you need to believe strongly in your ability to overcome the obstacles and setbacks that are a daily part of your professional landscape.

People in Sales and Marketing need to be focused on making things happen through individual effort, and that requires a consistently High degree of Positive Expectancy.

Persistence in the face of failure is at the heart of Positive Expectancy. Persistence is different from motivation because persistence is what keeps you going after you've experienced failure. Persistence is the voice inside you that tells you to plow ahead.

Here is how jobs Low and High on Positive Expectancy demands can be described:

Low Positive Expectancy	*High Positive Expectancy*
Few difficult challenges	Very difficult tasks
Attitude does not matter	Positive attitude critical
Little chance to fail	Frequent failures viewed as setbacks

To succeed as a Teacher (page 414) requires a High level of Positive Expectancy. When a student catches on to what you've been trying to communicate, you feel duly rewarded, but this reward may come only after many repetitions of the message. On the other end of the scale, persistence and optimism are wonderful traits, but ones not *necessary* for success as an Auditor (page 279). One can do an excellent job as an Auditor with Low levels of Positive Expectancy.

While Positive Expectancy is not critical for the successful execution of duties in all jobs, it is a behavioral resource you will want to be able to tap to help you through the rough spots everyone experiences in a career.

PERSONAL INFLUENCE: COMMUNICATION WITH A PURPOSE

What It Is and Why It Is Important to Your Career
"He is a natural salesperson."
"She seems able to find common ground with anyone in the company."
"He displays influence and persuasion in his dealings."

Personal Influence is communicating with people to influence their thinking, or the way they act, toward a desired outcome. You need to understand whom you are communicating with, and adjust your style to the needs of the person and the purpose of the communication.

Personal Influence skills refer to the way you speak and the way you listen;

it's the way you dress and the messages your body sends; it's your technical communication skills and how well you get along with people. Personal Influence is all the ways you give expression to your wishes and sway other people to your cause.

Although many jobs in this book do not include the word "sales" in their title, they are actually very similar to Sales positions: these jobs require you to understand your audience, formulate a message, deliver it, and persuade others. If the message doesn't work, then you adjust it, using your Personal Influence to get your point across.

Here is how jobs Low and High on Personal Influence skills can be described:

Low Personal Influence	*High Personal Influence*
Interact with same people	Communicate with varied audiences
Can use single communication style	Must be able to adapt communication style
Little need to influence others	Critical need to persuade and influence others

Working with others and communicating effectively with them is an important part of the work of a Human Resources Manager (page 309). This career requires High Personal Influence. While even Scientists must sell their ideas, and often in writing, Personal Influence is less critical to the performance of Biological Scientists (page 183) than to professionals in other careers; consequently, this career is rated Low on its Personal Influence skill requirements. However, it's Personal Influence skills in the scientific field that are likely to land the clients, the research money, and the promotions.

SMART DECISIONS: USING REASON, SAVVY, AND COMMON SENSE TO REACH CONCLUSIONS YOU FEEL CONFIDENT TO ACT ON

What It Is and Why It Is Important to Your Career

"*She knows how to evaluate her options, and invariably makes great decisions.*"

"*Once he decided to use what he knew to get to where he wanted to go, he landed a job and got on with his life.*"

"*As an auditor, she knows how to evaluate businesses, and she applied that knowledge when she chose not to accept the job offer. Six months later there was a merger, and what would have been her job was eradicated.*"

Good decision-making skills mean that you are able to apply all your business experience and all your professional competencies to guide your decision-making process. In other words, your decisiveness combined with your experience results in Smart Decisions.

Decisiveness is critical in some jobs, because a delay simply cannot be afforded. There is only a window of opportunity, or a short period of time in which you must decide and then act. If you wait and collect more information or second-guess yourself, then the opportunity can pass on by.

The ability to make good decisions is earned over time by professionals serious about their passions. The benefits are directions and actions that work toward Career Buoyancy.

Here is how jobs Low and High on Smart Decisions are often described:

Low Smart Decisions	*High Smart Decisions*
Not called on to be decisive	Must make decisions
Judgment not called for	Requires good judgment
Can wait to decide	Must make quick decisions

Stuff happens, and often it happens quickly. Attorneys (page 327) find themselves in situations where they need to maintain their cool and make decisions that are consistently good. This career is rated High on its decision-making requirements. However, decisiveness is not an important part of the daily work of a Dental Assistant (page 154), a career which is Low on decision-making requirements.

INFORMED RISK: TAKING INFORMED CHANCES WHILE LOOKING AHEAD

What It Is and Why It Is Important to Your Career
"He looks before he leaps, but he still leaps when he needs to."
"Investing in the new equipment was a big budgetary risk, but he believed the expenditure would expand his market and position him appropriately."
"She implements novel ideas for traditional challenges. Everyone says she thinks 'outside the box.'"

You live in a world that is changing so rapidly, you will never have all the facts at your fingertips before a particular decision has to be made. To wait for all the facts is to be frozen into indecision—and you know what happens to indecisive rabbits caught in highway headlights. Informed Risk enables you to move forward with confidence while, at the same time, it encourages you to expect circumstances to change and to be prepared with alternate plans. People with developed Informed Risk skills understand the need to develop contingency plans, because when you know your professional territory, you know circumstances will change.

Informed Risk dares you to be different through change, through trying something new. An Informed Risk is one where you have considered the options, know your stuff, and stand ready to alter your direction as the situation changes. It is not a bet-the-farm-on-one-roll-of-the-dice risk. Informed Risk is flexible planning in the light of your professional practical know-how. In your career, Informed Risk increases the odds in your favor by continually providing escape hatches and contingency plans for reaching your career goals.

Here is how jobs Low and High on Informed Risk demands can be described:

Low Informed Risk	*High Informed Risk*
Minimal risk necessary	Calculated risk is required and rewarded
Little need for alternative plans	Need for backup plans
Plans can be determined ahead of time	Plans must be open to modification

Dashing off to respond to an emergency call, a Firefighter (page 441) has to have a game plan or two. Before heading into the flames, or another less life-threatening situation, you need to have options and a backup to minimize the risk. Not that you don't take risks—you take ones that are *Informed*. Firefighter is one of the careers requiring a High level of Informed Risk. However, staying flexible, having options, and knowing the odds is not a critical part of the job of an Air Quality Specialist (page 438), a career in which you can succeed with a Low level of Informed Risk skills.

INNER OPENNESS: HAVING THE SELF-AWARENESS, EMOTIONAL ADAPTABILITY, AND OPEN-MINDEDNESS NEEDED TO RECOGNIZE AND BUILD ON PERSONAL STRENGTHS, TOLERATE CHANGE, AND RELATE FLEXIBLY AND CONSTRUCTIVELY WITH OTHERS

What It Is and Why It Is Important to Your Career
"He is self-aware and open to divergence and complexity."
"She is always looking for ways to improve her craft."
"He is turning his weaknesses into strengths."

Inner Openness means being aware of your strengths and weaknesses, asking for and accepting feedback, and being open to new ideas and change. It means that you know yourself and understand how your style of interaction affects others.

In your career, Inner Openness gives you the wisdom to fearlessly evaluate where you stand, to accept the facts and face the challenges of eradicating personal weaknesses by turning them into strengths.

Here is how jobs rated Low and High on Inner Openness demands can be described:

Low Inner Openness	*High Inner Openness*
Little need to understand self	High self-awareness
Little need for feedback	Requires openness to feedback and input
Inflexible	Get along with others

Open-mindedness and tolerance define how a Special Education Teacher (page 415) approaches his work situations. Without these traits, his work is doomed to fail. It's a career that requires a High Level of Inner Openness. Inner Openness is not required as much in the career of a Botanist (page 185 in the Biological Scientists group) as it is in other careers, and so a Botanist job is rated Low on Inner Openness needs.

FLEXIBLE THINKING: CREATIVELY SOLVING PROBLEMS

What It Is and Why It Is Important To Your Career
"She is an innovator and an effective problem solver."
"She is always coming up with new ways to revamp the old products."
"He can get right to the core of a client's problem, whether the client states the problem or not."

Fish gotta swim and birds gotta fly, and you must always learn and grow if you are to stay buoyant in the new world of work. New techniques must be learned, and skills brought up to date. You must have a desire to learn, know, and discover, because a questioning mind is a flexible mind, and flexible minds are in demand.

Flexible Thinking refers to your originality, curiosity, and analysis. It is creative adaptability in a variety of different contexts, including problem-identification and problem-solving skills, analytical ability, and an aptitude for seeing new patterns, directions, and approaches. If you have developed your Flexible Thinking skills, you are inquisitive and curious, eager to tackle a challenging problem and develop new solutions. You love to learn new things, to explore, and to create.

In your career, Flexible Thinking helps you anticipate and adapt to change, using it to your gain. Here is how jobs Low and High on Flexible Thinking demands can be described:

Low Flexible Thinking	High Flexible Thinking
Use existing ideas	Create original ideas
Use predetermined methods	Invent your own methods
Static thinking style	Dynamic thinking style

Original ideas that work and that solve unique problems are part of what makes an Urban Planner (page 434) tick. This is a career that requires a High level of Flexible Thinking skills. The work of a Dental Hygienist (page 153) does not require inventiveness and so is rated Low on Flexible Thinking skills.

ORGANIZED ACTION: COORDINATED ACTION, EFFICIENTLY FOCUSED ON A SPECIFIC OUTCOME

What It Is and Why It Is Important to Your Career
"She always takes the initiative to get the job done."
"She has organized her schedule to accommodate her job, her voice lessons, and carpooling the kids."
"He always gets the job properly finished on time because he plans it that way, and his organization makes the plan happen."

Organized Action is the ability to get things done efficiently, without wasted effort or time. It is a learned behavior that enables you to break down overwhelming tasks into small daily steps. Organized Action involves analysis, planning, and achievable-milestone schedules; each deadline is reached by a hundred measured steps. It's organized action that helps you make your dreams a reality.

Without Organized Action, projects just don't get completed. As companies strive for efficient operations and reengineer themselves to do more with less, Organized Action is a recognized skill set of the employee who can function with less management and more autonomy. If your Personal Preferences call for a job with High Autonomy, it's your organization skills that will get you there.

Here is how jobs Low and High on Organized Action skills are often described:

Low Organized Action	High Organized Action
Priorities set already	Must set and manage priorities
Handle one job at a time	Handle multiple projects
Projects are straightforward	Projects are multi-phase

Getting things done, and being able to set priorities on an ever-changing slate of projects, is the key to the successful performance of a Secretary (page 385). This job requires a High level of Organized Action skills. The daily chores of a Psychiatric Aide (page 163), on the other hand, are not as project-oriented as other careers. A Psychiatric Aide generally does not have to juggle priorities and tasks; therefore this career is rated Low on Organized Action.

AN IN-DEPTH LOOK AT A SAMPLE PROFESSIONAL COMPETENCY PROFILE

Let's take a look at the Professional Competency Profile for a Writer. As you can see, a writer needs great abstraction skills (High on Abstraction), must be able to experiment (Average on Experimentation) in terms of his writing, but does not need to analyze the big picture as much as people in some other jobs (Low on System Thinking).

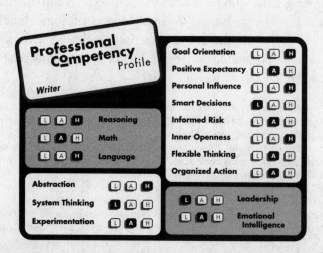

Writers have to understand others' emotions, but need not be experts at it (Average on Emotional Intelligence), and given that they mostly work independently, do not need Leadership skills (Low on Leadership).

They need a strong sense of direction and motivation to keep going (High on Goal Orientation), and must have a positive outlook (Average on Positive Expectancy), especially if their work encounters some rejections. They must be expert in the area of persuasion (High on Personal Influence), and they need to have a reasonable degree of organizational skills and be accomplishment-oriented (Average on Organized Action). But they also need to take chances once in a while (Average on Informed Risk), and to have some new ideas (Average on Flexible Thinking). In their job it's important that they be very self-aware and open-minded (High on Inner Openness), and they can take their time making decisions (Low on Smart Decisions).

Writers also need High Reasoning and Language skills, and Average Math skills.

CONNECTIONS

As you read through this chapter, you may have noticed that certain patterns emerged among the Professional Competency and Personal Preference characteristics. For instance, in reading about the Professional Competencies, you may have noticed that careers that require a high level of Emotional Intelligence often need a high level of Inner Openness as well. There are many such relationships among these characteristics[6]—in fact, there is a good deal of overlap between these traits and behaviors. When you read about System Thinking and Abstraction skills, you may find that the concepts resonate with descriptions of Flexible Thinking skills. And these traits *do* share some common characteristics.

Yet these traits are measuring *different* aspects of competencies. System Thinking looks at the big picture, Abstraction creates patterns, and Flexible Thinking generates original ideas. So, while they are certainly related, they are just as certainly not duplicating each other.[7]

6. When this information was analyzed statistically, using simple correlations, we found that some of the competencies correlated with others. That is, when one competency was high, another would be high, and vice versa. These correlations were moderate for the most part.
7. By using a statistical technique known as principal components analysis, we discovered that there are four related groups of competencies. All of the competencies can be divided into four groups, which have some characteristics in common:
  - *emotional traits*—emotional and personal characteristics
  - *thinking traits*—analytical and problem-solving abilities
  - *decision-making traits*—ability to make quick decisions and exercise good judgment
  - *creativity traits*—ability to come up with new and original ideas and implement them

Always keep in mind that certain skills are often required for certain jobs and not for others. Even if you have a job that is rated low on one, or all, of the Professional Competency knowledge areas, that in no way reflects on who you are; it reflects the competencies required to efficiently discharge the duties of that job.

But also bear this in mind: no matter where your skill bank stands today, or the needs of the job you start tomorrow, consciously developing your Professional Competencies will enhance your employability throughout your work life.

Looking For Your Match: Putting Both Halves of Your Career Brain into Action

If your Mobility Profile (the summation of your Professional Competencies) matches the professional requirements of a job, you can probably land the job and succeed; if your Affinity Profile matches the Workplace Realities of a job, you'll probably enjoy your work life. If you have the affinity for a certain kind of work but lack the competencies for that job, the odds are that such a job will be difficult for you to succeed in. In this instance, your time and energy are best spent on other career options, or on the development of skills that would help you succeed in that type of work. The reverse side of the coin holds true as well: with the right competencies, but low affinity, for a job, you can probably do the job but you may not enjoy it. The important thing is to evaluate your options with both sides of your career brain, and figure out what is the best fit for you.

I talk to thousands of people every year about their jobs, their careers, and their lives. I hear many, many stories of career decisions gone bad. Not all of these bad situations could have been avoided, but many of them could have. By understanding both your Professional Competencies and your Personal Preferences, and by matching them with the jobs slated for greatest growth in the future, you will be taking a balanced and insightful approach to your career decisions.

CHAPTER THREE

Establishing Your Personal Preferences and Professional Competencies: A Self-Appraisal

If you want to do the best by your career and your job hunt, now is the time to give your personal preferences and professional competencies twenty minutes of careful appraisal.

This self-appraisal comes in two parts. In the first part you will respond to statements designed to prioritize your interests, preferred activities, and workplace preferences. You will rate each statement according to a five-point scale, and there is no right response. The scale is simply designed to help you clarify and order those factors *most likely to predict your affinity for a particular job*. Once you total your scores, you will be able to fill in a template with your ratings on page 60. This is your personal *Affinity Profile*. To judge your affinity for a particular job, compare it with the Workplace Realities Profiles that appear in the job descriptions in Part 2 of this book.

In the second part of the self-appraisal you will get the chance to evaluate your skill level in each of the professional competency areas sought by employers hiring for the jobs of the future. Not all professional competencies are needed to succeed in all jobs, so this isn't a test in which your goal is a perfect score. In fact, you need to give yourself an objective look in the mirror, to see what skills you have today to get you where you want to be tomorrow. Just as in the first part of the self-appraisal, there are no right ratings; the more honest your responses, the better the handle you will get on your strengths and weaknesses. In a modern career, self-knowledge offers the power to step forward in your personal development, and in your career.

Once you have answered the questions, it will be time to total your scores and transfer the ratings to your personal *Mobility Profile* on page 70. You can then use it to evaluate your professional mobility and skills against the Professional Competencies Profile presented for every job description in the book.

You will find that your Mobility and Affinity Profiles can be used as excellent tools to:

- Develop a list of all the jobs you would *enjoy* doing (Affinity);
- Develop a list of all the jobs you *can* do (Mobility);
- Find out which jobs most accurately match your needs (Affinity) and current abilities (Mobility);
- Identify compatibilities between the job and career you are *in*, and the job or career that you *want* (Affinity and Mobility);
- Find out what you have that employers of in-demand professionals want in today's competitive marketplace (Affinity and Mobility);
- Evaluate your real-world options in the event of a downsizing at your place of work (Affinity and Mobility);
- Objectively rule jobs in or out for your further consideration (Affinity and Mobility);
- Identify areas for personal development (Affinity and Mobility);
- Pinpoint what causes your feelings of unhappiness or insecurity in your current job, so you can develop skills to make the job more secure, or work toward a job that will give you a more supportive working environment (Mobility and Affinity);
- Evaluate strengths to emphasize at job interviews (Mobility and Affinity);
- Convince potential employers that the work you have done has relevance to the work you want to do (Mobility).

Personal Preferences Self-Appraisal: Your Affinity Profile

ASSESSING YOUR INTERESTS

Each of the following Career Interest areas will help you better understand your general preference for activities dominant in different careers. For each activity in the following appraisal, think about whether you would enjoy it— find it interesting or satisfying—by using this scale:

Not At All Interesting	0
Of Little Interest	1

Somewhat Interesting	2
Very Interesting	3
Extremely Interesting	4

As you go through the interest categories, *stay open-minded*. If you have never attempted one of the activities, do not immediately give yourself a low score; think about whether you believe you'd like it. Of course, if you have engaged in an activity listed in this section and concluded that you really don't care for it, that's a different story. In that case, go ahead and give the activity a *low* interest rating.

CAREER INTERESTS

Invention

RATING	QUESTION
_____	Express my thoughts or ideas
_____	Develop new ideas or products
_____	Create something new
_____	Work with theories or concepts
_____	Discover new ways of doing things
_____	**Total Score** - *Invention*

Problem Solving

RATING	QUESTION
_____	Solve complex problems
_____	Figure out the root cause of a problem
_____	Conduct experiments or research
_____	Use analytical thinking
_____	Search for information
_____	**Total Score** - *Problem Solving*

Financial

RATING	QUESTION
_____	Work with numbers
_____	Follow the stock market
_____	Explain financial information to others
_____	Manage investments
_____	Manage budgets and finances
_____	*Total Score - Financial*

Technology

RATING	QUESTION
_____	Use state-of-the-art technology
_____	Work with complex systems
_____	Use software programs
_____	Set up equipment, understand how it works
_____	Design or write computer programs
_____	*Total Score - Technology*

Development

RATING	QUESTION
_____	Teach people
_____	Train others in area of expertise
_____	Help people to feel better
_____	Help people to improve their lives
_____	Help people to solve their problems
_____	*Total Score - Development*

Project

RATING	QUESTION
_____	Manage complex projects
_____	Plan and schedule activities
_____	Organize information and records
_____	Determine resources required for a project
_____	Get things accomplished
_____	*Total Score - Project*

Persuasion

RATING	QUESTION
_____	Debate and negotiate
_____	Understand people's needs
_____	Communicate ideas and concepts
_____	Persuade others to a course of action
_____	Be convincing
_____	*Total Score - Persuasion*

ASSESSING YOUR PERSONAL PREFERENCES

The following should help you better understand your personal workplace preferences, and build your Affinity Profile so you can match them against the Workplace Realities of different jobs. Use the following rating scale to respond to the Personal Preferences statements:

Of No Importance	0
Of Little Importance	1
Somewhat Important	2
Very Important	3
Extremely Important	4

Read each statement, and rate your preference on this scale of 0 to 4. Do not spend too much time thinking about the statements, since your first response usually reflects your true feelings. There is no right or wrong here; it's a case of what feels good for you, in your life.

PERSONAL PREFERENCES

Social Environment

RATING	QUESTION
_____	Work with other people
_____	Meet and discuss my work with colleagues

_____   Work with people I enjoy
_____   Work on group projects rather than alone
_____   Be part of a team
_____   *Total Score* - *Social Environment*

Autonomy

RATING   QUESTION
_____   Not being told what to do
_____   Not having a boss who micro-manages me
_____   Make my own decisions
_____   Set my own schedule
_____   Be my own boss
_____   *Total Score* - *Autonomy*

Creativity

RATING   QUESTION
_____   Be creative on the job
_____   Think up new ideas
_____   Solve problems in unique ways
_____   Invent or discover
_____   Express myself
_____   *Total Score* - *Creativity*

Variety

RATING   QUESTION
_____   Steady work routine
_____   Not knowing what to expect each day
_____   Think and act on my feet
_____   Work with a varied group of people
_____   No need to plan my day
_____   *Total Score* - *Variety*

Altruism

RATING   QUESTION
_____   Job works toward improving the community
_____   Help people

_____ Change the community
_____ Give something back to the community through work
_____ Positively impact people's lives
_____ **Total Score** - *Altruism*

Stress

RATING   QUESTION
_____ A fast-paced job
_____ Tight deadlines
_____ Have a career in the fast lane
_____ Juggle multiple projects
_____ Stay busy and active
_____ **Total Score** - *Stress*

TOTALING YOUR SCORES

By now you should have added up the points for every Career Interest and Personal Preference. For each individual score, determine whether it is Low, Average, or High by comparing your results to the table below:

Low   0 to 5
Average   6 to 14
High   15 to 20

Now, check the appropriate box in the summary chart below:

SUMMARY CHART: AFFINITY SELF-APPRAISAL

Career Interests	Low	Average	High
Invention	[ ]	[ ]	[ ]
Problem Solving	[ ]	[ ]	[ ]
Financial	[ ]	[ ]	[ ]
Technology	[ ]	[ ]	[ ]
Development	[ ]	[ ]	[ ]
Project	[ ]	[ ]	[ ]
Persuasion	[ ]	[ ]	[ ]

Personal Preferences	Low	Average	High
Social Environment	[ ]	[ ]	[ ]
Autonomy	[ ]	[ ]	[ ]
Creativity	[ ]	[ ]	[ ]
Variety	[ ]	[ ]	[ ]
Altruism	[ ]	[ ]	[ ]
Stress	[ ]	[ ]	[ ]

HOW TO USE THE RESULTS FROM YOUR AFFINITY SELF-APPRAISAL

Start with your Career Interests. Take your Career Interest categories in the High range and compare them to each of the major job categories that follow. Each class of jobs has one or more interest categories. Simply match your High interests to these categories.

If you do not have any High ratings, or you have already matched your High ratings, expand into the Average range; this is important, since there may be one or more jobs that would interest you in a category that, overall, is rated only Average.

If all of your Interest areas are rated Low, look at the actual score numbers and then examine those categories with the highest ratings.

For example, if you scored High for Persuasion, then you should examine all job opportunities that tap these interests. In this case, you would definitely look at some of the jobs in Human Resources, Sales and Marketing, and Financial Services. However, you will want to consider steering clear of those jobs that tap into a low-rated interest area; a career which is High on a need in which you score Low may turn out to be a disappointment for you.

Job Category	**Interest Area(s)**
HEALTH CARE	
Administration	
Health Care Service Manager	Development/Project
Medical Records Technician	Project/Problem Solving
Medical Assistant	Development/Project
Medical Secretary	Project/Development
Nursing	
Registered Nurse	Development/Problem Solving
Licenced Practical Nurse	Development/Project
Home Health Care Nurse	Development/Project
Nursing Aide	Development/Project
Physical Health	
General and Family Practitioner	Problem Solving/Development
Podiatrist	Problem Solving/Development
Audiologist	Development/Problem Solving
Medical Therapist	Development/Problem Solving
Medical Technologist	Development/Technology
Dispensing Optician	Problem Solving/Development
Dentistry	
Dentist	Problem Solving/Project
Dental Hygienist	Development/Problem Solving
Dental Assistant	Development/Problem Solving
Mental Health	
Psychiatrist/Psychologist	Problem Solving/Development
Psychiatric Aide	Development/Project
THE TECHNOLOGIES	
Biotechnology and Environmental Technology	
Biological Scientists	Problem Solving/Invention
Medical Scientists	Problem Solving/Development
Conservation Scientists	Problem Solving/Project
Geoscientists	Problem Solving
Engineering	
Engineers	Problem Solving/Technology
Information Technology	
Computer Software Engineer	Technology/Problem Solving
Systems Analyst	Problem Solving/Technology

Computer Programmers	Technology/Problem Solving
Information Systems Manager	Technology/Persuasion
User Support Analyst	Problem Solving/Development
Computer Service Technician	Technology/Repair

BUSINESS AND PROFESSIONAL SERVICES
Financial Services
Banking:

Loan Officers/Counselors	Financial/Development

Securities:

Broker/Trader	Persuasion/Financial
Brokerage Clerk	Project/Financial

Accounting:

Accountants	Financial/Project
Auditors	Financial/Project

Insurance:

Insurance Agents	Financial/Persuasion
Actuary	Financial/Project
Underwriter	Financial/Project

Human Resources

Benefits Managers	Financial/Development
Human Resource Managers	Development/Persuasion
Training Managers	Persuasion/Development
Labor Relations Specialist/ Diversity Manager	Persuasion/Project
Management Consultant	Problem Solving/Invention

Law

Attorneys	Problem Solving/Persuasion
Paralegal	Project/Problem Solving

Media/Communications/Public Relations

Editor	Invention/Project
Writers	Invention/Project
Public Relations Professional	Invention/Persuasion

Sales and Marketing

Sales Representative	Persuasion
Retail Sales Associate	Persuasion
Travel Agent	Persuasion/Development
Flight Attendant	Project/Development

Food Service

Chefs/Cooks	Invention/Project
Restaurant/Food Service Manager	Project/Persuasion
Waiter/Waitress	Project/Development

Support Services

Record Clerks	Project
Secretaries	Project
Legal Secretary	Project

PUBLIC SERVICE

Social Services

Social Service Administrator	Project/Development
Social Workers	Development
Human Services Worker	Development
Counselors	Development/Project

Education

Teacher	Development/Project
Adult Education Teacher	Development/Project
Teacher's Aide	Development/Project
Librarian	Project/Invention

State and Local Government

Urban and Regional Planner	Problem Solving/Project
Air Quality Specialist	Problem Solving/Project
Child Care Worker	Development
Firefighter	Project/Development
Police Officer	Project/Development
Corrections Officer	Project/Development
Security Guard	Project/Development

PROFESSIONAL COMPETENCIES APPRAISAL: YOUR MOBILITY PROFILE

The following sequence of questions[1] will help you evaluate the level of skill you feel you possess in each of the professional competency areas most in demand in today's professional workplace.

1. The assessment questions in this book are designed to get you to think about your professional competency and personal preferences in a serious, formal way. These questions do not represent a true test of these skills and traits, however. In a professional Mobility and Affinity test, test items would appear in a different order and would not appear after a description of the trait we are trying to measure. In addition, we have not provided norms for test interpretation.

For each question, answer using this scale[2]:

Little or No Skill	0
Some Skill	1
About Average Skill	2
Above Average Skill	3
Well Above Average Skill	4

BASIC FUNCTIONAL SKILLS

Reasoning

RATING	QUESTION
_____	Understand formulas and symbols
_____	Solve complex, abstract problems
_____	Employ logical, scientific thinking
_____	Collect data and develop conclusions from those data
_____	Understand complex instructions found in diagrams, graphs, etc.
_____	**Total Score** - *Reasoning*

Math

RATING	QUESTION
_____	Understand advanced calculus: limits, continuity, mean value theorems
_____	Geometry: circumference area, analytic geometry
_____	Statistics: probability, statistical inference
_____	Algebra: differential equations
_____	Ability to work with exponents, logarithms, quadratic equations
_____	**Total Score** - *Math*

2. There is an important distinction between self-rating scales and performance tests. We are presenting you with a self-rating scale, a *subjective* measure of your skills and affinities. In other words, a high rating on Abstraction indicates that *you* are confident in your Abstraction skill. In reality, your actual Abstraction skill may be Low, Average, or High. Still, your self-confidence is an important factor since this confidence is reflected in your interviewing style, search style, and job performance. (Note, too, that one of the best commercial tests in this area, the Campbell Interest and Skill Survey, uses a similar skill confidence approach.)

Language

RATING | QUESTION

Comprehend and write journal articles and critical reviews

_____

Write plays, stories, poems

_____

Understand principles and methods of effective public speaking

_____

Participate in group discussions of complex material

_____

Prepare business letters, reports, and presentations

_____

Total Score - *Language*

THINKING SKILLS

Abstraction

RATING | QUESTION

Take different bits of information from multiple sources, evaluate it, and construct a story/analysis based on it

_____

See new solutions for complex problems

Discover new problems to solve

_____

See patterns and meaning in unrelated pieces of information

_____

Integrate huge amounts of data using formulas and theories

_____

Total Score - *Abstraction*

System Thinking

RATING | QUESTION

Look at the big picture

_____

Understand relationships among the parts of a complex system

_____

Understand the *real* cause of a problem

Consider multiple variables at the same time

_____

See how one part of a problem is related to another problem

_____

Total Score - *System Thinking*

Experimentation

RATING	QUESTION
_____	Develop and test different solutions to problems
_____	Understand the experimental method
_____	Excellent powers of observation
_____	Record accurately the results of new methods
_____	Generate and test new ideas
_____	**Total Score** - *Experimentation*

CAREER BUOYANCY BEHAVIORS

Goal Orientation

RATING	QUESTION
_____	Set goals and objectives
_____	Work very hard to achieve personal goals
_____	Excel and achieve
_____	Have clear goals
_____	Motivate myself
_____	**Total Score** - *Goal Orientation*

Positive Expectancy

RATING	QUESTION
_____	Keep on trying when things get difficult
_____	Failure is not a major setback
_____	Able to persist under difficult conditions
_____	Possess positive attitude and self-confidence
_____	Do not easily give up
_____	**Total Score** - *Positive Expectancy*

Personal Influence

RATING	QUESTION
_____	Strong communication skills
_____	Easily persuade people
_____	Change my approach depending upon who the other person is

_____ Can get people to change their minds
_____ Can motivate others
_____ **Total Score** - *Personal Influence*

Smart Decisions

RATING   QUESTION

_____ Make good decisions
_____ Have common sense
_____ Have business know-how
_____ Understand how things really work
_____ Be decisive
_____ **Total Score** - *Smart Decisions*

Informed Risk

RATING   QUESTION

_____ Prepared to act when necessary
_____ Usually have a back-up plan in place
                   Evaluate my options and the odds of success, and
_____ if they are reasonable, I take the chance
                   Employ contingency planning skills
_____ Calculate odds of success
_____ **Total Score** - *Informed Risk*

Inner Openness

RATING   QUESTION

_____ Open-minded, introspective
_____ Tolerant and flexible about other people
_____ Can adjust to the demands of the situation
_____ Tactful and sensitive to others
_____ Solicit criticism and feedback
_____ **Total Score** - *Inner Openness*

Flexible Thinking

RATING   QUESTION

_____ Learn new things
_____ Solve complex problems

_____ Generate new and original ideas
_____ Learn quickly
_____ Evaluate ideas, connect them with others, and apply
          them in different contexts
_____ **Total Score** - *Flexible Thinking*

Organized Action

RATING	QUESTION
_____	Set priorities
_____	Efficient and organized
_____	Get things done by breaking down large projects into small steps
_____	Obtain necessary information
_____	Know how to get things done
_____	**Total Score** - *Organized Action*

PEOPLE SKILLS

Leadership

RATING	QUESTION
_____	Often volunteer to lead groups or meetings
_____	Considered to be a strong leader
_____	Make decisions for myself and for others
_____	Have supervisory skills
_____	Can easily get people to do things at work
_____	**Total Score** - *Leadership*

Emotional Intelligence

RATING	QUESTION
_____	Always open to my feelings
_____	Know what makes people feel angry, sad, or happy
_____	Can get myself into and out of moods
_____	Can identify emotions in others, art, language, and behavior
_____	Can control emotions in myself and in others
_____	**Total Score** - *Emotional Intelligence*

TOTALING YOUR SCORES

Add up the points for every Mobility trait or skill. For each total score, determine whether it is Low, Average, or High by comparing your results to the table below:

Low   0 to 5
Average   6 to 14
High   15 to 20

Then check your results in the appropriate box.

SUMMARY CHART: MOBILITY SELF-APPRAISAL

Basic Functional Skills	Low	Average	High
Reasoning	[ ]	[ ]	[ ]
Math	[ ]	[ ]	[ ]
Language	[ ]	[ ]	[ ]

Thinking Skills	Low	Average	High
Abstraction	[ ]	[ ]	[ ]
System Thinking	[ ]	[ ]	[ ]
Experimentation	[ ]	[ ]	[ ]

Career Buoyancy Behaviors	Low	Average	High
Goal Orientation	[ ]	[ ]	[ ]
Positive Expectancy	[ ]	[ ]	[ ]
Personal Influence	[ ]	[ ]	[ ]
Smart Decisions	[ ]	[ ]	[ ]
Informed Risk	[ ]	[ ]	[ ]
Inner Openness	[ ]	[ ]	[ ]
Flexible Thinking	[ ]	[ ]	[ ]
Organized Action	[ ]	[ ]	[ ]

People Skills	Low	Average	High
Leadership	[ ]	[ ]	[ ]
Emotional Intelligence	[ ]	[ ]	[ ]

HOW TO USE THE RESULTS FROM YOUR MOBILITY SELF-APPRAISAL

Your Mobility Profile can be a powerful career-planning tool when compared with the Professional Competencies Profiles offered with each job description in Part 2 of this book. Every job in the book identifies the level of Professional Competencies required for a good fit. This will enable you to immediately evaluate each job against the relevant skills you currently possess. And when you use these results in conjunction with your Affinity Profile, you'll discover a job content that resonates with your interests and is compatible with your way of interacting with the world.

A Low level rating for a specific competency in a job profile means that you are less likely to require that skill in great measure, *compared to the other jobs in this book*. An Average skill level means that you don't need to excel in that area, but you do need to have developed it to a reasonable level. A High level requires you to have expertise in that area.

Those who go farthest in every field of endeavor will be those who have the widest and most developed range of Professional Competencies. In other words, while a particular job may not demand that you have, for example, exemplary Abstraction skills, concern for your ongoing employability and pro-motability demands that you do.

When a job is rated Low on a skill, knowledge area, or behavior it should *not* become one of your goals to become low in that area. In fact, if you rate High on one of these areas, but want to pursue a career that is rated Low in the area, *don't worry!* However, one of your goals must be never to get worse in that skill area.

If you are concerned about too many of your ratings being in the Low range, don't let this cause you despair. You have actually taken two great steps forward: you have established where it is that you stand, and what it is that you need to develop to get to wherever it is you want to go.

HIGH DOESN'T MEAN IMPOSSIBLE

When your career dreams exceed your current professional competencies—and this happens to everybody—you can develop the skills, go back to school, choose another direction, or look to stepping-stone jobs with similar needs where the skill entrance fee is a bit lower. But *don't forget the dream*: work toward it over time, using the jobs you *can* do to develop the skills you will need to achieve your career goals.

YOUR WORK DOESN'T DEFINE YOU OR YOUR COMPETENCIES

If your work history includes jobs which are rated Low on several Professional Competency factors, one of your challenges will be to convince potential employers that you have these abilities, even though they normally wouldn't expect that of someone in your current field of work.

Take the example of a Billing Clerk we looked at earlier. This is a career which is rated low on Abstraction, System Thinking, and Experimentation skills, because in general, Billing Clerks don't require these particular competencies to do their work. They don't get much of a chance to use, or to show, these kinds of skills; in most cases the job just doesn't call for it. But it doesn't mean that if you are a Billing Clerk that *you* don't have these skills! It's the job's Professional Competency requirements we are rating, not *you*. Of course, if you have a skill that is not exercised on the job, it may atrophy over time.

A Low rating simply means you don't *have* to have that skill, knowledge area, or behavior highly developed in order to do that job well. If you happen to have a High skill where none is required for a job you want, then great! You can use it to grow professionally. You may be a bit different from other people in that career, but the difference is a positive one for you, because you can bring something unique to the table.

Making a Match Between You and the Job

Now it's time to transfer your Personal Preferences ratings to the Affinity Profile template, and your Professional Competencies ratings to the Mobility Profile template, both of which appear on the following page. These templates are exact mirror images of the Workplace Realities Profile and the Professional Competency Profile that appear for every job in the second part of the book. So after you fill in your ratings, you can copy the template and then match your preferences or competencies with the realities and requirements found in the job profiles. (*Note:* If you copy the templates onto overhead transparency film from a local stationery store, you then will be able to overlay them onto each job that interests you.)

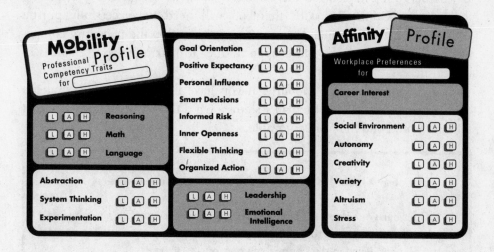

Putting It All Together

Sometimes, a person's Mobility and Affinity factors are in sync and fit the jobs in question; at other times, one or the other profile is either low or high for a particular career. When they are out of sync, here is a way of interpreting what path you should take next:

• *Low Affinity / Low Mobility:* If you do not have the Professional Competencies and your Personal Preferences are also not being met by a career, then it isn't worth going after the opportunity. Your time and energy are best spent on other career options.

• *Low Affinity / High Mobility:* With a skill set in a certain career area (High Mobility), but Low Affinity, you can do the job but you may not enjoy it. Or you can get a job but you ultimately may not want to keep it, because your needs aren't being met. For the long term, it's best to move on, or to grow into a different area where your Affinity needs can be met. Perhaps the right move is to remain in the same career area, but switch to a different environment. Experiencing burnout may signal that it is time for some change—but still not time to throw out the considerable experience and skills you have acquired in your career to date.

• *High Affinity / Low Mobility:* Having your Affinity needs met by a job but lacking its professional competencies spells a career nightmare for you. Rather than jumping headlong into the abyss, if you find yourself in this situation, start your long-term planning *right now*. The first question to ask yourself is whether you *can* acquire the necessary skills. If so, go about acquiring the experience and the skills that you will need to successfully pursue your dream. If you are unable or unwilling to develop the necessary competencies you must look for other opportunities to maximize your chances of career success.

• *High Affinity / High Mobility:* If you have the Mobility skills and the Affinity needs for a career, then all systems are go. You have the necessary skill sets and would find the work enjoyable.

For Those Just Starting Out, or Switching Careers

• Consider your interests first. However, if your interests don't completely match a career you want to investigate, don't let it stop you; compromise must always be considered in the context of your long-term goals.

• Make sure that you have adequate professional skills, or at least that your profile is close enough to make success on the job a probability, given your commitment to skill development and the sacrifices which that might require. If your ratings say you can do the job, and your ratings were honest, you will go into the job interview with greater confidence, and a knowledge of what the interviewer is likely to want to hear about. In most cases, focus your career search in a direction where you can use your professional competency strengths.

For Success over the Long Term

• Check out your career buoyancy behaviors. If your career is rated high on a behavior in which you are rated average or low, be warned that you'll need to spend some of your time boosting this behavior, or increase the risk of career atrophy.

• Constantly acquire new job-specific skills, and hone your transferable skills.

• Pursue additional interests via an entrepreneurial venture or hobby. These activities will develop your professional competencies, enhance your economic viability, and help you achieve a dynamic professional life.

In the Final Analysis

The approach I have developed includes a couple of important principles about career management that I want to share with you.

- *You're the best judge of your career and your work life.* This book is simply a guide—a set of *suggestions*. It can help you explore career options, but no expert can tell you how to live your life, or choose your career.
- *Career paths that closely match your interests, skills, knowledge, and professional behaviors offer the most opportunities for satisfaction and success.*
- *High is not Impossible.* If you take a good look at yourself and find that your dream job requires very different interests or greater skills than you have now, don't despair. Either change direction, or build the skill sets necessary to achieve your career goals, as you work just a bit harder than some of your colleagues to get wherever it is you want to go. You can learn the necessary skills and acquire the needed experience through stepping-stone jobs, moonlighting, an entrepreneurial venture, volunteer work, or further schooling.
- *Your new awareness of your professional competencies can provide you with a firm foundation on which to build throughout your work life.*
- *In terms of skills, you need the basics to get a job—usually.* For if you have the ability to learn, some employers may see your potential and give you a probationary period during which you acquire the needed skills. So you may not be down for the count if you don't have all of the Professional Competencies to the required level.
- *Change careers midstream only after carefully considering all of the reasons for dissatisfaction with your current career.* (See box.)

SWITCH JOBS, CHANGE CAREERS, STAY PUT?

Before switching jobs, or careers, you need to understand the reasons for your unhappiness. These are the usual reasons to seriously consider a career change:
- Your career isn't in one of your interest areas.
- You don't have the skills.
- You have interest and skill in another area.
- It's not a hot career, and your long-term prospects for survival and/or success are poor.

But it could be that you just need to change jobs, and not your *career*, if:
- You have a crummy boss who's not going anywhere.
- You enjoyed the work once upon a time.
- Your company is floundering, but the industry is not.
- Pay, benefits, or working conditions are below par at your company.

• *Lastly, if you like to do something, and you have the required competencies, go for it!* If you have the aptitude to acquire other skills along the way, even better. And if you have the necessary Buoyancy traits, you'll last for the duration of what is likely to be a long trip.

Good luck and be sure to keep in touch: see page 486 for contact information.

PART TWO

THE JOB DESCRIPTIONS AND INDUSTRY ANALYSES

Health Care

Health care is concerned with the delivery of preventive and curative medicine through the expertise of doctors, nurses, medical therapists, medical technologists, and dental and mental health professionals. Health care services, themselves, are delivered in many ways: through hospitals, clinics, outpatient centers, homes, and hospices.

Increasingly, this enormous industry is dominated by larger and larger health care deliverers such as HMOs (health maintenance organizations). At the same time it is also an industry that spawns successful new ventures almost every day.

Consequently, the health care business has its own world of supporting corporate structures, with their accompanying hierarchies of administrators and support staff—medical, dental, and mental health secretaries, computer programmers, accountants, and librarians. Just as in other professions, these people can work for a corporate behemoth or a solo practitioner who needs employees for only a few hours a week.

In examining the health care industry, we'll focus on the delivery of service, and not on the corporate support structure that delivers that service. Professionals who work in the administrative and corporate support structure can expect their futures to mirror those of the area of health care with which they are most closely associated.

Luckily, the health care industry is virtually recession-proof; whatever the economic climate, people still get sick. Which is not to say that the industry isn't changing or that it isn't subject to further change in the future. We are an aging society, living longer and surviving far more illnesses than ever before—

although the health care costs associated with this longevity are somewhat frightening. Solutions to this problem are revolutionizing the health care industry. There's a new and strong emphasis on cost containment in hospitals and throughout the industry, which is now emphasizing preventive medicine, outpatient services, at-home care, and enhanced responsibilities for the physician-supporting ranks. The health care industry is busily reinventing itself as steadily as it is growing.

And growing it is, *at twice the rate of all other jobs*. The government anticipates that the health care industry could generate about four million new jobs—or two out of every ten new jobs that we create in the entire economy—over the next ten years. About a million jobs will be created in hospitals, almost as many in doctors' and dentists' offices, and the balance in nursing, personal care facilities, clinics, and other aspects of at-home health care, which has been flagged as the hottest growth area in the field. For example, jobs for home health aides are expected by some to double, and by others to triple, by 2005.

While at-home health care will create many new jobs, there will also be growth in more traditional health care settings: hospitals, clinics, pharmacies, medical laboratories, private doctors' offices, HMOs, dental and mental health facilities, and so on. Positions will be available across the country, although the steadiest growth will be in California, New York, and the Central and Middle Atlantic states, because of the population density.

Administration

Health maintenance organizations (HMOs), which help employers manage the cost of health care for employees, are likely to further dominate the market, and physician practice management organizations (PPMs) will grow to facilitate the interface between the doctor's office and the HMO. PPMs manage the paperwork and relationship with the HMO, as well as other aspects of the practice. This frees the physicians to concentrate on the practice of medicine (and golf).

However, hospitals, which we are used to viewing as the beating heart of health care, will experience much slower growth than other areas of the industry because of these new and hopefully cheaper approaches to maintaining our health. Does this mean there will be no jobs in hospitals? Absolutely not. Hospitals will still account for 50 percent of all health care jobs. It's just that those big hospitals in metropolitan areas, the traditionally recognizable employers, will continue to trim the fat, and will hire a different type of health care professional. It is likely that there will be a decline in some administrative and support positions as hospitals consolidate and simultaneously apply the latest technological advances to the administration of the business.

Medical Practitioners

The advances in medical technology, which are enabling the medical profession to make such great strides in treatment, are also creating the need for more technically oriented professionals at all levels—and this has led to an escalation of costs. In short, we need and will use much more health care in the future, which is good news for the industry, yet health care companies and their employees can expect the same volatility as every other industry that is busy reinventing itself to survive. Still, lots of jobs *are* going to be created in an enormous profession, but there will be few safe havens.

Private duty nurses, medical assistants, home health care nurses, outpatient therapists, and others who provide in-person services will not only be in demand—these will be among the fastest-growing jobs in the economy—but their professional roles will also expand. Highly trained nurses and assistants, and certain dental and mental health professionals will provide primary care in place of doctors. Home health care nurses will oversee their patients' nutritional needs, as well as provide companionship and housekeeping services. And therapists will provide at-home services to patients, saving them hospital visits and reducing expenses.

In many areas of the country, the expanding health care industry has replaced a number of the jobs lost in manufacturing. However, when production line workers lose their jobs, it doesn't mean they all get new ones as doctors, nurses, and therapists. The new jobs are going to the people with the new *skills*. Education, especially in health care, is paramount.

INSIDER'S VIEW OF THE HEALTH CARE INDUSTRY

All aspects of the health care industry are going through a radical restructuring—including downsizing and outsourcing. To someone on the outside looking in, it may seem strange that health care is predicted to be a growth industry in the years ahead.

But insiders agree that, despite massive changes, the health care industry will continue to grow over the next decade. People will always need medical care, and an aging population in particular will fuel health care's growth. The problem is predicting how—not whether—health care will expand.

The emphasis in the Health Care industry is shifting away from sickness toward wellness. "Under managed care," explains Lucy J. Randles, C.L.S./CL.Dir., who is the president of Health Care Advantage in Ohio and a clinical laboratory director, "the incentive is to keep patients out of hospitals and prevent them from getting sick."

And, when patients do need care, Randles points out, they will be more likely to go to a rehabilitation facility, HMO, long-term care or nursing home, or even a retirement center than to a hospital or a residential mental institution. As a result, public health care facilities will downsize or close, and the need for employees in these traditional health care centers will decrease, as the number of alternative health care facilities increases.

Now for better news. Since workers will leave traditional health care employers for facilities, there will be growth potential for generalists who can do many different things. Randles offers an example: "People who have been doing the same thing for twenty-five years, like nurses, may lose their jobs. But new graduates who are familiar with all types of nursing and with all types of patients are more marketable." She advises those entering the health care professions to "get experience in and exposure to as many areas as you can."

James S. Todd, M.D., executive vice president of the American Medical Association, agrees. He advises even physicians to stay broad-based.

Randles also points out that people in the health care industry will focus on short-term jobs more and more. "Employers prefer someone who has not been in a job more than five years. They want people who have been exposed to different management styles."

Says Randles: "If you're in a profession that can take advantage of all the changes, and you're willing to adapt and take from your knowledge base what is useful, the opportunities are tremendous." Although she concedes that stability isn't a part of the health care industry today because of economic and regulatory reform, she believes that as things settle down again, the industry will be sound.

Marilyn Moffat, P.T., Ph.D., president of the American Physical Therapy Association, says that physical therapists will continue to be in great demand, with an increasing number of them possessing B.A.s and doctorates. However, she cautions that managed health care will create some changes for physical therapists as well. Because patients will have fewer visits to the hospital, physical therapists will have to do their job more quickly. "Physical therapists will have to refine their existing skills. Patient education has always been part of the job, but now it will have to be done in a smaller time frame. Everyone has to adjust to it."

She also sees computer skills as becoming an important part of physical therapists' knowledge base, as physical therapists put instructions for patients on-line. And there will be more program coordination, as social workers, nurse practitioners, mental health professionals and physical therapists combine their skills in a new approach to health care.

Finally, Moffat predicts, "The future looks excellent for physical therapists. As we show we can keep patients out of institutions, demand is going to continue to be there."

SUCCESS IN HEALTH CARE

According to James S. Todd, M.D., those who will be successful in the health care industry will have the ability to anticipate and be fully prepared to deal with all facets of the health care system. They will have to have an understanding of "not only the science and art of medicine, but management of organizations and an understanding of quality."

For medical assistants and nurse practioners, who are sometimes called "physican extenders," Melissa Webb, president of Circlewood Executive Search Group (a recruitment firm) located in Kalamazoo, Wisconsin, thinks the most important strengths for success include "good analytical skills, good people skills, attention to detail, and a sincere desire to help people."

Just as the delivery of other health care services is changing, delivery of dental services is changing, too. Gail Bemis, president of the Chicago-based American Dental Hygienists' Association, predicts that up to 80 percent of the insured population will receive its dental services through managed care in the next ten years. Harold E. Donnell, Jr., C.A.E., executive director of the Chicago-based Academy of General Dentistry, believes that managed care won't overtake the dental profession to the same degree that it will medicine, but he foresees that "dentists will rely more on dental auxiliaries and be more likely to practice with other dentists in group practices than as solo practitioners." This, he says, will "give them added efficiency in practice."

Bemis, too, expects change in dentistry to be enormous. She believes that dental professionals will increasingly work in alternate practice settings outside the traditional arena, including nursing homes, home health care programs, community outreach centers, schools, and prisons. The great array of work settings will assure employment for professionals and provide them with a semblance of job security.

Jobs with a Future in: Health Care

Administration

Health Care Service Manager . . . Health Care Generalist . . . Clinical Manager . . . Medical Records Technician . . . Medical Assistant . . . Medical Secretary

Nursing

Nurse . . . Registered Nurse . . . Licensed Practical Nurse . . . Nurse Practitioner . . . Geriatric Care Nurse . . . Rehabilitation Nurse . . . Home Health Care Nurse . . . Private Duty Nurse . . . Integrated Care Deliverer . . . Nurse Anesthetist . . . Medical Surgery Nurse . . . Intensive Care Nurse . . . Nursing Aide

Physical Health

Physician . . . General and Family Practitioner . . . Internist . . . Geriatric Physician . . . Preventive Medicine Physician . . . Podiatrist . . . Medical Therapist . . . Physical Therapist . . . Occupational Therapist . . . Recreational Therapist . . . Respiratory Therapist . . . Audiologist . . . Speech-Language Pathologist . . . Dispensing Optician . . . Medical Technologist . . . Radiological Technologist . . . EEG Technologist . . . Nuclear Medicine Technologist

Dentistry

Dentist . . . Orthodontist . . . Pediatric Dentist . . . Prosthodontist . . . Oral and Maxillofacial Surgeon . . . Dental Hygienist . . . Dental Assistant

Mental Health

Psychiatrist . . . Psychologist . . . Psychiatric Aide

ADDITIONAL OPPORTUNITIES
IN THE HEALTH CARE INDUSTRY

You will also find the following jobs in the health care industry. These jobs appear in most companies in all industries. You will find the particulars of these jobs on the pages noted.

Job Category	Interest Area(s)	Page
Biological Scientist	Biotechnology & Environmental Technology	183
Medical Scientist	Biotechnology & Environmental Technology	185
Biochemist	Biotechnology & Environmental Technology	186
Computer Software Programmer	Information Technology	214
Systems Analyst	Information Technology	213
Auditor	Financial Services	279
Accountant	Financial Services	273
Chief Financial Officer	Financial Services	284
Corporate Controller	Financial Services	284
Benefits Manager	Human Resources	302
Compensation Manager	Human Resources	303
Human Resources Staffing Specialist	Human Resources	309
Director of Training	Human Resources	313
Corporate Training Specialist	Human Resources	313
Labor Relations Specialist	Human Resources	318
Diversity Manager	Human Resources	318
Management Consultant	Human Resources	323
Insurance Agent/Broker	Insurance	289
Attorney	Law	327
Public Relations Professional	Media/Communications/PR	346
Restaurant or Food Service Manager	Food Service	370
Records Clerk	Support Services	378
Secretary	Support Services	385
Social Worker	Social Services	400
Human Services Worker	Social Services	404
Counselor	Social Services	409
Librarian	Education	426

Administration

HEALTH CARE SERVICE MANAGER: HEALTH CARE GENERALIST/CLINICAL MANAGER

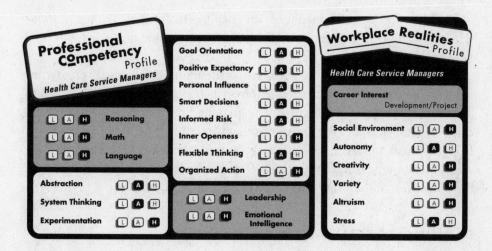

Health care service managers are the business managers of the health care industry, providing all the nonmedical services required to smoothly operate a medical facility. Health care managers specialize in designing, integrating, and instituting health care services so that the service works effectively for patients, and economically for employers.

Health care managers can be divided into two primary groups:

Health care generalists are the top administrators: *chief executive officers* (CEOs) and their primary managerial staff. They set the overall goals of a facility, both internally—for what they hope to achieve—and externally—for how they hope to be perceived. For example, an urban hospital may make a commitment to provide services to impoverished people in its community who cannot afford to pay for their treatment. Top administrative managers develop programs to educate community members with regard to the hospital's services, and then raise the funding for this program from the government and the business community.

The top administrative managers' involvement includes planning and policy making, community outreach, and ensuring that all governmental regulations are observed. As well as business credentials, these individuals typically have a great deal of former experience at the clinical level, so they are familiar with the various operational aspects of a health care facility.

A primary area of employment for health care managers is in group medical practices. In those settings, managers work closely with the doctors to meld the policies of the doctors and the business realities of the marketplace. Typical duties of health care managers in group practices include planning, budgeting, human resource matters, billing and collection, equipment outlays, and patient flow.

Health care service managers in health maintenance organizations (HMOs) handle all the responsibilities of group practice managers, but on a larger scale.

Clinical managers are the specialists with training in a relatively narrow field of health care services such as *physical therapy* or *medical technology*. These heads of specialized departments in a medical facility are typically educated in their distinct area of expertise and have practical experience in that field. Clinical managers oversee staffing and personnel decisions in their department, prepare and submit budgets to the financial administrator, and set the objectives for their staff that reflect the goals of the facility.

EARNING POTENTIAL

Health care service managers' salaries are as varied as the services they provide and the facilities they operate. Their income will very much depend on the size and revenue of the medical practice they represent.

A recent survey found that half of all hospital *chief executive officers* (the very top administrators) earn at least $140,900, with salaries ranging between slightly less than $77,000 to more than $223,600. The competition for these higher-end jobs is acute.

The median salary for health care managers in small group practices with net revenues of $2 million or less is $46,600. For those in very large group practices with net revenues over $50 million, the median salary is $166,700.

The salaries for *clinical department managers* vary according to department. In the areas listed below, clinic managers average approximately the following yearly salaries:

Medical Records Manager	$41,500
Home Health Industry Manager	$52,500
Manager in Imaging or Radiology	$53,300
Physical Therapy Manager	$54,700
Rehabilitation Services Manager	$58,800
Nursing Services Manager	$65,700

Nursing home administrators earn a median annual salary of $44,100, with the salary ranging from $36,500 to $68,200, depending on the size of the facility.

EDUCATIONAL REQUIREMENTS

Most top management administrators at hospitals and large nursing facilities have a master's degree in health services administration or business administration. Some managers also have previous work experience in one of the health care professions, along with graduate business credentials.

There are only twenty-nine colleges and universities that offer a bachelor's degree in health services administration. However, according to the Accrediting Commission on Education for the Health Services Administration, sixty-four schools have accredited graduate programs leading to the master's degree in health services administration. These unusual numbers emphasize the fact that most health care service administrators are general undergraduate business majors who then concentrate on health services management at the graduate level.

Because there are not many academic programs specifically geared toward health services administration, applications far outnumber the available spots in classes, and this will remain true for the next several years. Eventually more schools will offer majors in this field, but the competition is still bound to be fierce. Applicants with good academic records and relevant work experience will stand a better chance of acceptance in such programs.

A DAY IN THE LIFE

Over half of all health care service managers in the United States work in hospitals. One in seven works in a nursing or personal care facility; one in eight works in a physician's office or a clinic; the rest work in home health agencies, medical and dental laboratories, and other health and allied services.

While their environment is generally clean and comfortable, health care service managers work long hours because many of the facilities in which they work are open twenty-four hours a day. Administrators in these facilities are on call day and night, just like doctors.

Health care managers may travel a great deal and often address audiences and deliver presentations on the state of their facility.

JOB GROWTH

While the health care industry enjoys a strong growth pattern, there will be an even greater demand for qualified managerial personnel. Employment for health care service managers is expected to grow much faster than the average rate for all occupations between 1995 and 2005, with as many as 120,000 new positions projected to be filled. Hospitals will remain the primary employers, but growth will not be as fast in hospitals as in other areas.

Due largely to a growing population of elderly people, the growth in home health care agencies, nursing homes, and long-term care facilities will provide numerous job opportunities for well-qualified managerial staff. As medical group practices and HMOs grow, opportunities for managers in these organizations are expected to grow proportionately.

For those who enjoy a challenge, work well under pressure, and have benevolent aspirations, health care service manager positions are a perfect option. Although managers do not treat patients directly, their contributions can have a beneficial effect on the overall care of all the patients treated in their medical facility. The compensation and prestige associated with managerial positions make this profession an attractive one, and an excellent career choice for young people to consider, as well as for those with management or financial experience considering a new career path.

MEDICAL RECORDS TECHNICIAN

Medical records technicians organize and evaluate the data on patients' charts, then record the information into computer files. The records maintained and reviewed by technicians include information pertaining to examination results, X-ray and laboratory test reports, and the doctor's diagnosis and treatment plan.

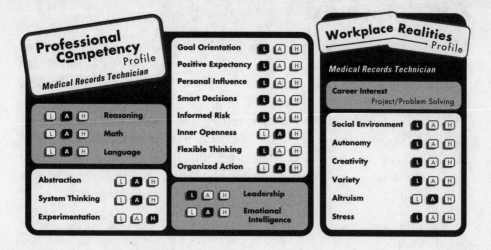

Because the health care industry generates so much paperwork, hospitals and insurance companies have created a diagnosis and procedure code that serves as a shorthand for reporting purposes. When technicians in hospitals review a patient's reports, they translate the written procedures into code for entry on the computer.

Health insurance carriers' need to contain costs has led to the creation of designations for patients suffering from certain diseases. When reviewing reports, medical records technicians must assign many patients to a diagnosis-related group (DRG). It is the patient's designation into one of the hundreds of these groups that determines the amount an insurance carrier will reimburse the hospital for the patient's treatment. Since insurance companies compile records on the average cost of treatment for individual diseases, technicians can determine in advance the probable cost of treatment, and will attempt to keep the hospital's costs within the average range. Technicians who specialize in these coding functions are called *medical record coders*, *coder/abstractors*, or *coding specialists*.

Medical records technicians also provide data to insurance carriers to determine average costs, and analyze data for their hospitals in order to reduce costs, improve care, assist in legal actions, and respond to surveys.

Many organizations maintain records on the family members of patients who suffer from some diseases, to determine a possible genetic link. Medical records technicians supply information to these organizations to help in their research.

EARNING POTENTIAL

A recent survey conducted by the American Health Information Management Association (AHIMA) found that accredited medical records technicians working as coders earned an average of $11.30 per hour. Unaccredited coders made less: $9.77 per hour.

Salaries increase for experienced coders who move into management positions. Since these are full-time positions, the average annual salary of $29,600 is enhanced by medical benefits and, in some cases, retirement plans. The federal government, which also offers its employees benefits packages, pays medical records technicians an average annual salary of $22,008.

EDUCATIONAL REQUIREMENTS

Most entry-level medical records technicians hold a two-year community college or junior college degree. These institutions offer formal training for the occupation. Courses offered in this field include medical terminology and diseases, anatomy and physiology, legal aspects of medical record-keeping, the coding and abstraction of data, statistics, building and interpreting databases, quality assurance methods, and computer training.

This training is rigorous, but the nature of the job requires it. Acquired knowledge, logical thinking, and accuracy are all essential components of this job.

Although in the recent past hospitals promoted medical records clerks to technician jobs, this practice is expected to grow much less common in the future. Employers want to hire Accredited Records Technicians (A.R.T.s) who have passed an examination administered by the AHIMA. This accreditation procedure requires that the candidate possess an associate degree from a program that is, in turn, accredited by the Committee on Allied Health Education and Accreditation (CAHEA) of the American Medical Association or that they be graduates of an independent study program in medical records technology and have completed thirty semester hours of class credits in specific classes related to the field.

Applicants seeking medical records technician training in community colleges and junior colleges are advised to determine whether or not the program they apply to is accredited by CAHEA. In 1992, there were ninety accredited programs for medical records technicians, but there are also unaccredited programs. Graduates of unaccredited programs are not permitted to sit for the accreditation exam, and not taking the exam may hurt their future employment chances.

A DAY IN THE LIFE

Medical records technicians are almost unique in the health care field because they have very little or no contact with patients. They generally work a forty-hour week, and may be required to work occasional overtime hours because of the volume of information generated in hospitals. Many hospitals schedule their medical records technicians in shifts and keep the departments open twenty-four hours a day, providing medical records technicians with some flexibility in scheduling their work hours.

Insurance companies, accounting firms, and law firms also hire medical records technicians to review and analyze information from patient and hospital records for auditing, tax reporting, or litigation purposes. Public health departments need medical records technicians to supervise data collection from health care facilities and to aid research. Some self-employed medical records technicians work on a contract basis as consultants to nursing homes and physicians' offices.

The working environment for medical records technicians is clean and comfortable. They work at computer display terminals, so strained eyesight is an occupational hazard. The work demands attention to detail and accuracy.

JOB GROWTH

There are approximately 76,000 medical records technicians employed in the United States, half of whom work in hospitals. Most of the others work in nursing homes, group medical practices, HMOs, and health clinics.

Even though the outlook for all hospital-related jobs is not as encouraging as it is for jobs in the area of outpatient care, hospital jobs should be plentiful for medical records technicians. Many of the job openings will result from replacement needs. Experienced medical records technicians may choose to specialize in Medicare coding, or they may move into management positions, leaving openings for generalist technicians. Part-time positions are plentiful in the occupation.

In addition to hospital staff positions, job growth for medical records technicians is expected in such sites as doctors' offices, medical clinics, HMOs,

HELP WANTED
MEDICAL RECORDS TECHNICIAN

Review patient reports, and translate the written procedures into code for entry on the computer. Assign patients to a diagnosis-related group (DRG). Provide insurance carriers with data to determine average costs, analyze data to reduce costs for hospital and improve care, assist in legal actions, and respond to management and industry surveys. Salary Range: $20,300–$88,000.

nursing homes, and home health care agencies (such as Visiting Nurse organizations). Overall growth in this field is expected to exceed the national average through the year 2005.

Medical records technicians will continue to have extraordinary job opportunities because data, billing reports, and insurance carrier requirements have created a two-tier health care industry: the people who provide care to patients (doctors, nurses, medical assistants, nurse practitioners, and nursing aides) and those who review and report the data generated by the actual care. Although it is the service providers who produce income for the industry, the complexity that has arisen due to government regulations, reporting procedures, and increased awareness of providers' liability has created a need for a separate staff to process the information that keeps the industry running.

MEDICAL ASSISTANT

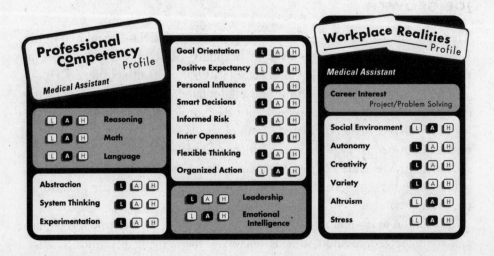

Clinical duties vary according to what state laws permit. Many *medical assistants* take medical histories and record vital signs. They also explain treatment procedures to patients, prepare patients for examination, and assist physicians during examinations. Medical assistants collect and prepare laboratory specimens or perform basic laboratory tests on the premises. They are usually responsible for sterilizing medical instruments and disposing of contaminated supplies.

Medical assistants may also handle the routine clinical and clerical tasks that enable hospitals and doctors to operate efficiently. Their duties vary according to the location and size of the facility and to the medical specialty practiced there. For example, many hospitals are research facilities as well as medical facilities. Many medical assistants perform routine experimental tasks and report the results to the doctors or scientists who work in the facility. At the National Institutes of Health (NIH) or the Centers for Disease Control (CDC), most medical assistants work with researchers intent on finding a cure for such diseases as AIDS and cancer.

Medical assistants also instruct patients on medication and special diets. They prepare and administer medications as directed by a physician. They deliver prescriptions and authorize drug refills by telephone to pharmacies as directed by physicians, draw blood, prepare patients for X rays, take electrocardiograms, remove sutures, and change dressings.

Medical assistants perform many clerical duties that medical secretaries and administrative assistants in all office settings perform. These include answering telephones, transcribing correspondence, and scheduling appointments. The duties related specifically to medical research include updating and filing medical patient records, filling out insurance forms, arranging for hospital admissions and laboratory services, and handling billing and bookkeeping.

Medical assistants may also arrange examining room instruments and equipment, purchase and maintain supplies and equipment, and strip and clean examining rooms between patients.

Medical assistants who specialize in particular fields will assume additional duties:

• *Podiatric medical assistants* make castings of feet, expose and develop X rays, and assist the podiatrist in surgery.

• *Ophthalmic medical assistants* help ophthalmologists provide eye care. They use precision instruments to administer diagnostic tests, measure and record vision, and test the functioning of eyes and eye muscles.

They show patients how to use eye dressings, protective shields, and safety glasses, and also how to use and care for contact lenses. They maintain optical and surgical instruments and assist the ophthalmologist in surgery. Under the direction of the physician, they may administer medications, such as eyedrops.

EARNING POTENTIAL

The earnings of medical assistants vary widely, depending on their experience, skill level, and location. According to recent surveys conducted by the Committee on Allied Health Education and Accreditation and the American Association of Medical Assistants, the average annual starting salary for graduates of medical assistant programs ranged from approximately $11,000 to $15,000. Medical assistants with ten years of experience or more averaged $24,000.

EDUCATIONAL REQUIREMENTS

Although formal training is available for medical assistants, it is not always required. Some medical assistants are hired and then trained on the job. Applicants usually need a high school diploma or G.E.D. certificate. High school courses in mathematics, health, biology, typing, bookkeeping, computers, and office skills are helpful.

Although many medical assistants do not need a college degree, many colleges and universities offer programs that train students for this career. High schools, junior colleges, and vocational technical institutes also offer training courses in this field. College-level programs usually last either one year, resulting in a certificate or diploma, or two years, resulting in an associate degree. Vocational programs can take up to one year and lead to a diploma or certificate. Courses include anatomy, physiology, and medical terminology. Instruction in typing, transcription, record keeping, accounting, and insurance processing is also pertinent. Students learn laboratory techniques, clinical and diagnostic procedures, pharmaceutical principles, medical administration, and first aid. They are also instructed in office practices, patient relations, and medical law and ethics. Since much of the patient information they prepare is confidential, a grounding in ethics is important for medical assistants.

Medical assistant programs can be accredited by either of two organizations:

• the American Medical Association's Committee on Allied Health Education and Accreditation (CAHEA), which in 1993 accredited 207 medical assisting programs;

• the Accrediting Bureau of Health Education Schools (ABHES), which in 1993 accredited 136 medical assisting programs.

Accredited programs may include a clinical externship that provides practical experience in health care facilities. In addition, the Joint Review Committee for Ophthalmic Medical Personnel has approved thirteen programs in ophthalmic medical assisting.

States do not issue licenses to medical assistants, but some states require them to take a test or a course before they are permitted to provide such basic care as taking X rays, drawing blood, or giving injections. There are also national examinations that grant certification to medical assistants:

• The American Association of Medical Assistants awards the Certified Medical Assistant credential.

• The American Medical Technologists award the Registered Medical Assistant credential.

• The American Society of Podiatric Medical Assistants awards the Podiatric Medical Assistant Certified credential.

• The Joint Commission on Allied Health Personnel in Ophthalmology awards the Ophthalmic Medial Assistant credential at three levels: Certified Ophthalmic Assistant, Certified Ophthalmic Technician, and Certified Ophthalmic Medical Technologist.

Although certification does not ensure someone a job, it does prove to be a valuable credential to anyone either looking for a job in the field or already working as a medical assistant.

A DAY IN THE LIFE

Medical assistants work in comfortable and clean yet often bustling environments. Over 70 percent are employed in physicians' offices, while approximately 12 percent work in offices of specialized health care practitioners, such as chiropractors, optometrists, and podiatrists. Other medical assistants work in hospitals, nursing homes, and clinics. They constantly interact with people, and often must handle several responsibilities at once.

Most full-time medical assistants work a regular forty-hour week. Some work evenings and weekends.

HELP WANTED
MEDICAL ASSISTANT

Take patients' medical histories and record vital signs. Explain treatment procedures to patients, prepare patients for examination, and assist physicians during examinations. Collect and prepare laboratory specimens or perform basic laboratory tests. Instruct patients on medication and special diets. Arrange examining room instruments and equipment, and purchase and maintain supplies and equipment. Salary Range: $11,000–$24,000.

JOB GROWTH

Medical assistants currently hold approximately 181,000 jobs. As the health care industry expands, employment of medical assistants is expected to grow by as much as 70 percent by the year 2005. Because of the prohibitive cost of hospital care, outpatient treatment has become, and will remain, the most commonly used form of medical care. The continued growth of outpatient services will provide medical assistants with a great number of openings.

Because of the high turnover rate in the field and the demand for well trained personnel, job prospects should be excellent for medical assistants with formal training and/or experience, and particularly for those with certification. Since formal training for these positions can be pursued at all levels and price ranges, candidates are advised to receive at least a minimum amount of training in order to provide themselves with a competitive edge in the marketplace.

MEDICAL SECRETARY

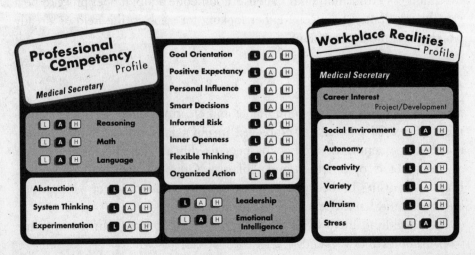

Medical secretaries are a necessary component of a medical office. They serve as intermediaries for doctors who lack the time to respond personally to all of their patients' questions and requests, and they have the responsibility for many of the nonmedical functions that are a large part of running a medical practice.

They perform the standard duties of all qualified secretaries, including scheduling appointments, organizing and maintaining files, preparing preprinted forms, and typing from dictation and notes. Since medical secretaries prepare medical reports and transcribe dictation that includes the findings of a doctors' examination—much of which is dictated in "professional shorthand"—they must be familiar with medical terminology and procedures.

Additionally, medical secretaries spend a good deal of time coordinating patient billing, insurance requirements and forms, and hospital procedures to the exacting standards of the insurance companies.

EARNING POTENTIAL

The average annual salary for technical secretaries, the category into which medical secretaries fall, is $16,700. Experienced medical secretaries may earn an average of $22,700, depending on location and level of responsibility.

EDUCATIONAL REQUIREMENTS

Medical secretaries must be equipped with a general education, some specialized training, and above all, common sense.

Although many secretarial jobs require only a high school education, medical secretaries work with computers and medical billing procedures that require experience and education beyond the norm. However, they need not be college graduates. Interested candidates should consider taking training courses in bookkeeping, word processing, and an elementary introduction to medical terminology and medical procedures.

Interpersonal skills are important for medical secretaries. The manner in which they communicate with sick patients and their relatives, who may be anxious or upset, is very important. They must be accurate in conveying information from the doctor—which again requires an understanding of basic medical procedures—and discreet in providing only the information the doctor wants passed on.

They must also exhibit these qualities in their dealings with insurance

---

HELP WANTED
MEDICAL SECRETARY

Schedule appointments, organize and maintain files, and take doctor's dictation and notes. Must understand medical terminology and procedures, and prepare medical reports. Coordinate patient billing, insurance requirements and forms, and hospital admission procedures for insurance companies. Salary Range: $16,700–$22,700.

---

company personnel. Although these dealings may at times be frustrating, good communication with insurance carriers is essential for the smooth running of a medical practice. Common sense and attention to detail and accuracy are all necessary for this aspect of the job of a medical secretary.

A DAY IN THE LIFE

Medical secretaries work in the clean, comfortable environment of doctors' offices and medical clinics, where the atmosphere is generally pleasant though often hectic. Full-time medical secretaries usually work a forty-hour week that often includes Saturdays and sometimes evenings.

JOB GROWTH

Although overall growth in the secretarial field is forecast to proceed at a rate below the national average over the next ten years, the news is better for medical secretaries because the demand for their professional expertise will grow along with the increasing demand for doctors and the general growth in the field of medicine. And while technological advances may continue to threaten the security of general secretarial positions, automation will enable medical secretaries to perform more efficiently, allowing them to take over more duties that busy doctors do not have time for, as well as provide more personal service to patients.

Look toward the growing medical fields of *geriatric care* and *preventive medicine* for numerous opportunities.

Nursing

NURSE: REGISTERED NURSE/LICENSED PRACTICAL NURSE/NURSE PRACTITIONER/GERIATRIC CARE NURSE/REHABILITATION NURSE/HOME HEALTH CARE NURSE/PRIVATE DUTY NURSE/INTEGRATED CARE DELIVERER/NURSE ANESTHETIST/MEDICAL SURGERY NURSE/INTENSIVE CARE NURSE

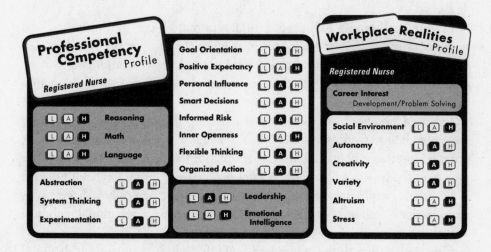

Because of changes in health care—fewer and shorter hospitalizations of patients, more preventive and wellness programs, increasing input from insurance carriers on approved procedures, and the needs of an aging population—the field of nursing is changing rapidly. **Nurses** are now even more involved in patient care than they were in the past, and much more involved in handling some relatively straightforward functions formerly handled by physicians. The nursing occupational titles described here represent the fastest-growing areas for today's and tomorrow's nurses.

Registered nurses (R.N.s) administer care to the sick and injured and help people stay well. They are trained to care for the whole person, providing for their patients' physical, mental, and emotional needs. They are often the first health care professionals a patient sees. It is they who observe and weigh a patient and record initial symptoms before a doctor examines the patient. They also provide continuous care for hospital patients in a doctor's absence.

Registered nurses assist physicians during treatments and examinations. They administer medications and assist in rehabilitation. R.N.s develop and oversee nursing care plans. They teach patients and their families ways to provide proper care for invalids. Although a registered nurse's duties are limited by law to certain tasks, the tasks they actually perform are determined by their individual jobs.

Since hospital nurses form the largest group of nurses, many R.N.s are hospital staff nurses who provide bedside care and carry out physicians' orders. Hospital nurses usually specialize in one area of care, such as surgery, maternity, pediatrics, the emergency room, intensive care, or oncology. They may also rotate among different departments, but it is rare for experienced nurses to do so.

In nursing homes, R.N.s concentrate primarily on administrative and supervisory duties. They do, however, oversee the care of the residents and assess their condition. They develop treatment plans, in conjunction with a doctor's orders, and supervise other nurses with less training and fewer qualifications.

Licensed practical nurses (L.P.N.s) made up the majority of the nursing profession before registered nurses (R.N.s) became the industry standard. The primary difference between the two designations is that registered nurses are now required by law to have either an associate degree or a bachelor's degree in their field, while licensed practical nurses are required only to have a two-year associate degree or just the training provided by a vocational/technical school.

Almost all of the duties performed by both registered nurses and licensed practical nurses are the same, although a licensed practical nurse's duties are also limited by law to certain tasks. The typical duties performed by an L.P.N. include bathing and feeding patients, and taking and noting temperature,

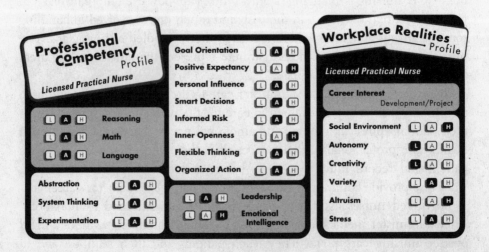

pulse, and blood pressure readings. L.P.N.s change dressings and treat wounds and infections. They also administer medications and prescriptions.

Nurse practitioners provide general care and treatment to patients in medical facilities and doctors' offices. Although they work under a physician's supervision, nurse practitioners are responsible for performing physical examinations and providing preventive treatments. Nurse practitioners also order diagnostic tests and evaluate the test results. They then pass along their findings and recommendations to the doctor.

Nurse practitioners take part in discussions involving patient care plans, and because of their training, their opinions are given significant weight. They may recommend (but not prescribe) medication or other forms of treatment, such as physical therapy or emotional counseling.

Many nurse practitioners specialize in a particular area of practice, such as pediatrics, geriatrics, obstetrics, or family planning. In some states, nurse practitioners may engage in independent practice.

Geriatric care nurses treat older patients exclusively. Since older Americans are the fastest-growing segment of the population, geriatric care nurses will have increasing job opportunities in the future. There are two main areas of care required by elderly people: treatment and maintenance.

Treatment care will remain relatively straightforward: nursing specialists in this practice will treat patients according to a doctor's diagnosis. Growing numbers of geriatric care nurses will find jobs in life care facilities, the treatment wings of retirement communities.

Maintenance care is the field that will create a real boom in geriatric nursing. Never before has a country been faced with such a large number of people who are not sick, but simply old. Aging brings with it problems of memory, loss of control of bodily functions, loss of appetite, and other gradual signs of declining control of one's mental and physical capabilities. Many of these people will live in retirement homes and elder care facilities. These facilities will provide most of the new jobs for geriatric care nurses.

Rehabilitation nurses are a combination of nurse and physical therapist. This is a stressful, demanding job. Patients requiring rehabilitation range from those suffering minor injuries to those recovering from strokes, heart attacks, or paralyzing accidents. A rehabilitation nurse oversees a patient's treatment and sets a schedule based on the average patient's progress from such injuries.

Rehabilitation hospitals are facilities that specialize in the therapy needed by patients recovering from traumatic illness or injury. Patients are admitted to these facilities after they have been treated and released from the hospital.

Rehabilitation nurses, therefore, normally see patients when their condition has stabilized sufficiently to begin treatment. Depending on the injury involved, rehabilitation nurses may see patients for long periods of time. This is a field that demands greater personal interplay between nurses and patients than many other areas of nursing, and in that respect it requires a person with a temperament suited to long, slow, tedious work while a patient improves incrementally.

Home health care nurses perform the same duties as nurses in hospitals and doctors' offices: they give patients shots, check on patients' vital signs, and examine a patient to check his or her condition. The main difference is that home health care nurses provide an alternative for patients who cannot get to a doctor's office. They also provide a more cost-effective method for monitoring and maintaining a patient's condition than would be possible in the hospital.

Home health care services are an increasingly popular trend in nursing because they cut down on health care costs and allow nurses to work a flexible schedule. Home health nurses range from *visiting nurses* who visit a number of patients in their homes to *private duty nurses* who usually care for one bedridden patient.

Many visiting nurses are registered nurses who have worked in hospitals but who seek a change from the long hours and stress of hospital nursing. Others are working nurses who supplement their full-time income with part-time hours.

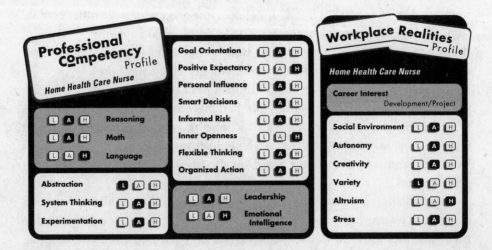

Private duty nurses minister to the needs of one patient only. Often they live in the house with the patient and his or her family because their patient needs constant attention. Most private duty nurses are paid for by the patients themselves, with a small percentage of the cost paid for by insurance carriers. They also work, on a contract basis, for patients in hospitals or rehabilitation facilities who need continuous care.

Integrated care deliverers are instructors as well as nurses. They provide nursing services and teach health education and disease prevention to families and community groups. They visit patients' homes to observe and determine the specific needs of the patients and their families. Some of these potential needs include financial assistance, hospital beds, and other medical devices.

Integrated care deliverers' duties overlap with those of home health care nurses in that they provide treatment to patients according to a physician's instructions. But they also evaluate patients on a broader scale and can recommend additional sources of treatment, such as psychological treatment. Their concern is not only with a patient and his or her specific ailment, but also with a larger unit: the family or the community. An integrated care deliverer is a bridge-builder who is interested in the sources, not just the care, of a problem.

Nurse anesthetists administer local, intravenous, spinal, or other anesthetics under a doctor's supervision, often in a hospital setting. They prepare the solutions according to prescribed standards and observe the patient's reactions to the anesthetic. Nurse anesthetists also work in dental offices or in doctors' offices, where they administer local anesthetics for minor dental or surgical procedures.

Medical surgery nurses are the people who typify, for many, the image of a nurse. It is they who assist surgeons in the operating room, coolly functioning under great stress, not only aware of the patient's condition but also anticipating the surgeon's needs for instruments. Regardless of the nature of the procedure, surgery nurses must remain observant and objective under all operating room conditions.

Their duties may include preparing the operating room, sterilizing instruments, and handing the instruments to the doctor. It is very important that the surgery nurse maintain an accurate count on all instruments, sponges, and other surgical tools used in the procedure. Care, accuracy, and attention to detail are all important elements in a surgery nurse's makeup.

Intensive care nurses closely monitor a patient's condition postsurgery. All patients in intensive care units are connected to monitors situated both in their room and at the central nurses' station. Intensive care nurses observe and record monitor readings while other nurses minister to the patient's personal needs.

Working in an intensive care unit demands constant vigilance. Since every patient is at great risk of death, intensive care nurses work in a very stressful atmosphere. The difference between intensive care unit nurses and nurses working in other units of a hospital is largely the concentration required by the job and the ability to resuscitate patients. Because intensive care nurses work with people who often lack physical mobility, they must have a better than average degree of strength.

EARNING POTENTIAL

Salary figures for these specialized professions are not as readily available as figures for registered nurses and hospital staff nurses. And since many of the growing fields in nursing employ people on a part-time basis, salary statistics are not as definitive as they would be for full-time employees.

	Starting Salary	Median Salary	Experienced Salary
Registered Nurse	$26,000	$34,000	$46,000
Licensed Practical Nurse	$16,000	$21,500	$24,000
Nurse Practitioner	$28,000	$43,500	$45,000+
Geriatric Care Nurse	$20,000	$30,000	$40,000
Integrated Care Deliverer	$24,000	$30,000	$37,500
Nurse Anesthetist	$40,000	$66,500	$70,000+

Registered nurses in the fields of **home health care** and **integrated care** should expect to make salaries comparable to most other registered nurses. **Rehabilitation, private duty, medical surgery,** and **intensive care** nurses may expect to earn a bit more.

Note: The figures cited above reflect the entire profession. Salaries may be higher in big cities and for nurses who work in a large medical practice.

EDUCATIONAL REQUIREMENTS

There are 1,470 entry-level registered nursing programs. The two major degrees are the bachelor of science in nursing (B.S.N.) and the associate degree in nursing (A.D.N.). A third program, the diploma program, is given in hospitals and lasts two to three years. Only a small number of graduates come from this program.

The B.S.N. is the degree most employers are looking for. This involves the completion of a four-year college program as well as clinical experience in nursing. The B.S.N. provides job candidates with a greater ability to advance in the profession or even to change into a different health care–related field. Approximately 30 percent of nursing students graduate with a B.S.N. degree. The two-year A.D.N. degree is achieved by approximately 60 percent of nursing graduates.

Nursing education includes a combination of classroom instruction and supervised training in hospitals and other health facilities. Among the courses students take are anatomy, physiology, microbiology, chemistry, nutrition, and psychology and other behavioral sciences.

Nursing is a licensed profession. State licensing requirements include graduating from an accredited nursing school and passing a national licensing examination. Nurses may be licensed in more than one state, either by examination or by endorsement of a license issued by another state. Licenses must be renewed periodically, and many states require continuing education as a requirement for renewal.

Licensed practical nurses are generally high school graduates who have completed a one-year practical nursing program and passed a state licensing exam.

Most **nurse practitioners, geriatric care nurses, rehabilitation nurses, home health care nurses, private duty nurses,** and **integrated care deliverers** are L.R.N.s, licensed registered nurses.

Geriatric Care Nurse

Care for elderly patients according to doctor's directions. Administer medication, perform and analyze diagnostic tests, and assist patients with daily functions such as eating, bathing, and dressing. Salary Range: $20,000–$40,000.

Rehabilitation Nurse

Oversee a patient's treatment and set a rehabilitation schedule. Much one-on-one contact and interplay with patients necessary. Requires a person with a positive and patient temperament, as patient may improve only incrementally over a long period of time. Salary Range: $20,000–$40,000.

Home Health Care Nurse

Visit patients at their homes to give shots, check on patients' general and specific health concerns, and evaluate patients' condition. Salary Range: $20,000–$40,000.

Integrated Care Deliverer

Provide nursing services and teach health education and disease prevention to families and community groups. Visit patients' homes to observe and determine the specific needs of patients and their families, such as financial assistance, hospital beds, and other medical devices. Evaluate patients on a broader scale and recommend additional sources of treatment, such as psychological counseling. Salary Range: $24,000–$37,500.

Most **medical surgery** and **intensive care nurses** require additional education, and all must be fully qualified and experienced before assuming major responsibilities.

Nurse anesthetists must undergo considerable additional schooling before they are permitted to practice their trade. They must first graduate from a B.S.N. program. The additional education and training involved in becoming a fully qualified nurse anesthetist may last up to ten years.

A DAY IN THE LIFE

Nurses work for the most part in comfortable surroundings: clean hospitals, nursing homes, or doctors' offices. Their duties may be stressful and the hours long and irregular, including night and even weekend shifts. Even though nurses work under the supervision of doctors, they generally have their own responsibilities that require a degree of independence. Nursing is a profession that appeals to team-oriented individuals who also have an independent streak and a strong sense of personal responsibility.

One hazard of nursing is the exposure to infectious diseases. Although most hospitals maintain rigid guidelines to protect employees from the dangers of disease and from radiation and chemicals used in treatments, accidents occur and nurses do occasionally contract the diseases they are exposed to.

Another occupational hazard for nurses is back injury. Because they have to

Private Duty Nurse

Minister to the needs of one patient only, in either a hospital or a home setting. Must live with patient and provide constant care. Salary Range: $28,000–$60,000.

Nurse Anesthetist

Administer local, intravenous, spinal, or other anesthetics under a doctor's supervision. Prepare the solutions according to prescribed standards and observe the patient's reactions to the anesthetic. Salary Range: $40,000–$70,000+.

Medical Surgery Nurse

Assist surgeons in the operating room, by preparing operating room, sterilizing instruments and passing them to surgeons, and maintaining an accurate count on all instruments, sponges, and other surgical tools. Must not only be aware of the patient's condition, but also anticipate the surgeon's needs for instruments. Accuracy, efficiency, and attention to detail critical. Familiarity with medical instruments necessary. Salary Range: $40,000–$70,000.

Intensive Care Nurse

Responsible for closely monitoring a patient's condition post-surgery, observing and recording monitor readings, and ministering to the patient's personal needs. Position requires constant vigilance. Salary Range: $40,000–$70,000.

lift patients regularly, nurses are always in danger of straining their backs. They also spend a good portion of their time on their feet.

Although **nurse practitioners** may be required to visit patients at their homes occasionally, most of their duties are centered around medical offices. Many nurse practitioners report overtime hours as being a standard element of their practice, due largely to the amount of paperwork the job requires. One benefit of the occupation, though, is that nurse practitioners normally work under minimal supervision. Although they work in conjunction with doctors, they are fully responsible for their own duties.

Geriatric care nurses work in the offices of gerontologists (physicians who specialize in treatment of the elderly), in hospitals, retirement communities, and in life care facilities. The majority of these facilities are clean, neat, and orderly. Geriatric care nurses may also be involved in community programs, visiting elderly people in their homes in order to check on their health. Because many of their patients may require extensive care, geriatric care nurses may be required to perform many physical duties, such as lifting, bathing, and feeding patients.

Rehabilitation nurses work almost exclusively in rehabilitation facilities. These facilities house all of the equipment necessary for patient therapy. This job may require heavy lifting, depending on a patient's condition, and can prove alternately stressful and tedious. As the rehabilitation process can be a long one, this profession requires great patience on the part of the nurses.

Home health care nurses and **private duty nurses**, as their titles suggest, work in private homes. Their working conditions vary according to the patient's circumstances. Nevertheless, many home health care and private duty nurses enjoy the variety of visiting different locations, as opposed to being situated in a hospital department or a physician's office. Much of their time is spent in the car, with additional time spent in an agency's office or at home filling out paperwork.

Integrated care deliverers work in homes, community health centers, and hospitals. Much of their job involves paperwork; recommending different programs and coordinating different types of treatment require careful planning and follow-up.

Nurse anesthetists, medical surgery nurses, and **intensive care nurses** work in hospitals, and often perform their duties in crisis or emergency situations. They must be able to endure their patients' suffering and to function capably under stress.

JOB GROWTH

There are over three million nurses employed in the United States. Two-thirds of those work in hospitals; one-third work in physicians' offices and clinics, nursing homes, home health care agencies, temporary help agencies, schools, and government agencies. About one-quarter of all R.N.s work part-time.

Job prospects in nursing are good, even though large wage increases have attracted more people to nursing and dampened the vigorous demand that existed a few years ago. Projections for the profession estimate that there will be over one million additional employment opportunities for nurses between 1995 and 2005, with low unemployment and high earnings. Many of the new opportunities will be part-time ones.

Employment of all **registered nurses** is expected to grow much faster than the average for all occupations through the year 2005. Because older people will live longer and require treatment of a greater number of problems, registered nurses will be in ever-increasing demand. Many of these job openings will arise from the need to replace experienced nurses who retire or simply leave the profession due to its stressful nature.

The opportunities that will exist are likely to be in the same areas that need additional R.N.s today. For example, R.N. recruitment in rural areas remains a problem, as does recruitment in some inner city hospitals, and in specialty areas such as **intensive care, rehabilitation, geriatrics,** and **long-term care**. These specialty areas involve extreme stress, which often causes nurses to burn out.

The emphasis on Health Maintenance Organizations (HMOs) and wellness programs will mean a decline in the demand for hospital nurses. The number of hospital inpatients will decrease, but the overall effect will be a need for more nurses in preventive medicine and outpatient care in such areas as **geriatric care**, **integrated care**, and **rehabilitation nursing**.

The **home health care** field is also expected to grow rapidly. This is due in large part to a growing number of older persons with functional disabilities, rising consumer preference for less expensive means of care, and advances in technology that will make home treatment a sound alternative to hospitalization.

The need for **nurse anesthetists** will increase, as they will be needed not only in hospitals but also in outpatient care facilities. The employment outlook for this field is considered to be very good. **Medical surgery** and **intensive care nurses** will also continue to be in demand as the medical industry experiences growth and the turnover in these stressful positions continues to be high.

Most promotions within the nursing profession are to supervisory positions, such as head nurse in a hospital department. Other management positions within nursing—such as director or assistant director of nursing—normally require a graduate degree in health services administration.

Many registered nurses find a second career in the business side of health care. Their nursing expertise and experience on a health care team equip them to manage such care services as home care nursing organizations. Others are employed by large health care insurers in the health planning and development, marketing, and quality assurance areas.

Although technology may make some other occupations obsolete, nursing is a field that will always require the human touch: judgment, decision making, and awareness of people's particular needs. Although nurses assist doctors, theirs is still a leadership position, and nurses can expect to take over more responsibilities in patient care during the next decade. The sheer numbers of patients and the economics of health care dictate that different nursing careers evolve to meet the increasing need for cost-contained care. Nurses trained to work with a minimum of doctor supervision, or who can work comfortably in different environments, will have an edge over the competition.

Years ago the nursing profession was limited almost exclusively to women, and most nurses were L.P.N.s. Now that the requirements of the nursing profession have been raised to reflect modern standards, opportunities for both men and women exist, and inevitably all nurses will be required to have a bachelor's degree in the future.

NURSING AIDE

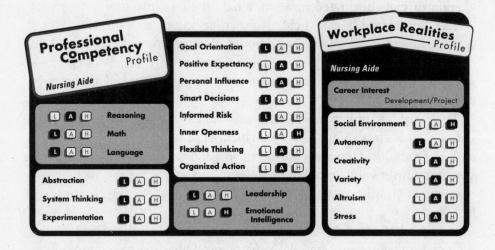

The medical profession is highly esteemed, in part because of the glamour long associated with doctors and nurses as they are depicted in popular culture. There is, however, another side to medicine that doctors, nurses, and patients know well, and this side has little to do with glamour.

Medicine is similar to many professions in that its emergencies and dramatic procedures punctuate long periods of routine maintenance care. Doctors cannot attend to most of these routine chores, and nurses often find themselves so overwhelmed by their responsibilities that they must seek help. *Nursing aides* supply nurses with the help they need to provide routine—but necessary—care to all of their hospital, nursing home, or residential care patients.

Nursing aides, for example, respond to patients' call bells; deliver messages for doctors, nurses, and even patients; serve meals; make patients' beds; and feed, dress, and bathe patients. Aides may also give massages to patients in danger of suffering from bedsores and apply skin care products to those same patients. They can take temperatures; check pulse, respiration, and blood pressure; and assist patients who need help going to and from their bed. Nursing aides often accompany patients to operating or examining rooms, and may clean the patients' rooms during their procedures or examinations.

Because nursing aides often have close contact with patients, they are charged with observing a patient's physical and emotional condition. They report any significant changes in the condition to the doctors or nurses. This is especially true of nursing aides who work in nursing homes. Geriatric patients require a great deal of care and observation, and it is usually a regular nursing aide who has the most frequent close contact with the patients. Nursing aides are often better able to determine changes in a patient's condition or demeanor than doctors or nurses who see the patient infrequently.

Medical technology is capable of establishing a stable condition for many patients who remain incapacitated—to varying degrees—for long periods of time. Because the patients' conditions do not change dramatically, there is no call for them to be attended by medical professionals trained to provide emergency care. Although there is very little that is purely "medical" in terms of the care they offer patients, nursing aides fill the greatest need in patient care today: keeping patients comfortable.

EARNING POTENTIAL

Median annual earnings of full-time nursing aides in 1992 were approximately $13,800. The middle 50 percent earned between $11,000 and $17,900. The lowest 10 percent earned less than $9,500. The top 10 percent earned more than $23,900.

Nursing aides who work in hospitals may also receive hospital and medical benefits, extra pay for late-shift work, and pension plans.

EDUCATIONAL REQUIREMENTS

Nursing aide jobs are often a first step into the working world for young people. Many nursing aide positions are available to people who lack a high school diploma or previous work experience, even though some employers require training or experience. Nursing homes, for instance, may hire inexperienced workers and put them through a mandatory seventy-five-hour training program, then require them to pass a competency evaluation program within four months of their start date. Nursing aides who successfully complete this training program are placed on the state registry of nursing aides, which provides them with transferable credentials for jobs in other settings.

People interested in becoming nursing aides will find training programs offered in high schools, vocational/technical schools, community colleges, and some nursing homes. Class work covers body mechanics (to help move patients without hurting them), nutrition, anatomy and physiology, infection control, and communication skills. Training in bathing, feeding, and grooming patients is also covered.

A DAY IN THE LIFE

Most nursing aides work in either hospitals or nursing homes. Most hospitals are clean and pleasant environments; however, nursing homes vary greatly, depending on their management.

Many nursing aides work a part-time schedule. Since most of the facilities that employ nursing aides need help on a twenty-four-hour basis, nursing aides can often choose the schedule they want to work, which may include night and weekend hours.

There are many unpleasant duties associated with nursing aide jobs: emptying bedpans, changing bed linens, and feeding disoriented patients. Furthermore, because many patients cannot move comfortably, nursing aides must be strong enough to lift and turn their patients.

JOB GROWTH

There are approximately 1,417,000 nursing aide jobs in the United States, one-half of which are in nursing homes and one-fourth in hospitals. The balance are in settings such as residential care facilities and private homes.

Opportunities for nursing aides are expected to remain good through the year 2005. Job growth will exceed the national average for all occupations due to the increased need for long-term patient care and medical breakthroughs that have allowed people to survive illness and injury, but have left them in need of rehabilitation. As in most jobs with low educational and skill requirements, however, turnover in nursing aide positions is always high. Even

JOBS WITH A FUTURE IN: HEALTH CARE   115

> **HELP WANTED
> NURSING AIDE**
>
> Provide routine care to hospital, nursing home, or residential care patients. Respond to patients' call bells, and deliver messages for doctors, nurses, and patients. Serve patients meals, make patients' beds, and feed, dress, and bathe patients. Take temperatures, pulse, respiration, and blood pressure, and assist patients who need help going to and from their bed. Observe a patient's physical and emotional condition and report any significant changes in the condition to the doctors or nurses. Salary Range: $9,880–$23,900.

though more facilities—such as nursing homes—that need nursing aides are being built, the majority of job openings will result from replacement needs rather than from newly created jobs. The good news is that there will be many thousands of jobs opening each year as people either change occupations or leave the workforce.

The nursing aide occupation offers people without postsecondary education a chance to acquire fundamental skills and to receive certification in a field that provides them with a credential to take to future employers. For that reason, this occupation should continue to prove attractive to young people.

For people looking to supplement their income or to work at odd hours, employment as a nursing aide provides round-the-clock opportunities for work.

Nursing aide is not a career job, but it can be a good first job, to provide someone with a work history, or a good part-time job that will always be available whenever someone needs or wants to work.

Physical Health

PHYSICIAN: GENERAL AND FAMILY PRACTITIONER/INTERNIST/GERIATRIC
PHYSICIAN/PREVENTIVE MEDICINE PHYSICIAN

Physicians are trained in and primarily deal with the diagnosis and treatment of disease and injuries. They perform physical examinations and administer diagnostic tests to detect health problems, and prescribe medication and/or therapy to alleviate or correct these problems. The following four specialties of doctors show a particularly promising growth rate.

General and *family practitioners* provide a broad range of services to their patients, usually on a regular basis, monitoring general health condition through physical checkups and treating routine illnesses. While some are trained in a specialty practice, for the most part general and family practitioners are primary care physicians who refer patients to specialists when additional expertise is required for treatment.

Internists diagnose and treat diseases and injuries of the internal organ system. When a patient comes in with an ailment, an internist will perform a physical examination and run a series of process-of-elimination tests to identify the problem and prescribe the appropriate treatment. While internists specialize in internal medicine, their area of expertise is very broad. Ultimately, however, they may refer the patient to a specialist for treatment of an illness that falls outside their expertise.

Geriatric physicians are a subset of the class of general practitioners, but the growing number of older Americans has dictated that the field become a specialty. Geriatric physicians are generally primary care physicians, much the same as family physicians, but with a focus on the particular needs of the aged. Examinations, reviewing patients' medical histories, diagnoses, and ordering medical tests are among their chief responsibilities. While some geriatric physicians specialize in particular disorders, most will refer patients to specialists for expert care for a particular ailment.

Preventive medicine physicians treat patients in order to help them avoid illness, promoting proper diet, good hygiene, and effective methods to prevent disease. They are typically primary care doctors whose patient treatments include diet, exercise, medication, and lifestyle changes. In some cases this is known as *wellness care*: treatment designed to keep people from needing expensive care that could have been avoided with proper education or behavioral changes. Insurance carriers are eager to promote such care because it reduces their long-term costs.

EARNING POTENTIAL

Earnings for physicians vary widely based on years of practice, geographic location, the number of hours worked, and the doctor's own experience, reputation, skill, and personality. Additionally, physicians who own or have a partnership interest in a medical practice may earn almost 50 percent more than those who work for others on a salaried basis. Keeping all this in mind, we can put the median annual salary for all physicians at $140,000.

Family practitioners have among the lowest earnings among physicians. The median annual income for family and general practitioners after expenses is approximately $98,000.

The median annual income for **geriatric** and **preventive medicine physicians** falls into a category similar to that of a general family practitioner, although as in all areas of medical practice, the income may vary widely.

The median annual income for **internists** is $125,000.

EDUCATIONAL REQUIREMENTS

There are two types of physicians: *M.D.s* (doctors of medicine) and *D.O.s* (doctors of osteopathy). The two different degrees reflect the fact that M.D.s and D.O.s attend two different types of medical school, each of which stresses slightly different treatment.

While both M.D.s and D.O.s use such accepted methods of treatment as drugs and surgery, D.O.s' training gives special emphasis to the musculo-skeletal system. D.O.s believe that a body's good health depends on the proper alignment of bones, muscles, ligaments, and nerves. D.O.s are particularly well-suited to preventive medicine, because a large part of their training underscores this philosophy.

All doctors must be licensed to practice. The licensing procedure requires graduation from an undergraduate institution, graduation from an accredited medical school, completion and passage of licensing examinations, and between one and seven years of residency. Many states offer reciprocity for doctors licensed in another state, but some impose limits on a doctor's ability to practice.

For undergraduate premedical studies, a prospective doctor should expect to study physics, biology, and inorganic chemistry. Other areas premed students should consider include mathematics, social sciences, and humanities.

Admission to the 141 accredited medical schools in the United States (125 of which award M.D. degrees, 16 of which award D.O. degrees) is highly competitive. Once admitted, students spend two years studying anatomy, bio-chemistry, physiology, pharmacology, psychology, microbiology, pathology, and medical ethics. The last two years involve practical work with hospital and clinic patients under the supervision of licensed physicians.

Upon graduation from medical school, all M.D.s go on to their practical graduate medical education known as residency. A residency, depending on the specialty of the resident physician, may last as long as seven years. Graduate students applying for a residency in their field take the National Board of Medical Examiners' standard examination.

D.O.s serve a twelve-month rotating internship after graduation from medical school. Before beginning the internship, they must pass an examination given by the National Board of Osteopathic Medical Examiners. After completing the internship, many D.O.s take a one- to three-year residency in a specialty.

Most doctors seek board certification after completing their residency and possibly after one or two years in practice. A board certification proves that the doctors are fully qualified to practice their specialty. For *medical doctors*, examinations for board certification are given by the American Board of Medical Specialists. *Doctors of osteopathy* must pass a board examination given by the American Osteopathic Association. There are specific board certification examinations for internal medicine and general/family practice.

Geriatric physicians must complete a three- to eight-year residency, depending on the extent of their medical school education. They may specialize in internal medicine or family medicine with a subspecialty in geriatrics.

Preventive medicine physicians must complete a one-year residency and may seek board certification as a Preventive Medicine Specialist after completing one practical year of training, research, or teaching, and two to five years in practice, depending on the extent of their medical school education.

All in all, a physician's education never ends. Practicing physicians must remain current with changes in their field. Most doctors attend seminars and read medical journals on a regular basis in order to stay aware of new techniques and discoveries.

A DAY IN THE LIFE

Physicians generally work in clean, quiet, comfortable offices and hospitals. **Family** and **geriatric** physicians may also make house calls.

More recently, **geriatric physicians** have begun to work in retirement communities that have an agreement with a local hospital to provide care for patients on a general-retainer basis. Doctors who are part of a group will visit the community to see patients, rather than require elderly patients to go through the difficulty of visiting the doctor's office. A geriatric physician may also serve as a staff doctor at a large retirement community.

While physicians work with little or no supervision, they frequently work long and irregular hours (though this may not be so much the case with **preventive care specialists**). Statistics show that at least half of all full-time practicing physicians work more than sixty hours a week. Night and weekend hours may be a necessary part of their practice, and they are often on call for emergencies. These long hours are especially typical for young physicians trying to build a practice.

Although many doctors continue to practice beyond normal retirement age, they also then tend to reduce their patient load to provide themselves with more free time.

JOB GROWTH

A recent study found that approximately 560,000 physicians are practicing in the United States.

Of that number 61,600 are **general/family practitioners**. Over the next decade that number is expected to increase by 2,750 per year based on growth

HELP WANTED

Family Practitioner

Conduct physical examinations and clinical tests. Responsible for treating routine illnesses and prescribing medication/therapy. Refer patients to specialists for specialized treatment. Average Salary: $98,000.

Internist

Diagnose and treat internal organ maladies. Perform physical exams and clinical tests. Prescribe treatment and medication for conditions. Average Salary: $125,000.

Geriatric Physicians

Specialize in care of elderly patients. Perform physical exams and clinical tests. Prescribe treatment and medication. Average Salary: $98,000.

Preventive Medicine Physicians

Consult with patients regarding good health practices to avoid health problems. Provide patients with diet plans, exercise plans, lifestyle programs, and medical alternatives. Average Salary: $98,000.

and replacement needs. With many incumbent physicians having studied in specialized medicine, a shortage of general/family physicians will create a demand in this field.

The same study found that approximately 93,500 **internists** are practicing in the United States, a number that can be expected to rise by around 4,200 per year through the year 2000, based on growth and replacement needs.

There are currently no accurate statistics available to quantify the number of physicians specializing in the field of **geriatric medicine**. However, all indications show that with the aging of the nation's population, employment of geriatric physicians can be expected to grow faster than the average for all occupations in the United States over the next ten years.

Current statistics reflect that there are only 1,120 practicing specialists in **preventive medicine**, but because of the marketplace demand to reduce health care costs, preventive care will become an increasingly important growth area in the future of medicine.

There is some dispute among experts as to whether or not there is an oversupply of doctors. One thing is certain among physicians, though: an oversupply does not equate with an inability to find employment or to establish and build a sole practice. Because of the demand for health care, doctors should always be able to make a good living.

If medical schools do produce an oversupply of doctors, more doctors may be forced to begin practices in rural areas and small communities. Others may forgo a sole practice in favor of a salaried position in a group practice, clinic, or HMO. These opportunities allow doctors to work reasonable hours and avoid the excessive cost of starting a practice.

Additionally there are two trends in health care that are giving rise to great concern, since both facts present a problem for the health care industry that cannot be solved. The first is that people are living much longer than in the past. Health care in this country has succeeded in providing people with longevity; now it must learn to care for an aging population. This makes specializing in geriatric medicine a particularly prudent choice.

The second is that health care costs escalate at an average of 15 percent every year. Individuals and companies are continually paying more for health insurance, and insurance companies are, in turn, continually looking for ways to save money. The active pursuit of wellness is a trend that is finding favor with a large segment of the population—people who are enthusiastic about exercise and nutrition—as well as with insurance companies, which want to contain costs. Preventive care is a relatively new and growing phenomenon with a healthy future.

PODIATRIST

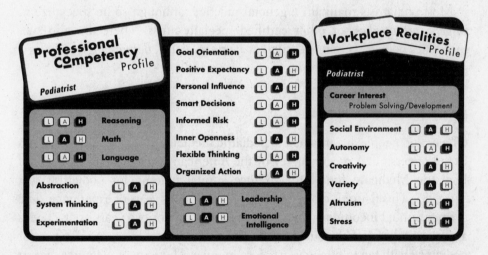

Feet, don't fail me now. *Podiatrists* are the medical specialists who treat injuries and disorders of the foot. Although it may strike many as unusual that a body part so seemingly simple as the foot requires a specialized profession, the foot is a much more important and complicated structure than it seems. The human foot contains twenty-six bones in addition to its nerves, muscles, ligaments, and blood vessels. It also has different types of skin: the skin on a person's heel is unlike the skin on any other part of the body. The complex nature of the foot, its design, which both supports and balances the body and provides for mobility, and its many potential ailments all serve to warrant a separate profession for doctors of podiatric medicine (D.P.M.s).

Some of the foot conditions podiatrists treat include corns, calluses, ingrown toenails, bunions, heel spurs, arch problems, ankle and foot injuries, deformities, infections, and foot complaints associated with diseases such as diabetes.

Treatment methods employed by podiatrists include prescription drugs, physical therapy, and surgery. D.P.M.s also take molds and design and fit corrective shoe inserts, or orthotics. They design custom-made shoes to correct foot deformities.

Podiatrists rely on physical examinations, X rays, and laboratory tests to diagnose foot problems. Occasionally, particularly in cases involving systemic diseases, conditions suggesting other serious illness may first manifest themselves as foot disorders. For example, one common symptom associated with diabetes is foot ulcers. These erupt as a result of the poor circulation of many diabetes sufferers. Podiatrists are trained to spot such symptoms and refer their patients to medical specialists in other fields for additional treatment.

Most podiatrists maintain a general practice, although some specialize in *surgery*, *orthopedics*, or other certified specialty areas. There are also subspecialties podiatrists practice, such as *sports medicine*, *dermatology*, *radiology*, *geriatrics*, and *diabetic foot care*.

EARNING POTENTIAL

One reason people are attracted to podiatric medicine is the potential earnings in the profession. A recent survey by the American Association of Colleges of Podiatric Medicine found the *average* annual income for podiatrists was $100,287. This figure is closely tied to a practitioner's years of experience. The average annual income for podiatrists with only one or two years of practice is approximately $35,578, but the figure rises considerably—to $119,674—for podiatrists with ten to fifteen years of experience. These income figures suggest why many podiatrists continue to practice past traditional retirement age, and why there is little turnover in the profession.

EDUCATIONAL REQUIREMENTS

Podiatric medicine is a licensed medical practice in all states of the United States. Although licensing requirements vary from state to state, general qualifications for podiatrists include graduation from an accredited podiatric college and the successful completion of written and oral examinations. Twenty-five states also require podiatrists to complete an accredited residency program. Some states grant reciprocity to podiatrists, which means that they are permitted to practice in a state if they have qualified for a license in another state. Thirty-one states have continuing education requirements for the renewal of podiatric licenses; requirements vary by state.

Although some podiatric colleges do not require applicants to be graduates of accredited colleges, they all require applicants to have completed at least ninety semester hours of undergraduate study. Applicants are advised to check with the podiatric colleges for their admissions standards, and to complete their undergraduate degrees before attending a podiatric college. An undergraduate degree enhances one's chances of being accepted.

Undergraduate classes that serve as prerequisites for admission to podiatric college include eight semester hours each of biology, inorganic chemistry, organic chemistry, and physics, and six hours of English. Applicants must also take and receive an acceptable score on the Medical College Admission Test (M.C.A.T.).

Colleges of podiatric medicine offer a four-year program. The curriculum parallels that of other medical schools, including two years of classroom instruction in anatomy, chemistry, pathology, and pharmacology, and two years of clinical rotation experience. It is during the last two years of the program that students receive their first practical experience treating patients under the direct supervision of senior podiatrists.

Podiatrists receive their D.P.M. degree after completing the four-year program, but most subsequently complete a one-year hospital residency program. During the course of that year, doctors of podiatric medicine serve clinical rotations in anesthesiology, internal medicine, pathology, radiology, emergency medicine, and orthopedic and general surgery. Some residencies continue past the first year and provide extensive training in specialty areas.

There are three certifying boards in podiatric medicine that recognize and administer qualifying examinations in four specialty areas of practice. These are:

• American Board of Podiatric Surgery
• American Board of Podiatric Orthopedic and Primary Podiatric Medicine
• American Board of Podiatric Public Health

HELP WANTED
PODIATRIST

Diagnose and treat foot ailments. Perform physical exams and clinical tests. Prescribe medication, therapy, and/or surgery. Fit patients for orthotics, and refer patients to specialists for specific disorders. Salary Range: $35,600–$119,700.

A DAY IN THE LIFE

Most podiatrists work in private practice, maintaining their own offices and hiring their own staff. Some serve on staff in hospitals. A few large cities have facilities that serve as teaching hospitals for podiatrists.

Private practice allows podiatrists to set their own hours, but they may also find themselves working long hours, nights, and weekends in order to establish their practice. Otherwise their work lives parallel the rigors of the rest of the medical profession: you are expected on the first tee early every Wednesday—unless you have a doctor's note.

JOB GROWTH

A recent survey showed that there are approximately 8,200 podiatrists in the United States, most of whom have solo practices. As has been the trend in medical practice, though, many more podiatrists are forming partnerships or developing group practices. This joining together allows podiatrists and other professionals to treat a greater number of patients and share the expenses of medical practice. Many podiatrists also work in hospitals, nursing homes, and clinics. Some work in teaching hospitals, where they both teach and maintain a practice.

An interesting feature of podiatric medicine is that only seven states—California, Florida, Illinois, Iowa, New York, Pennsylvania, and Ohio—have colleges of podiatric medicine. Because most graduates of podiatric colleges tend to establish a practice near these colleges to draw on their resources, there are large portions of the United States that have very few practicing podiatrists. The South, the Southwest, and large rural and suburban areas where there are insufficient numbers of podiatrists are areas of great opportunity. In these areas general practitioners and orthopedists currently provide patients with primary foot care.

In part because of the relatively small number of podiatrists and the growing need for their services, the profession will grow at a rate exceeding the national average for all occupations through 2005. The largest patient base will be the increasing number of elderly people who suffer greatly from foot disorders. In addition, the more active lifestyle of modern times will continue to bring about more sports-related foot ailments, requiring treatment from podiatrists.

People interested in entering the field of podiatric medicine should be advised that podiatric care has typically proved to be something tied into patients' disposable income. Many people choose not to have routine foot care performed if it is not covered by their medical benefits plan. Although coverage typically includes nonelective surgery and other medical emergency care, routine foot care is often not covered.

MEDICAL THERAPIST: PHYSICAL THERAPIST/OCCUPATIONAL THERAPIST/RECREATIONAL THERAPIST/RESPIRATORY THERAPIST

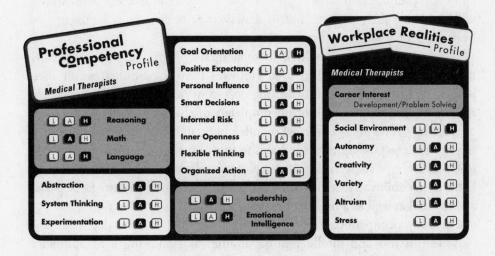

Medical therapists plan, organize, and conduct therapeutic/rehabilitation programs for patients who suffer from debilitating physical or mental injury or disease. The following four specialties in this field show particularly promising growth.

Physical therapists oversee the recovery programs of patients suffering from muscle, joint, bone, and nerve injuries or diseases. Once a patient has recovered sufficiently from an illness or injury to begin physical activity again, he or she will be referred by the doctor to a physical therapist for specific treatment. Physical therapists follow a doctor's orders to assist patients in their rehabilitation. Their goal is to restore a patient's functions as fully as possible, to relieve pain, and to prevent further disability or a recurrence of the disabling condition.

In order to perform their tasks, physical therapists first put their patients through a battery of tests. These tests serve to determine a patient's strength, motor development, sensory perception, functional capacity, and respiratory and circulatory capacity. Then, using these determinations, physical therapists devise a treatment program that includes manual exercises; instruction and assistance in using canes, crutches, prostheses, and other supportive devices; and such therapeutic treatments as hydrotherapy, traction, heat and ice applications, and ultrasound. As the patient's condition evolves during treatment, the physical therapist adjusts the level of activity and degree of intensity to push the patient toward further improvement.

One important element of physical therapy is motivation. Patients who have conditions that improve only gradually often find themselves growing depressed over the slow pace of their recovery. Physical therapists must continually motivate their patients not to despair over temporary setbacks or slow improvement, and praise them for their successes.

Occupational therapists help to rehabilitate people who are physically, mentally, or emotionally impaired (or who have a combination of these problems) and provide them with the tools to work again. Many people who suffer disabling injuries are not so completely disabled that they are incapable of working. Yet some people who suffer permanent injuries are unable to return to the job they previously held, so they must develop new skills for the jobs that are now viable. And since a person's self-esteem is closely connected to his or her ability to work at a job, many injury victims find work to be a therapeutic tool as well as a means of making a living.

One way occupational therapists help their clients is by determining a person's physical and intellectual capabilities and tailoring a rehabilitation program suited to that individual. A program may range from such activities as learning to use a computer, to such fundamental tasks as dressing oneself. The nature of the rehabilitation program depends entirely on the level of activity the client can hope to achieve.

At a more sophisticated level, occupational therapists organize activities that aid the sensorimotor and intellectual capacities of their clients, as well as activities that teach handicapped clients how to adjust to and work within the limits of their handicap.

People with permanent disabilities need to be trained in the use of adaptive equipment, such as wheelchairs, eating and dressing aids, and computers that enable them to communicate effectively with others. People who have mental disorders have different needs, and occupational therapists assist them in developing such skills as time management and financial budgeting. Other occupational therapists, called *industrial therapists*, help patients to find and then keep jobs that are appropriate to their skills.

Understandably, the job of an occupational therapist can be emotionally draining. Many patients show improvement in small increments. Therefore, occupational therapists must have great patience and the ability to empathize with their clients.

Recreational therapists help individuals with mentally, physically, developmentally, or emotionally disabling conditions to develop, recover, or maintain daily living and work skills.

People who suffer disabling injuries or contract debilitating illnesses often need activity in order to begin reclaiming their life. Many such patients will never regain their full physical capacity, but they can learn to enjoy life within the boundaries of their condition. Recreational therapists help patients by teaching them ways to enjoy physical activity despite their limitations.

Recreational therapists plan, organize, and direct medically approved recreation programs for patients in hospitals and other institutions as part of a recovery program. The typical responsibilities of a recreational therapist include directing and organizing sports, dramatics, games, and arts and crafts to assist patients in developing interpersonal relationships, socializing effectively, and developing the confidence necessary to participate in group activities. They regulate the content of the program to accommodate the patients' capabilities, needs, and interests. They instruct patients in relaxation techniques (such as deep breathing and concentration) to reduce stress and tension. And they also instruct patients in calisthenics and stretching, and individual and group sports.

Recreational therapists also counsel and encourage patients to develop leisure activities. They organize, coordinate, and accompany patients on special outings and prepare progress charts and periodic reports for medical staff and other members of the treatment team regarding the patients' reactions and progress.

Some recreational therapists may also supervise and conduct in-service training of other staff members, review their assessments and program goals, and consult with them on selected cases. They train groups of volunteers and students in techniques of recreation therapy; serve as consultants to employers, educational institutions, and community health programs; and prepare and submit requisitions for needed supplies.

Respiratory therapists specialize in breathing disorders and general respiratory systems. Thousands of people suffer from respiratory ailments such as asthma, allergies, and emphysema—potentially deadly conditions that often require advanced treatment and skilled care. Respiratory therapists work under the direct supervision of doctors or from prescriptions to administer therapeutic respiratory care and life support to patients with cardiopulmonary deficiencies and abnormalities.

The typical responsibilities of a respiratory care therapist include following prescribed instructions, measuring arterial blood gases, reviewing patient information to assess the patient's condition, and determining the requirements for treatment and medication. Respiratory therapists also determine the most suitable method for administering inhalants to patients.

Respiratory therapists set up and operate equipment such as mechanical ventilators, therapeutic gas administration apparatus, environmental control systems, and aerosol generators to ensure observance of the specified parameters of treatment. These treatment parameters include the volume of oxygen, the gas concentration, humidity, and temperature. This equipment and these calibrations are designed to provide relief for patients suffering from advanced respiratory illnesses.

Respiratory therapists administer medicinal gases and aerosol drugs to patients. They monitor patients' physiological responses to therapy and may perform bronchopulmonary drainage to eliminate fluid buildup in patients' lungs. Respiratory therapists assist patients in performing their breathing exercises and perform pulmonary function tests to be used by physicians in diagnosis.

In addition, respiratory therapists maintain patients' charts, inspect and test respiratory care equipment, and demonstrate respiratory care procedures to trainees and other health care personnel. They also notify and consult with physicians in the event of patients' adverse reactions to treatment.

Medical science has yet to discover cures for many of the ailments that afflict the respiratory system, and so a large part of a respiratory therapist's job is to maintain a patient's level of health and breathing for as long as possible. Many people who suffer from respiratory ailments gradually grow worse, for there are few cures. Therefore, respiratory therapists work to slow down the debilitating effects of respiratory illnesses.

EARNING POTENTIAL

Beginning **physical therapists** can expect to earn between $17,500 and $24,000 a year; those with more experience, between $20,000 and $55,000 a year, according to 1995 statistics.

Beginning **occupational therapists** can expect to earn between $26,000 and $34,000 a year; more experienced therapists, between $30,000 and $40,000 a year.

Beginning **recreational therapists** can expect to earn between $18,000 and $28,000 a year; more experienced therapists, between $25,000 and $40,000 a year.

Salary growth for the therapists mentioned above should be good, somewhat better than the rate of inflation. Occupational and recreational therapists in private practice typically earn more than salaried therapists.

Beginning **respiratory therapists** earn between approximately $16,300 and $26,000 a year; more experienced therapists, approximately $18,000 to $42,000 per year. Salary growth in the field is expected to be limited, despite the demand for respiratory therapists, by the fact that educational requirements in the field are not as intense as for many other therapist occupations. Also, because respiratory therapists require expensive equipment to perform their job and must work under a doctor's supervision, they have few opportunities to work as independent contractors or consultants.

EDUCATIONAL REQUIREMENTS

Physical therapists must graduate from an accredited physical therapy program and pass a mandatory state licensure exam before they can practice their occupation. In 1992 there were seventy bachelor's degree and sixty-four master's degree physical therapy education programs available in the United States. Competition for entry into these programs is stiff, and a good high school record in math and sciences is essential. Program courses include biology, chemistry, and physics, as well as human growth and development, therapeutic procedure, biomechanics and neuroanatomy. Practical experience in physical therapy is part of the training. A master's degree is recommended for those interested in progression into an administrative position. Many states require continued education for renewal of licensure.

Occupational therapists also must obtain a minimum of a bachelor's degree in occupational therapy before they qualify to take the licensing exam that is now mandatory in thirty-six states and the District of Columbia. In 1992 there were sixty-seven entry-level educational programs, ten post-bachelor's programs, and fifteen master's programs available in occupational therapy. Curriculum courses comprise physical, behavioral, and biological sciences and occupational therapy theory and skills. Students must also complete a six-month supervised clinical internship.

Recreational therapists should have a four-year undergraduate degree in therapeutic recreation, although an associate degree in recreational therapy may be sufficient for some positions. There are approximately one hundred educational programs that prepare recreational therapists, half of which are acknowledged by the National Council on Accreditation. Courses include human anatomy, physiology, psychology, and medical terminology, as well as general therapeutic recreation and a 360-hour internship.

Respiratory therapists must have either a bachelor's degree or an associate's degree, or must have graduated from a vocational/technical school that offers a certificate program in the field. Respiratory care students must take courses in mathematics, biological science, and physical science, as well as in technical procedures and equipment and clinical testing. In 1992, 283 respiratory therapist educational programs were accredited by the Committee on Allied Health Education Accreditation of the American Medical Association. All graduates may take the C.R.T.T. (certified respiratory therapy technician) examination, and C.R.T.T.s with the required educational and practical experience are eligible to take the registry exam to become an R.R.T. (registered respiratory therapist).

A DAY IN THE LIFE

Medical therapists generally work in hospitals, clinics, and other health care settings. These are generally clean, comfortable, and quiet environments. Many of these therapists work in rehabilitation facilities that exclusively serve patients who have been released from the hospital but who require training to recover their physical functions—typically the case with stroke victims.

Some **physical therapists** work for orthopedic surgeons who treat patients suffering from sports-related injuries. These therapists usually have a room housing several pieces of equipment—including weight-lifting and range-of-motion equipment—where they see patients and treat them according to the doctor's orders.

Private practice physical therapists work on a consulting basis for retirement homes and rehabilitation facilities. They may also be referred to individual patients by doctors or home health care agencies.

Physical, occupational, and **recreational therapists** work under little direct supervision but must work in cooperation with others. **Respiratory therapists** work under the supervision of physicians, but much of their work is performed without direct supervision.

HELP WANTED
MEDICAL THERAPISTS

Physical Therapist
Oversee recovery programs of patients suffering from muscle, joint, bone, and nerve injuries or diseases. Devise and implement a treatment program. Encourage patients, praising them for success and sympathizing with them over setbacks. Salary Range: $17,500–$55,000.

Occupational Therapist
Help rehabilitate people who are physically, mentally, or emotionally impaired and provide them with the tools to work again. Determine a person's physical and intellectual capabilities and tailor a rehabilitation program suited to the individual. Organize activities that aid the sensorimotor and intellectual capacities of clients, as well as activities that teach handicapped clients how to adjust to and work within the limits of their handicap. Salary Range: $26,000–$40,000.

Recreational Therapist
Help individuals with mentally, physically, developmentally, or emotionally disabling conditions to develop, recover, or maintain daily living and work skills. Plan, organize, and direct medically approved recreation programs for patients. Direct and organize sports, dramatics, games, and arts and crafts to assist patients in developing interpersonal relationships. Instruct patients in relaxation techniques to reduce stress and tension. Salary Range: $18,000–$40,000.

All of these therapists' jobs may entail overtime, night, or weekend hours. Often, there are physical demands that require strength and agility. Some therapists may have to lift equipment or disabled patients on a regular basis and spend much time standing or walking. The particularly stressful aspect for these therapists, however, is the degree of frustration involved in working with patients whose condition often does not improve quickly or significantly. Temperamentally, these therapists must be able to exercise both leadership and patience.

JOB GROWTH

A recent survey indicated that approximately 95,000 **physical therapists**, 55,000 **occupational therapists**, 28,000 **recreational therapists**, and 82,000 **respiratory therapists** were employed in the United States. Most jobs were located in hospitals, but a small and rapidly growing number are in private practice.

The fields of **physical, occupational, and recreational therapy** will grow at a faster than average rate during the next decade. Many more physical therapists will be needed to treat the ever-increasing number of elderly people and those who experience incapacitating injury. The growth of nursing homes and life care communities will provide therapists with a large number of job openings during the next ten years. Statistics indicate that the job market for all physical-activity therapists will grow by 43,000 jobs between

Respiratory Therapists
Assist doctors in improving a patient's condition. Help determine required treatment and medication. Set up, operate, inspect, and test respiratory equipment. Administer and teach use of respiratory aids to patients. Responsible for maintaining patient charts. Salary Range: $16,000–$42,000.

1995 and 2005. Hospitals will continue to supply the largest percentage of positions for therapists, but home health care and outpatient services as well as retirement and nursing homes will also employ numerous therapists. There will also be a moderate number of **occupational therapists** employed in schools due to extended services for handicapped students.

The future holds abundant opportunity for **respiratory therapists**. While most of their positions are in hospitals, respiratory therapists will also find employment in nursing homes, medical clinics, and as emergency medical providers working for ambulance services. Although the field itself is relatively small, it should grow at a significant rate as people continue to live longer and require greater respiratory care.

Although this occupation requires a less demanding academic background than some other therapist professions, the occupational demands placed on **respiratory therapists** are no less rigorous—and the risks involved for the patients are often greater. This is an occupation that should appeal to people who want to provide a valuable service to patients often too weak to help themselves. It requires strength and sensitivity to the needs of sick people.

While the largest part of job growth in the physical therapies will result from the increased demand for rehabilitative services brought about by medical advances and the aging population, another significant factor is that members of the baby boom generation now reaching middle age will require therapy as a result of the many maladies associated with middle age, stress, and overwork, such as heart attacks and strokes.

Many people leave the therapy field due to its inherently stressful nature. This "churning" of jobs means that there should be many available openings to accommodate therapists new to the occupation.

One major development in the field of physical therapy is the recent change in legislation that permits therapists to bill Medicare directly for their services. Since these bills formerly had to be submitted through a hospital or health care agency, physical therapists were limited to working for health care employers. Direct billing allows therapists greater flexibility in self-employment. Because the requirements are fairly strict, the field is not an easy one to enter. Once a therapist has begun to practice, though, the amount of business he or she can expect will continue to grow. This is an excellent career choice for those with the intelligence, drive, and inner strength to meet the requirements and help disabled people. It also provides the opportunity to turn a salaried job into an entrepreneurial career and far surpass the wages of a salaried employee.

AUDIOLOGIST AND SPEECH-LANGUAGE PATHOLOGIST

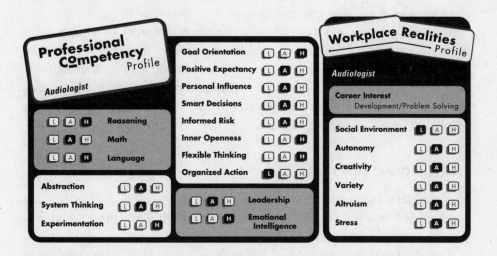

Speech and hearing therapists both work with patients who have difficulties with verbal communication, often caused by a hearing disorder. Although they specialize in different aspects of therapy, their work is often interdependent.

Audiologists diagnose hearing disorders through a series of tests such as air and bone conduction and speech reception, using audiometers and electro-acoustic instruments to determine at what level the patient detects and distinguishes sound. Once the source and extent of the problem is ascertained, the audiologist prescribes a method of treatment, which can include ear canal cleaning, or fitting amplifiers, alerting devices, or other hearing aids and auditory training. The audiologist works in conjunction with the patient's family, school, and workplace, counseling the parties involved on communication, perhaps offering training in lipreading, and helping them deal with the stress of living or interacting with someone with a hearing disorder.

Speech-language pathologists evaluate and treat patients who have problems with articulation, voice rhythm, and fluency; comprehending or expressing language; pitch control; or eating and swallowing. Many of these problems stem from hearing disorders, so audiologists often may refer their patients to speech-language pathologists for further treatment. Speech impediments may also be the result of stroke, cleft palate, brain injury, or emotional problems. Speech-language pathologists conduct instrumental, oral, and written tests to record and evaluate speech irregularities. They then recommend a course of treatment, from simple verbal exercises to automated devices and sign language, depending on the severity of the problem. Like audiologists, they train and counsel the patient's family, friends, and colleagues in techniques for communicating with the speech-impaired.

Some audiologists and speech-language pathologists work in schools (often they are categorized as *special education teachers* [page 415]), assisting teachers and hearing/speech-impaired children to adjust to a classroom routine, or running special speech classes. Others conduct research and develop treatment and activity plans for the speech- and hearing-impaired in schools, hospitals, clinics, and nursing homes.

EARNING POTENTIAL

The median salary for audiologists and speech-language pathologists is approximately $36,000. Starting salaries average $26,000, while those with ten or more years' experience can earn around $58,000.

Audiologists tend to earn slightly more than **speech-language pathologists**. Salaries vary also depending on geographical location (generally higher in the Northeast and lower in the South and Midwest) and college degree. A doctorate will practically guarantee you an additional $10,000 per year.

EDUCATIONAL REQUIREMENTS

A master's degree is the standard credential for those wishing to practice in audiology or speech-language pathology. Most states require licensure, with a prerequisite of 375 hours of clinical experience, passing of a national examination, and nine months of postgraduate work experience.

There are 235 colleges that offer master's degrees in speech-language pathology and audiology. In order to obtain this degree you must complete courses in anatomy, physiology, psychology, acoustics, and speech therapy and communication disorders.

Compassion, patience, and, obviously, communication skills are important for anyone considering a career in this field.

HELP WANTED

Audiologist

Diagnose and prescribe treatment for hearing disorders using audiometers and electroacoustic instruments. Counsel clients about living with a hearing disorder. Also counsel patient's family, friends, and colleagues in effective communication techniques. Job requires compassion, patience, and excellent communication skills. Salary Range: $26,000–$58,000.

Speech-Language Pathologist

Diagnose and treat patients with language, articulation, comprehension, and hearing disorders. Conduct tests to record and evaluate speech irregularities. Recommend treatments from verbal exercises to automated devices and sign language. Train and counsel patient's family, friends, and colleagues in communication techniques. Requires compassion, patience, and excellent communication skills. Salary Range: $26,000–$58,000.

A DAY IN THE LIFE

While the physical demands on audiologists and speech-language pathologists are minimal, the same cannot be said for the psychological and emotional demands. They generally work forty-hour weeks, in clean, comfortable offices, clinics, schools, or hospitals, and spend a good deal of time sitting, consulting, and working with patients. They work under very little direct supervision and there is a good deal of record-keeping involved.

The strenuous aspect of the profession is mental, with the intense concentration that is involved in conducting tests, the repetitive nature of the rehabilitation techniques, and the frustration level for both audiologist/speech-pathologist and patient when improvement is slow. However, those blessed with a combination of patience and a desire to help others will find this a rewarding career.

JOB GROWTH

There are approximately 73,400 audiologists and speech-language pathologists employed in the United States today. This number is expected to increase to 97,000 by the year 2005. This growth can be attributed largely to the aging of the population and the hearing and stroke-related problems that come as we all slip into life's sunset years. Therefore there will undoubtedly be lots of opportunities in retirement homes and home health care agencies for audiologists and speech-language pathologists. There also will be openings for these professionals in school systems, where state laws require children with problems in speech and hearing to receive special aid.

There will be an increasing need for these specialists in hospitals and clinics as technology finds new ways to increase the survival rates of accident, trauma, and stroke victims. Audiologists and speech-language pathologists are opening their own clinics and may contract themselves out to hospitals and institutions, or treat private patients.

As school enrollments appear to be holding steady in this field while demand for qualified practitioners increases, there is a good likelihood those who are trained will have no difficulty in obtaining employment.

DISPENSING OPTICIAN

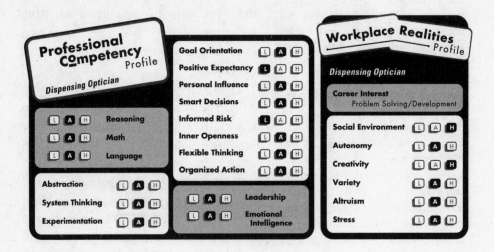

A medical doctor (*ophthalmologist*) or a trained eye expert (*optometrist*) examines a person's eyes to determine what degree of correction by eyeglasses or contact lenses is required. **Dispensing opticians** are the people who actually fit eyeglasses and contact lenses according to the prescriptions. Dispensing opticians order the necessary laboratory work for customers and adjust the finished eyeglasses. They issue orders that direct technicians in grinding lenses, or they grind and insert the lenses in frames themselves. In some states, dispensing opticians fit contact lenses under the supervision of an optometrist or ophthalmologist.

Dispensing opticians also serve as salespeople. They assist customers in their selection of the appropriate frames for their glasses, and they recommend lenses and lens coatings for customers. The typical duties of a dispensing optician include examining written prescriptions to determine lens specifications, and taking measurements for a client's eyeglass size, including the distance between the centers of the pupils and the distance between the eye surface and the lens. Dispensing opticians may obtain a customer's previous record, or verify a prescription with the examining optometrist and ophthalmologist. After the glasses are made, dispensing opticians verify that the lenses have been ground to specifications. Then they may reshape or bend the frame with the aid of a heating instrument, so that the eyeglasses fit the customer properly. Dispensing opticians also fix, adjust, and refit broken frames and instruct clients on the necessary care of eyeglasses.

There are specialists in the field who fit contact lenses, artificial eyes, cosmetic shells that cover blemishes in the eye, and devices that serve to aid clients with poor vision. Fitting contact lenses properly requires the dispensing optician to measure the eyes' shape and size, choose the proper type of material for the lenses, and draft work orders specifying the prescription and lens size. This procedure requires skill, precision, and patience.

Many dispensing opticians manage their own small practices. These individuals must order and stock inventory, maintain customer records, and handle bookkeeping duties.

EARNING POTENTIAL

A study by the Opticians Association of America has found that salaries for dispensing opticians in retail stores average approximately $26,000. The starting salary for licensed and certified opticians is in the range of $20,970. Those with three to five years of experience average $21,875; six to nine years, $25,876; ten years or more, $29,640.

Noncertified opticians average about $6,000 less at each level of experience. Beginning apprentices earn an average of about $13,000 a year, while experienced opticians can earn more than $30,000 a year. Those who run their own stores usually earn considerably more than salaried workers. But in addition to base salary, employers often pay commissions and bonuses, and sometimes offer profit-sharing programs.

EDUCATIONAL REQUIREMENTS

Although some employers hire people with no previous experience in opticianry, most candidates in the field will have received some formal training before applying for a job. Some large employers still offer structured apprenticeship programs for employees, and some small employers offer less formally structured on-the-job training. In the twenty-one states that license dispensing opticians, applicants without formal college experience train from two to four years as apprentices. Apprenticeship or formal traineeship is offered in most of the other states as well.

Apprentices receive training in the technical aspects of the craft and in office management and sales. Apprentices work directly with patients, under the supervision of experienced opticians, fitting eyeglasses and contact lenses. In states requiring licensure, information about apprenticeships and licensing procedures is available from the state board of occupational licensing.

Formal opticianry training is offered in community colleges and in some colleges and universities. There are about forty programs, twenty-three of which are accredited by the Commission on Opticianry Accreditation and award two-year associate degrees in ophthalmic dispensing or optometric technology. There are also shorter programs, including some under one year. Some states that license dispensing opticians allow graduates to take the licensure exam immediately upon graduation; others require up to a year of experience prior to sitting for the exam.

Dispensing opticians may also gain credentials through voluntary certification or registration by the American Board of Opticianry or the National Contact Lens Examiners. Certification must be renewed every three years; renewal requires continuing education.

Dispensing opticians with a college background have typically studied physics, basic anatomy, algebra, and geometry. Courses in mechanical drawing are particularly valuable because training usually includes instruction in optical mathematics, optical physics, the use of precision measuring instruments, and other machinery and tools. All of these skills are essential for opticians.

A DAY IN THE LIFE

Dispensing opticians work indoors in a bright, clean, comfortable environment. They may work in small stores where they provide service to customers on an individual basis, or in large stores where several dispensing opticians serve a number of customers at once. Because it usually takes an hour for a customer to present a prescription, decide on lenses, and select frames, small shops that cater to one customer at a time may find it difficult to compete with the large chains that offer quick service to almost all customers and advertise one-hour fitting services.

All opticians deal with customers, so they must have a sense of salesmanship as well as expertise in their craft. Most dispensing opticians work a forty-hour

HELP WANTED
DISPENSING OPTICIAN

Fit eyeglasses and contact lenses according to prescriptions. Take measurements for a client's eyeglass fitting, order the necessary laboratory work, oversee lens grinding, assist customers in frame selection, and recommend lenses and lens coatings for customers. Fix, adjust, and refit broken frames, and instruct clients on the necessary care of eyeglasses. Salary Range: $13,000–$30,000+.

week, although some work longer hours preparing lenses for customers or maintaining shop hours that accommodate their clientele.

JOB GROWTH

Dispensing opticians hold approximately 63,000 jobs, and half of the jobholders work for ophthalmologists or optometrists who sell glasses directly to patients. Many of the others work in optical shops, including large optical stores. These large stores offer customers the convenience of having their glasses prepared while they wait. Customers at small shops, in contrast, may have to wait a week for glasses to be sent to an optical laboratory for grinding and fitting. Some opticians work in optical departments of drug and department stores.

The primary source of business for opticians is middle-aged and older people. Since the population is rapidly growing older, and people continue to live much longer than in the past, the client base for opticians will continue to grow at a pace faster than the average for all occupations through the next ten years.

Fashion, as well as necessity, influences the demand for corrective lenses. Frames come in thousands of styles and colors, and the fashion trend is for people to have more than one pair. Technology that has created photochromatic lenses (which grow darker or lighter to adjust to the brightness of a light source) and disposable or colored contact lenses has added to the public's desire for variety in eyewear.

The need for eyeglasses is one people cannot ignore, but the demand for different types of eyeglasses is discretionary and corresponds to the health of the economy. Dispensing optometrists are susceptible to slower periods during economic downturns, but the growth in the field, and the need to replace opticians who move into other jobs, such as sales positions for eyeglass or lens manufacturers, will provide a large number of future job openings.

As in so many other professions that will grow over the next ten years, the trade practiced by dispensing opticians is closely connected to the aging population. While there is always a steady base of customers of all ages who need prescription glasses, the fact is that older people make up the largest market for opticians, and also have the most disposable income.

MEDICAL TECHNOLOGIST: RADIOLOGICAL TECHNOLOGIST/NUCLEAR MEDICINE TECHNOLOGIST/EEG TECHNOLOGIST

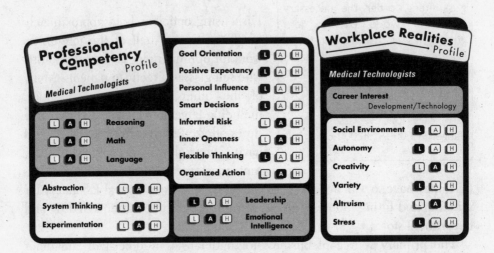

Technologists in the medical field are the clinical laboratory workers who perform medical tests. Because the health care field is growing rapidly, medical practitioners are going to need thousands of support personnel to run tests and examine samples that enable doctors to detect, diagnose, and treat their patients' medical problems.

Medical technologists are called upon to perform complex tests involving chemical, biological, and hematological reactions. They perform microscopic examinations of cultures to determine the level of bacteria, fungi, parasites, and other microorganisms. Medical technologists also look for abnormal cells and cell counts when checking for different types of infections or cancers.

Medical technologists use automated equipment and instruments, as well as microscopes, cell counters, and other laboratory equipment, to run and analyze their tests, and then they forward their findings to doctors. Because of their complexity, these tests call for a high degree of competency on the part of the technologist.

The duties assigned to a medical technologist depend largely on the lab in which he or she works. Those employed in general testing laboratories may perform many diverse tests, while those in specialized laboratories will usually be assigned to one specific task or type of test—for example, those labs that process preemployment drug test samples.

There are several different designations for speciality medical technologists, including *clinical chemistry technologists*, who analyze the chemical contents of body fluids; *microbiology technologists*, who identify microorganisms and bacteria in samples; *blood bank technologists*, who analyze and type blood for transfusions; and *immunology technologists*, who study the effects of antigens (foreign substances) on the human immune system. Due to the rise of infectious diseases such as AIDS, many more medical technologists have been needed to run and study test results. The following medical technologists show particularly strong growth.

Radiological technologists specialize in radiological clinical and laboratory testing, assisting doctors in injury and disease detection and treatment through the use of advanced imaging equipment such as X-ray machines, computerized tomography scanners, and magnetic resonance imaging machines.

Radiological technologists evaluate the accuracy and quality of the images and provide technical assistance to doctors. They prepare and position patients for examination and treatment, set up and operate the equipment, develop the test results, and maintain the files. Their function is partly administrative (preparing and organizing paperwork) and partly mechanical (preparing and operating the equipment for use). The difference between radiological technologists and doctors of radiology is that the technologists are not trained to read the finished X rays or MRI reports in order to diagnose a patient's condition.

Different designators of radiological technologists include *radiation therapy technologists*, who are trained in the use of high-tech linear accelerators with electron capabilities used in treating cancer patients; and *sonographers* (ultrasound technologists), who prepare patients for, and take, ultrasound images of specific body parts, survey the image for idiosyncrasies, and determine whether the image is legible for analysis by the attending physician.

Nuclear medicine technologists administer radiopharmaceuticals (radioactive drugs) to patients and monitor the changes and reactions in tissue and organs in order to detect an abnormality (areas affected by disease will show a higher or lower reading of radioactivity than normal tissues and organs). When working with radioactive material, nuclear medicine technologists must be particularly careful to follow safety standards that minimize the risks of exposure both for patients and for other workers.

In some respects, a nuclear medicine technologist's work mirrors that of a radiological technologist's. Both operate equipment to take photographic images of patients, but the nuclear medicine technologist uses gamma cameras (scanners) that first detect a radioactive drug in a patient's body and then map its progress through the body. The technologist then produces these images on a computer screen or develops them on film for a physician to analyze.

Nuclear medicine technologists record and maintain patient records as required by federal law, and are also responsible for monitoring the amount and types of radionuclides they receive, use, and dispose of.

EEG technologists operate electroencephalograph machines to test patients for brain and nervous system disorders. Applying electrodes to designated spots on the patient's head, they choose the most appropriate combination of instrument controls and electrodes to produce a reading of the brain for analysis by neurologists and physicians, who look for such disorders as brain tumors, strokes, toxic/metabolic maladies, and epilepsy, as well as the effects of infectious diseases and organic causes for mental/behavioral problems.

EEG technologists often assist in the determination of cerebral death, the absence of brain activity, and help to assess the probability of a recovery from a coma. Increasingly EEGs are performed in operating rooms, a circumstance that requires the technologist to understand anesthesia's effect on brain waves.

EEG technologists are often called upon to perform ambulatory monitoring and nerve conduction tests. Specialized EEG technologists also administer sleep studies and perform quantitative EEGs (brain wave mapping).

EARNING POTENTIAL

The following table shows average salaries recorded by several recent studies. As is generally true in the medical field, the earning potential of technologists is very much dependent on experience, size of the medical facility, and geographic location.

	Starting Salary	Median Salary	Experienced Salary
Medical Technologist	$25,000	29,600	40,000
Radiological Technologist	$22,000	28,200	48,000
Nuclear Medicine Technologist	$26,400	32,800	60,000
EEG Technologist	$20,000	25,500	35,000

EDUCATIONAL REQUIREMENTS

Although in the past some **medical technologists** have qualified for their jobs by combining experience and on-the-job training, it is much more typical these days for employers to hire college graduates for clinical laboratory posts. Most bachelor's degree programs in medical technology require classes in chemistry, biological sciences, microbiology, mathematics, and specialized courses devoted to knowledge and skills used in the clinical laboratory. Most programs also include computer science classes.

People interested in specialized medical technologist positions should consider continuing their education to the graduate level. Since specialized jobs require additional training, many specialist technologists hold master's degrees. Of course, technologists can begin work in a general field and receive experience while studying part-time for a graduate degree.

Some, but not all, states require that clinical laboratory personnel be licensed or registered in their specialty. This procedure is done on a state-by-state basis. On a nationwide scale, the Board of Registry of the American Society of Clinical Pathologists, the American Medical Technologists, the National Certification Agency for Medical Laboratory Personnel, and the Credentialing Commission of the International Society for Clinical Laboratory Technology certify clinical laboratory workers in their specialties. Most employers require that applicants be certified as competent in their jobs, and many insist upon certification when considering employee promotions.

Most **radiological technologists** graduate from a vocational/technical school that awards certification or receive an associate's degree from a two-year college program. A four-year college program that leads to a bachelor's degree is recommended to those who wish to be considered for supervisory positions. Additional education or a master's degree in business and health administration is advised for those with a desire to become a department administrator such as *chief radiological technologist.*

The Committee on Allied Health Education and Accreditation (CAHEA) accredits most formal training programs in radiological technology. Most employers prefer to hire registered technologists, and registration generally requires graduation from a CAHEA-accredited program.

There are nearly 700 accredited radiography programs available, 120 radiation therapy programs, and 50 sonography training programs. High school graduation or equivalency is necessary for acceptance into the programs and a good background in math and science is recommended. The radiography courses offer training in anatomy, physiology, radiation physics,

imaging, and safeguarding, as well as general medical procedures, terminology, and ethics.

There are various programs leading to the career as a **nuclear medicine technologist**; the programs offer a certificate, an associate degree, or a bachelor's degree.

Certificate programs, which last one year, are usually offered in hospitals. These programs accept people already employed in health care fields, especially radiological technologists and ultrasound technologists eager to specialize in nuclear medicine. Other medical technologists and some nurses also apply for certification in these programs.

In all programs, from a one-year certificate to a four-year bachelor's program, the course work covers much of the same material: physical sciences, the biological effects of radiation exposure, the use of radiopharmaceuticals, imaging techniques, radiation protection, and procedures and computer applications. There are currently 112 CAHEA-accredited programs in this field.

Nuclear medicine technologists must meet federal standards on the administration of radioactive drugs and the operation of radiation equipment. Furthermore, approximately one-half of all states require nuclear medicine technologists to be licensed.

Most **EEG technologists** learn their skills on the job, but some complete formal training programs. A high school degree is required and some positions require further educational training or college degrees.

Additional education is available in hospitals and community colleges. The Joint Review Committee on Education in Electroneurodiagnostic Technology has approved thirteen formal programs. These programs usually last from one to two years and include laboratory experience as well as classroom instruction in human anatomy and physiology, neurology, neuroanatomy, neurophysiology, medical terminology, computer technology, electronics, and instrumentation. Graduates receive associate's degrees or certificates.

The American Board of Registration of Electroencephalic and Evoked Potential Technologists awards the credential Registered EEG Technologist to qualified applicants. Although registration is not usually required for staff-level jobs, it does indicate professional competence and usually is necessary for supervisory or teaching jobs.

A DAY IN THE LIFE

The working conditions for laboratory personnel depend on the size and quality of the laboratory. Because medical laboratories must be clean and bright, the typical work setting for all **medical technologists** is pleasant. In some hospitals, where laboratory work is performed throughout the day and night, there are shift work opportunities. In some smaller laboratories, medical technologists may be required to work on a rotating shift basis.

Although medical technologists often work with infectious samples and specimens, their risk of infection is minimized by the proper use of protective gear, sterilization, and infection control procedures. Therefore, the risk associated with this occupation is low.

Radiological technologists work under the direct supervision of a physician, and must work in cooperation and coordination with others. The job may entail overtime, nights, and/or weekend hours, particularly in twenty-four hour establishments such as large hospitals. The physical demands on radiological technologists are sometimes burdensome, with some lifting and a significant amount of walking or standing. The emotional demands may also be taxing, as some technologists are in constant contact with extremely and terminally ill patients. There is also the potential of radiation exposure, though this is uncommon with the correct use of precautionary equipment.

Nuclear medicine technologists work standard forty-hour weeks, but they may work on different shifts. Since all hospitals are open on a twenty-four-hour basis, nuclear medicine departments may operate on an extended schedule, requiring some weekend and night hours for technologists. Although there is certainly some potential for radiation exposure in this occupation, safety standards are strictly adhered to, significantly reducing the risk. All nuclear medicine technologists wear safety badges that show readings of radiation levels in the immediate area. As a result of monitoring and safety practices, these badges rarely approach readings in the danger zone.

EEG technologists work under little direct supervision, but must work in cooperation and coordination with others. The physical demands are moderate, although they spend about half of their time on their feet. The job may entail overtime, night, and/or weekend hours. Emergencies may be particularly stressful.

HELP WANTED

Medical Technologist

Conduct laboratory tests on cultures, tissues, and blood samples to detect abnormalities/disease. Clinically test new drugs. Analyze and record test results. Salary Range: $20,000–$60,000.

Radiological Technologist

Prepare patients for testing. Operate advanced imaging equipment, develop test results, and evaluate quality of images taken. Maintain files. Salary Range: $22,000–$48,000.

Nuclear Medicine Technologist

Administer radiopharmaceuticals to patients. Monitor response to the tests in their tissues/organs. Develop test results for analysis by physician. Salary Range: $26,400–$60,000.

EEG Technologist

Prepare patients for EEG tests. Operate electroencephalograph machines. Preview EEG reading prior to analysis by physician. Salary Range: $20,000–$35,000.

JOB GROWTH

Of the approximately 300,000 medical technologists employed in the United States, there are roughly 192,000 **radiological technologists**, 13,000 **nuclear medicine technologists**, and 7,300 **EEG technologists**. Fifteen percent of technologists work part-time.

The overall growth outlook for medical, radiological, nuclear medicine, and EEG technologists is expected to be especially good over the next ten years. While much of the growth in this area will come from attrition, the aging population will also increase the need for medical testing and diagnosis. The use of imaging equipment and nuclear technology for diagnosis and treatment of disease and injury should eventually replace the more hazardous and invasive use of exploratory surgery.

As is the case with many other occupations that involve peripheral medical work, the greatest job growth will occur in settings other than hospitals. An increased demand for imaging, and the inability of hospitals to accommodate the backlog, has triggered the opening of many private imaging clinics, providing technologists with ample opportunities for part-time and full-time positions in the next several years.

The salaries, promotion possibilities, and prestige associated with this occupation make it a very attractive career path. But because this field, like all technical fields, demands up-to-date professional knowledge, applicants with an advanced degree and an area of specialization will be more attractive to employers than applicants with a bachelor's degree and generalized work experience. Medical technologists currently working in the occupation are urged to study toward a master's degree, and undergraduates interested in this career are similarly urged to continue toward their master's.

Dentistry

DENTIST: ORTHODONTIST/PEDIATRIC DENTIST/PROSTHODONTIST/ORAL
AND MAXILLOFACIAL SURGEON

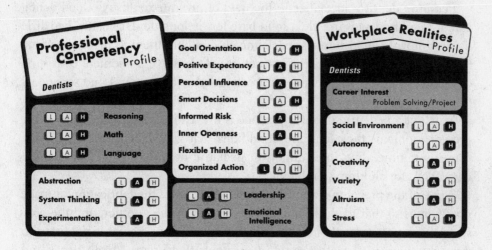

Good dental health mandates regular visits to the most dreaded of medical experts, those who probe and pry in your mouth with ungodly instruments in order to examine and treat problems of the teeth and gums.

Dentists who specialize in *orthodontics, pediatric dentistry, prosthodontics,* and *oral* and *maxillofacial surgery* are likely to experience the most opportunities in the future.

Orthodontists constitute the largest group of specialists in the dental profession, and also the busiest. Orthodontists treat conditions resulting from abnormal jaw development or tooth positioning. Their area of expertise extends to all dental-facial structures rather than just the teeth and gums. Many teenagers and adults dislike wearing braces, but very few regret the results brought about by braces and other treatment provided by their orthodontist.

A large part of an orthodontist's work occurs in the preliminary stages before actual treatment. During this period the orthodontist will examine the patient by using cephalometric (i.e., head) measurements, height and weight measurements, dental X rays and photographs, and teeth, gum, and jaw impressions. These recordings indicate to the orthodontist the treatment required to create proper alignment for a patient's teeth.

Orthodontists then fit a patient's teeth with braces and other corrective devices, such as space maintainers and retainers, in order to bring the teeth and jaw into correct alignment. Since most orthodontic changes occur over a period of time, another part of the doctor's treatment is to examine the patient on a periodic basis and to make adjustments to the fitted devices as the teeth and jaws shift gradually into alignment.

Pediatric dentists specialize in the field of juvenile dentistry. Good dental care for children can provide a solid base for lifelong dental health. Pediatric dentists provide for children's special needs and help them to maintain strong teeth, gums, and oral supporting structures. They serve a clientele consisting of infants, children, and teenagers, treating baby (or primary) and secondary (or permanent) teeth.

Much of a pediatric dentist's practice is preventive medicine. Many of the present problems they treat are conditions that will, if left untreated, grow worse over time. The intervention of pediatric dentists provides permanent corrections for children's problems.

Some of the preventive work they perform includes the fabrication of space maintainers so that teeth do not overlap or crowd one another, and the construction and placement of dental bridges and dentures. Pediatric dentists also treat children's teeth with fluoride or sealants that prevent tooth decay and allow the teeth to grow stronger.

The practice of pediatric dentistry includes a good deal of counseling and teaching. Because pediatric dentists recognize problems in early stages of development, they must advise parents on the conceivable outcomes if a condition is or is not treated immediately. They also instruct young patients in proper dental hygiene.

Prosthodontists are the prosthetics experts in the field of dentistry. Like practitioners in all specialized fields of medicine, prosthodontists offer services and skills that the general practitioners—in this case, family dentists—cannot provide. Prosthodontists perform reconstructive work on mouths, jaws, and teeth that have suffered traumatic injury or have developed in a deformed manner. Their prosthetic devices provide stability and strength to a patient's mouth and jaw. Prosthetics is, and will continue to be, a growing field in many areas of medicine.

Prosthodontists primarily replace missing teeth and the structures that surround and support the teeth. Prosthodontists record a patient's physiologic (or normal functioning) jaw position in order to determine the proper shape and size of the dental prosthesis they make. They take their measurements with the instruments of their trade, including such tools as face bows and dental articulators. Much of their work involves preparation of the prosthetic itself. This is exacting work that requires patience and a particular attention to detail. The normal next step is to insert artificial teeth or dentures that conform to the patient's physiologic oral structure.

Prosthodontic work may serve a cosmetic function—by correcting the appearance of natural and acquired mouth and jaw deformities—but it also serves a practical one: improved speech and chewing functions are among the other benefits of prosthodontia. These prosthetic corrections also allow patients to retain surrounding teeth rather than lose them as a result of the abnormality.

Oral and *maxillofacial surgeons* are the dental specialists who perform surgery on a patient's mouth and jaw, as well as on the head and neck structures that surround and support the mouth and jaw. For example, while a generalist dentist can extract a tooth in his or her office, oral and maxillofacial surgeons perform more difficult operations, such as removing impacted wisdom teeth. These procedures used to be performed in hospitals, and typically involved an overnight stay. Now oral and maxillofacial surgeons, who are trained to administer local and general anesthetics, perform such operations in their offices and patients are permitted to return home after recovering from the anesthetic.

Oral and maxillofacial surgeons do not, however, limit their practice to the teeth and gums. They also remove tumors associated with lip and mouth cancer and any other abnormal growths in the mouth. They correct abnormalities of the jaw by mandibular or maxillary revision, and treat and repair fractures of the jaw. They also perform preprosthetic surgery in preparation for the insertion of dental prosthetic devices and other reconstructive procedures.

EARNING POTENTIAL

A recent study by the American Dental Association showed that the net median income of dentists in private practice is $90,000 per year. Dentists in speciality practices, such as **orthodontics, prosthodontics,** and **maxillofacial surgery**, have net incomes of approximately $130,000 per year.

Since many dentists are self-employed, they must provide their own health insurance, life insurance, and retirement benefits. Also, all dental practices require a large capital investment for equipment, and continuing expenses for staff and assistants. Many dentists start out as a partner in an existing practice while saving to invest in a private practice. Starting salaries for such dentists range from $22,000 to $30,000.

EDUCATIONAL REQUIREMENTS

In the United States, all dentists must be licensed. Licensure requirements vary slightly from state to state, but in most instances a candidate for licensure must have graduated from a dental school approved by the American Dental Association's Commission on Accreditation and have passed both written and practical examinations.

Many candidates fulfill the written part of the licensing procedure by passing the National Board for Certification in Dental Technology. Other written tests and the practical examination are administered by individual states.

Although many dental schools require applicants to have completed only two years of college-level predental education (two years of classwork in the sciences and humanities), most dental school applicants choose to finish their bachelor's degree before attending dental school.

Dental schools require applicants to take a standardized admissions test, the Dental Admissions Test (D.A.T.). The score on this test, grade point average, and recommendations are the primary factors dental schools consider when evaluating applications.

Dental school is a four-year program, which includes classes in related sciences. Students take classes in anatomy, microbiology, biochemistry, and physiology during their first years, then treat patients in dental clinics during the last two years. This clinical training takes place under the supervision of a licensed dentist.

Dental schools award either one of two equivalent degrees: doctor of dental surgery (D.D.S.) or doctor of dental medicine (D.M.D.).

Approximately fifteen states require specialists, such as **orthodontists**, **prosthodontists** and **oral surgeons**, to obtain a specialty license before beginning to practice. Requirements for these licenses include an additional two to four years of graduate specialty education following completion of dental school and, in some states, passing an examination in the specialty field. The normal training period for these specialized dentists, including dental school, is ten years.

A DAY IN THE LIFE

Dentists work almost exclusively in light, bright, comfortable offices. Some dentists work in hospitals and outpatient clinics. Most dentists and dental specialists work a standard forty-hour week, though beginning practitioners may work fewer hours while building up a steady practice. However, on the golf courses of America, Wednesday is usually referred to as Doctors and Dentists Day.

Orthodontists may fit patients with orthodontic devices on only two or three days each week, and spend the rest of their work hours seeing patients in preparation for treatment or in follow-up to adjust the devices and determine a patient's progress.

Oral and **maxillofacial surgeons** work four or five days a week. Like many other surgeons, they may perform operations on only two or three days each week, and spend the rest of their work hours seeing patients in preparation for surgery or in follow-up to a surgical procedure. Since they perform many of the relatively straightforward procedures in their offices, the offices must contain sufficient space for a waiting room, surgery, and recovery room.

Many specialists in all medical fields, including dentistry, are either sole practitioners or partners in a small practice. Because of the expense involved in maintaining a private dental practice, many specialists form small partnerships with others in their field or related dental specialists.

JOB GROWTH

In the 1960s the federal government lent support to the expansion of dental schools. The result was a glut of graduates by the early 1970s, just when the economy took a nose-dive. This led to a significant number of **dentists** who were unable to sustain their practices. Beginning in 1979, dental school enrollments began dropping, and the number has not picked up over the past fifteen years. And while overall *growth* in dentistry is expected to progress at a slower than average rate through the year 2005, the *demand* for dentists will increase at a faster than average rate because the demand for dentists will exceed the number of new dental school graduates. Job prospects, therefore, are expected to be excellent over the next ten years, particularly for dental specialists.

Dentists in all areas of practice hold approximately 144,000 positions. Statistics show that almost 90 percent of dentists are in private practice. The remainder work in private and public hospitals and clinics and in dental research.

Orthodontists have experienced excellent career growth and will continue to do so. Like **pediatric dentistry**, orthodontics should continue to be a good field for dentists to enter because many couples in two-income households are having children at a later point in life. These parents are better able financially to provide excellent medical and dental care for their children. Similarly, many adults are having orthodontic work done, now that they are in a position to afford it.

HELP WANTED
DENTISTS

Orthodontist
Treat conditions resulting from abnormal jaw development or tooth positioning. Fit braces and other corrective devices and examine patients on periodic basis and to make adjustments to their devices. Examine patients by using cephalometric measurements, height and weight measurements, dental X rays and photographs, and teeth, gum, and jaw impressions. Salary Range: $27,500–$130,000+.

Pediatric Dentist
Specialize in treating children's teeth. Focus on maintaining strong teeth, gums, and oral supporting structures. Construct and place dental bridges and dentures; fabricate space maintainers. Treat teeth with fluoride or sealants, and instruct young patients in proper dental hygiene. Salary Range: $22,500–$105,000+.

Prosthodontist
Perform reconstructive work on mouths, jaws, and teeth. Replace missing teeth and the structures that surround and support the teeth. Make prosthetics when necessary for reconstruction. Average Salary: $130,000.

Oral and Maxillofacial Surgeon
Perform such operations as removing impacted wisdom teeth or tumors associated with lip and mouth cancer. Perform preprosthetic surgery in preparation for the insertion of dental prosthetic devices and other reconstructive procedures. Correct abnormalities of the jaw. Administer local and general anesthetics. Average Salary: $130,000.

The good news for dentists and dental specialists, such as **prosthodontists** and **oral/maxillofacial surgeons,** is that today's younger generation focuses more on preventive care and regular monitoring, while the aging population will require greater dental care. Middle-aged baby boomers will need the greater dental care associated with aging, while elderly people, who will be more likely to retain their natural teeth than in previous generations, will require continued maintenance. And even though many people choose not to see a dentist on a regular basis, people in need of oral surgery usually have no choice but to receive treatment.

The bad news for the whole dental profession is that many dentists practicing today have fewer clients than they can treat. Some companies are dropping the dental plan part of the health benefits package, and this is affecting many dentists' practices. Competition for patients remains keen in the field, and so many dentists find themselves working past retirement age, which adversely affects the number of opportunities for young dentists.

Still the factors of the aging population and the younger generation's focus on prevention, along with the shortage of recent dental graduates, suggest the future of dentistry has much to offer.

Dental Hygienist/Dental Assistant

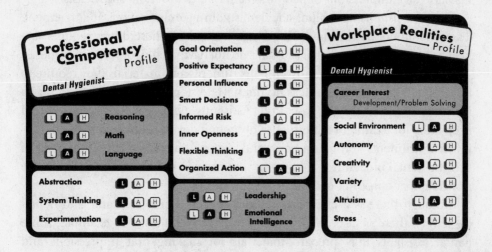

Dental hygienists provide people with dental care maintenance, such as cleaning and polishing teeth, and they educate patients in dental hygiene to reduce the risk of serious oral and dental problems. They also examine patients' teeth and record any irregularities that must be called to the dentist's attention.

They remove stains, plaque, and other harmful substances that eventually cause damage or tooth decay, and apply preventive agents such as fluoride and sealants. They may take and develop X rays, which dentists then read to determine further treatment; put temporary fillings and periodontal dressings in place; remove sutures following oral surgery; and polish and recontour amalgam restorations (that's "caps" to those of us who are dentally challenged). In some states, hygienists can administer local anesthetics and nitrous oxide–oxygen anesthesia, and place and carve filling materials.

Some dental hygienists develop and promote community dental health programs which may include teaching how to practice good oral hygiene as part of the promotion of their employer's practice. Therefore, dental hygienists with good presentation skills can expect to develop better, higher-paying jobs over a career. In these programs they also may explain the relationship between diet and oral health, inform patients on how to select toothbrushes, and show patients how to floss their teeth—all necessary elements of normal tooth care.

In dentists' offices, dental hygienists use hand and rotary instruments to clean teeth, X-ray machines to take dental pictures, syringes with needles to administer local anesthetics, and models of teeth to explain oral hygiene. They may also take impressions of people's teeth in order to mold study casts.

Dental assistants work alongside dentists during examinations and treatment. They should not be confused with dental hygienists, whose duties require state licensure. The duties of dental assistants do not have such rigorous requirements.

Dental assistants hand dentists the instruments and materials they require to treat patients so that the dentists do not have to stop work in order to reach an instrument or prepare a compound. Assistants clean a patient's mouth and keep it dry for treatment with the use of suction devices. They sterilize and disinfect instruments and equipment, and prepare tray setups in anticipation of specific dental procedures. They may also provide patients with postoperative instruction and instruct patients in oral health care.

Although there is a clear distinction between dental assistants and dental hygienists, there is also an occasional overlap of duties. For example, some dental assistants may prepare materials for making oral impressions and restorations, and they may process dental X rays. They may also remove sutures and apply anesthetic and preventive agents to the teeth and gums.

Dental assistants with laboratory duties make casts of the teeth and mouth from impressions taken by dentists, clean and polish removable appliances, and make temporary crowns. Of course, these responsibilities require specific training in addition to their general training.

In smaller practices, dental assistants may also serve as clerks, taking responsibility for such office duties as arranging and confirming appointments, receiving patients, keeping treatment records, sending bills, receiving payments, and ordering dental supplies and materials.

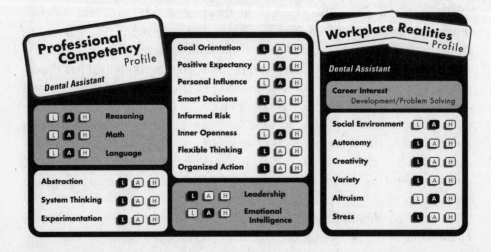

EARNING POTENTIAL

According to the American Dental Association, **dental hygienists** who worked 32 hours a week or more averaged $609 a week in 1991; the average hourly earnings for all dental hygienists was $18.50.

A 1992 survey showed that weekly earnings for full-time **dental assistants** averaged approximately $322. The middle 50 percent of dental assistants earned an average of $362 per week. Hourly earnings for all dental assistants averaged approximately $9.20.

As with employees in other fields, a dental hygienist's and assistant's benefits vary according to the practice in which they work. Some may be required to work full-time in order to qualify for benefits. Dental hygienists who work for school systems, public health agencies, the federal government, or state agencies usually have substantial benefits that add value to their job.

EDUCATIONAL REQUIREMENTS

All **dental hygienists** must be licensed by the state in which they practice. Licensure requirements include graduation from an accredited school of dental hygiene and the successful completion of a written and clinical examination.

The written examination is administered by the American Dental Association Joint Commission on National Dental Examinations and is accepted by all states. The clinical part of the exam is administered by the state itself.

In 1993 there were 208 programs in dental hygiene that were accredited by the Commission on Dental Accreditation. Although some of these programs result in a bachelor's degree, most grant an associate's (or two-year) degree. There are also five universities that offer master's degree programs in dental hygiene.

For most hygienists, though, an associate's degree is sufficient for private practice in a dentist's office. Hygienists who receive a bachelor's or master's degree usually work in research, teaching, or clinical practice settings for public or school health programs. Approximately half of the dental hygiene programs prefer to accept applicants who have completed one year of college, but requirements vary from school to school. Dental hygienist programs offer instruction in subjects such as anatomy, physiology, chemistry, microbiology, pharmacology, nutrition, radiography, histology (the study of tissue structure), periodontology (the study of gum diseases), pathology, dental materials, clinical dental hygiene, and social and behavioral sciences.

Dental assistants, unlike dental hygienists, are not licensed by any state agencies. They may, however, become certified by the Dental Assisting National Board. Unlike licensure, which is a mandatory process, certification is voluntary, but will prove helpful in looking for a job.

Many dental assistants learn their skills on the job, but an increasing number are being trained in dental assisting programs offered in community and junior colleges, trade schools, and technical institutes. Regardless of their technical training, dental assistants must embody the qualities medical professionals need in assistants: reliability, manual dexterity, and the ability to work well with others.

There are in the United States 232 training programs for dental assisting that are approved by the American Dental Association's Commission on Dental Accreditation, and all require applicants to be high school graduates. The programs include classroom, laboratory, and preclinical instruction in dental assisting skills. Many of the students in these programs also get practical experience working in clinics, dental schools, or dentists' offices. Most of the accredited programs take one year to complete and issue a certificate or diploma to graduates. There are a few two-year programs, but these are offered by community colleges and junior colleges and result in an associate's degree; they involve other course work in addition to the dental assistant classes. Some private vocational schools offer four- to six-month courses in dental assisting, but these are not accredited by the Commission on Dental Accreditation.

Many states that have adopted formal standards for dental assistants who perform radiological procedures accept the successful completion of the certification examination as evidence of having met the standards. Candidates for certification may qualify to take the examination either by graduating from an accredited training program or by having two years of full-time experience as a dental assistant. In addition, applicants must have taken a course in cardiopulmonary resuscitation (CPR).

A DAY IN THE LIFE

One attractive feature of a dental hygienist's and assistant's work is that it frequently permits employees to maintain flexible schedules. Dentists may hire them to work only two or three days a week, allowing them to hold jobs in more than one dental office. They are often required to work Saturdays and evening hours to accommodate working patients who cannot make appointments during normal office hours.

Dentists' offices are usually clean and bright, and the working conditions for dental hygienists and assistants are generally cheerful. As a result of infectious disease warnings, though, they should wear safety glasses, surgical masks, and gloves. And, because they often take X rays of patients, they must be careful to adhere to proper radiological procedures. Hygienists must also be trained in recommended aseptic technique and in the use of appropriate protective devices when administering nitrous oxide–oxygen anesthesia.

JOB GROWTH

Surveys have shown that **dental hygienists** hold approximately 121,500 jobs and **dental assistants** 200,000 jobs in the United States. These figures do not take into account the fact that many dental hygienists and assistants hold more than one job, which suggests that the number of jobs exceeds the number of hygienists. Approximately half of all **dental hygienists** work on a part-time basis, averaging less than thirty-five hours a week, while one-third of **dental assistants** work part-time in more than one office. Almost all work in private dental offices. A small number work in dental schools, private and government hospitals, state and local public health departments, or clinics.

Employment opportunities for **dental hygienists** and **assistants** are expected to grow much faster than the average for all occupations through the year 2005 because of the increasing demand for dental care. Demand will be stimulated by the population growth; by the fact that many middle-aged and elderly people, who have benefited from good dental care, are retaining their teeth much longer than in the past; and because, although dental care has always been considered a necessity by many families, it has historically done better in times when people had higher incomes and more disposable income. As incomes are expected to rise over the next ten years, opportunities should be good for all people involved in the dental profession.

Because the real earning potential for dentists lies in their reconstructive and oral surgery work, many more dentists are hiring **dental hygienists** and **assistants** as an alternative to handling routine work themselves, thereby providing themselves with more time to perform their specialty (read "high dollar return") skills.

The number of people enrolling in dental hygiene programs has increased in recent years after declining in the 1980s. Nevertheless, unless the numbers grow dramatically, job opportunities will remain very good for **dental hygienists**. Dental hygienists can expect to find excellent job opportunities in the

HELP WANTED
DENTAL HYGIENIST
AND ASSISTANT

Dental Hygienist

Examine and clean teeth. Use dental instruments and X-ray machines. Administer local anesthetics. Educate patients in dental hygiene. Salary Range: $22,000–$37,000.

Dental Assistant

Work alongside dentist during examinations and treatment. Knowledge of dental instruments a must. Sterilize and disinfect instruments and equipment and prepare tray setups. Clean patient's mouth and keep it dry for treatment. Good office clerical skills and phone manner necessary. Salary Range: $9,900–$21,800.

marketplace because their skills match a present and future need. People want to take care of their teeth, for both health and cosmetic reasons, and dental hygienists help them to do so. A youthful appearance is something many people have been concerned about for years. This is especially true of people now in middle age, who realize they are a part of a booming youth culture. This group (of which your aging author is a member) will be particularly eager to maintain their teeth.

Most of the job openings for **dental assistants** will develop from the need to replace assistants who leave the occupation. Many assistants leave the job market to take on family responsibilities, return to school, or transfer to other occupations. Dental assistants will find many job opportunities exist for them in dental offices, but they may have to be flexible and accept having to work part-time at a few different locations rather than full-time in one office; like big business, small businesses want to save on the overhead and benefits costs associated with full-time employees wherever possible. The downside of this arrangement is that many dental assistants will not receive full medical benefits from one employer. The upside is that dental assistants can often create a schedule that suits their needs and allows them to work at other endeavors as little or as much as they like.

The medical field is growing very fast, and it will continue to grow at an extremely fast rate over the next ten years. Semiskilled positions for assistants will grow with the profession, and the fact that the turnover among dental assistants is high means that thousands of job openings will exist every year. A dental assistant's job is a wonderful starting job for a young person, or a good part-time job for someone looking to supplement a family income.

Mental Health

PSYCHIATRIST/PSYCHOLOGIST

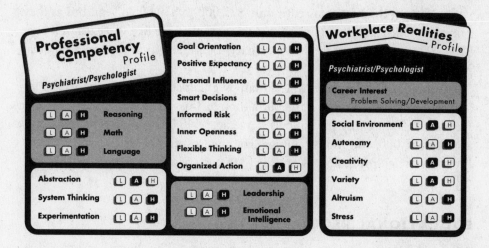

Psychiatrists and *psychologists* treat patients with mental, emotional, and behavioral disorders. The difference between the two professions is that psychiatrists are medical doctors (M.D.s) who undergo the same training as all who graduate from medical school, while psychologists are doctors of philosophy (Ph.D.s) holding an academic degree. Because they are licensed to practice medicine, psychiatrists are able to prescribe medication for their patients, whereas psychologists cannot.

Psychiatrists and psychologists analyze human behavior. They study how a person thinks, feels, and behaves, and look for ways to change behavioral patterns through counseling, or sometimes, in the case of psychiatrists, medication or institutionalization.

Most patients are referred to psychiatrists or psychologists by a primary care physician. The initial treatment procedure is almost the same for both psychiatrists and psychologists. Each interviews the patient to gain information about his or her family and medical history. This may be followed by diagnostic testing. After evaluating all of this information, the psychiatrist or psychologist determines the patient's mental or emotional condition and formulates a treatment program.

Psychiatrists and psychologists often specialize in a specific area, such as *family psychotherapy, child psychotherapy, rehabilitation psychotherapy, geropsychiatry, schizophrenia,* or *mental retardation.*

EARNING POTENTIAL

Earnings for psychiatrists and psychologists may vary widely based on the number of years of practice, geographic location, number of hours worked, and the doctor's reputation, skill, and personality.

Starting **psychiatrists** may earn only $25,000 to $30,000 a year, but as they gain experience and their client base increases, they are likely to earn well over $100,000, particularly if they own or have a partnership interest in a medical practice.

Psychologists generally earn less than psychiatrists. The median income for all psychologists is around $50,000, although this varies depending on their specialty. Counseling psychologists average $48,000, school psychologists average $55,000, and industrial/organizational psychologists average $76,000. Private practice psychologists are likely to earn as much as their psychiatrist colleagues.

EDUCATIONAL REQUIREMENTS

All **psychiatrists** must be licensed to practice. The licensing procedure requires graduation from an undergraduate institution, graduation from an accredited medical school, completion and passage of licensing examinations, and between one and seven years of residency. At this point the average psychiatrist is considered ready to practice — or to be committed.

Most psychiatrists seek board certification after completing their residency and possibly after one or two years in practice. Board certification proves that a doctor is fully qualified to practice his or her specialty. For medical doctors, including psychiatrists, examinations for board certification are given by the American Board of Medical Specialists.

Practicing psychiatrists must remain current with changes in their field. Most attend seminars and read medical journals on a regular basis in order to stay aware of new techniques and discoveries.

Psychologists with only an undergraduate degree in psychology are limited to assisting psychologists in clinical settings. Those with a master's degree in psychology can conduct psychological evaluations, counsel patients, and assist in research projects. A master's degree in psychology usually requires two years of full-time graduate study.

A Ph.D. will qualify psychologists for a wide range of positions in teaching, research, and counseling in schools, private industry, and government. A doctoral degree in psychology generally requires five to seven years of graduate work, including a year or more of internship.

All states require practicing psychologists to be licensed, and although the laws vary from state to state, most require a doctorate in psychology, internship, and one to two years professional experience. Most states also require that psychologists pass a state exam, and limit their practice to areas where they are trained and experienced.

A DAY IN THE LIFE

Psychiatrists and psychologists typically work from their offices, which may be located in a hospital, clinic, office building, or frequently a private home. Their offices are usually a comfortable environment, designed to put patients at ease and make them feel comfortable.

Psychiatrists and psychologists must be self-directed. They work with little or no supervision and are responsible for making decisions that may have a major effect on their patients. All doctors exercise a large degree of autonomy in their practice, but psychiatrists and psychologists often treat conditions that cannot be clinically proven by tests. For that reason, they must have great confidence in their own abilities, and must be mature, patient, sensitive, compassionate, perceptive, and emotionally stable. They must also be able to listen objectively and to make clear judgments. They also must be excellent communicators.

The practice of psychiatry and psychology has few physical demands, but the emotional demands of dealing with the likes of you and me and a sea of wacked-out postal workers is enormous. In addition, they remain on call to their patients at all hours, except for when they take a vacation to maintain their sense of balance.

JOB GROWTH

Approximately 40,000 **psychiatrists** practice in the United States, either as sole practitioners or as partners in a group practice. **Psychologists** hold about 144,000 jobs. Forty percent of them are involved in counseling, research, education, and administration; 30 percent are employed by hospitals, clinics, and other health care facilities; and the balance are in private practice. Psychologists also work in social services and in management consulting firms, market research companies, and other businesses.

The mental health field is expected to grow faster than the average for all occupations in the United States over the next ten years. Projected growth is attributed to several factors: the increased stress levels we face in our daily

HELP WANTED PSYCHIATRIST AND PSYCHOLOGIST

Psychiatrist

Interview patients to gain information about the patient, his/her family and medical history, then determine the patient's mental or emotional condition and formulate a treatment program. Study not only how a person thinks, feels, and behaves, but look for ways to change behavioral patterns through counseling, or sometimes through prescribed medication or institutionalization. May assess a patient's functioning through formal testing. Salary Range: $25,000–$100,000.

Psychologist

Interview patients to determine mental/emotional condition. Conduct psychological tests. Counsel patients using therapy methods such as psychoanalysis and behavior modification. Refer patients to psychiatrists for further treatment and/or medical prescriptions. Salary Range: $25,000–$76,000.

lives, the increasing acceptance of psychiatric and psychological treatment, and the mental health problems associated with an aging population. Additionally, baby boomers, who have grown up on therapy and enjoy having someone in their lives who will listen for forty-five minutes at a stretch without interruption, are aware of the benefits such treatment will have for their children, making child psychiatry and psychology a growth area.

Job opportunities for **psychologists** and **psychiatrists** will be most abundant in nursing homes and in the health care provider organizations that specialize in mental health. Alcohol and drug rehabilitation, family strife and violence counseling, and crime prevention programs are also on the rise, and all will need qualified psychiatrists and psychologists. These specialists also will be needed to assist in behavior modification programs which deal with general physical health such as weight loss and smoke stop programs. Increasingly, psychologists are also being utilized by business in both human resources and marketing as part of the strategic planning process.

Applicants who hold a doctorate in such specialities as school, clinical, counseling, industrial, or educational psychology will find themselves in demand throughout the next ten years. Extensive experience in quantitative research methods and computer science will be helpful for those candidates who wish to pursue the research side of this profession.

PSYCHIATRIC AIDE

Professional Competency Profile

Psychiatric Aide

L **A** H	Reasoning
L A H	Math
L **A** H	Language

Abstraction	**L** A H
System Thinking	L **A** H
Experimentation	L **A** H

Goal Orientation	L **A** H
Positive Expectancy	L **A** H
Personal Influence	L **A** H
Smart Decisions	L **A** H
Informed Risk	L **A** H
Inner Openness	L A **H**
Flexible Thinking	L **A** H
Organized Action	**L** A H

L A H	Leadership
L A **H**	Emotional Intelligence

Workplace Realities Profile

Psychiatric Aide

Career Interest
Development/Project

Social Environment	L A **H**
Autonomy	**L** A H
Creativity	**L** A H
Variety	**L** A H
Altruism	L A H
Stress	L A H

The demands of the mental health field, like those of every other medical care field, are growing so rapidly that there are not enough trained professionals to provide care to all the patients who require it. Very often, doctors and nurses in demanding fields need assistance in providing basic human services to their patients. In the mental health field, the people who provide patients with these services are **psychiatric aides**.

Psychiatric aides, also known as *mental health assistants*, *psychiatric nursing assistants*, or *ward attendants*, help care for mentally ill and emotionally disturbed people who are confined to hospitals, clinics, and other mental health settings. They typically work as part of a team that includes psychiatrists, psychologists, psychiatric nurses, social workers, and therapists.

Most of their duties revolve around the effort to create a comfortable environment for patients. Although these duties are not, strictly speaking, medical functions, they nevertheless serve to provide psychiatric patients with a stable environment and a routine schedule of activities. Psychiatric aides help the patients to bathe, dress, eat, and groom themselves. Additional responsibilities include socializing with the patients and leading them in educational and recreational activities. Psychiatric aides may play games, such as cards, with the patients, watch television with them, or participate in group activities such as sports or field trips.

Psychiatric aides observe patients and report any signs that might be important for the professional staff to know. If necessary, psychiatric aides will help restrain unruly patients and also accompany them to and from wards for examination and treatment. Because they have the closest contact with patients, psychiatric aides have a great deal of influence on patients' outlook and treatment, and an excellent opportunity to observe them for clinical changes.

EARNING POTENTIAL

The median annual income for psychiatric aides is $13,800, with the middle 50 percent earning between $11,000 and $17,900. Some aides at the lower end of the scale may earn less than $9,500, while those near the top may earn over $24,000.

The hourly wage ranges from $4.75 for beginners to between $5.00 and $8.00 for more experienced aides. Future increases can be expected to keep slightly ahead of inflation.

These low wages reflect the fact that psychiatric aides are not highly trained. Some very competent people are attracted to this occupation because of their desire to help patients with significant needs; others, because it provides them with an entry-level job in the field.

EDUCATIONAL REQUIREMENTS

Although employers may prefer to hire job applicants with previous experience in the field of psychiatric patient care, many hire young people looking for a relatively unskilled job and train them to care for the patients.

A high school diploma or experience is not necessary, but either is helpful and some employers require both. Some states require psychiatric aides to complete a formal training program. (Similar programs exist for nursing aides and other types of health care providers.) Since the duties of psychiatric aides resemble those of nursing or geriatric aides, people interested in this field would be well advised to take background classes in a nursing aide program, especially since many of the nursing aide functions are transferable to a job as a psychiatric aide—and vice versa; this provides greater career opportunities and employment flexibility.

A DAY IN THE LIFE

Psychiatric aides generally work in hospitals, clinics, and other mental health facilities. These are typically clean, comfortable, and relatively quiet environments. The physical demands are moderate, with a fair amount of time spent walking around and standing, with some medium lifting, carrying, and moving.

Psychiatric aides work under the direct supervision of doctors, and must also work in close cooperation with other members of the staff. Most full-time aides work forty-hour weeks, but because patients need care twenty-four hours a day, some aides work evenings, nights, weekends, and holidays. Working under emergency conditions or with out-of-control patients may be particularly stressful and aspects of the job may require extreme patience and prove frustrating.

Many psychiatric aides work on a part-time basis, which allows them to organize their work schedule around other activities, such as school, as they pursue an education that will advance their professional careers.

JOB GROWTH

A recent survey indicated that there are roughly 88,000 psychiatric aides employed in the United States. Most of these positions are in state and county mental institutions, psychiatric units of general hospitals, private psychiatric facilities, and mental health centers.

The overall job outlook for psychiatric aides is good, and employment is expected to grow faster than the average for all occupations. As the population grows and the stigma formerly attached to psychiatric care proves less imposing, the need to provide care to people with mental and emotional problems will create an increasingly large demand on the health care industry, as will the need for geriatric care. Many of the people who will require the services of psychiatric aides will be elderly people whose mental faculties have diminished over time. For many of these patients there will be no cure: the only treatment is to maintain the patient in as much comfort as possible.

Most of the employment growth will take place in private facilities because spending on public mental hospitals will be reduced along with all public spending over the next ten years. Communities simply cannot afford to spend their tax revenues on institutions that provide services to a relatively small number of people, no matter how important that service may be.

There will, however, be many job opportunities in this field as a result of job turnover. Like many other occupations that have modest entry requirements, psychiatric aide jobs typically undergo a great deal of turnover because many people find work in the field as a way to enter the job market. After working as a psychiatric aide for a while, many of the workers find other employment or

---

HELP WANTED
PSYCHIATRIC AIDE

Care for mentally ill and emotionally disturbed people who are confined to hospitals, clinics, and other mental health settings. Work as part of a team that includes psychiatrists, psychologists, psychiatric nurses, social workers, and therapists. Create a comfortable environment for patients. Help patients to bathe, dress, eat, and groom themselves. Additional responsibilities include socializing with the patients and leading them in educational and recreational activities. Observe patients' conduct and report any signs that might be significant to the professional staff. Salary Range: $9,880–$24,000+.

---

transfer into another health aide job. Two other reasons for the high turnover rate in the occupation are low wages and small possibility for job advancement.

This job is demanding, but rewarding. It requires only a small investment of time on the part of the psychiatric aide trainee, but it offers the opportunity to start work in the fastest-growing segment of the employment market: the health care industry. For these reasons, this will remain an appealing entry-level job for many people.

The Technologies

The four major growth technologies have invaded and impacted every corner of academia, industry, and commerce. They have ushered in a new era, and revolutionized the way we communicate and interact with each other.

- *Biotechnology* is changing the way we take care of our health and our food sources.
- *Environmental technology* is changing the way we take care of our environment and nurture our resources.
- *Engineering technology* is changing the way we build our systems of manufacture and supply.
- *Information technology* is changing the ways we increase our knowledge, communications, and competitiveness.

These technologies often work hand in hand with each other to achieve new breakthroughs, so as each year goes by, it becomes more and more difficult to define exactly where one technology stops and another begins. The same applies to the technology jobs and job titles. Job titles such as *engineer*, *scientist*, and *analyst* are gradually becoming interchangeable, depending largely on the employer, context, and application of the work. The job title issue is further confused by the collaborative nature of many technology jobs, where a specialist in one area, over a period of years, can become largely qualified in another area through years of association and application.

It has been exactly this continuous cross-fertilization of skills and relationships that gives birth to groundbreaking inventions and companies. Because of this, professionals in any of these four major growth areas may well find themselves plying their profession in any of the other technological fields, or in any other profession besides. An example would be the handful of chemists/ chemical engineers/scientists from Stanford University in California who gave birth to the entire computer revolution. It is unknown to many that without chemical engineers there would be no computer revolution, because it is their expertise that allows the computer chips to be etched for the electronic circuitry.

In this technologies section we'll look at a wide array of scientists, technologists, analysts, and engineers. We'll look at their areas of research and application, such as chemicals, computers, and engineering, and we'll look at the frontiers of biotechnology and environmental technology.

Bear in mind that the jobs in this agglomeration are the ones that have ushered in the age of information and the global marketplace. These are the men and women whose job it is to identify the problems and opportunities facing society. These are the workers who define and research the optimal solutions, the professionals who design the molds and manufacturing processes to manifest the solutions and advances. And these are the people who design, build, and maintain the electronic information systems that allow the results of all this work to be built in one part of the world and sold in another.

With the embracing of all technologies and their applications, we're seeing the effects in all industries, because the work done in any of the technologies has applications throughout the world of work. One of the results is that companies that didn't even exist ten years ago—small, pioneering firms—are rapidly becoming some of the country's major employers.

Biotechnology

About 11 percent of all scientists in the country work somewhere in the chemical industry, and fully a third of them work for petrochemical companies. The future for these industries is healthy, as they supply other industries such as electronics, autos, and construction.

Environmental awareness and regulations are also driving research-and-development dollars into the paychecks of scientists. This has led established giants in the chemical industry, for example, to become involved in joint ventures with—and outright purchases of—fledgling environmental companies. In fact, scientists with environmental specialities somewhere in their background can expect some of the best career opportunities. For example, biologists, the majority of whom currently work in academia, will see substantial growth in the private sector with biotech and envirotech applied jobs.

The biotechnology industry, which recently reinvented the tomato by crossing it with the flounder, is a dream come true for clinical researchers, lab assistants, marketers, and a host of other professionals. And, as it revolutionizes the agriculture, health care, and environment fields, the biotechnology industry will create new jobs at the rate of more than 10 percent annually.

Genetically engineered foods, medicines, and other products often enhance life, and sometimes are the only chance for saving it. But high research costs, technical barriers, public resistance, and strict government regulations make it difficult—and sometimes impossible—to get a new product on the market. In the world of biotech, however, one new food or medicine can mean a global mass market—and a big score for everyone involved. And indeed, the sales of biotech products are rising dramatically. The United States leads the world in biotechnology research, especially in biomedicine, which comprises about half of the biotechnology industry. Studies are currently under way to develop biomedical vaccines and cures for deadly viruses (including AIDS), cancer, cardiovascular disease, Parkinson's disease, and a seemingly endless list of ailments.

The application of biotechnology to environmental woes is another area that can only grow as we strive to save the planet for our heirs with new environmental regulations and increasing community activism. Bioremediation, an experimental approach that uses microorganisms to clean hazardous wastes, looks promising. Patent owners, patent beaters, and smart marketers are going to do well here. Biological substances that can replace pesticides, herbicides, and fungicides; break down fertilizer; diagnose environmental toxins; and reduce manufacturing pollution are also being developed.

Genetically engineered vegetables, milk, and other food products are beginning to arrive on supermarket shelves amid a great deal of fanfare—and suspicion. Whether or not we should so readily accept the new and improved foods, we are going to see agriculture and biotechnology reinvent each other. And who knows where that could lead? According to some experts, sales of biotech agricultural products could increase between 15 and 20 percent annually.

Yet biomedicine dominates, with most new biotech products coming from medicine and diagnostics. Agriculture is the next largest area, and environment comes last. Future sales in nonmedical areas—environment and agriculture—ultimately will depend on the public's acceptance or disapproval of genetically engineered environmental and food products.

In 1970, fewer than 150 people were employed in the biotechnology industry; by 2000, that figure should grow to between 35,000 and 40,000. That's tremendous growth—but then again, it's not that many jobs overall. Projections anticipate new jobs developing at the rate of about 1,200 a year over the next few years. This is a volatile industry because the lead time for developing genetically engineered products is so long, and the costs are correspondingly high. This can make job security in the smaller companies iffy. However, if you are part of a major breakthrough, you might never be in want for the rest of your days. The costs of R&D are causing many of the smaller firms in the field to merge or engage in joint ventures. The larger companies will offer that much more stability (and that much less share of the pie).

Chemists, physicists, and engineers who want to cross over into the biotech industry are especially welcome, as are doctors, nurses, physical therapists, pharmacists, and other health care professionals—they're needed to help with testing and evaluation. The biotech industry is still in its infancy, with most companies researching products that may not be on the market until well into the twenty-first century. As the industry matures, and companies move from research to production, jobs requiring a background in business, business and patent law, manufacturing, or marketing will increasingly become available.

INSIDER'S VIEW OF THE BIOTECHNOLOGY INDUSTRY

Even though biotechnology is still a relatively young industry, it's showing signs of aging. As companies in the industry create and produce new products, they will reorganize and merge with other companies. With the development of new biotech products will come an increase in jobs (in sales and marketing, particularly), but the trend toward larger biotech companies will keep down the actual number of jobs available.

According to Vicki Geis, director of human resources at Biosys Inc. in Columbia, Maryland, "Biotech companies have chosen to get larger. Small companies are fodder for larger companies because it's easier that way."

Biotech companies have a propensity for mergers and joint ventures because they make money only after their products come to market, and because research and development costs are high for small companies to fund by themselves. So, for smaller biotech companies, a marriage to a larger company often makes sense; it provides the money that R&D requires. In return for their seed money, larger companies get a share of the profits when the product goes commercial.

However, as Geis points out, companies' changing and merging lead to instability. "You'll find a lot of movement, and people going in and out of companies."

WHO WILL GET THE JOBS?

Since there will continue to be comparatively few jobs in the biotechnology industry, regardless of how large the field grows, how can you beat the competition? It helps to have a background as a chemist, physicist, engineer, or health care professional (such as a doctor, nurse, physical therapist, pharmacist, or the like). These professions can help with research and development. Later, as more biotech products come to market, people with a background in government regulations, business, patent law, manufacturing, and marketing will be in demand.

"Biotechnology companies are looking for real diversity," explains Geis. "A worker may have a biotechnology degree and also a law degree or an M.B.A. The dual perspective is very helpful and very necessary for an industry that tends to ask a lot of its people." While she acknowledges that biotechnology professionals wear a lot of hats, she adds that it's important to have a scientific background. "A Ph.D. gives you a certain lift and brings you to a certain level," according to Geis.

So it goes without saying that it's difficult to break into the biotechnology field—even for the aggressive. One avenue that may help, Geis believes, is volunteering, and another is interning. Either provides a professional with a track record that might open doors.

Geis also suggests "making yourself visible and keeping yourself educated. Since technologies come and go, and things happen quickly in the industry, you have to be forward-thinking." She recommends reading as many trade publications as possible while you're working. "You have to continually feed yourself. You can't stop learning."

She also believes it helps to see science as an art. "I think there are always positions for innovative, creative people, because that's what the industry is all about."

Environment

The irrefutable facts about acid rain, ozone depletion, global warming, lead poisoning, and other consequences of ill-considered industrial-era actions have led to massive public support of environmental reclamation and protection. The resulting environmental legislation has yielded a whole new crop of jobs in both private industry and government.

Environmental engineers are in seriously short supply. It is said that there are ten jobs for every graduate, and pay scales are rising appropriately. These engineers work on noise pollution and abatement, solid waste management, standards establishment, and superfund project management. Those engineers prepared to clean up hazardous waste and step in after environmental disasters *really* clean up—to the tune of about 25 percent more than other engineers.

The changing worldview that is creating such a boom in environmental applications is not only generating jobs for all kinds of scientists, engineers, and computer types; it is also creating high-paying professional jobs for accountants, salespeople, lawyers, and insurance industry professionals.

INSIDER'S VIEW OF THE ENVIRONMENT INDUSTRY

We all want to live in a safer world. People like you and me are clamoring for safe solid-waste disposal, hazardous-waste cleanup, and solutions to other modern-day threats to the planet. In response, the U.S. government is beginning to create tougher laws to protect the environment. The environmental industry, as a result, is coming into its own.

Environmental professionals agree that new government regulations will drive the industry's growth. According to Richard A. Young, executive director of the National Registry of Environmental Professionals, the industry now focuses primarily on compliance. But, in the next decade, the focus will shift to environmental systems management: preventing and minimizing damage to the environment.

Paula C. McLemore, president of the Air and Waste Management Association as well as manager of regulatory affairs for the Pasadena, Texas–based Albemarle Corporation, agrees. "There will be a greater emphasis on eliminating problems in design rather than eliminating them once they are designed."

WE'RE ALL IN IT TOGETHER

McLemore also points out that the environment is no longer solely the concern of manufacturers: "Environmental issues will be a part of all businesses in the future," she foresees. Service companies, such as banks and insurance agencies, will join in the quest for competent environmental professionals. She predicts that, increasingly, educational programs geared toward many professional areas will encourage awareness of environmental responsibilities.

She also sees another imminent change in the environmental industry: it's going global. "Global standards will cross government lines and international lines. As we develop more trade agreements, such as NAFTA, we'll be challenged with defining harmonized standards for regulatory tracking and compliance." Environmental standards will become consistent from country to country, and from continent to continent. Governments will be challenged to work with businesses to establish acceptable risk.

PROFESSIONAL PROSPECTS

Although lifestyle and philosophical changes will create a demand for environmental regulations, Richard A. Young cautions that opportunities for employment may not be forthcoming. "Through these last couple of years, we've seen industries downsize and often eliminate environmental departments," he says. But because companies still have to comply with regulations, there has been a comparable growth in environmental consulting.

McLemore says, "There is definitely a future in the profession, because there will always be a need [for environmental regulations]." However, she admits that cyclical changes in regulation are always creating "dips, peaks, and valleys" in employment. "Niche professionals feel it more," she counsels. "Having a diverse knowledge of environmental issues gives you the best chance."

According to McLemore, people who are successful in the environmental industry are those who are capable of striking a balance between sustaining business and giving society the protection it needs, who help the public understand they are in a good and safe environment, even though they have the benefits of industry.

Engineering

We're living in a technological culture, and we couldn't have technology without engineering. Engineers develop new technology, design software, and rebuild the infrastructure. They are the professionals who give form to our future, who make ideas work.

Mechanical, electrical, electronics, chemical, civil, biomedical, computer software, and environmental engineers will pretty much be able to write their own tickets in the decade ahead. Already there is a shortage of trained chemical engineers. The Bureau of Labor Statistics predicts 25 percent more openings for engineers by the year 2000, and 40 percent job growth for electrical and electronics engineers.

The outlook for civil engineers has picked up with the need to rebuild the nation's infrastructure so that the United States may remain competitive in the global marketplace. Mechanical and industrial engineers will benefit from new products requiring design and manufacturing processes that are environmentally and ergonomically aware. Although manufacturing is diminishing across the board in America, we are still strong in the high-end, complex manufacturing areas where our technical know-how is still unsurpassed.

Environmental engineers also will experience strong growth and good earning opportunities, especially those who do the "dirty work"—that is, clean up environmental disasters—and command top pay. Environmental engineers who specialize in hazardous waste currently earn about 25 percent more than other engineers. The industry engages a high percentage of these engineers as independent consultants rather than employees. And we are seeing environmental engineering positions opening up at most mainstream companies, as they struggle to be more responsible about their products' impact on our environment.

Engineering in all disciplines has always been a predominantly white male preserve, and the shortage of qualified women and minorities in the field is good news if you fall into one of these categories. Further, because of the lack of engineers in these categories, there is a similar lack in the senior technical and management ranks, which bodes well for those with their eyes set high on the professional career ladder.

Regrettably, the outlook for mature engineers who have been downsized is not so strong. There are fewer senior positions than there were just a few years ago, and there is a feeling that some of these people have let technology pass them by. In addition, business looks toward the younger, cheaper, more technologically adapted engineering graduates to fill their ranks for the twenty-first century. A good idea for mature engineers having difficulty in transitioning from one job to the next is to consider how their experience and people skills fit them ideally for sales and marketing positions with technology companies, where their technical background will make them prime candidates.

INSIDER'S VIEW OF THE ENGINEERING INDUSTRY

Engineers are the shapers of our society. Whatever their discipline, engineers all have one thing in common: according to industry insiders, their chances of bringing home a paycheck into the next decade and beyond are excellent.

In fact, Jim Davis, CEO of the American Society of Civil Engineers (the oldest national professional engineering society in the United States), predicts as much work for civil engineers as they can handle. With the undertaking of megaprojects such as constructing dams for hydropower and building international trade centers, Davis foresees that, in the future, "Design will be done twenty-four hours a day, versus the current eight or ten hours a day."

TEAM PLAYERS

Does that mean engineers will be working twenty-four hours a day? Yes and no. Davis sees that the design process is rapidly evolving into a series of team projects: "A consultant will start designing in New York, and then send the drawing by electronic means to Asia. The designer in Asia will continue for eight hours and then send it to Europe." He says that the civil engineers of old, who were lone entrepreneurs with a vision, will give way to owners, builders, and contractors who will work together to get a project done.

Tony Tarkowski, president of Troy, Michigan–based Sygnetics Inc., adds, "I foresee that engineering teams will work to develop products from all over the world, linked by the Internet. These teams will consist of people who are imaginative and forward-thinking enough to develop clear, concise products utilizing the latest technologies."

PUT ON YOUR TRAVELING SHOES

Even though the Internet will connect workers, engineers will become more mobile. Jim Davis points out, "Civil engineers will have to move around the world to work. They'll have to go to where the work is." For example, if there's a dam under construction in China to provide water resources and hydroelectric power, people in this country may want to get involved, and will have to go to China to get the design and construction knowledge. "Then, ten years from now, when we're building a new dam in this country for additional water supplies or sources of power, we'll have people knowledgeable in that area."

AND THEN WHAT?

So, after we've built enough bridges and roads to go around the world, what's left for civil engineers to do? Jim Davis explains, "Bridges rust and roads get potholes. Along with constructing and designing major projects, we'll be maintaining them. As the cycle moves on, we'll be designing projects in third world countries, but we'll still be maintaining structures in this country on a continuing basis. . . . The public will demand a sound infrastructure. They're not going to let the Golden Gate Bridge deterioriate; they'll demand the bridge is maintained. Civil engineers will be critical to the rebuilding process."

Similarly, other branches of engineering will continue to grow. Tony Tarkowski offers, "In the ever-expanding world of production, the ability to create at a competitive pace will fuel the need for highly specialized engineers into the future."

Hugo Schluctor, a recruiter based in Virginia Beach, Virginia, also radiates optimism for the future of engineering: "Those who can conceive of ways to make a product or service more efficient or less costly will always be sought after."

SUCCESS IN ENGINEERING

"Hard-working, well-educated, imaginative, and flexible, with a diversified background" is how Tony Tarkowski characterizes successful engineering professionals.

Jim Davis contributes, "You have to have a sense of confidence. I push students to go back to grad school, but also to get good, practical experience; with education alone you can be arrogant." He also believes that engineers must be perceptive, analytical, and communicative, to be able to share their visions with other people.

Information Technology

Computerized workplaces have allowed corporations to do so much more, so much more effectively, for so much less, but they have also led to the corporate restructuring that has cost millions their careers over the last few years. The impact of computers on the workplace has completely changed the way every corporation conducts its business.

Computers are everywhere, and they do just about everything—even Windows. But, except for the notebook and laptop categories, and such up-and-coming areas as virtual reality, computer hardware is no longer where the industry is at. The focus now is on applied technologies for the next decade. These include:

Software-Related Professional Services
- custom programming
- integrated systems design

Information Services
- creating information
- storing information
- manipulating information
- payroll
- credit reporting

The industry employs people with a wide range of skills and education. And, while size and location of a company often determine pay, because the computer industry demands more skills and greater education, it pays more than other industries.

The growth in the industry is centered on the traditional corporate user market and the exploding personal computer/home business marketplace that computers, in many ways, made possible. However, the industry, despite its growth and impact on every facet of our lives, is anything but stable. Technology is about innovation, and because of this, all computer-related jobs and companies are in a constant frenzied sprint for the next technological breakthrough. Which, if it doesn't put them at the front of the industry, might still save them from being left behind and going bankrupt. In other words, this is not a profession for the faint of heart.

Given these sobering facts, it still is an industry that could well double its employment of professionals over the next decade. This growth will be especially strong in information systems throughout most industries.

As corporations rely ever more heavily on computerized databases and their access to and manipulation of information, information systems (IS) professionals will continue to grow in importance on the corporate landscape. Technical jobs will abound not only in the database information service companies and their clients, but in sales, marketing, and customer service.

Information systems will be integrated with local area networks (allowing many users within one location access to data) and the growing field of wide area networks (allowing access from multiple remote locations to central repositories of data). These communication trends will further enhance the work opportunities for IS professionals. Industries that are seen to have special use for these technologies are insurance, health care (particularly HMOs), higher education, retail, and telecommunications.

The majority of technical professionals in the information technology industry can probably trace their first paying jobs in the field back to the day they started coding as a programmer. In twenty short years, this job title has grown to number over half a million professionals, and it is projected to grow by an additional quarter of a million people by 2005.

Systems analysts are the people who computerize manual tasks and upgrade existing computerized functions. The profession is anticipated to grow *at more than 100 percent* through 2005. Now, as systems analysts frequently start as programmers, this reinforces the great work potential here, as well as the opportunity for almost certain professional, and therefore monetary, growth.

But the fastest-growing job in the computer industry—and the one that's getting the most media hype—is that of "software developer." As companies use computers more and more, the job of developing appropriate software will continue to be challenging and rewarding. Which means that those with the right background—a technology degree as foundation, great analytical and creative skills, and practical project management know-how—will be able to command a six-figure salary.

Computer companies range from gargantuan to small, with the typical computer firm having eighteen employees. The odds are you will work in an entrepreneurial start-up or growth company; expect spartan surroundings and a gung-ho attitude (maybe not surprising, given the fact that 75 percent of all computer industry workers are between twenty-five and forty-four years old).

Work environments in the information technology field also vary greatly. Consultants, salespeople, and programmers often work at, or frequent, their clients' job sites. Word processors and other data entry professionals, and others whose work can be done at a terminal, may increasingly telecommute from home.

If you plan a career in information technology, you cannot be someone who likes the status quo; change and volatility are the passwords of this industry. Your goal is not to find a lifetime employer, because that would be like looking for the needle in the proverbial haystack, but to maintain your employability. This will require constant upgrading of your skills on your own time, and an awareness of industry trends so that you do not get caught being overpaid in a technological backwater. Interpersonal skills applied with non-technical people will be paramount to your success, and, because of the increasing influence of overseas markets, languages and multicultural awareness will stand anyone's career in good stead.

INSIDER'S VIEW OF THE INFORMATION
TECHNOLOGY INDUSTRY

Insiders in the computer industry agree that today's fierce competition among hardware and software vendors will continue. There is a consensus, too, about the consequences that will have for the employment picture.

"The computer industry is moving into the maturity stage," cautions Elizabeth Berglund, director of communications for the Lombard, Illinois–based Computing Technology Industry Association, "and job stability is not a by-product of that." Still, she emphasizes that the growth potential of the industry, because of the application of information technology to all strata, is "phenomenal."

Lenley Farmer, who is a senior technical recruiter for TM Floyd & Company in Columbia, South Carolina, recalls how the early 1990s brought downsizing and "trimming the fat." With acquisitions, mergers, and partnering, computer programmers and others were pushed out of their jobs. "If you weren't a hands-on person," she remembers, "your position got cut." She and other insiders predict there will be more of the same ahead.

The computer warfare will, Farmer believes, push many professionals off company payrolls (and accompanying benefit programs) and into temporary work. "As companies downsize, they're more likely to hire contractors," she points out. Still, according to Farmer, demand for qualified workers will remain high; they will just work for themselves rather than for employers. "More and more college graduates with computer science backgrounds will go directly into contracting," Farmer forecasts, "and they'll make as much money as old-timers who have been in the business for years."

TRAINING PAYS OFF

Competition between computer vendors will create the need for professionals in product development, sales, and marketing. It will also increase the need for highly trained workers.

As Perry Anthony, executive director of the Des Plaines, Illinois–based Institute for Certification of Computing Professionals, puts it, stable employment in the industry will be "dependent upon one's ability to demonstrate competence against a standard of knowledge and the willingness to obtain and utilize that knowledge. There remains a strong demand for documented and universally recognized computing industry competence."

Lenley Farmer concurs. "You'll need to be a certified this or a certified that.

A specialty is a must." Berglund, too, advises that computer professionals will need "more and more education, both formal and informal."

There are at least two ways in which professionals can receive the certification many say they will need for success. First, computer companies such as Microsoft and Novell provide special training that leads to certification. Second, the Institute for Certification of Computing Professionals offers qualified individuals with at least four years of professional computing experience the opportunity to earn the C.C.P. designation.

It is generally accepted in the information technology industry that people with the most education are the most sought-after workers in this growing but volatile field.

TELECOMMUNICATIONS

Soon, offices around the world will not only be computerized but will also be wireless, according to Tim Ayers, spokesperson for the Cellular Telecommunications Industry Association in Washington, D.C. Ayers predicts growth in wireless communication but, because of the major changes expected in the industry, says that "stability is another matter."

More optimistic about the future of telecommunications is Mike Zarneck, of First Search, a leading technology recruitment firm, in Chicago. He boasts that the growth in the industry is "phenomenal," and that it's being driven by the push toward wireless in the cable and multimedia industries.

"Wireless is changing the way we live. It will bring about so much change in the next ten years," Zarneck predicts, "that it will be like going from black-and-white to color television. There's so much expansion and activity." In his view, these rampant changes will help maintain stability in the industry. Although companies will be laying off employees whose skills no longer meet their current needs, the same (or other) companies will hire at least as many replacement employees on a temporary or contract, if not a permanent, basis.

Zarneck adds that the telecommunications industry can use, along with professionals in engineering, data communications, and telecommunications, people in most professional disciplines. "If you do enough research on the industry, you'll find a place where you can fit in. It might be on the construction side, building thousands of new cell sites and towers; or in real estate, moving in for site acquisition or dealing with zoning regulations." The key to success, he believes, is a willingness to take risks and to keep your skills up to date.

KEEPING UP WITH THE CHANGES

With the rapid developments in high technology, new products, languages, and programs spring up faster than you can gain specialized knowledge in each of them. "It will get harder to predict the technologies you should be studying," Elizabeth Berglund admits.

She stresses that professionals can retain their career buoyancy as long as they're creative about where and how they apply their skills. Many people look for jobs in all the wrong places, she notes. The solution, as she sees it, is to keep an eye out for opportunities to transfer your know-how, whether it's in marketing or R&D, to new areas. Perry Anthony, too, believes that "technical professionals who can truly anticipate business opportunities and problems, initiate action, and communicate effectively to nontechnical employees have the best chance of success."

Insiders agree that the future of information technology will be exciting but volatile.

Jobs with a Future in: The Technologies

Biotechnology and Environmental Technology

Biological Scientist . . . Ecologist . . . Microbiologist . . . Physiologist . . . Botanist . . . Aquatic Biologist . . . Zoologist . . . Medical Scientist . . . Geneticist . . . Biochemist . . . Conservation Scientist . . . Forester . . . Range Manager . . . Soil Conservationist . . . Geoscientist . . . Geologist . . . Geophysicist . . . Geological Oceanographer . . . Hydrologist . . . Petroleum Geologist . . . Mineralogist . . . Paleontologist . . . Seismologist . . . Stratigrapher

Engineering

Engineer . . . Electrical and Electronic Engineer . . . Civil Engineer . . . Environmental Engineer . . . Mechanical Engineer . . . Chemical Engineer . . . Industrial Engineer . . . Metallurgical and Materials Engineer

Information Technology

Computer Software Engineer . . . Systems Analyst . . . Computer Programmer . . . Systems Programmer . . . Applications Programmer . . . Information Systems Manager . . . User Support Analyst . . . Computer Service Technician
[Note: These computer industry jobs can be found in many companies in all industries.]

ADDITIONAL OPPORTUNITIES IN THE TECHNOLOGIES

You will also find the following jobs in the technology industries. These jobs appear in most companies in all industries. You will find the particulars of these jobs on the pages noted:

Job Title	Industry	Page
Accountant	Financial Services	273
Auditor	Financial Services	279
Chief Financial Officer	Financial Services	284
Corporate Controller	Financial Services	285
Benefits Manager	Human Resources	302
Compensation Manager	Human Resources	303
Human Resources Manager	Human Resources	308
Human Resources Staffing Specialist	Human Resources	309
Director of Training	Human Resources	313
Training Manager	Human Resources	313
Corporate Training Specialist	Human Resources	313
Labor Relations Specialist	Human Resources	317
Diversity Manager	Human Resources	317
Management Consultant	Human Resources	323
Attorney	Law	327
Public Relations Professional	Media/Communications/PR	346
Sales Representative	Sales and Marketing	351
Records Clerk	Support Services	378
Secretary	Support Services	385
Librarian	Education	426
Air Quality Specialist	State & Local Government	438

Biotechnology and Environmental Technology

BIOLOGICAL SCIENTIST: ECOLOGIST/MICROBIOLOGIST/PHYSIOLOGIST/ BOTANIST/AQUATIC BIOLOGIST/ZOOLOGIST/MEDICAL SCIENTIST: GENETICIST/BIOCHEMIST

Biological scientists, also commonly known as *life scientists*, conduct research to enhance our understanding of living organisms and their relationship to the environment. They combine their findings with those of other scientists to develop new medicines, to help farmers increase crop yields, and to help improve the environment.

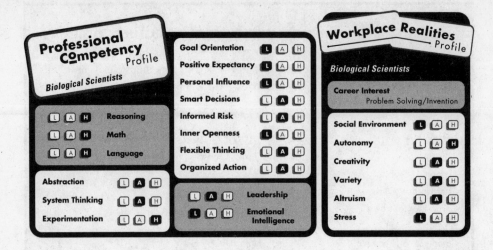

Biological science is one of the more wide-ranging specialities of the scientific fields; most biological scientists are also classified by the type of organism that they study. As biological studies grow, the present classifications for biologists will also evolve. Some of the more commonly known subcategories are listed below:

Ecologists are biological scientists who study the interrelationship of organisms and the environment. Ecologists work in two major fields of study, environmental pollution and the ecosystem, conducting research in methods for pollution abatement. They draw on their knowledge of scientific and engineering principles to identify pollutants, the dangers they pose, and their specific impact on the ecosystem. They study pollution emission measurements, atmospheric monitoring readings, meteorological and mineralogical findings, and soil and water samples to gauge the level of danger presented by a pollutant's presence in an environmental system. They also study the short-term and long-term effects of industrial pollutants on plant and animal populations. They may study the changing patterns of rainfall, temperature, and climate and the way that these changes affect various environmental conditions.

Microbiologists investigate the growth and characteristics of microscopic organisms such as bacteria, algae, or fungi and their effects on tissue and matter. They may specialize in environmental, food, or agricultural studies, or in virology, immunology, or industrial microbiology.

Physiologists study the cellular and molecular structure and life functions of plants, animals, and humans, exposing organisms to a variety of environments in order to measure the effects. Physiologists may specialize in functions such as growth, reproduction, photosynthesis, respiration, or movement in the physiology of a specific part of the organism.

Botanists study all aspects of plants and their environment. Some study all aspects of plant life, while others specialize in areas such as the identification and classification of plants, the structure and function of plant parts, the biochemistry of plant processes, or the causes and cures of plant diseases.

Aquatic biologists study plants and animals living in the water. Subcategories of aquatic biology include: *marine biologists*, who study saltwater organisms; *oceanographers*, who study the physical characteristics of oceans and the ocean floor; and *limnologists*, who study freshwater organisms.

Zoologists study animals' origins, behavior, diseases, and life processes. Some experiment with live animals in controlled or natural surroundings while others dissect dead animals to study their structure. Zoologists are usually identified by the animal group studied: *ornithologists* (birds), *mammologists* (mammals), *herpetologists* (reptiles), and *ichthyologists* (fish).

Medical scientists are biological scientists who do biomedical research to discover more effective treatments for serious diseases and other health problems. This research usually involves comprehensive studies of various biological structures. Medical scientists who have earned a medical degree often work in conjunction with doctors in clinical trials, administering treatments to patients suffering from serious disease. They then monitor and test the results. Medical scientists may sometimes direct their research toward prevention of ailments, disorders, and diseases.

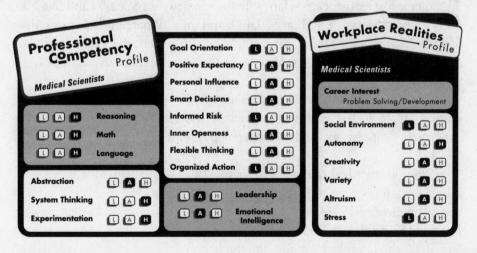

One particularly strong subcategory of medical scientist is *Geneticists*, medical research scientists who examine the biological characteristics related to heredity. Some of the topics studied by geneticists include the role of genes in human and animal development, the transmission of physical and mental characteristics from generation to generation, the development of new mutations, and the effects of outside influences on heredity. Geneticists attempt to discover the reasons behind similarities and differences of family members' hair, eye, and skin coloring, height and physical build, and resistance or susceptibility to disease.

Biochemists study the chemical composition of living things and explore the complex chemical combinations and reactions involved in metabolism, reproduction, growth, and heredity. They conduct experiments to register the effects of substances such as food, drugs, and hormones on tissues and body functions. They may specialize in studying chemical functions that contribute to life, such as the formation of antibodies, or the effects of aging and the process of death. Specialists in this field include *enzyme chemists*, *protein chemists*, and *pharmaceutical chemists*.

EARNING POTENTIAL

The salaries paid to scientists are notoriously low for the amount of education and training required, suggesting that most scientists are motivated more by their inquisitive nature and dedication to the field than by the promise of a fiscally rewarding career. A recent study found that the median annual salary for all **biological scientists** was approximately $34,500. The middle 50 percent of all biological scientists earn salaries that range between $26,000 and $46,800. Only 10 percent earn less than $20,400, and only 10 percent earn more than $56,900. According to the College Placement Council, the beginning salary offered to bachelor's degree recipients in biological science averages $21,850 per year.

Microbiologists earn an average salary of $49,440; **physiologists**, $55,326. General biological scientists employed by the federal government in non-supervisory, supervisory, and managerial positions earn an average salary of $45,155.

Salaries for **medical scientists** differ slightly. The median annual salary for medical scientists averages approximately $32,400, with the middle 50 percent earning between $25,800 and $52,200. Ten percent of medical scientists earn less than $20,000, but 10 percent earn more than $77,600. **Geneticists** earn $55,709, which ranked among the higher end of salaries for specialized research scientists.

Entry-level **biochemists** average $23,700 to start, while experienced professionals in the field typically earn $29,800 a year and senior biochemists average $37,900. Those in supervisory positions earn around $45,725, and administrators earn salaries ranging near $60,000.

EDUCATIONAL REQUIREMENTS

Most colleges and universities offer both bachelor's and advanced degrees in **biological science**. Curricula for these advanced degrees vary according to the specialty being studied. Advanced degree work includes classroom and field study, laboratory research, and a thesis or dissertation.

A bachelor's degree is adequate for positions in biological science which do not involve research; it is highly unusual for graduates with bachelor's degrees to be performing independent experiments in laboratories. Some, however, may be eligible for positions as research assistants, biological technicians, medical laboratory technologists, testers, or inspectors.

A master's degree in a designated biological science specialty is sufficient for a candidate entering applied research, or interested in management, inspection, sales, or service. For both long-term research projects and for college teaching positions, biological scientists must hold a Ph.D.

A Ph.D. is the minimum educational requirement for **medical scientists** and **biochemists**. Since their work is almost completely research-oriented, there is no substitute for the background and training provided by doctoral studies. The Ph.D. qualifies medical scientists to perform research on life processes or diseases, and also to analyze the results of experiments performed on patients. Many medical scientists also hold a medical degree, since they must often administer drugs to patients or experiment with gene therapy. Because the Ph.D. is the minimum credential for medical scientists and biochemists, most spend many years in postdoctoral research before they receive offers for permanent jobs. These postdoctoral positions often involve highly sophisticated experiments that provide researchers with additional expertise they later use in their jobs.

All scientists should be able to work both independently and as part of a research team, and should possess exceptional oral and written communication skills. In order to complete their projects, they need patience, physical and mental stamina, and endurance.

A DAY IN THE LIFE

Biological scientists work in a wide variety of locations. Some **ecologists** may conduct experiments on laboratory animals or greenhouse plants; others may

HELP WANTED BIOLOGICAL SCIENTISTS/ LIFE SCIENTISTS

Biological Scientists

Conduct research on living organisms and their relationship to the environment. Help develop new medicines and improve the environment. Salary Range: $19,000–$57,000.

Ecologist

Work in either of two major fields of study: environmental pollution and the ecosystem. Conduct research on methods for minimizing pollution. Identify pollutants, and gauge their danger levels and ecological impact in an environment. Study the changing patterns of rainfall, temperature, and climate, and their effects on various environmental conditions. Salary Range: $19,000–$57,000.

Microbiologist

Investigate the growth and characteristics of microscopic organisms such as bacteria, algae, or fungi, and their effects on tissue and matter. Salary Range: $19,000–$57,000.

Physiologist

Study plants, animals, and humans, in particular their cellular and molecular structure and life functions. Expose them to a variety of environments in order to measure the effects of such factors on life processes and functions. Salary Range: $19,000–$57,000.

Botanist

Study all aspects of plants and their environment, including identification and classification; the structure and function of their parts; the biochemistry of their processes; and/or the causes and cures of plant

conduct their research outside of laboratories, for example in tropical rain forests. Many scientists work in the field, gathering samples or setting up equipment to take readings of conditions, although **microbiologists** and **physiologists** are more likely to spend the bulk of their time conducting experiments in laboratories. **Botanists** and **zoologists** frequently take field trips that require working or living for periods of time outdoors. They may be in charge of activities at a botanical garden or zoo. These activities may require a great deal of overtime, particularly for biological scientists who work as consultants. **Aquatic biologists** spend a good deal of time outdoors, on and in the water, in every imaginable weather condition.

Medical scientists and **biochemists** usually work in offices, clinics, and hospitals, and in laboratories that contain a wide variety of sophisticated scientific equipment such as electron microscopes, number-crunching computers, and thermal cyclers. Since most of their experiments must be performed in a controlled environment, these laboratories must be kept clean and bright. Some, however, work in less predictable surroundings, dealing with dangerous microorganisms or toxins, or in diverse, and relatively hostile, climatic conditions in order to study the environment and habitats of various organisms. Certain studies demand that scientists safeguard themselves from infection by wearing protective gear.

Scientists often work alone, but they may also be a part of a larger research diseases. Salary Range: $19,000–$57,000.

Aquatic Biologist
Study those plants and animals living in the water. May experiment with live and dead aquatic lifeforms, including dissection. Salary Range: $19,000–$57,000.

Zoologist
Study animals' origins, behavior, diseases, and life processes. May experiment with live animals, or dissect dead animals to study their structure. Salary Range: $19,000–$57,000.

Medical Scientists
Conduct biomedical research to discover more effective treatments for serious diseases and other health problems. Work in conjunction with doctors in clinical trials, administering treatments to patients infected with serious disease. Monitor and test results. Salary Range: $19,000–$77,600.

Geneticist
Examine the biological characteristics related to heredity and the genetic factors in resistance or susceptibility to disease. Study the role of genes in human and animal development, the transmission of physical and mental characteristics from generation to generation, the development of new mutations, and the effects of outside influences on heredity. Average Salary: $56,000.

Biochemist
Study the chemical composition of living things, and explore the chemical reactions in metabolism, reproduction, growth, and genetics. Conduct experiments on the effects of food, drugs, and hormones on tissues and body functions. Salary Range: $23,700–$60,000.

team. Naturally, since they perform research that must be correctly recorded, they are responsible for doing considerable paperwork. In order to complete their experiments and studies, scientists often do overtime and evening work.

JOB GROWTH

A recent survey reported that **biological** and **medical scientists** held nearly 117,000 jobs in the United States. Almost four out of ten of those surveyed were employed by federal, state, and local governments. Federal workers were largely employed by the Departments of Agriculture, Interior, and Defense, and the National Institutes of Health. One-fifth of those surveyed worked in the pharmaceutical industry, hospitals, or research and testing laboratories. Many of these research scientists hold faculty positions at colleges and universities, where they perform their own experiments while they train the next generation of scientists.

Employment of **biological scientists** is expected to increase at a rate faster than the national average for all employment over the next ten years. It is estimated that there will be approximately 20,000 new positions created in addition to the openings that result from normal attrition rates. The next century will continue to provide abundant opportunities for biological scientists, as scientific breakthroughs will open up new areas where their expertise will be required.

Efforts to clean up and preserve the environment will continue to add to growth in this field. More biological scientists will be needed to determine the environmental impact of industry and government actions, and to correct existing environmental problems. Increasing interest in preserving wildlife and plant species from damaging human contact is creating a greater interest in the specific fields of *ecology* and *environmental biology*. And as the earth's population grows, biotechnology will help to support the food supply through *agricultural engineering*.

Medical scientists and **biochemists** will continue to explore possible cures for diseases and to develop new products through biological methods. Based on greater advances in genetic science, expansion is expected in related research fields such as AIDS and cancer research. For individuals who have a strong scientific orientation without the interest in becoming a medical doctor, a career as a medical scientist is an interesting and challenging option.

An anticipated decrease in government budgets and funding may mean that scientists will be more successful holding jobs in private sector scientific research. Private sector funding can be affected by economic recessions, although scientists who are involved in long-term projects need not be concerned. One concern among scientists, though, is the recent trend toward making them partly responsible for soliciting funds to continue research projects or to begin new projects. As in so many other professions, research scientists are discovering that they must develop talents for communication, sales, and marketing in order to continue working in their area of expertise.

Some of the most significant contributions to the future of life on earth are made by scientists, and their work cannot be overvalued. The requirements for these jobs are among the most intellectually challenging found in this book; however, the reward for someone who contributes to a research breakthrough that improves life is immeasurable.

Because of the tentative nature of many research projects, researchers should be versed in a number of areas. Prospective research scientists are encouraged to pursue additional degrees and gain significant laboratory experience in biological science so that they can move to research projects in other areas if necessary.

One growing trend is for environmental scientists to work as independent contractors on a project basis. Since many of these positions require specialized training, it makes sense that scientists may be better able to market their skills and talents to an entire industry rather than to one employer who may not have the need for full-time staff scientists. Environmental scientists may also work as consultants to businesses or—as is more frequently happening—to state and local government agencies.

Even though government funding may not be as readily available as it has been in the past, the public's need, and private industry's demand, for new scientific discoveries will ensure that there is a ready job market for capable scientists. Regardless of where funding comes from, the need for continued research to find ways to protect our fragile environment, to enhance agricultural production, and to find cures for deadly diseases and debilitating conditions will demand that studies in biological science and biotechnology continue without pause.

CONSERVATION SCIENTIST: FORESTER/RANGE MANAGER/SOIL CONSERVATIONIST

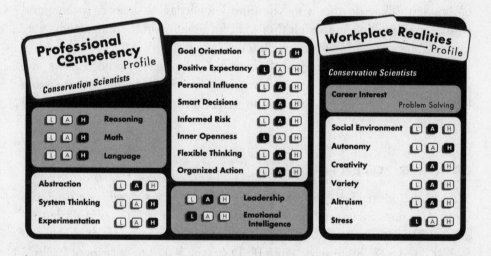

Conservation scientists manage, develop, oversee the use of, and protect natural resources. They manage timberland and natural wildlife habitats. This challenging work is also essential for the preservation of thousands of living species.

Conservation scientists fall roughly into four categories: *ecologists* (see page 184), *foresters*, *range managers*, and *soil conservationists*.

Foresters work for private industries to purchase timber from landowners. Their purchases are made with consideration not only for the economic benefit to their employer, but also with concern for the environmental impact of deforestation on the land. In determining what trees are to be cut down, foresters analyze the wildlife habitats and water sources in the area, and check the water quality and soil stability to ensure compliance with environmental regulations. Foresters are ecologists who take into account the entire biological system of a forest.

Foresters and ecologists supervise the regeneration of a deforested area, choosing the sites and placing the trees for planting. The foresters continue to monitor the trees' growth to ensure their health and the biological system's continued integrity.

Range managers protect rangelands in order to preserve their use without destroying their environment. There are approximately one billion acres of rangeland in the United States, primarily in the west and in Alaska. These rangelands provide food and living habitat for many animal species—grass and shrubs for grazing, water from protected watersheds—as well as recreational facilities for campers and tourists, and mineral and energy resources.

Range managers also work with ranchers to assist with livestock growth and production. They do this with scientific knowledge of grazing systems and animal reproduction. Although they plan for grazing on the rangelands, they must also be aware of soil conservation needs.

Soil conservationists work with farmers and ranchers who rely on the soil for their livelihood. Soil conservationists develop programs that enable farmers and ranchers to use the soil to maximum benefit, while maintaining its nutrients.

EARNING POTENTIAL

Most bachelor's degree graduates recently hired by the federal government as foresters, range managers, or soil conservationists earn a starting salary of around $18,340 per year. Candidates with a master's degree are paid between $22,717 and $27,789 to start, while Ph.D.s receive starting salaries of $33,623 in field positions and $40,298 in research positions. The average salary for all foresters employed by the federal government in 1993 was $42,440. For soil conservationists, the average salary was $39,448.

In private industry, the starting salaries for those with a bachelor's degree are comparable to the federal government pay scale. The starting salaries are lower, though, for those working at the state or local government level.

EDUCATIONAL REQUIREMENTS

In 1993 there were forty-five accredited college programs offering a bachelor's or higher degree in earth and conservation science. Curriculum in these programs centers around science, mathematics, communication skills, and computer science, as well as technical subjects. People hoping to become **foresters** should also study land use policy matters and environmental regulatory laws.

Range managers can study their specialty at thirty-one colleges and universities that offer degrees in this particular field. Range management classes include studies of plant, animal, and soil sciences with emphasis on the principles of ecology and resource management. Electives for range management include economics, forestry, hydrology, agronomy, wildlife, animal husbandry, computer science, and recreation.

Because there are very few schools that offer majors in **soil conservation**, most soil conservationists take their degree in one of the following related majors: agronomy, general agriculture, or crop or soil science.

A DAY IN THE LIFE

Most conservation scientists balance their laboratory or office work with many hours in the field. The duties of a conservation scientist involve more time spent working in cooperation with animals and nature than with people. Although much of their work is solitary, they also work alongside farmers, ranchers, and loggers, to name a few, and they also must deal with tourists and campers.

The working conditions can be very rough for conservation scientists. They may be required to work outdoors in all weather conditions, and they regularly can cover considerable distances on foot. It's an exciting career for someone who likes the outdoor life and who wants to make a contribution to the ecosystem.

JOB GROWTH

There are approximately 35,000 conservation scientists in the United States. Almost 33 percent of this number work for the federal government, primarily in the Department of Agriculture's Forest Service and Soil Conservation Service, and in the Department of the Interior's Bureau of Land Management. The Forest Service alone employs over 5,000 foresters and 400 range managers. Twenty-five percent of conservation scientists work for state governments, and eight percent for local governments. The remainder work for private employers, primarily in the forestry and logging industries.

Due to budgetary cutbacks by the federal government, employment growth

---

HELP WANTED CONSERVATIONIST SCIENTISTS

Forester

Work for private industries to purchase timber from landowners. Consider economic benefit to employer, as well as environmental impact of deforestation on the land. Analyze the wildlife habitats and check the water quality and soil stability to ensure compliance with environmental regulations before trees are cut down. Supervise the regeneration of a deforested area, choosing the sites and placing the trees for planting. Salary Range: $18,300–$78,000.

Range Manager

Protect rangelands in order to enable the public to use them without destroying the environment. Work with ranchers to assist with livestock growth and production, while considering soil conservation needs. Salary Range: $18,300–$60,000.

Soil Conservationist

Work with farmers and ranchers who rely on the soil for their livelihood. Develop programs that enable farmers and ranchers to use the soil to maximum benefit, while maintaining the soil's nutrients. Salary Range: $18,300–$36,000.

---

figures in the conservation field may look deceptively low. There will be opportunities, though, as a large turnover is expected in this field as a result of the number of foresters and range managers due to retire in the near future.

Job opportunities in private industry are expected to grow more quickly than in the public sector. Also, although government cutbacks will affect employment, state and local governments will continue to need conservation scientists in order to comply with federal laws governing environmental protection and responsible land use.

State-level jobs will also be created as a result of the nationwide Stewardship Incentive Program, which is funded by the federal government. This program provides money to the states to encourage landowners to practice multiple-use forest management. States will hire foresters to work with landowners in making decisions about how to manage their forested property. In private industry, more foresters should be needed to increase productivity and plan regeneration for future timber harvesting.

The dream that first brought people to America was open land. Conservation scientists know the true worth of this open land, and what it means to wildlife and to the ecological balance of the northern hemisphere. These careers will continue to attract those adventurous souls who have an affinity for the land and understand that what the land produces is every bit as important as industry and technology.

GEOSCIENTISTS: GEOLOGIST/GEOPHYSICIST/GEOLOGICAL OCEANOGRAPHER/HYDROLOGIST/PETROLEUM GEOLOGIST/MINERALOGIST/PALEONTOLOGIST/SEISMOLOGIST/STRATIGRAPHER

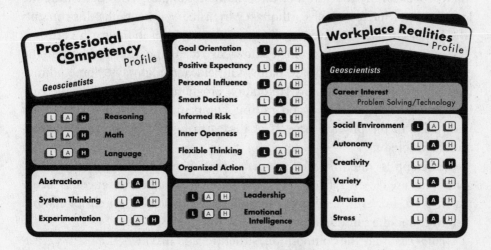

Increasingly, **geologists**, **geophysicists**, and other **earth scientists** are becoming known as *geoscientists,* a term that better describes their role in studying all aspects of the earth. Geoscientists study the physical structure, composition, and history of the earth, its forces and its resources.

The typical responsibilities of geoscientists include identifying and examining rocks, studying information collected by remote sensing instruments in satellites, conducting geological surveys, constructing maps, and using instruments to measure the earth's gravity and magnetic field. Geoscientists also analyze information collected through seismic prospecting, which involves bouncing sound waves off buried rock layers. Some search for oil, natural gas, minerals, and underground water.

Geoscientists play an important role in studying, preserving, and cleaning up the environment. Many design and monitor waste disposal sites, preserve water supplies, and reclaim contaminated land and water to comply with stricter federal environmental laws and regulations. They also help locate safe sites for hazardous waste facilities and landfills.

Additional responsibilities include examining chemical and physical properties of specimens in laboratories, sometimes under controlled temperature and pressure. They may study fossil remains of animal and plant life or experiment with the flow of water or oil through rocks. Some specialists use two- or three-dimensional computer modeling to portray water layers and the flow of water or other fluids through rock cracks and porous materials. They use a large variety of sophisticated laboratory instruments, including X-ray diffractometers, which determine the crystal structure of minerals, and petrographic microscopes for the study of rock and sediment samples. They determine the locations and intensities of earthquakes by using seismographs, instruments which measure energy waves resulting from movements in the earth's crust.

Geoscientists also apply geologic knowledge to engineering problems in the construction of large buildings, dams, tunnels, and highways. Some administer and manage research and exploration programs, and others become general managers in petroleum and mining companies. They often apply their knowledge of the physical aspects of the earth to solve or prevent environmental problems.

Geoscientists often specialize in a particular subfield. Geology and geophysics are closely related fields, but with some major differences. Specialists in both, however, commonly apply their skills to the search for natural resources and the solution of environmental problems.

Geologists study the composition, structure, and history of the earth's crust. They try to find out how rocks were formed and what has happened to them since their formation.

Geophysicists use the principles of physics and mathematics to study not only the earth's surface but its internal composition, ground and surface waters, atmosphere, and oceans, as well as its magnetic, electrical, and gravitational forces.

Geological oceanographers study and map the ocean floor. They collect information using remote sensing devices aboard surface ships or underwater research craft. *Physical oceanographers* study the physical aspects of oceans, such as currents, and the interaction of the surface of the sea with the atmosphere. *Chemical oceanographers* study the chemical composition, dissolved elements, and nutrients of oceans. Although biological scientists who study ocean life are also called oceanographers (as well as *marine biologists*), the work they do and the training they need are related to biology rather than to geology or geophysics.

Hydrologists study the distribution, circulation, and physical properties of underground and surface waters. They study the form and intensity of precipitation, its rate of infiltration into the soil, and its return to the ocean and the atmosphere.

Petroleum geologists explore for oil and gas by studying and mapping the subsurface of the ocean or land. They use sophisticated geophysical instrumentation, statistical analysis, and computers to collect information.

Mineralogists analyze and classify minerals and precious stones according to composition and structure.

Paleontologists study fossils found in geological formations to trace the evolution of plant and animal life and the geologic history of the earth.

Seismologists interpret data from seismographs and other geophysical instruments to detect earthquakes and locate earthquake-related faults.

Stratigraphers help to locate minerals by studying the distribution and arrangement of sedimentary rock layers and by examining the fossil and mineral content of such layers.

EARNING POTENTIAL

Beginning geoscientists earn annual salaries in a range between $20,000 and $35,000, while more experienced specialists earn from $25,000 to $60,000 and above. Salaries vary widely, depending on the employing industry. The oil and gas industries typically provide the highest salaries. Although the petroleum, mineral, and mining industries offer higher salaries, the competition in these areas is normally intense, and the job security is not as great as in other areas.

The federal government's average annual salary for geologists in managerial, supervisory, and nonsupervisory positions is approximately $52,000; for geophysicists, $58,000; for hydrologists, $48,000; and for oceanographers, $55,000. Salary growth should be roughly consistent with inflation.

EDUCATIONAL REQUIREMENTS

A bachelor's degree in geology or geophysics is adequate for entry into some lower-level geology jobs, but better jobs with good advancement potential usually require at least a master's degree in geology or geophysics. Persons with strong backgrounds in physics, chemistry, mathematics, or computer science also may qualify for some geophysics or geology jobs. A Ph.D. is essential for most college or teaching positions, and is important for work in federal agencies that involve basic research.

Over five hundred colleges and universities offer a bachelor's degree in geology, geophysics, oceanography, or other geoscience fields. Other programs offering related training for beginning geological scientists include geophysical technology, geophysical engineering, geophysical prospecting, engineering geology, petroleum geology, and geochemistry. In addition, more than three hundred universities offer advanced degrees in geology or geophysics.

HELP WANTED
GEOSCIENTISTS

Geologist
Study the physical structure, composition, and history of the earth, its forces and its resources. Identify and examine rocks, conduct ecological surveys, construct maps, and use instruments to measure the earth's gravity and magnetic field. Analyze information collected through seismic prospecting and remote sensing instruments in satellites. Manage research and exploration programs. Salary Range: $20,000–$60,000.

Geophysicist
Study the earth's surface and internal composition, ground and surface waters, atmosphere, and oceans, as well as its magnetic, electrical, and gravitational forces. Salary Range: $20,000–$60,000.

Geological Oceanographer
Map the ocean floor using remote sensing devices. Study the physical aspects of oceans and the interaction of the surface of the sea with the atmosphere. Analyze the chemical composition, dissolved elements, and nutrients of oceans. Salary Range: $20,000–$60,000.

Traditional geoscience courses emphasizing classic geologic methods and concepts (such as mineralogy, paleontology, stratigraphy, and structural geology) are important for all geoscientists. However, those students interested in working in the environmental or regulatory fields should also take courses in hydrology, hazardous-waste management, environmental legislation, chemistry, fluid mechanics, and geologic logging.

In addition to meeting the formal educational requirements, geoscientists should be able to work as a part of a team. Computer modeling, data processing, and effective oral and written communication skills are important, as is the ability to think independently and creatively. Those involved in fieldwork must have physical stamina.

A DAY IN THE LIFE

The workplace of the geoscientist is as diverse as the science itself. Some geoscientists spend the major part of their time in an office, while others divide their time between fieldwork and office or laboratory work. While offices and laboratories are typically clean, quiet, and comfortable environments, work in the field may be demanding. Geoscientists often travel to remote field sites by helicopter or four-wheel-drive vehicles, and cover large areas by foot. Some work overseas, and job relocation is not unusual. **Oceanographers** may spend a considerable amount of time at sea. The physical demands of office and laboratory work are modest, but fieldwork may involve strenuous physical activity and somewhat

Hydrologist

Study the distribution, circulation, and physical properties of underground and surface waters. Analyze the form and intensity of precipitation, its infiltration into the soil and return to the ocean and atmosphere. Salary Range: $20,000–$60,000.

Petroleum Geologist

Explore for oil and gas by studying and mapping the subsurface of the ocean or land. Salary Range: $20,000–$60,000.

Mineralogist

Analyze and classify minerals and precious stones according to their composition and structure. Salary Range: $20,000–$60,000.

Paleontologist

Study fossils found in geological formations to trace the evolution of plant and animal life and the geologic history of the earth. Salary Range: $20,000–$60,000.

Seismologist

Interpret data from seismographs and other geophysical instruments to detect and predict earthquakes and locate earthquake-related faults. Salary Range: $20,000–$60,000.

Stratigrapher

Locate minerals by studying the distribution and arrangement of sedimentary rock layers and by examining the fossil and mineral content of such layers. Salary Range: $20,000–$60,000.

primitive living conditions. One certainty is that the 9 to 5 office blues rarely occur in this occupation.

Geoscientists work with little direct supervision but must work in close cooperation with others. The job usually involves regular hours, but overtime, night, or weekend hours may be necessary.

JOB GROWTH

A 1992 survey found approximately 48,000 geoscientists in the United States. Of these, almost 25 percent were employed by oil and gas companies or oil and gas field service firms. Many others worked for consulting firms and business services, especially engineering services, which often provide services to oil and gas companies. Approximately 10 percent were self-employed, with most working as consultants to industry or government. Nearly 15 percent were with the federal government, and some worked for state and local agencies. Most of the remaining specialists worked for nonprofit research institutions.

The overall employment of geoscientists is expected to seesaw in the short term. Many jobs are in or related to the petroleum industry, which is subject to cyclical fluctuations. If low oil prices, higher production costs, improvements in energy efficiency, and restrictions on potential drilling sites continue, the resulting drop in exploration activities will reduce opportunities in this industry. However, an increase in oil prices is always a possibility, and then a market for geoscientists will assuredly follow in the quest to find and maximize oil sources.

In contrast, the demand for professionals in environmental reclamation and environmental protection has been growing rapidly. Geoscientists will be needed to help clean up contaminated sites in the United States and elsewhere, and to help private companies to comply with environmental regulations. In particular, jobs requiring training in engineering geology, hydrology, and geochemistry should be in demand.

The number of opportunities for geoscientists will depend on the particular subfield. Most jobs pay relatively well, and for individuals interested in physical and earth sciences, this broad field presents excellent options.

As the challenges presented by the earth's limited and decreasing natural resources become more defined, their potential solutions increase in complexity. In consequence, the training and education demanded of today's geoscientists will increase. As in most professions, lifetime learning will become the norm for geoscientists. For these reasons, persons interested in this field are encouraged to continue beyond the bachelor's degree level and to pursue graduate training as a boost.

Engineering

ENGINEER: ELECTRICAL AND ELECTRONIC ENGINEER/CIVIL ENGINEER/ENVIRONMENTAL ENGINEER/MECHANICAL ENGINEER/CHEMICAL ENGINEER/INDUSTRIAL ENGINEER/METALLURGICAL AND MATERIALS ENGINEER*

Engineers design, develop, and oversee the practical application of ideas, theories, and formulae developed by others. For example, the theory of jet propulsion, first applied during the early 1940s, has led—many stages and many discoveries later—to space shuttles that can travel through outer space and return to earth. Many of the stages of discovery between the original jet engines and space shuttle technology came about because engineers, in building actual working aircraft and spacecraft, realized that a change to the process could result in greater efficiency and power for engines. Engineers take theoretical discoveries and help make them work.

*For this job description, see page 211.

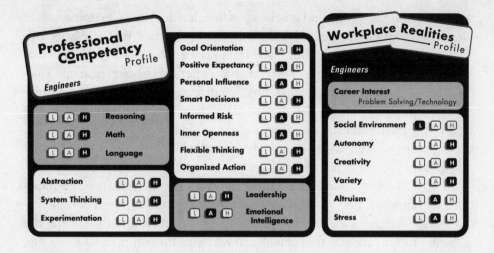

They design machinery and products, systems and processes, children's toys and luxury cars. Their concern is with the practical functioning of an object in the most efficient form possible. Cost and product effectiveness, reliability, safety, and efficiency are some of the major concerns they have when approaching a project.

There are twenty-five recognized major specialties in the engineering field. Within these specialities are subspecialties that allow engineers to pursue their particular interests in almost any imaginable field. Some specialty fields of engineering are *architectural engineering* (which involves the design of a building's support structure), *environmental engineering* (a growing field concerned with the treatment and prevention of pollution and other environmental hazards), and *biomedical engineering* (the application of engineering principles to medical and physiological problems).

The engineering industry has been through some turbulent times over the last ten years, with government employees being the hardest hit. The good news is that the long-term outlook for engineers is much improved. The decline in engineering majors in colleges and an increase in demand for up-to-date engineer trainees spells promise for the future. Engineers specializing in *electrical* and *electronic engineering, civil engineering, mechanical engineering, chemical engineering,* and *industrial engineering* are expected to find the best employment opportunities over the next decade.

Electrical and electronic engineers conduct research on electronic components and systems. Subsequently they design products and services for consumer and commercial use. On a more elemental level they are basically experts at transmitting electricity and electronic impulses. They are responsible for the design and efficiency of the electrical and electronic conveniences that surround us in our daily lives, from computers that supply us with information at work to lighting, heating, and air conditioning systems that keep us comfortable at home. These engineers perfect the electrical and electronic designs of cars and airplanes, washing machines and ovens, video equipment and robots—you get the picture. They have been instrumental in the technology boom that shows no signs of slackening by not only aiding in the development of technology but, more important, by developing additional practical uses for emerging technologies.

Subspecialties in electrical/electronic engineering include: power generation, transmission, and distribution; computer electronics; the communications field; designing electrical equipment and facilities; and developing the applications for controls, instruments, and systems for commercial uses (e.g., information and data processing systems), domestic uses (everything from timer-activated coffee makers to alarm systems), and industrial uses (such as the design and installation of industrial robot control systems and the development of aviation electronics).

Since electrical and electronics engineers are so integrally involved in every aspect of daily life, the field has been and remains a busy and popular one.

Civil engineers, of all engineering professionals, may be the most familiar to people. We can all grasp and appreciate the solidity of a road, the grandeur of a dam, or the majesty of a great bridge. Although we experience the results of work done by electrical, chemical, and *nuclear engineers* (who deal largely with electrical impulses, chemical reactions, and nuclear fission), we see the tangible results of the work of civil engineers.

Civil engineers design the basic structural aspects of roads, bridges, tunnels, airports, and buildings, and supervise their construction. Some civil engineers may design water supply and sewage systems for large urban areas or small rural communities. As in other specialized fields of engineering, civil engineers may practice particular subspecialties, such as *structural, environmental, construction, transportation, water resources*, and *geotechnical engineering*.

Civil engineers analyze reports, maps, drawings, and blueprints, geologic and topographic data, and other information to determine the feasibility of projected construction. They may inspect the actual construction sites in advance of breaking ground, to investigate potential problems.

During the construction of a project, civil engineers may supervise the building process, direct workers in their functions, and serve as inspectors to be sure construction conforms to the specifications and regional safety and construction standards. For example, a structural engineer's concerns for a building in San Francisco, which must conform to codes seeking to limit damage from potential earthquakes, are different from those of an engineer in New York, where the need to ensure the durability of underground pipes is a local concern.

Environmental engineers apply the theories and principles of science and mathematics to the economical solution of practical technical problems related to the environment. Often their work is the link between a scientific discovery and its application. Environmental engineers design machinery, products, systems, and processes for efficient and economical performance, toward the betterment of the many ecosystems that make up our environment. Environmental engineering is a subdivision of civil engineering.

The typical responsibilities of environmental engineers include supervising the design, construction, and operation of water distribution and storage systems, waste and wastewater treatment plants, and plumbing systems. Environmental engineers develop and supervise the collection, treatment, and disposal of liquid and solid waste. They may also be involved in other types of pollution control, such as air emission control and regulation for corporations or other bodies. They may even be involved in recommending methods for insect and rodent control.

Whether it's the development of a consumer product or of waste utilization equipment and processes, environmental engineers consider many factors. They will determine precisely which function the product needs to perform; design and test its components; fit them together in an integrated plan; and evaluate the design's overall effectiveness, cost, reliability, and safety. Environmental engineers will often work in testing, production, and maintenance. All this is done in the context of the product's impact (and that of the process used to make it) on the environment.

Mechanical engineers perform research and also plan and create the designs for a variety of items, including tools, engines, machines, and other mechanical and electromechanical products and systems. They research and analyze data to determine whether or not a proposed design is feasible. They also design instruments, controls, and power-producing engines such as internal combustion engines, steam and gas turbines, and jet engines.

Mechanical engineers provide a vast range of services, depending largely on the industry they work in and the functions for which they are responsible. Many mechanical engineers specialize in such fields as *applied mechanics, design engineering, heat transfer, power plant engineering, pressure vessels*, and *piping* and *underwater technology*. One of the primary functions of

mechanical engineers is to design tools that other specialist engineers use for
working in their own areas of expertise.

Among the specialty areas associated with the engineering profession,
mechanical engineering is considered to be the broadest discipline. It extends
across many of the other interdependent engineering specialties, and includes
such broad areas as production operations, maintenance, and even technical
sales.

Chemical engineers must be familiar with not only chemistry, but also
physics, mathematics, and the physical sciences. Their job might involve the
production of a new process for manufacturing chemicals, or the design of
equipment needed for such a process. At the postproduction end, chemical
engineers may be responsible for testing the newly produced chemicals to
determine acceptable quality levels and to judge the merits of the new manufacturing process.

But chemical engineering is not a field limited only to the process of chemical production. Chemical engineers can be found in such broad fields as *electronics* and *aviation*; slightly narrower fields, such as *environmental* and *pollution control*; and in such specific areas as *oxidation* and *polymerization*.
Likewise, chemical engineers have always played a major part in the development of the *computer industry*, both as the founding fathers of leading computer technology companies, and as the engineers who chemically etch the
intricate patterns on microscopic printed circuit boards and computer chips.

Some chemical engineers work as on-site consultants and supervisors in the
construction of new manufacturing facilities. Chemical engineers working in
the field of manufacturing operations oversee aspects of production and serve
as troubleshooters for problems that arise on the locations, such as the environmental impact and management of the effluent and chemical wastes produced by the manufacturing processes in the facility.

Chemical engineers may work in laboratories under controlled conditions,
conducting research and experiments that lead to the discovery of new chemical formulations for a multitude of uses.

Industrial engineers work in industrial plants, where they oversee production methods and processes in order to develop the most efficient production
methods possible. They are the coordinators who design and then supervise
the implementation of new or modified industrial facilities.

Industrial engineers work closely with production planners in order to
determine a production schedule for an industrial project. Some of the most
important factors they consider in planning the schedule are the sequence of
the production process, the amount of lead time necessary for preparation and

completion of the project, and the sales forecasts and actual orders that must be filled by the production schedule.

When they develop a new production plan, industrial engineers go over the production specifications, including materials used, degrees of stress in the fabrication process, and cost of bringing the industrial plant up to the level required by the process. They examine the manufacturing capacity of the plant and the resources required, both in worker hours and equipment. Then, they analyze the sequence of production and lead time projections they had prepared, and coordinate them with the work schedules of the plant employees.

Industrial engineers must also supervise production workers in the early stages of the manufacturing process so that there are no major problems and no unanswered questions. The process devised by industrial engineers ordinarily requires that each worker serve a specific role. If one worker is uncertain of his or her duties in the process, the entire production schedule can be held up.

In order to plan such complicated processes, industrial engineers must have knowledge not only of manufacturing, but also of production design, materials and parts used in manufacturing, fabrication processes, assembly methods, and quality control standards. All of these aspects of the manufacturing process are required elements of an industrial engineer's expertise.

EARNING POTENTIAL

An engineer's starting salary depends largely on his or her area of specialization. Starting salaries are higher for engineers with a bachelor's degree than they are for entry-level B.Sc.s in almost any other field.

A recent College Placement Council survey showed starting salaries for **engineers** with a bachelor's degree to be approximately $34,000, ranging from $40,675 for **chemical engineers** down to $29,375 for **civil engineers**. Applicants with a master's degree and no experience averaged $39,200 as a starting salary, while a Ph.D. in engineering averaged $54,400 to start.

Studies surveying earnings for engineers in the prime of their career showed median annual earnings of about $52,500 for mid-level engineers with no supervisory duties. Engineers at senior managerial levels earned a median annual salary of approximately $87,000, ranging from $60,000 to well over $100,000. The average 1993 annual salary for experienced engineers in the federal government was $54,425.

The breakdown of salaries by specialty looks like this:

	Starting Salary	Median Salary	Experienced Salary
Electrical/Electronic Engineer	$33,750	$41,000	$53,000+
Civil/Environmental Engineer	$29,375	$39,000	$50,000+
Mechanical Engineer	$34,465	$43,000	$57,000
Chemical Engineer	$40,675	$46,500	$65,000+
Industrial Engineer	$32,350	$41,300	$63,900

EDUCATIONAL REQUIREMENTS

Engineering is a profession that requires intensive education. A bachelor's degree in engineering is only the beginning for many engineers. Many colleges and universities offer engineering programs that provide a general background in the field for the first two years of study, and then offer highly concentrated course work in the chosen specialty. A strong background in advanced mathematics and physical science is essential. Because engineering deals almost entirely with technical information, all colleges and universities require their engineering students to take courses in computer science.

Although most college engineering programs, even those with specific concentrations, are designed as four-year programs, the fact is that many engineering students take five years to graduate. In fact, some universities are now officially making engineering a five-year program because an engineering major is so demanding. Other universities now offer a five- or six-year program that includes working in the field while studying engineering. Although such a program takes longer to complete, students do receive practical experience to go along with their theoretical studies, as well as the opportunity to help finance an expensive course of study. Plus, on graduation, they already have a year's practical experience to leverage their candidacy in the job hunt, and they can also pull down a starting salary equivalent to that of a degreed engineer with a year's worth of practical experience.

Although advanced degrees are not normally required for starting positions in engineering, those with a master's degree or Ph.D. find their advanced degrees helpful in pursuing jobs in the highly technical engineering fields where jobs are more plentiful and salaries most rewarding. Their degrees also make them better candidates for future promotion into the higher-paying management positions.

Some 390 American colleges and universities offer engineering degrees. Most, but not all, are accredited by the Accreditation Board for Engineering and Technology. Students applying to college and university programs should plan to attend a school that offers an accredited program.

All engineers whose work is deemed to affect life, health, or property, or who offer their services to the public, are required to be registered in the state where they practice their profession. The requirements of state registration include a bachelor's degree from an accredited college or university program, four years of relevant work experience, and the passing of a state examination.

Aside from the educational requirements, prospective engineers should be analytical, self-motivated, and creative. An engineer must be able to work with precision and patience, both independently and as part of a team. Strong communication skills, oral and written, are also an important asset for an engineer's career success. Employers of engineers place "team work ethic" and interpersonal skills as high priorities on their list of desirable traits.

A DAY IN THE LIFE

Engineers work under many different conditions, depending on their specialty. Some engineers work in comfortable offices, but other engineers' jobs can be loud, dirty, and dangerous—for example, supervising the demolition and construction work in a burning oil field in Kuwait.

An **electronic** or **electrical engineer** is as likely to be conducting research in a laboratory facility as working at a construction site supervising the installation of an electrical system.

A **civil engineer** is more than likely to be found working outdoors, examining the structural progress of a building, bridge, or highway. Of course there are times civil engineers will work in offices, using computers to work out designs, impact studies, construction schedules, and cost-effectiveness reports. *Environmental civil engineers* may be found aboard ship, supervising off-shore construction sites, while *structural civil engineers* may be working on a research project in a laboratory.

Many **environmental engineers** work in laboratories, industrial plants, or construction sites where they inspect, supervise, or solve on-site problems. A certain percentage of their time may be spent outdoors. Other engineers work in offices almost all the time.

Mechanical engineers may work in offices designing products and then visit production plants to oversee the manufacturing and test the operation of their creations.

Chemical engineers work in many areas of engineering: in laboratories,

HELP WANTED
ENGINEERS

Electrical and Electronic Engineer

Design and conduct research on electronic components and systems. Apply technology to development of new products. Salary Range: $33,750–$53,000+.

Civil Engineer

Design the basic structural aspects of roads, bridges, tunnels, airports, and buildings, and supervise their construction. Analyze reports, maps, drawings, blueprints, and geologic and topographical data to determine the feasibility of projected construction. Salary Range: $29,375–$50,000+.

Environmental Engineer

Apply scientific and mathematical principles to solve technical problems related to the environment. Design machinery, products, systems, and processes for efficient and economical performance. Develop and supervise the collection, treatment, and disposal of liquid and solid waste. Salary Range: $29,375–$50,000+.

Mechanical Engineers

Plan and create the designs for a variety of instruments and controls, including tools, engines, machines, and other mechanical and electromechanical products and systems. Research and analyze data to determine feasibility of proposed design. Salary Range: $34,450–$57,000.

chemical plants, and environmental waste and construction sites, to name a few. The nature of their specialty will often mean they are exposed to dangerous chemicals and conditions where they must wear protective clothing and masks.

Industrial engineers work in their offices at industrial locations, or they spend a good deal of time in the industrial facility itself because they are integrally involved in the production process and in the earlier setup stages when the plant is preparing for a new production run.

Many engineers are employed by federal, state, and local governments. For them, a forty-hour week in an office is common. Those engineers employed in the private sector can expect to work considerable overtime when projects require, and engineers who offer their services on a consulting basis may find their time split between different projects, traveling from office to construction sites or manufacturing plants. The hours may be long and erratic, but boredom is rarely a factor.

Professors of engineering work in classrooms and university research facilities, which are generally pleasant, clean, and stimulating atmospheres.

JOB GROWTH

Engineering, in whatever field of specialization, will continue to offer great opportunities for many qualified job seekers. Consequently, engineering has been and will remain one of the most popular pro-

Chemical Engineer

Produce new processes and design new equipment for manufacturing chemicals. Test newly produced chemicals to determine acceptable quality levels and to judge the merits of the new manufacturing process. Familiarity with chemistry, physics, mathematics, and the physical sciences essential. Salary Range: $40,675–$65,000+.

Industrial Engineer

Design, coordinate, and supervise production processes and methods. Knowledge of the manufacturing process, and of production design, materials, and parts used in manufacturing, fabrication processes, assembly methods, and quality control standards required. Salary Range: $32,350–$63,900.

Metallurgical and Materials Engineer

Study internal structure of matter; extract and analyze matter from metals and their alloys. Create and develop alternative materials for manufacturing of high-tech products. Salary Range: $29,375–$50,000.

fessions for all college graduates. Because the field offers such diversity and opportunity along with good financial remuneration, there will always be large numbers of people attracted to it.

There are approximately 1.5 million engineers employed in the United States. The bad news is that with the downsizing of the defense industry, many experienced engineers lost their jobs. Not all of them have found their skills transferable to the contemporary engineering market and will either retrain or change careers.

The good news is that consumers are hungry for new products and conveniences, and as companies expand to meet the consumer needs, they will be hiring engineers with technological savvy to help design and produce these high-tech products.

The highest-growth area will be the **electronic** and **electrical engineering** field. There are approximately 385,000 electronic/electrical engineers employed in the United States, and this figure is expected to increase to nearly 445,000 by the year 2005. The bulk of this growth is expected to occur in the area of *communications* and *computer technology*. Businesses and government require faster and better means of communication and information processing, and consumers demand more and better electronic goods and services. Also, the world market will continue to demand sophisticated electronic merchandise. Emerging nations should create an increased demand for the technology supplied by electrical and electronics engineers.

One important note: If you want to remain marketable, *stay on top of the latest technology.* For engineering professionals, ongoing education is an integral part of your professional life.

Civil engineers will always be in demand. There are nearly 177,000 civil engineers employed in the United States, but the ability to update roads, bridges, and buildings to the standards attainable through ever-changing technology often depends on the ability of federal and local governments to fund such projects. Still, the reality is that our nation's infrastructure is aging, inevitably requiring major restructuring if we are to remain competitive in the global marketplace. Additionally, natural disasters ensure ongoing demand. A conservative estimate is that 27,000 additional civil engineers will be added to the workforce over the next ten years to take on this enormous and long-term task. They will be needed to design and construct new and better roadways; replace outmoded transportation systems, bridges, water systems, pollution control systems, and buildings such as schools and hospitals; and plan and implement general urban renewal projects.

The overall employment of **environmental engineers** is expected to increase steadily over the next ten years. Employers will need more environmental engineers as they increase investment in plants and equipment to improve productivity and expand the output of goods and services while conforming to the increasingly strict environmental guidelines of the EPA (Environmental Protection Agency). Competitive pressures and advancing technology will also force companies to improve and update product designs more frequently. In addition, deteriorating roads, bridges, water, and pollution control systems and other public facilities located primarily in major cities will require more environmental engineers to bring them up to date.

Mechanical engineers will enjoy a steady growth period through the turn of the century as the demand for construction services and manufacturing innovations continues. The current employment of mechanical engineers numbers 233,000, a figure that could increase by 25 percent over the next ten years. Increased demand for modern machinery and machine tools and the increased complexity of industrial machinery and processes should create opportunities for mechanical engineers.

There are only about 52,000 **chemical engineers** in the American workforce, and it is anticipated that there will be 5,000 additional positions in this field by the year 2005. Chemical engineers will find the most opportunities in the area of *environmental evaluation* and *waste cleanup*, although many chemical engineers will also be employed in the *computer field*.

Industrial engineers will find moderate growth on the job front in the short term. The largest number of engineering jobs for industrial engineers will be found in high-tech fields requiring a great deal of *computer simulation* and *communications technology*.

An up-and-coming specialty in engineering that has all the ingredients of a high-growth industry is *metallurgical and materials engineering*. These specialist engineers, of whom there are only 19,000 employed at present, study the internal structure of matter, extracting matter from metals and their alloys. They also develop new types of materials for use in creating technically advanced products, for example to make lighter-weight alternatives to glass and plastic without compromising on strength. These types of engineers will be increasingly required by product developers worldwide, and will find their expertise particularly in demand within the consumer goods, environmental, and recycling industries.

Relatively few engineers leave the profession each year. This may suggest job satisfaction or just the fact that many engineers are trained to perform their specific functions with no easy way to transfer into an unrelated field. Many of those who transfer from the field of engineering do so because they accept promotions to management-level jobs or professorships, move to sales-related jobs that benefit from engineering expertise, or take another specialized job in a related field.

Career-oriented engineers should pursue ongoing education in growth areas to increase the odds of finding and keeping a job and protecting their marketability in the ever-changing workplace. Those defense engineers who lost their jobs over the last decade would have been well-advised to study computer or environmental engineering during their careers as government employees, which would have better prepared them for the career crisis they now face. Keeping abreast of current technology is the key to success in this growing but competitive profession.

Information Technology

COMPUTER SOFTWARE ENGINEER/SYSTEMS ANALYST/
COMPUTER PROGRAMMER/SYSTEMS PROGRAMMER/
APPLICATIONS PROGRAMMER

Although computers have been used in business for years, computer capability grows so rapidly that professionals on the cutting edge ten years ago are now obsolete, unless they have striven mightily to keep up with the changes. Companies need no longer adjust their computer use to conform to a handful of available systems; now, computer operating systems and their attendant applications are tailored to every corporate user's needs. These systems will continue to change and develop at a breathtaking rate. The programming of these individual systems is essential to both the efficiency of information processing and the security of information management.

There are a multitude of positions with varying titles within the industry, many of which share the same or similar responsibilities. Of the many titles, most fall into one of the following categories: *systems analysts, programmers, engineers, managers* (page 221), and *user support analysts* (page 224). The picture is complicated further by the fact that a company may offer a fancy title instead of a better employment offer or raise at the end of the year; titles don't cost that much.

Computer software engineers may perform many of the same duties as other computer professionals during any given workday, but their jobs are distinguished by the theoretical expertise they use to address complex problems and generate innovative ideas for the application or creation of new technology. Computer software engineers in private industry work in areas such as applying theory, developing specialized languages, or designing programming tools, knowledge-based systems, or computer games. Computer software engineers often work as part of a team that designs new computing devices or computer-related equipment. In short, they are the people whose professional responsibility it is to examine the opportunities for development and change, and then formulate the proper ways to introduce that change.

Computer software engineers specify the files and records to be accessed by the system, design the processing steps, and design the format for the output that will meet the user's needs. They must be sure that the system they design can easily be learned by the user and that any problems encountered can be

quickly overcome. They also ensure security of the data by making it inaccessible to those who are not authorized to use it.

Software engineers coordinate tests and observe use of the system to ensure that it performs as planned. They prepare specifications, work diagrams, and structure charts for computer programmers to follow, and then work with them to debug, or eliminate errors from, the system.

Systems analysts are largely responsible for new developments in the software field. They are often known as *computer systems analysts, information systems analysts,* or *information systems specialists*. The job titles all sound similar because the functions are similar. This is a field in a state of flux: the need for analysts is so great that it has outpaced uniformity of job titles and designations.

Systems analysts work with the users of a computer system to develop and implement hardware and software that will provide users with the information processing capabilities they require; update and alter their current system to meet new needs; or assist them in purchasing new systems deemed most suitable for anticipated needs, and then tailor them accordingly.

Systems analysts work closely with information systems (IS) managers or chief information officers (CIOs) to determine a company's particular needs. The first step in designing or fixing a system is usually outlining the business needs into defined programmable categories. Next analysts utilize structured analysis, data modeling, information engineering, mathematical model building, computer sampling, and cost accounting techniques to construct a model of the desired system.

Systems analysts also oversee installation and setup of the hardware and are there to help integrate the programming necessary to customize the newly configured system. They prepare the specifications, charts, and diagrams that programmers use to input information into the system. Analysts run tests on the system and design modifications necessary for the system's smooth operation. They must ensure that the system is user-friendly, so that the employees who will be using the programs will not be intimidated by its complexities.

Another major area for systems analysts is *networking*. In networking, the analysts connect all the computers used by a business so that they can "talk" to one another. Systems analysts are concerned with the flow of information. Their job is to develop means to process information, make the means accessible to the users, provide security measures to make information inaccessible to unauthorized users, and provide easy means of communication throughout an entire system, whatever its size. The work of designing computer systems is so highly specialized that people tend to become experts in a field, like business, science, engineering, or microcomputer applications.

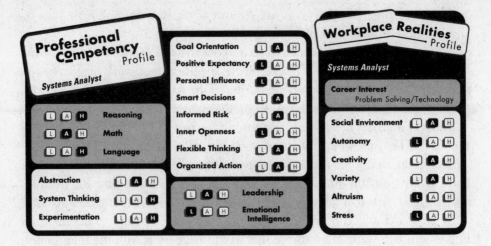

Computer software programmers write the detailed instructions (software programs) that direct the computer in performing its functions. They create programs by separating each step of the process and writing instructions in a language the computer can follow. These instructions are then coded into conventional programming language so that users can follow them.

In most large organizations, programmers follow the instructions of systems analysts who design the original systems. Programmers then make changes to the system over time as they discover better ways to perform tasks. Programmers test their programs to ensure that they work according to the plan. If errors occur, they must debug the program (correct the mistakes). In smaller organizations, computer programmer–analysts may design software as well as program it into the computer.

Programmers are frequently divided into two large groups: *systems programmers* and *applications programmers*.

Systems programmers design, develop, and maintain the software that controls the operation of an entire computer system. They revise the instructions that other programmers key into the system—regulating, for example, how quickly or efficiently the central processing unit handles tasks it has been programmed to perform. They may also write the technical information manuals.

Applications programmers are those whose work is geared toward the user end of computers. They write the programs that the rest of us use on our computers at home and at work. For example, if you buy a word processing program at the local Egghead Software, it was an applications programmer (or more likely a team of them) that wrote it.

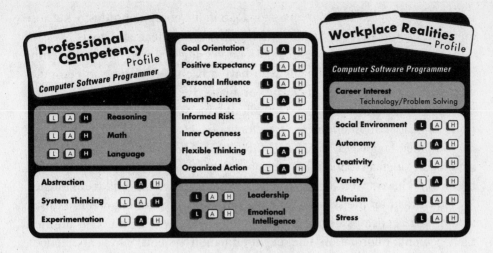

EARNING POTENTIAL

According to a 1992 study, the following were the estimated incomes of computer engineers, analysts, and programmers.

	Starting Salary	Median Salary	Experienced Salary
Computer Software Engineers	$17,000–$25,000	$42,000	$23,000–$65,000+
Systems Analysts	$25,000	$42,000	$65,500+
Computer Software Programmers	$19,000	$35,500	$58,000+

On average, **systems programmers** earn more than **applications programmers**, since system programming requires greater technical skill.

Salary growth for all computer engineers, analysts, and programmers should be considerably better than the rate of inflation.

EDUCATIONAL REQUIREMENTS

From the birth of the computer age, its acolytes have come from all walks of life and all educational backgrounds. While this will still hold true, more formalized educational paths have been developed.

Computer professionals have widely varying qualifications. There is no universally accepted way to prepare for a job in the computer industry because employers' preferences depend on their individual projects and goals.

A four-year undergraduate degree is increasingly a prerequisite for entry. Many employers seek applicants who have a bachelor's degree in computer engineering, electrical engineering, or math. Regardless of college major, prospective computer professionals should have familiarity with programming languages (most employers look for applicants with knowledge of a range of computer languages, such as FORTRAN, COBOL, and C++, fourth-generation languages, and other object-oriented programming languages) and they should have a working knowledge of computer systems and technologies.

A good road for the **systems analyst/computer software engineer** to follow would be a bachelor's degree in computer science with a minor in business management. Information science, information systems, physical sciences, applied mathematics, and data processing are other college majors for computer analysts and engineers. A graduate degree in engineering is also helpful. Computer engineers and analysts with aspirations to rise in their profession should certainly consider a graduate degree.

It is not unheard of for a high school graduate without a college degree, or a junior college graduate, to find a job in the **computer programming** world, starting as an applications programmer trainee and working her or his way up. But while more than a couple of major companies today were founded and run by college dropouts, these very same companies have some of the strictest educational requirements for their technical staff. In the computer world of the future, programmers will almost certainly be required to hold a bachelor's degree in computer science or information systems. In addition, experts recommend they complete courses in management information systems (MIS), accounting, inventory control, and business. And it is increasingly unlikely that a programmer with less than a bachelor's degree would be promoted to software engineer or systems analyst. The lesson here is that for the next few years you might still get your foot in the door despite some scholastic shortcomings, but subsequently you are going to need to pursue a degree to maximize your ongoing employability and foster your professional growth.

Technological advances come so rapidly that continual study is necessary to keep skills up to date. As a result, continuing education is available through employers, hardware and software vendors, colleges and universities, private training institutions, and professional seminars. A broad educational base kept current is the single greatest guarantee for a successful career in the computer industry.

For job seekers interested in a further competitive advantage, the Institute for Certification of Computing Professionals offers the designation Certified Systems Professional (C.S.P.) to those who have four years of experience and who pass a core examination plus exams in two speciality areas. Similarly, the Quality Assurance Institute awards the designation Certified Quality Analysis (C.Q.A.) to those who meet requirements for education and experience, pass an exam, and endorse a code of ethics.

Increasingly, as the computer industry becomes more service-oriented, communication skills—which in the past were a reputed shortcoming in computer industry—are becoming an important attribute. So in addition to the formal educational requirements, computer professionals should have good communications skills and like working with ideas and people. The most successful computer professionals tend to be those who think logically and are focused, patient, self-motivated, and creatively analytical.

A DAY IN THE LIFE

Systems analysts, computer software engineers, and **computer software programmers** usually work in clean, comfortable offices or laboratories and generally work a standard forty-hour week. However, they are often required to work overtime under pressure of a deadline or an emergency. In order to modify programs they may be required to report to work either before or after the scheduled workday for computer users. Consultants in the field may have to travel to examine the systems they need to modify or replace.

Systems analysts and **software engineers** do not work under much direct supervision but do work closely with others. **Programmers** often work under the supervision of systems analysts.

The physical demands are modest, with a great deal of time spent sitting at desks and computer keyboards. These are jobs very hard on the back, the buns, the circulation, and the eyes. Those who work closely with computers over the long term also face the potential of a whole new series of health-related complaints of the carpal tunnel syndrome variety. (Carpal tunnel syndrome is an ailment of the wrist and hand that develops from overuse associated with keyboard work.)

JOB GROWTH

A recent study found that **systems analysts** held approximately 666,000 jobs; **computer software engineers**, 211,000 jobs; and **computer software programmers**, 555,000 jobs in the United States. These positions were primarily in

HELP WANTED COMPUTER PROFESSIONALS

Software Engineer
Design programming tools, knowledge-based systems, or computer equipment, devices, and games. Specify the files and records to be accessed by the system, design the processing steps, and design the format for the output that will meet the user's needs. Make data inaccessible to unauthorized users. Coordinate tests and ensure the system performs as planned. Prepare specifications, work diagrams, and structure charts for computer programmers to follow and then work with them to debug the system. Salary Range: $17,000–$65,000+.

Systems Analyst
Work with users to develop and implement hardware and software. Oversee installation and setup of the hardware and help integrate the new system. Prepare the specifications, charts, and diagrams that programmers use to input information into the system. Run tests and design modifications necessary for the system's smooth operation. Assist with purchasing new systems. Salary Range: $25,000–$65,500+.

Systems Programmer
Design, develop, and maintain the software that controls the operation of an entire computer sys-

computer and data processing service firms, insurance companies, financial institutions, colleges and universities, computer and electronics equipment manufacturers, and government agencies. The largest group of programmers worked in data processing service organizations, including companies that write and sell software and companies that provide engineering and management services.

These occupations are considered to be some of the fastest-growing for the turn of the century. *Money* magazine named **computer systems analyst** #1 in its list of the top one hundred jobs for 1994, and the Department of Labor Statistics lists it in the top ten fastest-growing jobs through the year 2005. It is estimated that the need for **software engineers** will double, and that 150,000 **computer programming** positions will open over the next 10 years. Growth should be particularly strong in the areas of *data communications* and *multimedia* and the evolving field of *artificial intelligence*.

The driving force behind the anticipated growth in this field will be business competition. As users develop more sophisticated knowledge of computers, they become more aware of the machine's potential and are better able to suggest operations that will increase their own productivity and that of their organization. The need to design computer networks that will facilitate the sharing of information will be a major factor in the rising demand for computer analysts, engineers, and programmers. A greater emphasis on problem definition, analysis tem. Revise the instructions that other programmers key into the system. May write technical information manuals. Salary Range: $19,000–$58,000+.

Applications Programmer

Create and write computer programs for users. Update the in-place system. Test programs to ensure smooth operation. Debugging of program often necessary. Salary Range: $19,000–$58,000+.

and implementation will guarantee a higher demand for computer specialists. In addition, falling prices for computers are helping to convince even the smallest of small businesses to computerize their operations, further stimulating demand for these workers.

Despite the fact that many more people are entering the field, the number of advanced degree recipients has been growing at a slower rate than the market needs, so job opportunities will be very good for computer professionals who hold advanced degrees in their specific field. The reports of a downturn in overall job growth in the computer industry are misleading, because the field will merely experience a slowdown from the initial astounding boom and days of rapid exponential growth. There are few areas in industry that will grow as quickly during the next decade as the area of computer technology. So even job candidates with a bachelor's degree in a related field will find a good job market. Since the projections for growth in this field are so positive, it is likely that there will be considerable competition as college students increasingly choose computer science as their major, and caution should be exercised in becoming overspecialized in a single area, as flexibility and adaptability are key to maintaining employability.

One general business trend that is affecting employment stability is the growing number of temporary employees in the field. Many businesses are retaining them on a project basis: a project may take a few months or a few years to complete, but its completion eliminates the need for the specialist on permanent payroll. This booming outsourcing trend is a business unto itself, and many computer and business professionals move out of corporations and into the professional computer service industry. These professionals often become known as *systems integrators*. And as these experienced programmers transfer to management or systems analyst positions in data processing service firms, software houses, and computer consulting businesses, the turnover will create a good number of job openings for new **programmers**.

As technology needs change, and as more corporations increasingly require the most advanced forms of data processing and computing, the need for **systems analysts** will steadily rise. **Systems analysts** also will be in continuous demand to make changes in business systems that will keep costs down. There is little threat of redundancy as we have just scratched the surface of technology's enormous potential. Developments in the field do not eliminate the need for specialists; they increase it. And as international and domestic competition continues to increase, both factories and offices will need greater telecommunications and information-sharing technology, effective office and factory automation, and increased scientific research; these organizations will all require systems analysts with superior knowledge of the most advanced and sophisticated computer programming technology and the use of CASE (computer assisted software engineering) tools.

People who have the technical skills necessary to develop sophisticated software and who like the challenge of working under pressure will do extremely well in this occupation. People who do not work well under extreme pressure should be warned, though, that **systems analysis** is a high-energy field that often requires long hours and intense commitment to achieving an end.

Opportunities for **computer software engineers** are expected to grow at such a fast rate over the next ten years that the number of jobs will more than double. There are very few occupations that offer such excellent opportunities for growth: if total jobs will double, then the number of middle and top management jobs will also increase, contrary to the trend in most occupations.

Prospects in **programming** will blossom over the next few years, especially in the areas of *multimedia systems, imaging technology, artificial intelligence,* and *business applications.* However, the competition will be stiff and a well-rounded education to ensure flexibility will be advantageous to job seekers. Computer programming is a challenging job that provides many opportunities for employees to advance within a company or venture into self-employment as a consultant. Many computer programmers eventually reach supervisory positions, and then go on to management posts.

Computer professionals must be aware that the real threat of obsolescence in the field is failure to remain current with changes in technology. Because such changes occur so rapidly and in so many fields, analysts, engineers, and programmers are forced to specialize simply to keep pace with others in their own niche. For this reason, although businesses will require in-house computer experts, consultants who can provide excellent service to companies on a contract basis may also find themselves in a good bargaining position, particularly if they have had previous experience with a large company.

INFORMATION SYSTEMS MANAGER

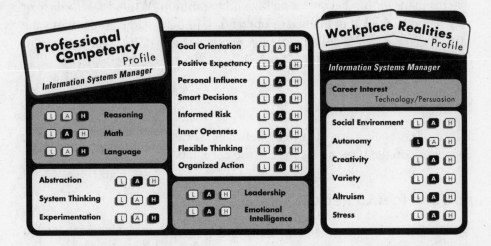

Professional Competency Profile
Information Systems Manager

	Reasoning
L A **H**	Reasoning
L **A** H	Math
L A **H**	Language

Abstraction	L **A** H
System Thinking	L A **H**
Experimentation	L **A** H

Goal Orientation	L A **H**
Positive Expectancy	L **A** H
Personal Influence	L **A** H
Smart Decisions	L **A** H
Informed Risk	L **A** H
Inner Openness	L A **H**
Flexible Thinking	L **A** H
Organized Action	L **A** H

| L **A** H | Leadership |
| L **A** H | Emotional Intelligence |

Workplace Realities Profile
Information Systems Manager

Career Interest
Technology/Persuasion

Social Environment	L **A** H
Autonomy	**L** A H
Creativity	L **A** H
Variety	L **A** H
Altruism	L **A** H
Stress	L A **H**

Information systems (IS) managers are responsible for coordinating the entire maze of an organization's information resources. They evaluate new software and hardware systems and tailor programs to help an organization use computer technology more effectively. These professionals are responsible both for understanding an organization's information needs and for keeping the company's technology up to date. They are aided in their work by software developers, systems analysts, and database managers. An IS professional also directs and coordinates the activities of computer personnel, and designs company computer operation policies.

Information systems managers research a corporation's particular information needs, through structured analysis, data modeling, information engineering, mathematical model building, sampling, and cost accounting. Once they have examined options on new systems and determined whether the proposed plan satisfies the organization's particular information needs, IS managers investigate whether the plan is user-friendly, secure, and financially feasible. They may decide to adopt additional hardware and supplementary software, and they may then be responsible for integrating the system with all the rest of the corporation's technological tools. The continued maintenance and update of the information network then becomes their primary function.

IS managerial professionals are responsible for the hiring and training of all the systems analysts, programmers, and technical staff in the information systems/data processing departments, and serve as the direct link between the corporate board and the IS/DP department. With the increased significance that information technology has for the success of a corporation, information systems manager has become a highly visible position. While an *MIS director* may report to the VP of finance or operations, in many large corporations the MIS director is now entitled *chief information officer* (CIO) and may report directly to the chief executive officer.

EARNING POTENTIAL

MIS professionals earn anywhere between $22,000 and $100,000 a year, depending on the size and location of the corporation.

EDUCATIONAL REQUIREMENTS

Anyone interested in a career as an IS manager should obtain at least a bachelor's degree in business management with a subspecialty in computer science, information science, computer information systems, or data processing. This degree will get you in the door at ground level, which is important because information systems managers are often promoted from within, usually after having some experience as a systems analyst or database manager. An employee may also have gained sufficient experience as a computer programmer or as an auditor in an accounting department, specializing in accounting systems development, to be considered for promotion into MIS. Employers almost always seek people with experience in analyzing computer systems' effectiveness in relation to both the needs of the people who use them and the corporation, and usually hire candidates with some grounding in business management or another closely related field in the business environment. Additionally, they often prefer applicants with degrees in computer science or engineering—the more advanced the better—or another related field. Scientific organizations prefer applicants with backgrounds in physical sciences, applied mathematics, or engineering.

Generally speaking, prospective IS professionals should have familiarity with programming languages, and a broad knowledge of computer systems and technologies. They must have an excellent sense of the machines with which their organization operates, and they must be able to understand the ideas brought to them by systems analysts, software developers, and computer software engineers.

As communications technologies change, IS managers must remain up to date with technological advances. It is highly recommended that they pursue

---

HELP WANTED
INFORMATION SYSTEMS
MANAGER

Coordinate organization's information resources. Evaluate new software and hardware systems, and tailor programs to help organization use computer technology more effectively. Understand organization's information needs and keep the technology up to date. Direct and coordinate activities of the computer personnel, and design company computer operation policies. Serve as the direct link between the corporate board and the IS/DP department. Salary Range: $22,000–$100,000+.

---

continuing education opportunities offered by employers, hardware and software vendors, colleges and universities, or private training institutions.

A DAY IN THE LIFE

MIS professionals usually work a forty-hour week in comfortable executive offices. They all work overtime and weekend hours to meet deadlines. They must remain aware of all new developments in computer use and software evolution, in order to find ways to save their employer money while providing easy-to-use technology for the entire company. The job can require extensive travel to stay abreast of technological change.

JOB GROWTH

Information systems managers are generally employed by public and private corporations, government agencies, computer and electronics manufacturers, insurance companies, banks, and universities.

Everyone agrees that employment of IS professionals will grow at a *much faster* than average rate compared to overall anticipated employment growth over the next ten years—although no one is prepared to commit to how much!

As international and domestic competition continues to increase, both factories and offices will need greater telecommunications technology, information sharing, problem analysis, and computer science research, and these organizations will all require IS professionals to direct their technological growth.

USER SUPPORT ANALYST

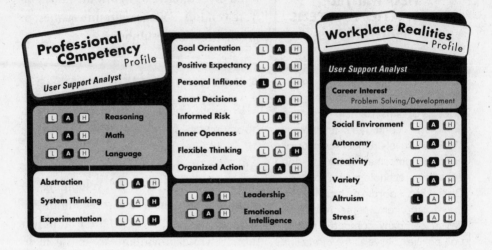

In the 1990s the use of computers and their attendant technologies, in both the home and the office, has increased to the point where the computer has become a standard piece of equipment in much the same way as the telephone. Along with this revolution in the ways we communicate and gather, process, and use information comes a need for technical support, and thus the creation of an entirely new occupation: *user support analyst*.

User support analysts assist computer users in resolving problems they may encounter with computer software and hardware. In person, or in most cases over the telephone, they talk the user through specific procedures in order to discover the source of the problem and attempt to correct it. For example, the copy of Microsoft Word you bought for your computer doesn't seem to be working as you'd hoped: you call the manufacturer's user support number, and then wait for forty-five minutes until it's your turn to present your problem to the user support analyst, who solves your problem with a quick word of advice or patiently works with you on the phone for an hour until your needs are met. If a system glitch or a recurring problem is discovered, the user support analyst will notify programmers, engineers, or software/hardware vendors and recommend changes.

Typically, when a large software developer introduces a program, the user support analysts receive thousands of telephone calls asking for assistance with the intricacies of the new application. User support analysts provide feedback to their employers on frequently asked questions, so that updated versions of the program will eliminate common problems.

Additional responsibilities may include testing software and hardware to evaluate "user-friendliness"; writing hardware and software evaluation manuals and procedures; developing training and user-aid materials, such as exercises and visual displays; training users on software and hardware or recommending outside contractors to provide training; and installing microcomputers, software, and peripheral equipment.

Some analysts also work as in-house consultants. They may be involved with office automation feasibility studies and may focus their area of specialization according to the type of software, computer language, or computer operating system with which they are most familiar.

EARNING POTENTIAL

The median annual salary for user support analysts is approximately $40,000. Beginners (usually the folks you'll talk to on the phone at the software vendor's 800 number) can expect to earn starting salaries in a range between $18,350 and $29,000, while more experienced analysts (typically the folks working as senior in-house or business-to-business consultants) can earn from $25,000 to $58,000 and above. Salary growth is projected to be better than the rate of inflation.

EDUCATIONAL REQUIREMENTS

A four-year undergraduate degree is increasingly a prerequisite for any job in the computer industry. Many employers seek applicants who have a bachelor's degree in computer science, information science, computer information systems, or data processing. Regardless of college major, employers look for people who are technologically adapted and who have a broad knowledge of computer systems and their attendant technologies. However, it is a job in which communication skills are at least as important as technology skills; put the two together, and you should be able to get your foot in the door without a four-year degree.

User support analysts should be able to think logically, have excellent communication skills, and like working with ideas and people. A great deal of patience, concentration, and attention to detail is a necessity for a successful user support analyst.

Technical advances are rapid, and most user support analysts keep abreast of changes by reading trade magazines and attending trade shows and training seminars regularly, and by taking continuing education courses

> ### HELP WANTED
> ### USER SUPPORT ANALYST
>
> Resolve problems a user may encounter with computer software and hardware. Talk user through specific procedures to discover the sources of the problem and correct them. Notify programmers, engineers and/or software/hardware vendors about common problems and recommend changes.
> Salary Range: $18,350–$58,000.

made available through employers, hardware and software vendors, colleges and universities, and private training institutions.

A DAY IN THE LIFE

User support analysts usually work in offices. These are typically clean, comfortable, and relatively pleasant surroundings. Many user support analysts are employed by software manufacturers. They work in large rooms with colleagues and take telephone calls from purchasers who have questions about the operation of a particular piece of software.

The physical demands are modest, with long periods of time spent talking on the telephone and sitting in front of a computer terminal typing on a keyboard. As is the case with most computer careers, user support analysts are susceptible to eyestrain, back discomfort, and hand and wrist problems.

User support analysts work under little direct supervision, but they do work in cooperation with others. They usually work forty-hour weeks, with occasional overtime, night, or weekend hours.

A great deal of patience and concentration is required of user support analysts when dealing with the problems of the many people coming fresh to computer usage without any technical knowledge of the hardware or software.

JOB GROWTH

Job opportunites for user support analysts are expected to grow faster than the average for all occupations; statistically, actual numbers are listed with the growth of systems analysts (see page 213). The growth will come mainly as a response to the explosive growth in the use of computers and the booming entertainment and educational software market. Additional opportunities will arise due to a high turnover rate, since workers will burn out or move into managerial or higher technical positions or other occupations. This is an excellent starting point for a career in the booming information services industry.

A career as a user support analyst will remain an attractive occupational option well into the next century. For entry-level employees seeking a challenging and evolving position in the computer field, this position will provide abundant opportunities, as the explosive growth in the use of computers will continue, and as information services and support will remain an all-important ingredient.

COMPUTER SERVICE TECHNICIAN

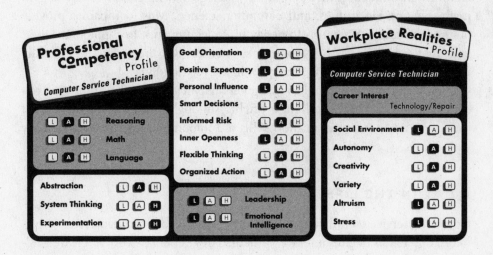

Also known as *data communication technicians, data processing equipment repairers,* and *computer machine repairers,* computer service technicians are the knights in shining armor who can fix the unfixable just as you are ready to tear your hair out follicle by follicle and throw your computer terminal through the window. They run diagnostic tests to identify why your user-friendly machine is being uncooperative, and determine whether it is a software or hardware problem (who cares . . . just fix it!). They use hand tools and test instruments to make the necessary adjustments, and replace or repair defective parts: splicing wires, connecting cables, dusting motherboards, and usually insisting on sharing every detail, as if the information will ever have any practical application in your technologically devoid lifestyle. They generally close the deal by filling out service report forms and presenting you with an enormous bill for their time. However, when you sit down to your newly functioning life mate and reglue your hair back on, you will sigh and truly appreciate that these technicians are worth their weight in gold.

EARNING POTENTIAL

Computer service technicians can earn anywhere from $18,000 to $42,500 and above, depending on experience, the company they work for, and the type of equipment they repair.

EDUCATIONAL REQUIREMENTS

Most computer service technicians have graduated from a vocational school, technical institute, or junior/community college, having completed courses in math, physics, electronics, and computer science. Most companies provide on-the-job training programs to newly hired technicians, to supplement their education and tailor it to particular specialties. Repairers must continually update their education, as technology changes so rapidly.

Computer technicians should have good analytical skills, the ability to concentrate, patience, and excellent eyesight. Although they generally work with little supervision, communication skills are important when dealing directly with clients.

A DAY IN THE LIFE

Computer service technicians are usually employed by manufacturers, wholesalers, or retailers of computer equipment. They generally work in clean, well-lit, air-conditioned computer service centers and manufacturing plants. They work forty-hour weeks, with overtime or odd hours sometimes required when they are called in for emergency repairs.

Some of these technicians may work for service organizations, which make office or house calls to repair computer equipment. The conditions will obviously vary depending on the location of the office: some may be large and comfortable, others cramped and noisy. Computer service technicians must have the ability to focus on the job at hand, despite the bustle surrounding them.

JOB GROWTH

The future is very bright for professionals trained in this field. Our society and businesses are more dependent than ever upon computers—a fact that becomes only too obvious when one of them breaks down. There are currently approximately 86,000 computer service technicians on American payrolls—a number expected to increase by nearly 15,000 new positions by the year 2005.

HELP WANTED
**COMPUTER SERVICE
TECHNICIAN**

Run diagnostics to identify software and hardware problems. Use test instruments and hand tools to adjust and repair defective parts. Requires people skills and analytical skills. Overtime and working odd hours for emergency repairs often required. Salary Range: $18,000–$42,500.

A computer repairer with an entrepreneurial streak could easily find a niche launching a privately run service business in this industry. Computer service technicians may also find themselves specializing in computer programming or systems analysis; they may even become successful sales representatives of computer equipment. There are many directions in which this career could lead you, and certainly there is room for growth in this booming area of computer expertise.

Business and Professional Services

The Business and Professional Services section is an amalgamation of financial services plus human resources, law, communications, sales and marketing, travel, food service, and support services. In the pages to come I'll address each industry in detail.

Financial Services

Financial Services includes four once entirely separate professions: Banking, Securities, Accounting, and Insurance. I have grouped them together because of the increasing homogenization of the four industries: each is developing products and services that were once the exclusive domain of another.

Financial Services once meant solely securities firms that trade stocks on behalf of their clients by taking companies public, and acting as merger and acquisitions agents. Now these firms are entering others' domains. The insurance industry faces encroachment by traditional financial service and mutual fund companies, which are now offering insurance. Regulatory changes allow banks to underwrite and sell insurance policies, but the banking industry itself is facing competition from firms like General Motors and AT&T, which are now selling credit cards—once the exclusive territory of the banks.

Insurance companies are making sorties of their own, offering competitive real estate and securities services. Simultaneously they are going into more collaborative marketing partnerships with banks, securities houses, and overseas insurers. Meanwhile the banks are now trading in securities, offering insurance, and developing whole new product lines of services in direct competition with the brokerage houses. In short, what were once four separate and dignified and secure professions are now rapidly becoming one vast financial free-for-all.

However, in a volatile job market this is *good* news, because it geometrically increases the number of places you can pursue a meaningful career in the finance profession.

BANKING

Fierce competition from each other and from everyone else in the voracious financial community defines the industry as banks reinvent themselves. The trend is toward sales- and marketing-oriented professionals. Regardless of your job title, the banking profession expects you to know how the money gets earned, and in this and every other profession it's the same: someone sells something to someone.

The banking industry is still restructuring and downsizing, and will continue to "aerobicize" old-school bankers out of existence. However, the industry is so big that plenty of jobs open up simply through promotions, job and career changes, and retirement.

INSIDER'S VIEW OF BANKING

Although competition will continue to play a role in the banking industry, and consolidation will lead to unemployment for many professionals, there is some good news.

For example, Bruce C. Anderson, president of Jamestown, New York–based Career Advancement Publications (their monthly newsletters include *Finance & Account Jobs Report* and *Sales & Marketing Jobs Report*), foresees dramatically higher rates of savings due to the aging demographics of our society and widespread uncertainty about the Social Security system. Also, because there will be an increase in larger financial institutions as banks consolidate, Anderson predicts that professionals with strong organizational and team-building skills will be in demand.

SECURITIES

As we noted earlier, securities firms trade stocks on behalf of their clients by taking companies public, and by acting as merger and acquisitions agents.

However, whereas trading stocks was once the exclusive province of the securities industry, now other firms—such as insurance companies—are entering this increasingly competitive arena. The securities industry in the next decade will be, as always, best suited to those who have high tolerance for risk and much stamina.

INSIDER'S VIEW OF SECURITIES

According to leading industry analyst Anderson, "The securities industry has historically been a volatile place to work, and there is no reason to believe this will change. Periods of great growth and huge profitability can very quickly turn to periods of little growth and vast unemployment. You need to make your money when times are good, with the full realization that these times may not last."

He acknowledges that a cutting-edge job in the securities industry, portfolio manager, has almost unlimited income potential. But he cautions, "Few manage to stay on top for long. It's a risky business; in fact, risk *is* your business. You can't rest on last year's results, and one bad quarter's performance can mean your job." He also offers, "You don't just walk in off the street and say, 'Make me a portfolio manager.' The starting point is usually as a low-level securities analyst or research assistant."

ACCOUNTING

Getting the right digits in the bottom right-hand corner of the quarterly profit and loss statement might not sound glamorous to some, but money makes the world go round, and accountants are experiencing one of the rosiest futures of any profession in the new world of work. In fact, accounting now permeates almost every company in an industry. For in business, all that really matters is the bottom line, and that is the accountant's jurisdiction.

Consequently, the profession will generate 300,000 new jobs over the next decade. This is attributable to the natural growth of industry through entrepreneurial endeavor and through the complexities of accounting in an economy which increasingly emphasizes foreign trade.

Accountants can pursue their profession in the industry of their choice; for example, an accountant working in banking may decide to develop mainstream banking experience, or she or he may decide to increase mobility by pursuing opportunities opened up by the homogenization of the financial services industry. Those who have studied languages, international management, tax law, accounting, auditing, and so on can pursue meaningful careers in the high-reward areas of international and management accounting, tax accounting, and auditing.

Accounting is not only a good bet to maintain career buoyancy, because it offers endless opportunities to segue from one industry to another, but it also offers an equal panorama of entrepreneurial opportunity, and the independence that path can provide.

INSIDER'S VIEW OF ACCOUNTING

Insiders share an optimistic vision: there will be a greater need for financial professionals in the years ahead than ever before. Increased business activity during the next decade will mean additional financial transactions. And that will translate into more jobs and higher-prestige positions for corporate treasurers and controllers, financial planners, loan officers, auditors, and other highly skilled finance workers.

According to Max Messmer, chairman and CEO of Robert Half International (as quoted in Robert Half/Accountemps' 1996 Salary Guide), the skill areas and specialities most likely to be in demand include: "[a] combination of public accounting and private industry experience; accounting professionals with SEC reporting experience; accountants with backgrounds in their respective industries; entry-level positions in accounts payable, accounts receivable, and payroll; cost accountants; tax accountants; and business consultants."

Diane O'Meally, executive vice president of accountants on call [sic], believes that clients' needs are changing, and they're looking for those with more business and nontechnical skills. "They're looking for more than just a number cruncher," O'Meally stresses. "They need someone with leadership skills who can operate as part of a team of executives to bring a company forward."

She also cites education and certification as important qualifications, as does Robert Half, who adds, "Companies are seeking candidates with C.P.A. and C.M.A. credentials, as well as a strong educational background and work ethic."

As Stewart Libes, president and CEO of Accountants on Call, points out, "There's always going to be a need for accountants, but there will still be competition for the top jobs."

INSURANCE

The insurance industry has traditionally provided retirement and savings programs for many Americans. However, if people continue to invest in mutual funds, this could put the pinch on the insurance industry. But even if that happens, it's only going to be a gnat's bite on an elephant's bottom; the enormous insurance industry will still be one of the biggest and most stable industries in the new world of work.

The proliferation of fax machines, entertainment systems, camcorders, and other at-home business and leisure equipment spells good news for the industry. As we buy high-ticket items, we'll have to insure them. New technology, combined with our increasing expendable income, will provide an endless supply of things that need to be insured.

Other factors behind the insurance industry's growth include women's ever-increasing need for life and disability insurance, brought about by their mass entry into the workforce; the complexity of the modern business world, which has increased demand for such types of insurance as product liability and pollution liability; and skyrocketing health and legal costs, which are pumping up sales of health and prepaid legal insurance policies.

The aging baby boom population is increasing the opportunities for selling health insurance, along with opportunities in financial and retirement planning services. Shifts like this always increase opportunities in other areas, too. In this instance, the need for new products and services will increase the need for insurance professionals to understand and learn how to sell them, which in turn increases the need for trainers within the insurance industry. This is good news for career changers, like a teacher who wants to get out of the public school system and who learns the insurance industry jargon and how it works.

With more than two million workers, the insurance industry is made up of two segments: the large insurance carriers that we all know, such as Metlife, and Blue Cross and Blue Shield, and everybody else who works in insurance, including the smaller companies, agents, brokers, and others. Although most jobs in the industry are created by insurance carriers, the balance is shifting. Until now, insurance carriers employed twice as many people as any other segment of the industry. Automation will temper insurance carriers' hiring, because fewer people will be needed to review applications and process claims. By comparison, other insurance workers, especially small-company employees who have direct contact with the customer base, are less likely to be affected by automation. Actuaries (who predict the probability of accidents, deaths, and so on, and what they will cost us monetarily) enjoy one of the fastest-growing jobs in the insurance industry, as well as in the whole economy. The Bureau of Labor Statistics expects the number of actuarial positions to grow almost 40 percent by 2005.

And because the industry is aggressively expanding its international business, with Europe and Asia as the main targets, this means increased opportunity and mobility for the bilingual and culturally aware.

INSIDER'S VIEW OF THE INSURANCE INDUSTRY

The insurance industry has seen hard times over the past few years. In the 1980s, companies sold a lot of insurance but made little money. Profit margins were small and competition was fierce. Insurance companies alternately undercut each other's rates and increased their own prices as they sought to survive intense competition. Like other fields, the insurance industry suffered downsizing, closings, and mergers.

Industry insiders agree that, in the next decade, the competition will continue. Also, over the next few years, nontraditional sources, such as mutual fund vendors, will compete with insurance companies. But for all its ups and downs, the insurance industry will continue to be enormous. We will buy more insurance than we ever did before, because we'll engage in a greater number of business transactions, sue one another more often, and face higher health and legal costs.

KEEP THE CUSTOMER SATISFIED

To beat the competition, insurance companies are going to shift their priorities back to where they belong; the customer's needs, once again, will come first. Says Sue Zeider, claims, customer relations and legislation manager of the Los Angeles–based Farmers Insurance Group of Companies, "Consumers will want more service and convenience. [They] need to have a single point of contact for all facets of the coverage and claim"—although this need may conflict with the increasing complexity of coverages and claims handling.

WHERE IS THE GROWTH?

While Zeider expects job stability in the insurance industry to be no better than in most other industries, she does predict there will be great growth, especially in entrepreneurial opportunities. Jane Seago, executive vice president of the National Association of Insurance Women, concurs. She emphasizes that many people will "open and manage their own agency of special interest."

In insurance, as in all industries, you should look at your job as an opportunity for on-the-job training for your own entrepreneurial ventures down the road.

Sue Zeider continues, "The insurance profession is so broad an individual can try various jobs within it such as sales, claims, risk management, regulation, actuarial, etc." She believes that, in the insurance industry overall, "the growing areas are in the alternatives to formal insurance, such as self-insured administrators and risk managers." Also, she foresees, "Jobs in claims will always be around, although the [particular] aspects of the job vary and change rapidly." Seago calls claims fraud investigation a "cutting-edge job."

Seago points out, "Growth potential abounds in the insurance industry, especially in the sales area." But she adds, "There are many, many people vying for good jobs."

For professional growth in the insurance industry, Zeider thinks you need computer skills. "The less obvious answer is a commitment to always learning. The insurance industry and the workplace are changing so rapidly, to succeed, you must be willing to constantly learn new skills and broaden your knowledge." Seago agrees with her. "Many states—in fact, most states—require continuing education to maintain certain insurance licenses." This bodes well for training opportunities in this industry.

"A good basic business background is always useful, but it should be tempered with substantial exposure to the social sciences and humanities. These disciplines help open eyes to differing cultures and a greater sense of ease with diversity," Seago continues.

Seago also offers, "Ambitious and motivated people, people able to set goals for themselves and discipline themselves to reach those goals, often do well in insurance." And, she stresses, "A strong desire—almost a sense of obligation—to help the customer is also an indicator of success, especially in the sales field."

A GLIMPSE INTO THE FUTURE

When asked what workplace changes she predicts for the next decade, Seago responds, "There will be an increasing focus on fraud: its identification, investigation, and elimination. Fraud simply exercises too great a drain on industry resources not to invest in cutting it down to size." She adds, "I also think there will be greater emphasis on niche marketing: developing products and marketing them to smaller and more specialized sections of the population. Finally, I look for an increase in professional liability products of all kinds . . . very important in these litigious times."

INSIDER'S VIEW OF FINANCIAL SERVICES

THE VALUE OF AGE AND EXPERIENCE

All industries are affected by the economic cycle, and the financial services professions are both the first to experience the effects of a downswing in the economy, and the first to benefit from the subsequent upswing. Not surprisingly, sales-oriented jobs have the best overall potential. What is surprising is that this is one industry where there is a trend to hire *older* salespeople, because of their professional maturity, business experience, and a wider network of contacts who are in their prime moneymaking years, and are either potential customers themselves or decision makers within their organizations.

BOOTING UP COMPUTER KNOWLEDGE

Whatever other qualifications a financial professional has, computer knowledge is a key to continued employment. Libes of accountants on call believes that workers will "really have to have a knowledge of how to utilize computer systems and office automation systems. Sophisticated jobs will require an ability to handle automation." The move from mainframe systems to PC-based computing is in full swing. As a result, there is a growing need for professionals who can help companies transition from traditional mainframe and legacy systems to client/server environments.

GETTING HIRED

There has also been a shift in the finance industry toward a greater reliance on a contingency workforce. Diane O'Meally remembers that, in the past, "You would send in a candidate who had 75 percent of the needed qualifications to a potential client, and he or she would probably get hired." Today, she says, "People have to be conservative in their hiring practices. They don't want to settle. They're hiring a lot of temps until they can find an A-1 candidate instead of a B-1 candidate."

Human Resources

The human resources (H/R) area is projected to grow by one-third over the next ten years. There will be plenty of jobs for trainers and employment interviewers, and all people in popular human resources jobs will keep training high on their own personal "to-do" lists to maintain employability in—yes, you've got it—another highly competitive field.

Training people and keeping them gainfully employed will become a bigger challenge—and a more profitable one—in the decade ahead, with the following questions to be answered: How much education and training will we need? What will students of all ages—including members of the workforce—need to learn, and how will they learn? How often will they need retraining? How permanent will any job be, and how flexible and extensive will their skill sets have to be for individuals to prosper in those jobs?

Because the entire way we do business in America is undergoing such fundamental change, it is not surprising that the human resources area will experience growth and a newfound importance. The shortage of technologically adapted workers means that finding and maintaining a competent workforce has real impact on the bottom line. It's human resources that plans and executes the corporation's expansion efforts, and it's human resources that analyzes and executes the downsizings. H/R people are involved in employee selection, training, OSHA (Occupational Safety and Health Administration), and equal opportunity compliance, wages and benefits, and union relations. Whatever it is that a company does to generate its revenue, it is the H/R function to see that the people, systems, and procedures are in place so that the revenue stream reaches optimum flow at minimum cost. The H/R function in a corporation does this partly in-house and partly by outsourcing some functions to the staffing industry.

HUMAN RESOURCES SERVICES OR STAFFING INDUSTRY

The staffing industry consists of employment agencies, executive recruiters, outplacement specialists, and a consultancy for every human resource function under the sun. Temporary help companies are rapidly becoming a mainstay of the economy, and have been darlings of the stock market for some years now as industry has shifted toward a contingency workforce.

Employment interviewers, in both temporary and permanent placement agencies, will have diverse qualifications depending on what type of workers their agencies provide. Companies that supply administrative workers, such as secretaries and word processors, will often hire staff who have professional experience in those areas; those that provide accountants, engineers, and others with specialized degrees may hire interviewers who themselves have experience and degrees related to those fields. Many staffing industry consultants work on some kind of incentive-based pay system. They may advance to managerial positions, and pursue a traditional corporate career path within the industry's larger employers; what was once a mom-and-pop industry now sports billion-dollar giants that support plenty of opportunity for career growth.

Human resources work on either side of the desk is well respected and decently rewarded—excellently rewarded if you survive to become a successful headhunter. On the corporate side, senior H/R people are now a common sight at board meetings and in the executive dining room, and the 1990s has seen the first wave of H/R professionals reaching CEO positions. On the staffing side, such events are even more commonplace.

Human resources has also proved to be an especially hospitable environment for women and minorities, many of whom already hold top positions.

INSIDER'S VIEW OF THE HUMAN RESOURCES INDUSTRY

Company mergers, closings, and layoffs are never good news. Yet there are professionals whose careers are, in fact, fueled by these events: outplacement specialists. These are the people who are paid to be helpful when the bomb is dropped on working people.

But that doesn't mean human resources professionals themselves are immune to downsizing. On the contrary: insiders will tell you that, when a company is cutting back, the human resources department is often among the first to find its functions outsourced. So stability isn't on the plate, even for those who work in personnel, in the next decade.

REPLACED BY COMPUTERS?

Laurence J. Stybel, of Stybel Peabody Lincolnshire, Massachusetts's oldest senior executive career consulting firm, believes that technology is already affecting generalists in human resources, and in some cases, replacing human resources professionals with networked personnel manuals. "If you want to fire someone now, instead of asking a human resources generalist how to do this, you can go to a computer and ask." He explains the difference between human resources generalists and specialists this way: "Generalists are such people as employee relations managers and vice presidents of human resources. Specialists might focus on compensation, benefits, or training." He does say that there appear to be growth opportunities for "people with five or less years of general experience." But he adds that, whereas in the past, when you'd had five years of experience, you had to decide whether you wanted to be a generalist or a specialist, "today, people are going to shuttle back and forth between being generalists and specialists." For example, a vice president of human resources who has corporate communications experience might be laid off, and then reposition himself as a benefits specialist.

Stybel suggests, "It's important for a human resources person to realize that, 'at some point in my career, I'm going to become a specialist.' " To become a specialist, he explains, you have to "stay in touch with one discipline and be on top of it." Thus he urges human resources professionals who are working for a company to broaden their responsibilities: "Push to redefine your role to include other things, such as employee communication, community relations, or total quality management."

Cocoa, Florida–based human resources professional Debbie Button believes that computers will work with, rather than instead of, human resources professionals. Major reengineering in the industry "will include complete computer interface with all employees. This will include terminals set up in common areas and networked with the H/R databases." She predicts, "Field-specific access will allow employees to find answers to their questions easily and privately. For example, they will have access to past evaluations, the date of the next scheduled evaluation, their tax status, and benefit information. Additionally, they will be able to enroll in classes, apply for tuition reimbursements, and post questions to the H/R staff."

Still, there are those industry insiders who take a more optimistic view of human resources' future, especially those in the H/R services industry. Bill Pate, Jr., president of Pate Resources Group, rates the growth and stability potential for human resources professionals as "Excellent. Our industry is a client-driven service industry offering solutions to the most difficult question facing all of business: who to hire."

THE CUTTING EDGE

Although it seems clear that outplacement will continue to be a growth industry within the human resources field, John Challenger, executive vice president of premier outplacement specialists Challenger, Gray & Christmas, hesitates to predict what shape outplacement might take in the future or which positions will be in most demand. But he does predict that the H/R and outplacement professionals who will be successful are those who "possess an altruistic nature, empathizing with the job seeker's dilemma while undauntedly reinforcing the importance of the aggressive finding and contacting of those who will bring the search for meaningful employment to an end."

He continues, "Unlike some professions, in which educational background is of paramount importance, in the outplacement industry the demand is directed toward those who authentically care and can help counsel others. In light of this," he concludes, "counselors and clergy are often the most viable candidates to enter the outplacement industry."

Stybel sees successful H/R professionals as those who have an understanding of "a business as a business, as opposed to a collection of individuals. This is a person who reads *The Wall Street Journal* every day and can talk to a finance person, and someone who has the fortitude to go up to the CEO and say 'This is wrong. We shouldn't fire people this way because it isn't the ethical thing to do.' " Good technicians can only go so far, Stybel believes. "It all goes back to sales, since human resources professionals are selling ideas and concepts."

Law

Law has always been a glamour profession and will probably remain so. With a growing population and increased business activity, especially in international trade, we'll need even more lawyers during the next ten years. But there is likely to be some industrywide restructuring.

Recently, law firms have come under fire for the high cost of their services. Now a whole industry is growing around helping clients get what they pay for. And many of us may soon be buying prepaid legal service plans, to counter the high price tag of counseling, or we'll be using paralegal services.

The legal profession isn't able to hold its corporate clients up to ransom quite so much as in the past, since corporate America finally began to choke on the tab for services. With a new fiscal awareness and stricter budgetary restraints, corporations are accounting for their legal dollars much more carefully. The result is that lawyers' fees are growing much more slowly than in the past. In turn, law firms are facing more competition and are likewise looking for ways to contain costs while increasing sales and profitability.

The law is an attractive profession because of the earning potential and prestige. The Bureau of Labor Statistics predicts that demand for attorneys will rise 31 percent by the year 2000. However, while there are jobs, there are also plenty of lawyers, so competition is *tough*. Once on board, those who hope to make partner had best be rainmakers, too—that's legal-speak for "bringing in business." The law has a great respect for professionals who can position and sell their services.

The changing law profession will make paralegals one of the fastest-growing jobs in the economy over the next ten years. Paralegals actually do much of lawyers' legal work and, in formulaic aspects of the legal profession (like much of real estate law), paralegals can do and are doing all of it. Some paralegals now stay in the profession for an entire career, becoming specialists in one of the hot growth areas, like litigation, trademark law, or trusts and estates. Others make the job a stepping-stone to becoming lawyers themselves, using it as a funding source for law school. Others take their legal background and make extremely effective executive assistants for movers and shakers throughout American industry. This is because an understanding of the law, and the organizational and detail skills developed in the legal profession, are assets in any business situation.

Today, competition among law firms is intensifying. Paralegal firms also compete with law firms—charging less than law firms and handling wills, name changes, uncontested divorces, and other routine tasks that have traditionally been the bread and butter of law firms. Moreover, lawyers themselves compete with other lawyers to become full partners in law firms. The process now takes at least ten years, and it will grow increasingly difficult to make the cut. New graduates compete with more established lawyers, many of whom are moving laterally rather than climbing the career ladder, and with other recent graduates for jobs and promotions.

The wide career horizons for paralegals are available for lawyers, too. Many who graduate from law school can find exciting and fulfilling careers in just about any profession, simply because the training of the lawyer is so well respected, and because the type of mind that survives law school can readily handle the complexities of most business situations. In fact, many students are now entering law school with advanced degrees, such as M.B.A.s and M.D.s, to increase their marketability.

Turnover in the field is low because of the investment of time and money involved in becoming a legal professional. And despite the stress, turmoil, and long hours—many lawyers work more than sixty hours a week—lawyers have the potential to make as much money as, or more than, any professional in America today.

INSIDER'S VIEW OF THE LAW INDUSTRY

People sue, and people countersue, at the drop of a hat. Sometimes it seems as if all of life isn't as much a stage as it is a colossal courtroom.

So you might think legal professionals of all disciplines could write their own ticket, but that isn't the case. Law firms, like other businesses, are concerned with the bottom line. Many law firms are downsizing rather than hiring, which is very bad news for law school graduates who are trying to build a career in an industry that has very little turnover. So how to succeed?

TRICKS OF THE LAWYER'S TRADE

For lawyers, the key to success according to industry insiders will be to specialize. The legal arena will grow more complex, and lawyers who bring a specific knowledge set to the job will find better employment opportunities than will generalists. Strong prospects for specialization include elder law, bankruptcy and taxes, and intellectual copyright. Also, thriving industries — biotechnology, engineering, health care, and more — will increasingly offer employment to lawyers.

FORGET LAW SCHOOL

But the best news in the industry isn't about lawyers at all. It's about *paralegals*, for whom employment opportunities are expected to increase exponentially in the years ahead. According to Susan A. Kaiser, vice president and director of professional development of the Cleveland, Ohio–based National Federation of Paralegal Associations, this is largely because paralegals can provide the public with more cost-effective legal services than lawyers can.

Whereas lawyers are information users, paralegals are information providers. According to Kaiser, a two-year degree with an emphasis in paralegal studies is acceptable to employers in some markets as the minimum criterion for individuals who enter the profession. But she points out that a bachelor's degree is becoming the hiring standard in many markets: "NFPA recommends that, based upon current hiring trends, future practioners should have a four-year degree to enter the profession. Students receiving a formal paralegal education should have twenty-four semester hours or the equivalent of legal specialty courses."

She adds that, like lawyers, paralegals also will do better if they have a specialty. For example, "Many nurses have successfully made the transition working in the areas of personal injury and medical malpractice. Additionally, those with backgrounds in accounting, computer programming, taxes, law enforcement, mediation, and real estate find their specialized knowledge an asset when moving into the paralegal profession."

BEYOND A DEGREE

A degree or a specialty alone won't keep paralegals employed. In this age of technology, it will be crucial for paralegals to feel comfortable using computers. Kaiser emphasizes, "Technology is playing an important role in the paralegal profession. Those with computer knowledge are moving into quasi-management positions in law firms and corporations to assist in developing and/or refining software programs to meet the needs of legal teams in various practice areas."

A TASTE OF FREEDOM

There is another reason why paralegals need computer skills, too. Because of budgetary constraints and attempts to cut overhead, many law firms and other employers are beginning to hire paralegals on a freelance basis. Freelance paralegals will have to use available technology to link home-based businesses with the workplace environment.

Kaiser explains, "Independent paralegals are relatively new to the profession and are challenging the boundaries for the delivery of legal services. Independent paralegals often provide assistance directly to the public and offer a wide variety of services, depending on their area of expertise. Services include document preparation (also referred to as *scrivener services*), representation where permitted by court rule or statutory authority, and providing information regarding the legal system and the various pro se procedures within various courts."

WHO ARE THE SUCCESSFUL PARALEGALS?

Kaiser describes a person who finds success as a paralegal this way: "Since the law is complex and often ambiguous, a paralegal must be intelligent, with an analytical and logical mind that is able to recognize and evaluate relevant facts and legal concepts. An individual should have the ability to organize, analyze, communicate, and administer."

Interpersonal skills that best serve paralegals, according to Kaiser, include "verbal communication, relating well to various types of people who are often in distress, and resolving conflicts." Those general attributes, Kaiser declares, have proven to be the foundation for success in the paralegal field.

Media/Communications/Public Relations

MEDIA/COMMUNICATIONS

There are a handful of hot jobs in the communications and public relations field that are slated for substantial growth, and that also allow their practitioners to cross industry lines with more ease than is possible in most other professions. The biggest problem with these jobs is that, since they have wide appeal, there is enormous competition.

The next decade will see a reshaping of the entire communications industry as multimedia technology becomes commonplace. The technologies of communication include television, computers, the telephone, videoconferencing, interactive television, and traditional and electronic publishing—but these are only the beginning. It will be up to the writers and editors to make these technologies useful to the community at large, and up to the PR people to tell us how happy we feel about the new capabilities and opportunities for success and fulfillment that come with these advances.

Currently there are about a quarter of a million professional writers, journalists, editors, and people in related positions. Although the profession will grow at almost a 30 percent rate over the coming years, the allure of these positions is so strong that competition is—yes, you've got it—fierce, just as in every other profession where there are jobs worth having.

In four years, the majority of Americans will be over thirty-five years old, and that will increase the demand for special interest magazines for adult audiences. Advertising agencies will employ tens of thousands of copywriters dreaming up Budweiser commercials and the like. Corporations will have insatiable needs for newsletter, speech, report, and manual writers. At the same time, professional and trade magazines will experience unheard-of demand, and the plethora of electronic products will further increase the already hot demand for technical writers.

The need for technical writers is understandable from a quick glance at that software documentation manual—in it you will quickly see that most currently employed technical writers have English as a second language. So this field is wide open to anyone who can take technical gobbledygook, cut through the irrelevancies, and explain the necessaries in plain English.

The 75,000-strong army of journalists will continue to grow—along with the fierce competition for their desirable jobs. The major dailies all require in-field experience; which means the inexperienced journalist is more likely to begin writing for the local town newspaper than for *The Wall Street Journal*.

Those going straight into the field out of college are more likely to have degrees in communications, journalism, or liberal arts than their predecessors.

Editors, those who sometimes make writers' work readable, will see a return to happier times, as the publishing industry went through its own restructuring in the last five years. The number of editorial positions in all publishing specialities will grow. Electronic, Spanish-language, and audio publishing will be among the strongest areas of growth.

One of the fastest-growing fields, not only within publishing but in the entire communications industry, is slated to be electronic publishing. In an era where the manipulation of knowledge is paramount, certain information that may once have been enshrined only within the covers of a book will now appear in electronic forms that offer more interactivity. This recycling of all written work will create a boom similar to the one when music went from vinyl to CD, and recording artists got to release their entire catalogs all over again.

Electronic publishing specialists, according to the current definition, edit, design, and produce books and magazines entirely on computer, and distribute them through on-line services or on CD-ROM. However, the title "electronic publishing specialist" is a bit of a misnomer; what we are really talking about here is an editor who has become technologically adapted, not only to the tools of his or her trade, but also to the applications and methods of distribution.

INSIDER'S VIEW OF COMMUNICATIONS

Insiders in the media/communications field observe cutthroat rivalry among professionals and those eager to get a job in the industry, and they predict more of the same for the next decade.

But even though this so-called glamour industry will remain as hard-nosed as ever in admitting newcomers to its ranks, it will have a heart (at least, those lucky enough to break into the industry will think so) in the coming years. This is because new media, and other up-and-coming trends, will create new job opportunities.

EXPOSING THE DUAL MYTHS

Myth # 1: All media jobs, particularly in publishing, are in New York.
According to *Guide to Careers in Magazine Publishing*, a publication of the American Society of Magazine Editors, "While it is true that New York City is

the hub of the magazine publishing industry, there are many opportunities available outside New York, particularly at trade publications and at the several hundred city, state and regional magazines currently being published."

Eugene Fixler, president of Ariel Recruitment Associates, a New York–based executive recruiter for publishers, concurs. "New York City is no longer the only mountaintop for publishing companies." In fact, the majority of his assignments aren't in New York anymore. Instead, publishers all over the country are importing talented New York people. "Those who love publishing and want to stay in it will have to open up their professional horizons and, if they and their families are willing to take a risk, think about relocation."

Creative people with a combination of design and computer skills will be in great demand to fill publishing jobs in the publishing cities of New York, Boston, Chicago, and San Francisco. You may also, of course, live in Bad Axe, Michigan, and telecommute if you're really good at your job.

Myth #2: You can only find work at a major media outlet.

"Don't limit yourself to the top 10 magazines in the country," urges the *Guide to Careers in Magazine Publishing*. "Remember that there are excellent trade magazines and smaller special-interest consumer magazines where entry-level jobs can lead to promising careers."

Eugene Fixler has on his client list, in addition to magazines, journals, and newsletters, major companies "such as the Microsofts and the AT&Ts" that hire publishing people in marketing and direct marketing. In addition, many of his clients are smaller companies, such as special interest consumer publishing, business-to-business information, professional-to-professional information, or personal information from experts to consumers (which includes everything from fitness and health to personal finance).

MERGERS TO COME

For in the long term, Fixler believes that the large general interest magazines are going to either combine with one another or fold. Because of pressure to keep up circulation and advertising dollars, multiple magazines with the same type of editorial content will consolidate, Fixler predicts. "Ultimately, one of the large magazines will acquire the other titles."

SHAKE-UPS CAN MEAN JOBS

In the media/communications field, mergers and reorganizations can mean employment opportunities. *Guide to Careers in Magazine Publishing* cites some figures to prove that magazine publishing is a dynamic industry. "There are an average of 1.3 magazines launched every day of the year. A typical adult American will purchase 36 magazines a year, up 20 percent from 10 years ago. Also, in the last 10 years, advertising revenue has doubled to $6.7 billion."

Guide to Careers advises people who are looking for a job: "Follow developments in the industry. If you read about a magazine start-up or a personnel shake-up, send off a few letters to the people involved. New magazines will need people, and new executives are often in a position to do some hiring."

BROAD-BASED EXPERIENCE

Although the print media will probably offer the greatest number of opportunities for employment, it's worth remembering that other avenues in communications are opening up, too. As Nancy Woodhull, of Pittsford, New York's, media recruitment firm Nancy Woodhull & Associates, points out, there is also about to be an explosion of other media, from on-line to cable.

"Media professionals cannot be defined by only one delivery truck," Woodhull cautions. "They have to be multidimensional in their backgrounds and approaches." She adds, "Unfortunately, the current educational system prepares someone for only one medium and not a multidimensional approach." Professionals who are successful in the media, according to Woodhull, have "a broad knowledge base, entrepreneurial and innovative approach, flexibility, and communicator strengths." She sees, at the heart of every successful media professional, an "information gatherer, whether from a data background or serious journalism background."

NEW MEDIA

Will new media create new job opportunities? Eugene Fixler notes, "Clients are nibbling on new media and putting some of their information on-line." And he predicts that the new media "will pick up some people." But he believes it will be a slow process, with industry professionals such as circulation people and editors "learning to apply their existing skills in an electronic environment."

Fixler echoes the sentiments of many other insiders: "Editors need two different communication styles—a visual style for on-line and a more elegant style for print. Print," he emphasizes, "is not going to go away. There will always be an audience that wants to . . . cuddle up with a good magazine on their pillow—similar to a book audience."

Public Relations

In a world where selling something to someone is at the heart of every business endeavor, image, positioning, and exposure are at the heart of all PR work. PR professionals are often hybrid animals: they're part writer, part editor, and part sales professional. They pull these divergent skills into a coherent whole to earn themselves a place in the ranks of one of today's most exciting, and stressful, professions. Public relations specialists work with health care, law, accounting, engineering, consulting, publishing, and many other types of firms to garner for them the right kind of print and broadcast media exposure.

PR is a profession that is blessed in that its potential customers span the length and breadth of American industry, and cursed in that it is particularly sensitive to the ebb and flow of the economy. Of particular interest to writers who have an outgoing side is the growth of the new super agencies in all major metropolitan areas. These super agencies are combining advertising and PR services to provide complete and coordinated public communication services to their clients. At the same time, many senior PR people, some of whom lost out in restructuring shake-ups, have now opened their own agencies and are experiencing success.

Agencies, though, whether large or small, have one thing in common: they're all trying to contain costs and maximize profits. One approach that is being shared is hiring cheaper, less experienced, but talented writers and publicists, and putting them under the tutelage of talented senior people. This gives the senior people variety, growth, and responsibility while keeping costs down.

Public relations employs selling and marketing skills. Public relations specialists and writers essentially sell editors, reporters, and producers on the idea of writing or producing stories that feature clients' companies, personnel, and products. And entrepreneurs in this field naturally must be able to sell potential clients on using their PR services. Like other salespeople and marketers, public relations professionals have to be resilient enough to handle frequent rejections.

Because public relations professionals work closely with the media, knowledge of the communications industry is a plus. And public relations is a great outlet for the talents of those with a background in television or radio production, or broadcast or print journalism, who are searching for meaningful career segues. Not only does public relations open up additional job possibilities for them, but it also provides ample opportunities to network with media professionals—and it offers communications-related work experience.

Public relations employees may work as research or account assistants, and later advance to positions as account executives or supervisors. And many experienced PR specialists eventually start their own firms. The start-up capital for a public relations business is minimal—all that's required is a telephone, a computer, and some media contact lists. It's another competitive growth field where experience and effort can result in entrepreneurial independence. And it's also a field that will benefit from the maturity and broad worldview that comes from a seasoned professional. Therefore PR is an attractive option for some midlife career changers.

INSIDER'S VIEW OF THE PUBLIC RELATIONS INDUSTRY

Selling is everything. Businesses of every description sell their products or services—and their reputations—through a combination of sales and public relations. To maximize their chances for positive (and, compared to advertising costs, inexpensive) exposure in the print, broadcast, and news media, companies rely on either in-house publicists or independent PR firms.

Unfortunately, the fact that public relations is largely dependent on the economy means that we can expect to see ups and downs in the industry. According to Luis W. Morales, president of the Public Relations Society of America, "Although the demand for PR professionals seems to be growing, the stability potential is questionable as corporate America continues its love affair with downsizing." Morales believes that PR is a great business to be in, but he agrees with other industry leaders' assessment that public relations often is one of the first areas to be looked at when companies talk about cutting back on expenses.

THE RIGHT BACKGROUND

According to Morales, not only is a degree in public relations beneficial, but journalism is still a good background for PR professionals. In fact, industry leaders often complain that too many public relations specialists lack solid writing skills. And, for all people who work in the field, Morales believes the key traits that lead to success are good skills, flexibility, hard work, and creativity.

Because audiences have become segmented, and smaller-audience media outlets are the trend of the future, professionals might find it helpful to have a specialty within the PR field. For instance, some people solely promote trade books, like the one you're reading; others specialize in crisis management; and still others focus on employee relations.

ENTREPRENEURIAL SPIRIT

Many public relations specialists eventually start an agency of their own, once they've built up enough experience in the corporate world. To that end, Morales suggests that all PR professionals "have a number of key courses in business, including accounting and writing." Of course, developing technology will continue to make it even easier for PR professionals to work right out of their homes.

Working on their own, in many cases, increases earning potential for publicists and cuts down on corporate stress—although, of course, it does bring with it the responsibility of constant marketing to bring in new business and the need to deal with frequent rejection.

Public relations is the business of creating a desired awareness of a product, service, or person, by a means other than paid advertising. There have never been more products, people, and services willing to pay for PR expertise than there are in today's service society. This is because creating awareness in your customer base, when that customer base is no longer just those people who walk past your door every day, is recognized as an important component of any successful sales and marketing plan.

In the years ahead, this promotion of goods and services will continue to be an indispensable part of doing business. However, E-mail, fax machines, and other technological innovations will change the way publicists deliver their messages to the media and to the public, and this means they are a group for whom technological adaptedness will be a part of professional survival.

Sales

There are sales positions in every company in every industry in America, and 38 percent growth is predicted for sales positions over the next ten years. The sales profession is tough, and turnover is high, so job opportunities for sales professionals abound everywhere.

Every sales job is a commission job. Even if it is "salary plus commission" or if it is positioned as a salaried job with a performance bonus attached, the facts remain the same: if you do not bring in a dollar sales volume appropriately in excess of the cost of your base plus bonus or commission, you do not get to keep the job.

The profession demands a high degree of inner strength and excellent inquiry and listening, focus, and organization skills. For those who can develop the behaviors, it is the field that ultimately enables people to make more money than any other. Nobody who tries his or her hand in sales ever fails, because even if you move on to other work, the communication, packaging, and negotiation skills you learn in the process will be of inestimable value throughout your career.

Sales experience will help you organize and execute a job hunt with a lot more confidence than is possible for others, because you will have a better understanding of yourself as a product that has to be packaged and sold, and you'll have practical experience in making sales pitches in different ways and environments. Sales skills will also allow you to move with relative ease between different industries. Like accountants and precious few others, you need never be without a job. Finally, sales skills coupled with accounting or legal skills is the combination that builds new companies and makes billionaires like Bill Gates.

So where do you begin? Well, traditional wisdom would have you look at the high growth areas and get a sales position there. Currently, the booming area is consumer electronics. And in sales, there is a simple equation: the bigger the sticker price on the product or service you are selling, the bigger the commission. So, while you may get your first sales job in consumer electronics working for the Wiz, that doesn't mean you will end up with the Wiz or even in consumer electronics. You may choose to leverage the sales experience you can get today for the sales entrée into the profession of your choice a couple of years down the road.

It will be easier to move out of sales into other rewarding areas once you have a foot in the profession's door. Sales is a wonderful entrée, especially if you are smart but didn't benefit from one of the world's great educations. While a good educational background is always sought in the more sophisticated areas of sales, the profession is so performance-oriented that educational requirements will invariably be waived for a top sales producer. If you can sell consistently, and you gain understanding of what drives sales in your industry in its larger context, you may even graduate into marketing, which is the creation, development, and positioning of products for other salespeople to sell. In this job, you are among the senior ranks at the irreducible core of the modern corporation, and as security goes in the new world of work, that's about as secure as it gets.

RETAIL SALES

Retail is projected to be the nation's largest employer by the turn of the century. Our growing disposable income will buy us more luxury items such as cars, compact disc players, large-screen television sets, and laptop computers. And with technology rapidly creating or improving the things that we "need," retail will reap the harvest.

The industry will also be fed by the entrance of even more women into the workforce. Working people require the clothes, uniforms, and accessories of their trade; apparel stores will therefore see some of the biggest growth in the industry. They also need reliable cars to get them to and from the office or wherever they work, so automotive dealers and service stations will also be among the fastest-growing segments of the industry.

The aging population will be another factor. A mature workforce has money to spend at specialty stores—for example, an Ethan Allen rather than a Sears. Which is not to say that discounters such as Wal-Mart will be hurting for business—they're growing with no end in sight.

Drugstores will also be a high-growth area of retail. An aging population will create an ongoing demand for new medicines, which we will see developed by pharmaceutical companies and the biotech industry in the years ahead.

INSIDER'S VIEW OF SALES

Technology has created a whole new world of products and services to sell. The more sophisticated or complex the product, the higher the sticker price, the higher the dollar commission, and the more competition for the jobs. Because of product complexity, selling will become more information-oriented, so you need the kind of mind that can absorb tons of apparently useless information and statistical data. Sales is also becoming much more team-oriented because of the increasing sophistication of the products, and because of a marketplace that frequently crosses time zones. Sales is a profession for those who thrive on pressure, variety, and challenge. They must also have the resilience to see things in the long term. In return, everyone in the field gets a shot at the American Dream.

Terra Downlain, founder of Career Advancement Publications, agrees that sales—particularly technical sales—always requires a technical background to some degree. She adds, though: "Mere technical skills, without good communications skills, are of little value in sales. Simply being a 'good talker' probably will remain the salesperson's most important asset . . . I see a degree in communications from a good university as an appreciating asset for the long term in either sales or marketing."

The best sales jobs in any industry go to those who have the appropriate skill sets, and who combine them with a specialist's knowledge of the industry and its products. Pharmaceutical companies love hiring chemists and pharmacy grads into their sales training programs; computer and software companies yearn for wireheads with the common touch; and the entire health care industry salivates over salespeople with some biology and chemistry in their backgrounds.

Yet specialists don't become that way by accumulating a certain number of academic credits. They become that way by maintaining a meaningful relationship with their chosen profession and its most dedicated players. To maximize the odds of long-term employability in any profession today, the modern professional needs to be connected, and that means becoming an active member of your professional community by joining and contributing to the activities of one or more professional associations. Nowhere are the contacts and connectivity more important than for people in sales. To find associations relevant to the meaningful pursuit of your profession, see *The Encyclopedia of Associations* at your local library.

TRAVEL SALES

The Department of Commerce tells us that the travel industry is the largest employer in thirty-nine of the fifty states, and travel agents will swell their numbers by 62 percent over the next ten years.

Like other industries, travel is experiencing its own restructuring in response to the changing needs of its customer base; it is catering more consciously to women, minorities, seniors, and the adventure- and ecologically-oriented baby boom and "post" generations.

Sales positions in travel aren't restricted to travel agencies; since deregulation, airlines, hospitality giants like Marriott and Disney, and cruise lines have all gotten into selling their products directly, thus increasing profitability by subtracting the travel agents' commission from the cost of doing business on that sale. But this is not expected to toll the death bell on the travel agency business; that's where we will still go for true choice, flexibility, and price.

INSIDER'S VIEW OF THE TRAVEL INDUSTRY

In the next decade, people will be taking to the skies (and the oceans, railroad tracks, and open road) more than they have in the past. Their professions will require more travel, with business activities increasing and companies in all industries going global. Also, with more disposable income, more people will be traveling even when their jobs don't require it.

But because it depends in part on discretionary income, the travel industry has its ups and downs. When unemployment is high or people are afraid of losing their jobs, the travel industry suffers. People and corporations cut back on extraneous travel when times are hard, because it's a relatively easy way to tighten the belt, and this makes it hard to predict how vigorous the travel industry will be from year to year, and from one economic season to another.

SPECIALTIES AND TECHNOLOGY

Even though it's hard for travel industry insiders to look into a crystal ball, they do predict that certain types of travel services will be in high demand. Marty Robinson, president of Boston-based Travel Career Network, says that the cutting-edge jobs in travel will include specialists in ecotourism and accessibility travel (sensitive to special needs). In fact, Robinson adds, travel agents increasingly will be specializing to stay competitive.

Also, Robinson explains that travel agents are telecommuting more and more. This means they have less client contact than before, and that they'd better know their way around the world of computers—particularly the Internet.

Ken Hine, president and CEO of the American Hotel and Motel Association, adds that technology is similarly expected to impact the lodging industry. In lodging, too, people are specializing in various areas. Hine suggests that financial management, communications, human resources management, and of course hospitality management backgrounds are in demand for lodging industry professionals.

WINNERS

Although Robinson believes that technology will decrease face-to-face contact between travel agents and customers, she suggests that customer service will remain a priority for successful travel professionals. Other important traits, according to Robinson, include enthusiasm, open-mindedness, and flexibility. Travel agents should also be good problem solvers and, more and more, employers want to see B.A.s. And, of course, it helps if they are well-traveled. Because the travel industry is so people-oriented, Robinson thinks people with backgrounds in education, nursing, and sales do well in it.

Ken Hine believes that lodging professionals, too, must be people- and service-oriented, with flexibility also being a key to success. He adds that many companies in the industry are increasing their in-house training programs to beef up employees' basic skills. He says that professionals from general business, financial management, applied technologies, and marketing will be able to shift into lodging positions most easily.

ON YOUR OWN

If you can telecommute, the next logical question is: Why not work for yourself? Many travel professionals are doing just that, and travel agents will continue to find entrepreneurial opportunities in the next decade. And they'll probably make better money, since many salaried jobs in travel (particularly the jobs that are growing fastest) are relatively low-paying.

But for those who want to work for travel agencies or corporations, Robinson predicts strong growth in the industry. Hine feels the same will be true for lodging professionals. "Although the lodging industry experiences its share of financial ups and downs," he says, "individuals with proven records of achievement will always be eagerly sought."

Food Service

With dual-income households, hardly anyone has time to cook anymore. Food service companies, particularly those establishments that offer delivery, takeout, and drive-through, are all in high gear supplying our three squares a day. Even though we are becoming a nutrition-conscious culture, fast foods—especially hamburgers, pizza, chicken, and french fries—are still among the hottest businesses.

The melting pot of America has given rise to a wonderful diversity of ethnic foods. Current awareness of cholesterol and saturated fat levels has also been a boon to the ethnic food market, as more and more people are trying different foods, not only for the taste treat, but because many of these foods are low in cholesterol and saturated fats.

Some say that food service is the third-largest industry in the country. According to the Bureau of Labor Statistics, the food service industry is expected to create more new jobs than any other small-business-dominated sector over the next decade.

Most eating and drinking places are small businesses, so unfortunately there is not much chance of advancement. In fact, according to the Washington, D.C.–based National Restaurant Association, three out of four restaurants are small businesses. Restaurants are small operators, but there are lots of them— so jobs should be plentiful in the decade ahead. Nevertheless, an industry dominated by giants and pygmies is not great news for those climbing the career ladder.

That said, traditional career tracks in the bigger food service companies are some of the best bets around. As foreign markets receive growing attention, particularly South America, Eastern Europe, and Asia, there will be special opportunities for food service professionals with diverse cultural and language skills.

INSIDER'S LOOK AT THE FOOD SERVICE INDUSTRY

Just as society is changing, the food industry is changing. These changes reflect the changes in our lifestyles, economy, demographics, and culture, and industry insiders agree that there's more of the same ahead. For the food industry, these changes spell good news and bad news. Market research says it's not unusual for people to eat outside their homes at least 50 percent of the time—that's the good news.

But the food industry, like other industries, is feeling the pressure to get lean and mean. Huge conglomerates like McDonald's dominate the industry, and that puts small businesses like Mom and Pop's Sandwich Shop in jeopardy. What follows is a familiar story by now: downsizings, shutdowns, and mergers. As Sharon Olson, head of the food service recruitment firm Olson Communications in Chicago, puts it, "professional growth is limited and stability is nonexistent. The industry is very mature at this point, and growth is only there for people who take a risk."

William P. Fisher, president of the Washington, D.C.–based National Restaurant Association, says that food service is "no more or less stable than other industries." But he contends the industry will continue to grow. He cites as some of the reasons for the growth "quality of life and the value people place on time."

He points out that "people will take hold of opportunities as other people leave the food service industry"—and people often do leave to move on to other careers. "We in the food service industry have the largest industry alumni of any industry in the country," Fisher says. "For a lot of people, food service is their introduction to the working world. . . . It's a great training ground for learning workplace disciplines."

As long as there is a high turnover in the industry, there will always be jobs available. "Careers are there for those who want to take advantage of them," Fisher continues. "People can come in and meet their personal objectives very quickly. Plus, the industry offers a lot of part-time opportunities to supplement income if you have another job." He believes the food industry will be especially appealing to parents because of the availability of before- and after-school shifts.

EFFICIENCY AND SERVICE

Keeping down costs and maximizing profits will be critical in the industry. To do this, industry insiders predict that companies will focus on their primary products and do away with secondary items. That means, for example, that a bakery that does great breadsticks might choose to deemphasize some growth opportunities, say soups and sandwiches, and instead focus energy on getting those breadsticks sold in supermarkets throughout the region.

People with training, and with computer skills or a background in nutrition, will be in high demand, according to Bill Fisher. Also, people who are used to dealing with systems, and who work in such behind-the-scenes areas as production, purchasing, storing of food, and so on, will have the right backgrounds to meet the food industry's needs.

As restaurants look for a way to distinguish themselves in a competitive arena, Fisher predicts that they'll turn to providing better service. The ideal job candidates, according to Fisher, will be "gracious hosts, gregarious people, people who are open and generous with their time. It will also help to be bilingual."

"More second- and third-career people are coming into the industry," he also points out. "As some of the major corporations downsize, we're going to have people in midlife, thirty-five to fifty-five, entering the industry." He believes that people of any age can succeed in the business, as long as their focus is on *service*. It's the nature of the person, not the person's age, that's important, according to Fisher.

Support Services

Much of this book addresses the work of the change makers—those professionals who make money or save money for their employers. But the work of those in *support services* is to make sure that each line and staff area has the tools at hand to function effectively.

There are estimated to be twelve to fifteen million support or clerical workers in the American workplace. They include secretaries; personal/administrative and executive assistants; and people in an endless array of clerking positions that include payroll, billing, filing, information, and order clerks. In some companies, in some industries, one person would combine all these jobs in one job title; in another company, in the same business, there might be fifty people assigned to each job area. What is certain is that somewhere around seven million jobs—half new jobs, half replacement jobs—will be filled in this area over the coming years, and that those jobs will go to the technologically literate.

The jobs in support services aren't glamorous in and of themselves, and many of them aren't particularly high-paying or prestigious, but they do provide a starting point for many worthwhile and satisfying professions. Medical and legal secretaries will do particularly well, working in pleasant professional environments in fields that will grow by 65 percent and 57 percent respectively.

INSIDER'S VIEW OF SUPPORT SERVICES

While all these jobs allow mobility throughout all industries, of these support positions, the secretarial/assistant positions offer the best combination of horizontal and vertical mobility. One of the criticisms of the profession is that you do much of the executive's work without the recognition, prestige, or other rewards. What you are getting, though, when you choose the right job, is a first-rate education at the seat of power in the industry of your choice. It translates into on-the-job training for climbing the corporate career ladder—or perhaps even more rewarding, the tools of success for an entrepreneurial endeavor of your own. Women and minorities who traditionally hold the majority of support jobs currently have high rates of success as entrepreneurs, in part because they have built their own successful businesses on the foundations of their support staff experience.

Jobs with a Future in:
Business and Professional Services

Financial Services

        Banking: Commercial Loan Officer . . . Consumer Loan Officer . . . Loan Counselor

        Securities: Broker . . . Trader . . . Brokerage Clerk

        Accounting: Accountant . . . Certified Public Accountant . . . Internal Accountant . . . Management Accountant . . . Government Accountant . . . International Accountant . . . Auditor . . . Finance Auditor . . . Forensic Auditor . . . Tax Examiner . . . Financial Manager . . . Chief Financial Officer . . . Corporate Controller

        Insurance: Insurance Agent . . . Insurance Broker . . . Actuary . . . Underwriter

Human Resources

        Benefits Manager . . . Compensation Manager . . . Employee Assistant Program Manager . . . Human Resources Manager . . . Human Resources Staffing Specialist . . . Director of Training . . . Training Manager . . . Corporate Training Specialist . . . Labor Relations Specialist . . . Diversity Manager . . . Management Consultant

Law

        Attorney . . . Bankruptcy Lawyer . . . Tax Attorney . . . Elder Law Attorney . . . Intellectual Copyright Lawyer . . . Environmental Lawyer . . . Paralegal

Media/Communications/Public Relations

        Editor . . . Writer . . . Communications Specialist . . . News Writer . . .

Columnist . . . Technical Writer . . . Publicity Writer . . . Copywriter . . . Public Relations Professional

Sales and Marketing

Sales Representative . . . Retail Sales Associate . . . Travel Agent

Food Service

Chef . . . Executive or Chief Chef . . . Assistant or Sous Chef . . . Prep Chef . . . Institutional Chef . . . Bread and Pastry Chef . . . Cook . . . Short-Order Cook/Fast-Food Cook . . . Restaurant or Food Service Manager . . . Waiter or Waitress

Support Services

Records Clerk . . . Billing Clerk . . . Bookkeeping Clerk . . . File Clerk . . . Information Clerk . . . Order Clerk . . . Personnel Clerk . . . Secretary . . . Executive Secretary . . . Administrative Assistant . . . Legal Secretary

---

ADDITIONAL OPPORTUNITIES IN BUSINESS AND PROFESSIONAL SERVICES

You will also find the following jobs in the business world. These jobs appear in most companies in all industries. You will find the particulars of these jobs on the pages noted:

Job Title	Industry	Page
Computer Software Engineer	Information Technology	212
Computer Software Programmer	Information Technology	214
Information Systems Manager	Information Technology	221
Systems Analyst	Information Technology	212

Note: Many employment opportunities in the legal profession are found with larger employers in all industries. Many media, communications, and PR jobs can be found at most medium-to-large companies in all industries. Sales jobs appear in all industries. Support services jobs appear in most companies in all industries.

Financial Services

BANKING

COMMERCIAL LOAN OFFICER/CONSUMER LOAN OFFICER/LOAN COUNSELOR

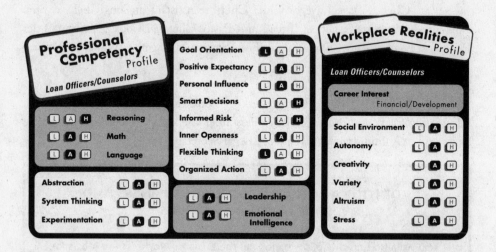

When a person or company applies to a bank or financial institution for a loan, the first people that they meet are loan officers and counselors. These financial institution employees speak to clients about their company's loan policies, and then provide the financial institution with relevant information on the individuals and companies applying for loans.

Loan officers may specialize in *commercial* loans, which help companies to pay for an expansion of operations, or they may work with *consumer* loans, which include home equity, automobile, and personal loans. They may additionally work with mortgage loans, which are used by customers to purchase real estate or to refinance an existing mortgage.

Loan officers prepare, analyze, and then verify loan applications. Once they finish processing an application, they request reports on the applicant's credit history from credit reporting agencies. This information is reviewed to ensure that the payment is within the borrower's capability to pay in accordance with the lending institution's guidelines. Based on the results of the credit rating reports, the loan officer recommends either granting or denying the loan.

Loan officers are a client's closest aide in the loan application process, but a loan officer represents the interests of the financial institution first and foremost.

For example, loan officers often require pledged collateral security from applicants in order to reduce their firm's financial risk. This collateral security might be in the form of the borrower's home. If the borrower were unable to pay back a loan, then the borrower would sell the home in order to raise the funds necessary.

Loan counselors, most of whom work for state or local government or nonprofit organizations, often meet with people who do not qualify for loans with banks. They may also work with people who are attempting to purchase a home, or with clients who wish to refinance debt. In these situations, clients must often prove that they are receiving some income, through self-employment or through assistance of some kind, to demonstrate that they can repay the loan. Counselors often work with people who have limited experience with financial matters, so they are also required to help their clients financially and psychologically—for example, with understanding the hidden costs and obligations of owning a home.

Loan counselors help borrowers learn what is expected in order for them to qualify for a loan. But more often loan counselors help clients locate federal loans and grants for a down payment sufficient to qualify them for a bank-financed mortgage loan. These are very common circumstances for those in strained financial circumstances who want to own their own home or move to a safer location. The loan counselor will help a client to fill out application forms, and will research federal, state, and local government programs that provide the client with additional funds. In this capacity, a counselor may select a single government program to help a client, or seek help from a combination of programs.

In order to work with their customers, loan officers and counselors need to be aware of all the most recent financial packages and services. There are, for example, a variety of mortgage products, including reverse equity mortgages, shared equity mortgages, and adjustable rate mortgages. Loan officers and counselors must fully understand and be able to explain and apply these different options to their customers.

EARNING POTENTIAL

The average yearly income of **consumer loan officers** is $25,400. Starting salaries average $21,000, and experienced officers earn around $28,900.

Commercial loan officers earn an average of $36,200, starting at an average of $29,500 and reaching a high of nearly $40,000.

Loan officers who deal solely with mortgages earn slightly less than general commercial loan officers. **Loan counselors** earn considerably less, starting at $15,000 and earning up to $35,000.

Loan officers are often given special checking privileges and lower interest rates on personal loans by the banks for which they work. Loan counselors who perform service for their communities often receive recognition from local governments, but do not get preferential financial treatment.

EDUCATIONAL REQUIREMENTS

Loan officers generally hold a bachelor's degree in finance, economics, accounting, or a related field. They also should have bank-related and computer experience. **Mortgage loan officers** require more training or experience in sales than is required for other loan officers. Almost all loan officers advance through the ranks of an institution after a number of years of experience in other banking positions. It's a job you can grow to, and beyond, from a start as a bank teller or counter service representative.

More highly educated loan officers may advance to bank managerial positions. Those with less advanced academic backgrounds are usually assigned to work at smaller bank branches, where promotion is generally less available than it is at larger city banks.

Like loan officers, **loan counselors** receive significant on-the-job training. They also have similar educational requirements, particularly accounting. More successful loan counselors may move up in the ranks to supervisory positions, but many loan counselors leave their field for better-paying positions elsewhere—often becoming loan officers, a position which receives preferential treatment.

Loan officers and counselors should have good mathematical skills, but they should also exhibit effective interpersonal skills. Their clients are their livelihood, so they should be able to communicate clearly in order to build a comfortable customer base. Loan officers should be willing to attend community events as representatives of their financial institutions. And loan counselors in particular should have an interest in helping others, especially those in need, and they should likewise be able to inspire trust and confidence. Patience and understanding are essential.

A DAY IN THE LIFE

Most **loan officers** and **counselors** work in offices, though they sometimes are required to travel locally. Mortgage loan officers, for example, often move from branch office to branch office and visit clients' homes in order to complete a loan application.

HELP WANTED
BANKING

Loan Officer

Work with commercial or consumer loans, and mortgage loans.
Prepare, analyze, and then verify
loan applications; request reports on
an applicant's credit history. Make
recommendations regarding an applicant's status as a loan recipient.
Salary Range: $25,400–$39,900.

Loan Counselor

Consult with individuals who do
not qualify for bank loans to assist
them in locating funds for a house
down payment, or in refinancing
debt. Understand, explain, and
apply financial options to customers, many of whom may have
limited experience with financial
matters. Salary Range: $15,000–
$35,000.

Commercial loan officers employed by large financial institutions also travel often in order to complete loan arrangements.

Loan officers and counselors generally work a 40-hour week, although additional working hours may be required, depending on the prevailing economic climate. A loan officer or counselor is always busiest when interest rates are low, as such conditions spur higher rates of loan applications.

JOB GROWTH

According to a recent survey, loan officers and counselors hold approximately 172,000 jobs in the United States. About seven out of ten **loan officers** surveyed were employed by commercial banks, savings institutions, and credit unions. Others were employed by mortgage brokerage firms, personal credit firms, or other non-banking institutions. Most **loan counselors,** on the other hand, work for state or local governments, or for nonprofit organizations.

Employment of loan officers and counselors is expected to grow faster than the average for all occupations through the year 2005. Nearly 70,000 new positions are forecast. As the population increases, the economy continues to grow, and a variety of new loans become available, loan applications will increase, providing more opportunities for loan officers and counselors. Many more job openings will occur from a need to replace those who leave the occupation or retire. College graduates will have the best opportunity to land and grow in these positions.

But beware! **Loan officers** lose their jobs in high numbers during difficult economic times. In this field, your current job and your general employability (real ability to pull down a steady paycheck) are directly applied to your sales ability to make loans—and *good* loans, where the client doesn't default. Loans are a major source of income for banks, so when the economy declines and the demand for loans decreases, loan officers sometimes face unemployment.

Loan counselors are less likely to lose their positions as quickly, particularly in regions that depend on local government services. For **loan counselors**, job security is dependent upon the dynamics of local government spending. A position as a loan counselor can provide a safety net for some displaced loan officers during tough economic times.

Securities

BROKER/TRADER/BROKERAGE CLERK

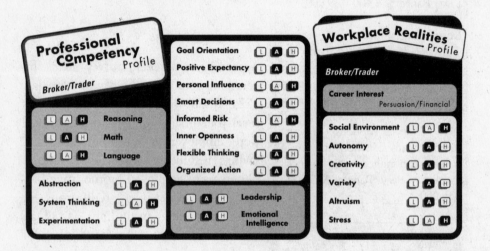

Brokers, also known as *securities sales representatives*, *registered representatives*, and *account executives*, buy and sell stocks, bonds, shares in mutual funds, insurance annuities, certificates of deposit, and other financial products included in the broad term "securities."

An investor interested in buying or selling securities contacts a broker and places an order. The broker conveys the order to representatives working on the floor of the securities exchange, or if a security is not traded on the floor of the exchange, transmits the order to the firm's trading department, where dealers in the over-the-counter (OTC) market make the transaction. Once the transaction is complete, the broker adds the purchased securities, or the proceeds from the sale, to the client's portfolio and reports the proceeds to the client.

It is important for brokers to understand their clients and anticipate their needs. For example, clients looking for low risk would invest in long-term safe stocks and bonds and would not be interested in investing in a risky venture, regardless of the potential return. On the other hand, short-term investors willing to take investment risks in order to make a large profit would be very interested in the type of venture just mentioned. Brokers must know which of their clients to contact regarding specific opportunities, and when, in the course of an investment's fluctuating value, to place their buy and sell orders.

Other services brokers provide for their customers include explaining the nature of investments and the products a company makes. Some clients with particular interests may invest in a security because the company manufactures a product the investor uses or likes, or because the company follows ecological safety procedures in its manufacturing process.

Brokers who oversee the client's entire portfolio can also be *financial planners*. They develop a clear picture of their client's total assets and investment goals before recommending a particular strategy that suits the client. A financial planner needs to know about the client's assets, liabilities, tax status, and retirement priorities, and may put together a personalized investment package that includes securities, life insurance, corporate and municipal bonds, mutual funds, certificates of deposit, and annuities.

Brokers tend to represent either individual clients or institutional investors. Most institutional investments concentrate on one type of item: stocks or bonds, for example, or commodity futures. Institutional investing has become a very large part of the securities business, and heavy trading by institutions can have a dramatic short-term effect on the stock market that directly influences individuals' investments.

There are two sides to success in the securities sales business: keeping up with the financial news and finding and keeping clients. Like all salespeople, brokers must find their own customers and develop a lasting client base that will lead to repeat business and referrals. Brokers can spend hours every day on the telephone making cold calls to prospective customers, trying to interest them in the securities firm's services.

Traders buy and sell commodities, securities, and currency, profiting from fluctuating prices.

Early every morning, radio and television business reports give the closing figures on the previous day's trading on the Tokyo Stock Exchange. Traders make sure they have the figures in their hands before the media announce the news, because they indicate what sort of day they can expect on American stock exchanges.

In a global economy, one nation's currency fluctuations also affect the economy of many other nations. If, for example, the Federal Reserve Bank raises or lowers its prime lending rate, traders in this and other countries make judgments about the strength or weakness of the dollar, and decide to buy or to sell.

Traders analyze the market conditions all over the world in order to know when to execute transaction orders placed by clients. Traders themselves work on the floor of a stock exchange. Their job is extremely hectic because they must make their purchases based on their study of market conditions and their own intuition.

Traders typically receive sales orders from brokers, who serve as intermediaries between customers and the floor traders. The brokers are responsible for ensuring the accuracy of the sales order information before acting on the order. They then contact the currency exchange or brokerage firm trading the requested securities to complete the transaction. The traders write up and sign the sales order confirmation forms, and they review all transactions to ensure that trades conform to Securities and Exchange Commission regulations.

Brokerage clerks work for investment and securities firms to produce the records associated with financial transactions. These clerks record the purchase and sale of securities for the firm. Footage of the trading floors at the New York Stock Exchange reveals that these financial transactions occur in the space of seconds—yet the orders are still accurately recorded in spite of the seeming chaos. The job of actually recording the transaction is the work of brokerage clerks.

Brokerage clerks, who work in the operations area of securities firms, perform many tasks to facilitate the purchase and sale of stocks, bonds, commodities, and other types of investments. Typical responsibilities include computing federal and state transfer taxes and commissions (using calculators and rate tables), verifying information (such as owners' names, transaction dates, and distribution instructions) on securities certificates to ensure accuracy and compliance with regulations, posting transaction data to accounting ledgers and certificate records, typing data on confirmation forms to effect the transfer of securities purchased and sold, receiving securities and cash, and scheduling the delivery of customers' securities.

Although some clerks perform a broad array of functions, many specialize in particular areas of financial transactions. For example, *purchase-and-sale clerks* match orders to buy with orders to sell. They balance and verify stock trades by comparing the records of the selling firm with those of the buying firm. *Dividend clerks* ensure the timely payment of stock or cash dividends to clients. *Transfer clerks* execute customer requests for changes to security registration and examine stock certificates for adherence to regulations. *Receive-and-deliver clerks* facilitate the receipt and delivery of securities among firms and institutions. *Margin clerks* post accounts and monitor activity in customers' accounts to ensure that customers make their payments and stay within legal parameters regarding stock purchases.

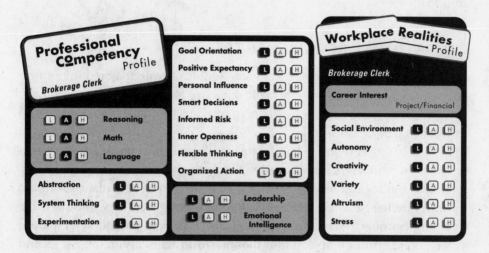

EARNING POTENTIAL

The median annual salary of **brokers** in the United States is approximately $40,700. They start at an average salary of $28,000 and with experience earn an average of $78,000. The average earnings for institutional brokers are typically much higher, approximately $156,000. Most of these earnings reflect the broker's ability to generate sales commissions. Although new brokers initially may receive a salary from their brokerage house, this arrangement changes to a full-time commission plus incentive bonus system within the first few months. Some brokers earn hundreds of thousands of dollars a year this way.

A **trader's** earnings depend upon his or her experience and capabilities, and are likely to be higher in large organizations and large cities. The median annual salary for traders is $39,700. Of this number, the lowest 10 percent earn $20,200 or less, while the top 10 percent earn over $77,800. It is estimated, however, that these numbers can be doubled when bonuses are factored in. And a small number of traders employed as *institutional traders* and *merger* and *acqusitions traders* earn from $600,000 to over $1 million per year.

Brokerage clerks' earnings range between $4.75 per hour and $6.25 per hour for beginners. Experienced clerks may earn between $5.25 and $10.00 per hour. An average annual salary for a full-time billing clerk is approximately

$18,400. Salary growth in this field will remain modest, keeping pace with, but not greatly exceeding, the rate of inflation. However, the job might provide a foot on the ladder for a person wanting to learn this business from the ground up.

EDUCATIONAL REQUIREMENTS

Almost all **brokers** have a college degree. Applicants who majored in business or economics in college are especially attractive to potential employers, even though, as in most sales jobs, there is no specific academic background required to perform this work.

State licensing is required for all brokers. This involves passing an examination to show competency and occasionally posting a bond for security. All brokers must also register as representatives of their firm in accordance with the securities exchange where they work. In order to register, they must pass the General Securities Registered Representative Examination and be employed by a registered firm for at least four months. Most states also require a second examination, the Uniform Securities Agents Law Examination. These examinations test a broker's knowledge of securities laws, customer protection laws, and bookkeeping practices.

Traders are almost all college-educated. In most cases, a bachelor's degree in accounting, finance, or business administration is the preferred academic preparation for traders. While a master of business administration (M.B.A.) degree is increasingly valued by employers, this is a field where lack of education doesn't kill the career of a focused professional with good communication skills. All traders must also pass a state examination in order to receive their license and become registered.

Because the laws regulating this field are increasingly complex, continuing education has become essential for traders, especially for those who want to advance in the field. Brokerage firms often provide opportunities for employees to broaden their knowledge and skills, and encourage them to take graduate courses and to attend industry conferences.

Because currency trading, like most other occupations, has undergone a technological revolution, traders must have a thorough knowledge of related computer applications in order to advance.

Most **brokerage clerk** positions require applicants to have a high school diploma or G.E.D. certificate. Mathematical aptitude is important in this position. Computer literacy is an essential ingredient in an applicant's résumé. High schools, business schools, and community colleges all offer courses that teach office skills. Most companies augment that sort of preparation with on-the-job training for new employees.

A DAY IN THE LIFE

Some **brokers** work for small investment firms, but the great majority work for a few large firms that have offices in major cities. These major players account for approximately 25,000 branch offices throughout the country.

Brokers work in large offices that they usually share with several other people. Securities firms hire large numbers of applicants and, after providing them with the basic necessary training, allow them to work for a period of time; the rigors of the job, such as long hours and high stress, quickly sort out those who aren't truly suited. The new hires typically have a desk and telephone of their own in a large room shared with many other young investment brokers. The pace is hectic and the noise can be distracting. An abundance of energy and a tough hide are helpful for surviving in this frantic environment. The strain of risk-taking is a natural part of the investment profession, because brokers know that they are constantly being evaluated for their performance. It is a business where you are only as good as your last few trades. As brokers prove themselves and take on more fiscal responsibility, they can be rewarded with private offices and administrative assistance.

Just as investments include a large element of risk, most jobs associated with securities investment involve risk. New brokers take a risk in trying to develop a career based on their knowledge, intuition, and personality. It takes a lot of self-confidence to succeed in the securities field, but those who do succeed will make a comfortable living or better.

Traders have offices close to the stock exchange floor, but they carry out their primary function on the crowded floor of the stock exchange itself. During the hours that an exchange is open, traders are in constant motion, yelling to be heard above the general noise of the exchange, talking on the telephone to market makers, listening to tips from other traders, and always fighting the crowd flow in order to make a purchase or sale in a timely way.

The work of stock exchange traders and commodities traders is physically and mentally demanding. Because of the amount of energy the job requires, most traders tend to be young people. This is a job demanding physical stamina, the ability to work well under extreme pressure, and attention to detail. After working a full day on the stock exchange floor, traders must study market conditions to prepare for the next day's work, or else they work on their efforts to become brokers. The job of a currency trader is not one a person usually

HELP WANTED
SECURITIES

Broker

Communicate with securities exchange representatives. Add the securities purchased through a trader to a client's portfolio and report the proceeds to the client. Understand and anticipate client's needs. Explain the nature of investments and the products a company makes. Salary Range: $28,000–$156,000+.

Trader

Analyze market conditions. Receive sales orders from brokers, ensure the accuracy of the information, and then buy and sell commodities, securities, and currency. Review transactions to ensure that trades conform to Securities and Exchange Commission regulations. Work on floor of stock exchange. Salary Range: $20,000–$77,800+.

Brokerage Clerk

Record the purchase and sales of securities for the firm. Compute federal and state transfer taxes and commissions. Understand and verify financial data. Ensure accuracy and compliance with regulations. Type data on confirmation forms. Average Salary: $18,400.

continues in for several years: it is a job that provides excellent background and training for a successful securities broker.

Although overtime may sometimes be required, traders typically work a forty-hour week. Attendance at meetings of financial and economic associations and similar activities is often required, especially for those traders seeking to advance in a securities-related career.

Brokerage clerks usually work in offices that range in size from a few people to over one hundred people. The physical demands are modest, although they must sit and work on computer terminals for several hours at a stretch. People who spend long hours at computer terminals are known to suffer from headaches, eyestrain, and repetitive motion injuries.

Most brokerage clerks work regular business hours, but it is not unusual for brokerage clerks to work night or even weekend hours in order to meet deadlines.

JOB GROWTH

Employment of **brokers** is expected to grow at a rate exceeding the national average for all occupations over the next ten years. This growth will result from economic growth, rising personal incomes, and the investment of inherited wealth. Deregulation has also allowed brokers to provide a broad variety of financial services, which will make them more in demand. There will be some 50,000 more brokers' jobs to fill through 2005.

Growth in institutional investment will also be strong, as employees increasingly invest in pension plans, IRAs, and trust funds. Competition will be tough for positions in the most prestigious firms; entry-level brokers will have much more success gaining experience in smaller organizations and smaller markets.

The changing nature of global trade and the economy will ensure the need for **traders**. A trader's job provides an invaluable introduction to the workings of the stock exchange to those who have the ambition to continue and ultimately work as brokers or elsewhere within the profession.

There are 57,000 **brokerage clerks** employed in the United States. The Department of Labor Statistics estimates that the number of jobs will increase by about 1,000 per year through the year 2005. Thousands of job openings for brokerage clerks will also result from the position's high level of turnover. As with most clerical jobs, many people transfer out of their clerical position for a promotion.

Brokerage clerks remain a necessary part of the financial reporting industry. They are needed to enter information into computers for trading by way of electronic data interchange (EDI). Computers may have largely replaced paper reporting, but clerks still enter and verify all transactions.

Accounting

ACCOUNTANT: CERTIFIED PUBLIC ACCOUNTANT/INTERNAL ACCOUNTANT/ MANAGEMENT ACCOUNTANT/GOVERNMENT ACCOUNTANT/INTERNATIONAL ACCOUNTANT

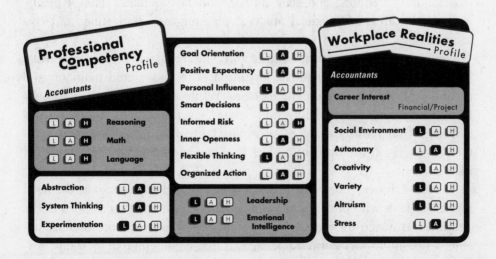

Wherever money is being made (or lost), **accountants** are on hand to manage the books. In every industry covered in this book, you will find accountants, each with a specialization and all with a broad application for their skills.

There are five major fields of accounting: *public, internal, management, government* and *international accounting*. In all of these areas, accountants prepare, analyze, and verify financial reports and taxes. They also monitor information systems and report on financial matters to managers in all areas of government and private business.

Certified public accountants (C.P.A.s) operate their own businesses or work for accounting firms. Their chief duties include consulting with clients ranging in size from large corporations to individuals in such areas as audits and taxation. Most public accountants concentrate primarily on their clients' tax matters, advising them of the advantages, disadvantages, and tax consequences of business decisions. Others may specialize in such areas as employee health care benefits and compensation or *forensic accounting* (investigation of bankruptcies and fraudulent transactions). They also may design accounting and data processing systems for companies of various sizes.

Internal accountants are employed exclusively by a corporation to set up and maintain its day-to-day financial records. They prepare financial reports such as profit and loss, income, expenditures, tax liabilities, inventory, and payroll. Because they work for one specific corporation, internal accountants generally have less flexibility in their practice than public accountants.

Management accountants serve as consultants to corporate executives, who make business decisions based on their accountant's interpretations of financial information. Management accountants also prepare financial reports for shareholders, creditors, and state and federal tax agencies. They typically work in the areas of financial analysis, planning and budgeting, and cost accounting.

Government accountants examine tax and financial records of private sector businesses and individuals for purposes of audits, and maintain and audit the records of government agencies. While many government accountants work for the Internal Revenue Service, overseeing the processing and auditing of tax returns, many other accountants work for individual government agencies in the areas of budget analysis, administration, and financial management.

As more businesses become an active part of the global economy, the need for accountants who understand the sometimes conflicting regulations of the countries in which their employers do business becomes more understandable. Since all businesses must operate within the guidelines of their host government, it falls to *international accountants* to help them understand and negotiate all of the various challenges that arise from foreign trade and foreign partnerships.

International accountants know the intricacies of trade regulations between any two countries, and the way trade regulations relate to the transport of goods and services across any intervening borders. They also provide information to management on foreign wage levels, so that a manufacturer has a clear idea of how to weigh bids for piecework from foreign industries.

International accountants must also know exchange rates, foreign governments' tax laws, and the rules of international law that apply to the sale, trade, and manufacture of goods and the sale and exchange of services. They must prepare and file tax reports not only with the corporation's home state and the IRS, but also with the foreign governments where the corporation engages in business. International accountants analyze and evaluate complicated tax laws so that their corporations are responsible for the least possible amount of tax consequences.

Like all management accountants, international accountants serve as consultants to corporate executives, who make decisions based on the accountants' interpretations of foreign and domestic financial information. International accountants also prepare financial reports for shareholders, creditors, and state, federal, and foreign tax agencies.

EARNING POTENTIAL

The many levels of accountants employed at innumerable organizations throughout the country (and worldwide) earn a wide range of salaries. The salaries for the nonexecutive positions in accounting run something like this:

	Starting Salary	Median Salary	High-End Salary
Public Accountant	$22,200	$29,300	$41,700
Internal Accountant	$23,000	$30,750	$42,250
Management Accountant	$37,000	$47,250	$61,000
Government Accountant	$18,300	$27,800	$48,200

As accountants move up the corporate ladder, their earning potential increases accordingly (see chief financial officer/corporate controller, page 284).

Statistics for **international accountants** are not separated from those of accountants in general, but because of the level of experience and expertise required to operate in this capacity, international accountants are likely to earn close to the top for the industry, in the $48,000 to $61,000 range.

EDUCATIONAL REQUIREMENTS

Corporations, accounting firms, and the federal government generally require accounting applicants to have a bachelor's degree in accounting. Many employers prefer job applicants with a master's degree in accounting or an M.B.A. with a concentration in accounting. Some large corporations will pay to send employees to school for graduate degrees.

In most states, **certified public accountants** (C.P.A.s) are the only accountants who are licensed and regulated. In order to gain licensure, an applicant must take and pass a demanding two-day, four-part examination. However, candidates for licensure are not required to pass all four parts at one time; most states require passage of two parts at a time, for partial credit. Note: Approximately one fourth of those who take the test each year pass each part they take.

But the educational requirements for the accounting field are in a transitional phase. Many states will soon require C.P.A. candidates to complete 150 semester hours of course work before qualifying to sit for the C.P.A. exam.

The Institute of Certified Management Accountants also administers a four-part examination, open to candidates with at least two years of experience as management accountants. Successful candidates are then designated Certified Management Accountants.

International accountants need not only a financial background, but also specialized knowledge in foreign business practices and customs that pertain to business. Programs in these fields have not been generally available in graduate business schools, but with the rise of multinational business, master's degree programs in business administration and management should place increasing emphasis on foreign businesses. Knowledge of a foreign language is also a great benefit to anyone seeking employment in this field. The ability to negotiate with foreign competitors or partners in their own language adds great value to an international accountant's already considerable stockpile of skills.

Those considering an accounting career should obviously have an aptitude for mathematics, good analytical skills, and good communication skills. Accuracy is essential to accountants, as is the ability to work without supervision. A high standard of integrity is expected from all accountants, wherever they work.

A DAY IN THE LIFE

Most accountants work in offices, although **public accountants** may travel to clients' places of business, and **management** and **government accountants** may travel to branch offices and other facilities. A good portion of the working day is spent analyzing and manipulating figures. Computers are rapidly replacing simple calculators as the accountant's tool of choice. Software packages allow accountants to prepare elaborate financial documents and records directly on-screen, eliminating the need to transcribe records to preprinted forms. Similarly, accountants consulting with clients can plug a laptop computer directly into the client's own computer system to have immediate access to necessary information.

Most **public**, **management**, and **government accountants** work a forty-hour week, although there may be seasons of the year (especially tax season, or the end of a fiscal year) when they are required to work long hours. Those **public accountants** who are self-employed in general work a longer work week. Studies have shown that four out of ten self-employed accountants report working more than fifty hours per week, as opposed to one out of four salaried accountants.

Most **international accountants** work long hours, in part because their responsibilities are so great, and in part because they need financial information from foreign markets as the information becomes available in different time zones. Many international accountants work both early and late at the office, and also have modems hooked up to their home computers so they can communicate with foreign markets even in the middle of the night. They are likely to travel to foreign countries. The position requires a lot of autonomy, but international accountants must also have the ability to work closely with many kinds of people and be capable of working within the diverse professional etiquettes of the foreign nations with which their employers do business.

Accounting as a profession is desirable not only for its mobility, stability, and respect, but because it also offers a clear and accessible path to entrepreneurial opportunity.

JOB GROWTH

There are 939,000 accountants and auditors in the United States, a number that is forecasted to increase by 150,000 positions by the year 2005. Future prospects for the profession are good, with growth exceeding the national average. Although the profession is large and subject to relatively little turnover, normal attrition (death, retirement, and transfers) and a growing economy will require more and more accountants. As start-up businesses grow and federal regulations become more exacting, the demand for accounting specialists will increase.

HELP WANTED
ACCOUNTANTS

Certified Public Accountant
Consult with clients in accounting areas, and, in particular, tax matters. Design accounting and data processing systems. Advise clients on tax consequences of business decisions. Consult with clients during audits. Salary Range: $22,200–$41,700.

Internal Accountant
Record and analyze financial information for the company. Salary Range: $23,000–$42,500.

Management Accountant
Consult with corporate executives. Prepare financial reports for shareholders, creditors, and state and federal tax agencies. Salary Range: $37,000–$61,000.

Government Accountant
Examine tax and financial records of private sector businesses and individuals for government audits. Maintain and audit the records of government agencies. Salary Range: $18,300–$48,200.

International Accountant
Know, understand, and negotiate accounting challenges that arise from foreign trade, specifically from trade regulations between any two countries, as well as exchange rates, foreign governments' tax laws, and rules of international law. Prepare and file tax reports. Analyze and evaluate complicated tax laws. Salary Range: $48,000–$61,000.

The role of **public** and **management accountants** is likely to change in the near future. Because of increasing pressure for them to assume liability, they will relinquish many auditing responsibilities to auditing specialists and take on greater management and advisory roles. In fact, many executives in positions such as controller, treasurer, financial vice president, and chief financial officer have accounting backgrounds.

As foreign businesses grow and federal regulations become increasingly elaborate, the demand for **international accountants** will increase. Since this is a relatively new area of expertise, and since corporations will continue to develop a business presence in foreign markets, the profession should experience substantial growth during the next ten years.

The global economy is a fact of life that affects everyone in the United States, not just big business. Businesses will look for employees with strong analytic ability, computer skills, and expertise in specialized areas such as foreign affairs and international law, and in developing programs for future trade practices. This exciting career provides enormous challenges and equally enormous rewards— some of the better rewards in the new world of work.

AUDITORS: FORENSIC AUDITOR/TAX EXAMINER

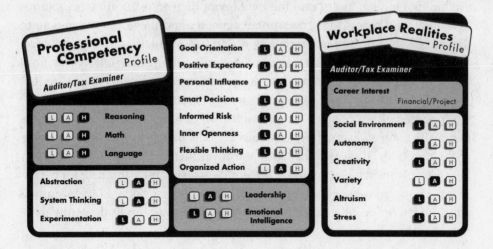

Auditors in the private sector, known as *internal auditors*, scrupulously examine a company's records to check for accuracy, compliance, and mismanagement, waste, and fraud. Auditors police the handling of all corporate monies for the corporation's financial management team. They might be thought of as fiscal efficiency experts, fine-tuning the best use of a company's financial resources.

In the public sphere, auditors maintain records for government agencies and examine the records of private corporations and individuals subject to taxation and governmental regulation. Auditors, along with accountants, make up a large number of the people employed by the Internal Revenue Service.

Auditors, both in the public and the private sector, use computers to examine and evaluate financial and information systems, management procedures, and internal controls in order to prevent fraud and waste. They also evaluate a company's operations for efficiency, effectiveness, and compliance with corporate policies and procedures, laws, and government regulations.

There are many types of highly specialized auditors, such as *electronic data processing auditors, environmental auditors, engineering auditors, legal auditors, insurance premium auditors, bank auditors,* and *health care auditors.* There are also *forensic auditors,* whose future looks particularly rosy; they are financial detectives who investigate allegations of fraud or embezzlement, particularly in bankruptcy situations. Although all these specialized auditors work in different fields and examine different types of records, they all strive for the same goal: total accuracy.

Tax examiners review tax returns to ensure that residents are paying their fair amount of state and local taxes. They usually have a professional background in auditing, and spend the majority of their time auditing tax returns. They maintain records for government agencies and they examine and audit the records of institutions, corporations, and individuals subject to taxation and government regulation. Tax examiners typically review tax returns from residents and businesses located within a state or municipality to ensure that the federal, state, or municipality represented is getting every penny it's due.

Computers have enabled tax examiners to develop financial applications that assist them in estimating residents' tax bills based on the size and value of their property, their income, and their investment holdings; such programs then flag anyone who falls outside the norms as a suitable candidate for harassment. They also manage internal audits on the services offered by a municipality to determine whether or not there is fraud or waste in its departments.

EARNING POTENTIAL

A survey by the Institute of Internal Auditors showed that salaries for **internal auditors** average from $26,500 (for those with less than two years' experience) up to $60,700 (for those with over ten years' experience). Candidates with outstanding academic records could make as much as $22,700 to start, while those with a master's degree or at least two years of professional experience could start at $27,800.

The starting salary in the federal government is approximately $18,300. On average, auditors employed by the government in nonsupervisory, supervisory, and management positions make $48,200 (some $2,000 more than the average for *government accountants*).

Salaries for state and local **tax examiners** do not keep pace with either private industry salaries or those of most high-ranking federal employees. They also are dependent on the geographic area covered: a starting salary could be as little as $9,976 in Vermont, but Wyoming reportedly pays its top tax examiners in excess of $50,000. Nevertheless, tax examiners working at the state level receive relatively good compensation and, as is true for most state, county, and municipal employees, a comprehensive benefits package.

EDUCATIONAL REQUIREMENTS

Most public accounting firms and businesses require applicants for auditing positions to have a bachelor's degree in a related field: accounting, business administration, or finance, to name a few. Most auditors employed by large accounting firms will have received a master's degree at an early point in their career. Virtually all **forensic auditors** must hold a master's degree. Employees may also be encouraged by employers to attend graduate school. In these cases the employer usually pays the tuition bills for the employee, rather than reimbursing him or her at the end of the semester. And employers today regard computer literacy as a given for entry into this profession.

The normal requirement for **tax examiners** and beginning government auditing positions is four years of college (including twenty-four class hours in auditing) or an equivalent combination of education and experience.

Since practical experience can often help an applicant get a job, many colleges offer intern programs that place students with businesses or accounting firms for summer employment or on a part-time basis. This hands-on training proves invaluable to students looking for permanent employment in the field. Forensic auditing, especially, requires a good deal of basic accounting experience and an ability to infer conclusions from limited information—a skill that grows sharper with experience.

Voluntary certification can attest to professional competence in a specialized field of auditing. Among the societies offering credentials is the Institute of Internal Auditors, which confers the designation Certified Internal Auditor (C.I.A.) upon graduates from accredited colleges and universities who have completed two years' work in internal auditing and who have passed a four-part examination. The EDP Auditors Association confers the designation Certified Information Systems Auditor (C.I.S.A.) upon candidates who pass an examination and who have five years of experience in auditing electronic data processing systems. Other organizations, such as the National Association of Certified Fraud Examiners and the Bank Administration Institute, confer additional specialized auditing designations.

Although many of these certification programs seem to apply more to the private sector than to the public sector, anyone working as a tax examiner for a state or local agency can also benefit from credentials that certify him or her as a highly qualified auditor or accountant. And such credentials are doubly valuable as career transition tools.

A DAY IN THE LIFE

Auditors work in varied office environments, most often in the offices of their clients. They spend most of their working hours either at a computer terminal or in a constantly changing array of environments, accompanied by their laptops.

Forensic auditors work primarily for accounting companies or governmental agencies. They serve as consultants to businesses and investigating agencies. They perform their work in offices—usually in the offices of institutions that are under investigation or have retained their firm's services.

Auditors work a standard forty-hour week, but they may need to work over-time during busy seasons when they review fiscal year–end reports for companies or when they examine reports to shareholders. **Forensic auditors** may be required to work a great deal of overtime during difficult investigations. In criminal matters, timely discovery of misappropriated funds can save investors a great deal of money. The demands for speed and accuracy can generate a great deal of stress.

Tax examiners work in state or local government office buildings. Some tax examiners for smaller municipalities may also work from their private offices, serving as municipal tax examiners on a part-time basis. Because they often send out tax bills to be paid at various times of the year (for example, the sewer and public use tax bills sent out during one quarter, the school tax bill during another), tax examiners at the local level rarely deal with the overwhelming amount of tax returns that flood the Internal Revenue Service offices each April.

JOB GROWTH

Taken together, accountants and auditors hold about 939,000 jobs, with nearly one-third of that number either employed by accounting, auditing, and book-keeping firms, or self-employed. That leaves more than two-thirds that are employed by the widest possible variety of businesses and industries. The Department of Labor Statistics predicts that the number of accountants and auditors will increase at a faster than average rate (by approximately 162,000 positions) by the year 2005.

For someone pursuing a traditional corporate career path, auditing may be just a first step, if you are prepared to obtain a broader educational background in business, finance, or accounting. An internal auditing background is a very solid foundation for those who wish to rise to the professional heights of controller and CFO. Many corporate executives have backgrounds in auditing and accounting.

As in many professions, demand for specialists will outstrip demand for generalists. This is good news for **forensic auditors**, whose skills are highly specialized in the review, investigation, and prosecution of corporate tax returns and financial statements. The Internal Revenue Service will have a growing need for auditors as the population continues to increase. Also, new technology will

---

HELP WANTED

Auditor

Examine company's records and operations to check for accuracy, efficiency, compliance, and mismanagement, waste, and fraud. Police the handling of all corporate moneys. Examine and evaluate financial and information systems, management procedures, and internal controls. Maintain records for government agencies. Salary Range: $22,700–$60,700.

Tax Examiner

Examine, audit, and/or maintain the records of institutions, corporations, and individuals subject to taxation and governmental regulation. Review tax returns from all residents and businesses located within a state or municipality. Salary Range: $9,976–$50,000+.

---

create opportunities for honest mistakes as well as opportunities for fraud. Forensic and audit accountants will be in demand to cope with these new challenges.

But although forensic auditors who prove their value will have no trouble finding jobs, they may not have the flexibility of auditors who work as independent contractors. Because the criminal investigations involving large-scale fraud or embezzlement are so exhaustive, many forensic auditors would not be able to perform their jobs without the support provided by a large accounting firm or a government agency.

State agencies will continue to grow over the next ten years as residents of states demand greater services from their elected officials. Furthermore, organizations that serve as watchdogs of public spending will increase their scrutiny of the ways public officials allocate public funds and tax revenues. For those reasons, the number of positions for **tax examiners** at the state level should grow by 16 percent before 2005, predicts the Department of Labor Statistics, and that translates into about 10,000 additional jobs.

Tax examiners' jobs are subject to the political climate in a state or municipality, but there is usually very little turnover in these positions. Of course, in the new world of work that status can change in the flick of a fiscal year. However, tax examiner positions at the local level will grow in areas that are enjoying new development and population growth. Areas in the South and Southwest should see the largest increase in this occupation, as northern businesses and a larger segment of the retired population continue to migrate to these areas. People interested in these positions must be aware, though, that the jobs will be very competitive on two levels: they will demand skilled auditors and accountants, and they may also require a civil service examination or knowledge of the workings of political patronage hiring systems.

Accounting

FINANCIAL MANAGER: CHIEF FINANCIAL OFFICER/CORPORATE
CONTROLLER

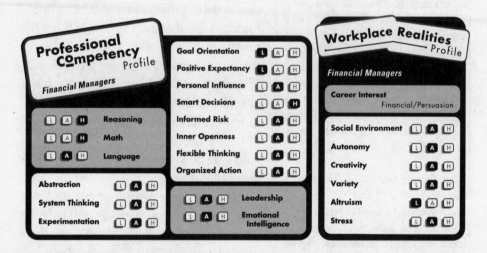

Professional Competency Profile

Financial Managers

L	A	H	Reasoning
L	A	H	Math
L	A	H	Language

Abstraction	L	A	H
System Thinking	L	A	H
Experimentation	L	A	H

Goal Orientation	L	A	H
Positive Expectancy	L	A	H
Personal Influence	L	A	H
Smart Decisions	L	A	H
Informed Risk	L	A	H
Inner Openness	L	A	H
Flexible Thinking	L	A	H
Organized Action	L	A	H

L	A	H	Leadership
L	A	H	Emotional Intelligence

Workplace Realities Profile

Financial Managers

Career Interest	
	Financial/Persuasion

Social Environment	L	A	H
Autonomy	L	A	H
Creativity	L	A	H
Variety	L	A	H
Altruism	L	A	H
Stress	L	A	H

Corporations exist to show a profit, so regardless of the industry, every company requires sound financial management. In medium-to-large corporations this is the function of the *financial managers*. These financial managers oversee the ebb and flow of income and expenditures, answer to shareholders, and are the cash architects of a company's strategic plans for the future.

The *chief financial officer* (CFO), sometimes titled *treasurer*, of a large corporation issues financial orders and directs financial planning. The CFO serves as part of the financial planning committee, controlling the expenditures and enhancing the profitability of the corporation. As corporate officers, CFOs delegate responsibility to accounting department employees such as controllers, budget analysts, and accountants.

One important aspect of a CFO's job is preparing the corporate budget—and seeing that it is closely adhered to. Planning a company's annual budget is an enormous enterprise on which the success of the company and all its jobs rests. First, managers and department heads submit their anticipated expenses for the upcoming year, including allocations for resources, payroll expenses, and other operating costs, such as capital expenditures for equipment and improvements. The budget proposals then go to the analysts, who apply cost-benefit analysis to the requests, to determine whether or not they benefit the company. They check to see if the departmental estimates conform to the company's standard procedures, and to standard spending practices. Once the analysts have determined which budget requests are fiscally viable, they submit revised budget proposals to the CFO for approval; ultimately the proposals are presented to the corporate board for authorization.

The CFO also reviews and analyzes industrywide financial records, performance reports, and projections to determine what rate of return the corporation can expect on investments, such as pension plans and investments used to raise capital.

In addition, since nearly every corporation routinely carries debt, a CFO must be aware of the debt and the cost of financing it. The CFO must maintain the debt at a level with which the corporation can operate comfortably and which will not adversely affect the corporation's credit rating and, where applicable, stock prices.

Working directly under the CFO is the *corporate controller*. The controller directs the financial operations of a corporation. Controllers are responsible for preparing all financial reports and statements, including income statements, balance sheets, and depreciation schedules that apply to capital assets. Controllers usually oversee the accounting, auditing, and budgeting functions of a corporation. They also coordinate the financial operations of different departments within the corporate structure to eliminate waste and unnecessary duplication of work.

Their function, though, is not merely to present to the corporation a picture of where it currently stands. Their main responsibility is to predict future profits, losses, and expenses based on a survey of past trends. Although they do not dictate a corporation's future plans, they do determine their feasibility. For example, in a corporation planning to expand into a new market, the controller will consider factors including the company's past success in expansion, the financial stability or growth potential of the proposed new market, and the anticipated expenses involved in expansion, in order to prepare a profit-and-loss projection for the project. Although controllers are rarely the visionaries who develop strategic plans, they must have sufficient vision to see beyond the immediate present, as well as have a solid grounding in past and present concrete realities.

Other duties handled by controllers include preparing reports for regulatory agencies, determining depreciation rates for capital assets (such as properties and equipment), and remaining up-to-date on daily operations in order to advise the management on changes that affect profitability.

Changing federal and state regulations are placing greater responsibility on financial managers, such as corporate controllers, to report financial data accurately. This responsibility not only increases the potential liability for corporations that report data inaccurately, but also increases the liability of controllers themselves as well as other financial managers. In addition, the expansion of many corporations into the global market has forced controllers to develop new reporting procedures.

Those who become corporate controllers have climbed the professional ranks over the years, having started with a good education, usually within the same industry and sometimes within the same organization. Their appointment as corporate controller may be the last step in their corporate career, or it could serve as a stage leading to CFO. By promoting corporate controllers from within the organization, a company can be certain that the controller has knowledge of the company and its unique business practices. Businesses also like to promote from within because choosing a known commodity for a high-ranking position reduces the risk of making an expensive mistake in selection. If a company does hire an outsider as controller, the person will almost certainly have had previous experience in that position with a similar kind of company. This isn't the kind of job that you get hired for without a track record.

EARNING POTENTIAL

The salaries of financial managers depend a great deal on the size and financial volume of the corporation. The nature of the business (a corporation, a banking institution, or a service institution) and its location also have a bearing on managers' incomes. Large corporations in private industry located in urban areas typically offer the highest salaries; banking and service institutions traditionally pay less than corporations.

A **chief financial officer** in a company that has a volume of $50 million would typically earn in the range of $56,000 to $80,000, whereas CFOs in large corporations with volumes in excess of $500 million receive salaries in the $250,000+ range. Large bonuses and generous benefits add significantly to the compensation package.

Corporate controllers working for the $50 million corporations earn $50,000–$64,000+; those working for the $500 million corporations, $129,000+. Salaries for assistant controllers range between $38,000 and $75,000.

EDUCATIONAL REQUIREMENTS

The minimum requirement for a position as financial manager is a bachelor's degree, but that requirement is changing. Because of the increased competition for jobs and the enormous responsibilities the jobs entail, corporations are increasingly looking to M.B.A.s for their financial management expertise.

Virtually every **chief financial officer** in a large American corporation has a master's degree in business administration (M.B.A.), as do most **controllers**. Many of them start off their careers with a bachelor's degree in accounting or finance. While rising through the ranks after starting as budget analysts or accountants, they study for their M.B.A., to enhance their chance of reaching the plum jobs.

But even a master's degree does not signal the end of a financial manager's education. The current business climate requires that managers be aware of changes in the global economy. Furthermore, state and federal regulations governing financial reporting are constantly changing, and it is necessary for financial managers to remain up-to-date. Companies encourage their employees to take numerous training programs and continuing education courses, and often help finance them. These programs and courses are necessary adjuncts to the experience a manager acquires on the job.

As in all fields that deal with the processing of information, financial managers have become increasingly dependent on computers to organize and analyze information. Anyone interested in the field of financial management must be proficient in the use of computers and their applications for the profession, and must stay abreast of the perpetual changes in the development of computer technology.

Financial managers must be unflappable people who can synthesize numbers and data in order to develop a coherent financial plan that serves the goals of the corporate officers and still provides individual departments with the resources necessary to perform effectively. They must have the ability to work independently, as well as be able to supervise and direct others. They must be able to analyze information and to communicate their findings and projections clearly and decisively.

A DAY IN THE LIFE

Chief financial officers work in very comfortable offices, usually located near the offices of other corporate officers. Much of their working day is spent in meetings. Because their jobs entail a great deal of responsibility, overtime becomes simply a part of the job. There is often considerable travel required, and there may be a great deal of stress at times. Their salaries, though, are typically commensurate with the demanding work they do.

**HELP WANTED
CHIEF FINANCIAL OFFICER
AND CORPORATE
CONTROLLER**

Chief Financial Officer

Direct the financial operations of a corporation. Prepare and review the corporate budget. Control expenditures and enhance profitability of the corporation. Issue financial orders and direct financial planning. Delegate responsibility to accounting department employees. Salary Range: $56,000–$250,000+. Bonuses and shares also add significantly to income.

Corporate Controller

Manage the financial operations of a corporation. Oversee the accounting, auditing, and budgeting functions of the corporation. Predict profits, losses, and expenses based on a survey of past trends. Prepare financial reports and statements for corporate executives and regulatory agencies. Salary Range: $50,000–$129,000+.

A **corporate controller** usually has a comfortable office located near the CFO and other corporate officers. Corporate controller can be a stressful job, especially in a diversified corporation. At least a forty-hour work week is to be expected, with most controllers working the same hours as the CFO. Since they work primarily with numbers, computers, and printouts, controllers do very little work-related traveling.

JOB GROWTH

There are approximately 701,000 financial managers in American businesses and service organizations. One-third of this number are employed by banks, savings and loans, finance companies, credit unions, insurance companies, and real estate firms. Another third are employed in health, social welfare, and management services. The Department of Labor Statistics forecasts that there will be an additional 170,000 financial managers hired over the next decade.

Relatively few people who rise to levels in financial management transfer to a different career path. Opportunities, therefore, will result from openings created by people either being promoted or retiring, and from the growth of American corporations and the new opportunities so generated. Many banking institutions are merging and consolidating their operations, so there will be less demand for financial managers in that field. Look for openings in the booming areas of business growth such as health care, environment, and international trade. The demand for skilled financial managers will increase with the growth of global trade, with the conflicting regulations that it will generate, and with the rapid changes in federal and state regulatory procedures.

Corporate controllers usually rise through the ranks of an organization. They may begin as accountants, be promoted to assistant controller, and then become controller.

Competition for the coveted and lucrative position of **CFO** is fierce. There are always a number of competent candidates waiting in the wings, whether it is someone from inside the corporation, a CFO from another corporation who can be wooed away, or an outside candidate with the right background and track record.

Highly skilled managers will succeed in the field, but competition for positions will grow increasingly intense in an employer-controlled job market. The downsizing trend in middle management may mean greater opportunity for advancement among those candidates who succeed in holding their jobs. They may be required to work longer hours and adapt more quickly to changing demands, but those who prove to be exceptionally well-qualified can expect to advance within their corporate hierarchy. Today's streamlined businesses operate on ability, not seniority. Young managers have the same opportunity as senior managers to advance within an organization.

Whether large businesses consolidate or diversify, they still will need astute financial officers and controllers to predict future trends and to steer them on the most financially prudent course in an uncertain time.

Insurance

INSURANCE AGENT/INSURANCE BROKER

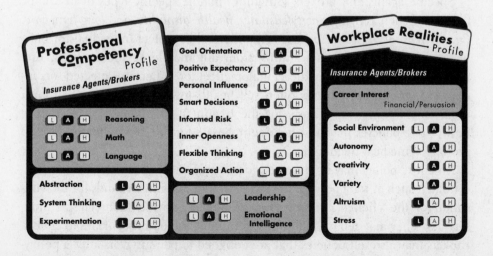

The primary difference between insurance brokers and insurance agents is that *insurance brokers* do not sell insurance for one specific company, but provide advice for their clients on the best insurance company, with the best rate and coverage, that suits the clients' needs. They are responsible for explaining the positives and negatives of various policies clearly to the client. *Insurance agents* often represent and sell one company's line of insurance policies (although independent agents may represent policies of various companies).

Insurance brokers and agents sell insurance policies to individuals, families, and large and small businesses. The correct policy may provide insurance protection for the lives of the policyholders, their health, automobiles, jewelry, personal valuables, furniture, household items, business, or other properties. Insurance brokers also service whatever policy these groups choose, and may also provide policy consultation to any of these groups. Finally, they may provide assistance with the retirement plans of their individual clients.

Insurance agents and brokers are responsible for compiling lists of prospective insurance clients, and making contact with these prospective clients. Sometimes initial contacts are made through referrals. Sales agents explain the merits of certain policies to these individuals, suggest a particular policy appropriate to a prospective client's needs, and calculate the full deductible and the premium for each policy. Once a policy has been successfully sold, the agent should continue to stay in contact with the new policyholder to see if there are any personal or business changes that affect the client's insurance needs. In the event of a loss on the part of a policyholder, the agent helps the policyholder settle any insurance claims. Agents or brokers may also be responsible for collecting weekly or monthly insurance premium payments.

Specific agents and brokers sometimes handle specific types of insurance for clients, such as *life, property/casualty, health, disability*, and *long-term care*. *Property/casual insurance brokers* sell policies that protect individuals or businesses from financial loss resulting from automobile accidents, theft, fire, work-related accidents, medical malpractice, or other unexpected occurrences. *Life insurance agents* often sell health insurance policies that cover medical or hospital care costs for the treatment of illness or work-related injury. The policies may also help compensate for the loss of income due to prolonged medical treatment.

An entire policy may be designed for an even more specific need of a policyholder, such as for a policyholder's retirement income, or funds for the education of the client's children. Some brokers provide financial planning services. They may sell mutual funds, annuities, and other securities to clients. Brokers may also sell policies that are designed to pay survivors after a policyholder's death. Life insurance agents who handle this kind of responsibility are also called *life underwriters*.

EARNING POTENTIAL

The median annual income of salaried insurance agents and brokers is $30,100. The middle fifty percent earn between $20,900 and $42,200 a year. The lowest ten percent earn approximately $15,400 or less a year, while the top ten percent earn over $64,600 a year. Agents and brokers are usually paid in one of three ways: regular salary only, salary plus bonuses, or salary plus commissions (the most common form of pay). Most independent insurance agents are paid on some commission structure, and this is especially true for those with the greatest experience, for whom commissions are usually high. Commissions depend mostly on the type of insurance that is sold and on whether the policy sold is new or a renewal. Some agents receive an hourly fee in place of commissions.

Insurance agents receive a wide array of benefits, including continuing education support, group insurance plans, and office space. Because agents must do a large amount of traveling, agencies usually pay for an agent's automobile or transportation expenses. They are likely to pay also for expenses accrued at convention meetings and in marketing or promotion enterprises.

Independent agents and brokers working for various agencies receive benefits, but they have no paid vacations or holidays. Their commissions, though, tend to be higher than those of non-independent agents because independent agents carry high marketing and promotional expenses.

All agents and brokers are legally responsible for any insurance mistakes they make. Independent agents consequently must buy their own insurance to cover any damages that arise from oversights or errors.

EDUCATIONAL REQUIREMENTS

Educational requirements for agents and brokers vary according to the different agencies. Most insurance companies prefer to hire college graduates who have majored in business or economics, but this does not imply that you must have a degree to get a job in this field; openings are available for applicants with only a high school degree if the applicant has a proven sales ability and excellent work experience. And since new brokers and agents often transfer from other occupations, many newly hired agents are significantly older than recent high school or college graduates.

Many colleges and universities offer courses in insurance, and certain colleges even offer students a chance to receive a bachelor's degree in insurance. Students enhance their preparedness for the insurance field by also taking courses in finance, mathematics, accounting, economics, business law, government, and business administration. All of these courses improve a student's understanding of social, marketing, and economic conditions relevant to the insurance field. Of course, an advanced degree from a business school is also extremely helpful for a prospective agent or broker, especially as the diversity of financial products sold by insurance companies increases.

Coursework in psychology, sociology, and public speaking are good preparation for work in the insurance field. Experience with computers is also very important, since computers provide instantaneous client information and deliver timely data on financial products available to the customer. It is important for an agent or broker to stay aware of any changes in tax laws, government benefit programs, and other state and federal regulations that affect the insurance needs of clients.

In order to sell insurance, every insurance agent and broker must receive a license from the state in which the agent works. In most states, licenses are obtained when applicants successfully complete specified courses and then pass written examinations that test knowledge of insurance fundamentals and state insurance laws. Separate licenses are required of agents and brokers who sell mutual funds and other securities. As licensed brokers continue to work, they may also pursue additional training at conferences and seminars sponsored by insurance organizations.

Several professional organizations offer professional designation programs that certify that an agent or broker is suitably experienced in a specific insurance field such as health, property, and casualty insurance, or financial consulting. These organizations require that applicants get additional education in order to receive such certifications of expertise.

Insurance is a sales profession, and thus the agents and brokers should possess certain personal qualities that inspire trust and respect in their clients. They should be affable, sincere, confident, and good communicators. Additionally, as they are for the most part self-employed or at least self-managed, they should be self-motivated and organized.

A DAY IN THE LIFE

Most insurance agents and brokers stay in contact with clients and prospective clients over the phone in small offices. They also spend a significant amount of time outside of these offices, traveling in local areas to meet with clients.

HELP WANTED
INSURANCE

Insurance Agent/
Insurance Broker

Sell insurance policies to individuals, large or small businesses, and families. Explain merits of policies, suggest appropriate policies, and calculate the full deductible and premium for each policy. Also stay in contact with the new policyholder to monitor any changes. Provide assistance with the retirement plans of individual clients. Compile lists of prospective insurance clients, and make contact with them. Salary Range: $15,400–$64,600+.

Insurance agents therefore have flexible schedules, with hours that they can design themselves and according to clients' needs. Evening and weekend hours are often required, and many insurance agents work more than forty hours every week.

Most agents work in cities, large towns, or other large population areas throughout the country. Some insurance agents are employed at the headquarters of insurance companies. Most agents and brokers, however, are employed at local insurance company offices or at independent insurance agency offices.

JOB GROWTH

There are approximately 292,000 insurance agents and brokers employed in this country. Employment of insurance agents and brokers in the United States is expected to grow much faster than the average for all occupations through the year 2005, with an additional 36,500 positions expected to open. Turnover is fairly high, so it is expected that many openings will arise out of the need to replace agents and brokers who leave the occupation. Many agents leave because of the highly competitive nature of the work.

The growth and volume of sales of insurance and financial products will ultimately determine the future demand for new insurance agents. As incomes rise, and as individuals become more concerned for their own long-term financial security, mutual funds, variable annuities, and other financial options will become more attractive. Since the number of retirees is expected to be high, so too will be the demand for long-term health care and pension benefits. Finally, in addition to items that traditionally need coverage, like homes and cars, new technology products, such as home computers, will also require insurance coverage, and this will gradually increase the need for insurance workers. This coverage of computers and advanced technology will be necessary on a wider scale—in both small and big businesses.

Companies are reducing the traveling needs of their agents by diversifying their marketing techniques to include direct mail and telephone sales. This reduces the amount of time and energy an agent puts into developing a sales lead, and it allows the agent to concentrate more on follow-ups. Customer service representatives are also more often performing duties like selling, expanding accounts, and sometimes generating new accounts, which once would have been handled by sales agents only. Each of these factors, along with the growth of multiline agents, self-insurance, and group policies, will make the work of agents and brokers more efficient, but it may impact hiring somewhat.

ACTUARY

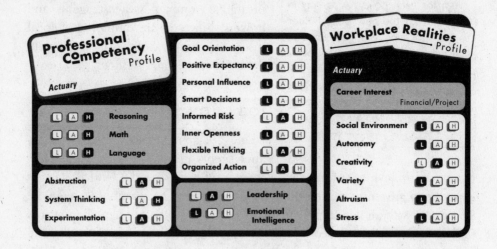

Actuaries are the original number crunchers, the people who digest large amounts of information to determine one's life expectancy, the likelihood that one's car will be stolen, or the growth rate of investments so that a company's pension plan will be able to make payments to retired employees. Actuaries are most frequently found working in the insurance industry, where they analyze past statistics (deaths, car thefts, stock gains and losses) in order to calculate future probabilities, thereby determining a policyholder's current payments.

It is essential that insurance companies have enough resources to compensate policyholders for their anticipated losses. The chief source of revenue for an insurance carrier is the premiums paid by policyholders. Calculating the premium rates and determining policy contract provisions is the actuary's job, and it is not a simple task. For example, in determining the premium for automobile insurance policies, the actuary looks at statistics for drivers by sex, age, and residence (home/apartment, city/suburb), type of automobile, and many other factors. The actuary then must set a premium payment that covers the probability of loss for the insured, makes a profit for the insurance carrier, and still remains competitive with premiums for similar policies in the industry. This same degree of calculation is used to determine premium rates and policy provisions for every type of insurance a company offers.

A skilled actuary is someone who has a facility with numbers and a strong background in mathematics, probabilities, and statistics, and the principles of finance. Actuaries must also remain abreast of changes in the economy, social trends, legislation, and general health in order to determine the accuracy of their statistics. Since the field is so complex, and since the information digested by an actuary changes constantly, it is no surprise that most actuaries concentrate on a particular area of expertise, for example, life, health, property and casualty insurance, and financial planning and investment.

Actuaries elevated to executive positions are not only technically proficient in their field but are also highly skilled communicators. Their role as executives includes explaining complex data to other company executives, policyholders and shareholders, and the general public. It is the executive-level actuary who testifies at public hearings concerning legislation affecting the insurance industry, premium rate increases, or policy provisions. They can also be visionaries in looking for new areas of business to explore, such as environmental risk or long-term health care for the elderly.

A small percentage of actuaries are self-employed consultants. They are often called upon as expert witnesses in legal matters in order to determine an injured party's wages lost due to injury, or the equitable distribution of anticipated proceeds in divorce cases. They may also set up pension plans, employer contributions for benefits packages, and unemployment compensation for small businesses. Still others work exclusively under the Employment Retirement Income Security Act of 1974, evaluating pension plans covered by the act and determining their financial stability.

EARNING POTENTIAL

A study conducted by the College Placement Council found that starting salaries for actuaries with a bachelor's degree averaged about $31,800. New college graduates who enter the field without having passed any actuarial exams average slightly lower salaries.

Typically, insurance companies and consulting firms give merit increases to actuaries as they gain experience and pass examinations. A Life Office Management Association survey of insurance and financial services companies indicated that actuarial students who have been designated associate, Society of Actuaries, received an average salary of about $46,000. Newly designated fellows, Society of Actuaries, received an average salary of nearly $65,500; fellows with additional years of experience can earn substantially more. In addition to base salary, actuaries receive other benefits, such as vacation and sick leave, health and life insurance, and pension plans.

EDUCATIONAL REQUIREMENTS

An actuary usually will have a bachelor's degree with a solid grounding in mathematics, actuarial science, statistics, economics, finance, and accounting. Courses in computer science and insurance are also very helpful to an aspiring actuary. Some companies prefer well-rounded individuals who, in addition to a strong technical background, have some training in liberal arts and business. Good communication and interpersonal skills are important, particularly for prospective consulting actuaries, where salesmanship is an element of securing and maintaining business. Although only about fifty-five colleges and universities offer an actuarial science program, hundreds of schools offer a degree in mathematics or statistics.

New actuaries serve what amounts to an internship (much like doctors), rotating among such jobs as marketing, underwriting, or product development in order to learn various actuarial operations and the different phases of insurance work. At first, they may prepare data for actuarial tables or perform other simple tasks as they develop the expertise that will determine the success of their employers.

Job advancement hinges on job performance and the number of actuarial examinations passed. These examinations, sponsored by the Society of Actuaries (life and health insurance and pension, finance, and investment) and the Casualty Actuarial Society (property and casualty), are given twice a year. Most actuaries begin the series while in school and complete it while serving their internship. It generally takes five to ten years to complete the exam series, which requires considerable independent study in such subjects as linear algebra, calculus, statistics, risk theory, and actuarial mathematics.

A DAY IN THE LIFE

Actuaries generally work a forty-hour week. An actuary spends most of her or his working hours at a desk, usually in a comfortable insurance office. Although some actuaries may travel to confer with clients, their tools are still a

HELP WANTED
ACTUARY

Determine insurance premiums. A facility with numbers, and a strong background in mathematics, probability, and statistics, and the principles of finance necessary. Must remain abreast of changes in the economy, social trends, legislation, and general health trends. Required to present and explain complex data to other company executives, policyholders, shareholders, and the general public. Salary Range: $31,800–$65,500.

computer, a calculator, and reams of statistical information.

JOB GROWTH

A recent study showed that there are approximately 15,000 actuaries in this country, a small percentage of whom are self-employed. More than half of the total number of actuaries work for the insurance industry, primarily for life insurance companies. The rest working within the industry work for property, casualty, and health insurance companies, and insurance agents and brokers. Most of the remaining actuaries work for firms providing consulting services, while a small number work for government agencies.

The outlook for employment in this field is very good, with positions for actuaries expected to grow faster than the average through the year 2005. But competition for jobs will be stiff, in part because favorable publicity about actuaries has increased the number of individuals entering the field. The best applicants for actuarial positions will be college graduates who have passed at least two actuarial examinations while still in school and exhibit a strong background in mathematics and statistics.

Advancement in the insurance industry generally takes place within two categories: Actuaries with expertise in the insurance, pension, and employee benefits fields often become administrators and executives in *underwriting*, *accounting*, or *data processing*. Those with a business background and supervisory ability may become managers in the areas of *marketing*, *advertising*, or *planning*. For any kind of advancement in the field, strong communication and problem-solving skills are considered a plus.

Despite the fact that the need for actuaries will continue to grow, the demand for them to work within the insurance industry will decrease. Mirroring the rest of the economy, insurance companies will turn to outside consulting agencies to replace in-house departments. Therefore, the major growth trend for actuaries will be with agencies that provide consulting services to the insurance industry.

Insurance

UNDERWRITERS

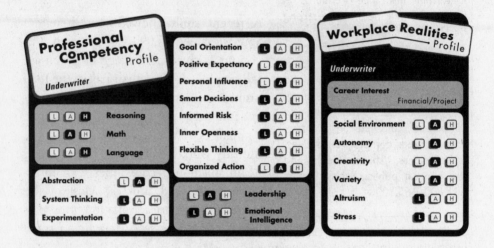

If an insurance company were run by its salespeople, the agents and brokers, it would go out of business quickly. In an effort to sell the greatest number of policies, the salesmen would insure many high-risk candidates, who would file too many claims. The company would go bankrupt because too much money would be paid out.

On the other hand, an insurance company run by actuaries would also go out of business quickly. Since actuaries are responsible for reducing an insurance company's risks, the company would never issue enough policies to cover overhead and the company would go bankrupt.

Underwriters occupy the middle ground between the two competing yet complementary functions described above. They are the professionals who appraise and choose the risks their company will insure. They base their decisions not only on data prepared by their company's actuaries, but also on facts supplied by the people applying for coverage. This process is not an exact science, although underwriters attempt to keep their company's risks within acceptable limits.

Underwriters must take into account factors such as, for life insurance coverage, a person's genetic predisposition to heart disease or cancer and that person's occupational exposure to factors contributing to the diseases. For property coverage, they might also study a region's cyclical weather patterns governing hurricanes or floods and the location of an insured's property in that region. They gather facts from medical reports, actuarial studies, insurance applications, and other sources to determine (a) whether or not the risks involved in a policy are worth taking, and (b) what premium to charge. What's the connection between an actuary and an underwriter? The actuary works out the overall range of risk, based on all possible variables. The underwriter uses the resulting guidelines to evaluate each individual customer profile and set a policy rate.

Because the amount of data they draw on continues to increase, many underwriters specialize in one of the three major categories of insurance: *life*, *property/casualty*, or *health*. These categories break down into additional subspecialties; for example, the property and casualty field includes fire, home, auto, marine, property, and workers' compensation. Furthermore, underwriters often focus on either group or individual policies.

Group policies make up the fastest-growing area of insurance sales. These policies, generally for life or health insurance, offer the same coverage to a group of people, all of whom pay the same premium rates. In determining the premium rates for such a group, an underwriter evaluates the group as a whole as well as certain factors pertaining to individuals. He or she then assigns a risk factor to the entire group's coverage and sets a premium.

Another form of underwriting involves the risk businesses and professionals face in the practice of their trade. What is the risk that a law firm will lose a big case due to its own negligence? What legitimate risks that fall under a doctor's control are involved in a surgical procedure? Many professionals are required by law to carry malpractice insurance as protection for their clients or patients. *Commercial accounting underwriters* study the risks and liabilities involved in running a business and determine the amount of coverage a company, law firm, or medical practice requires.

This career appeals to people who enjoy detail-oriented work and have good analytical ability. Underwriters must also have good judgment and the ability to make decisions.

EARNING POTENTIAL

Starting salaries for underwriters depend in part on the applicant's background. College graduates will initially earn more than applicants without a degree. Starting salaries are better in the field of commercial insurance, but salaries eventually tend to level off and stay constant with those in the personal insurance field. Here are the annual income averages:

	Personal Insurance Field	Commercial Insurance Field
Entry-Level Underwriter	$25,000	$28,000
Intermediate-Level Underwriter	$32,200	$32,800
Senior-level	$40,200	$40,600
Supervisor	$45,300	$45,500
Manager	$61,000	$61,000

Most insurance companies offer excellent benefits packages, which serve as an attractive inducement for applicants.

EDUCATIONAL REQUIREMENTS

A college degree is not necessary to get a job as an underwriter; however, insurance companies *prefer* applicants with a college degree in the field of business administration, finance, or accounting. Courses in business law may also prove helpful to aspiring underwriters.

Most companies have underwriter trainee positions available for those without a college degree, but these individuals should seek a degree in order to enhance their future job prospects. Large insurance companies offer training programs to prepare assistant underwriters for the profession. Underwriters are expected to take continuing education courses in the field as a part of the job. Companies usually pay the tuition involved. The American Institute of Chartered Property Casualty Underwriters offers the designations of Associate in Underwriting (A.U.) and Chartered Property Casualty Underwriter (C.P.C.U.). An A.U. designation requires a year and a half of class work and the passing of a comprehensive examination. The C.P.C.U. designation requires passing ten examinations on subjects such as personal and commercial risk management, business law, accounting, finance, economics, and ethics. This designation usually takes five years to achieve, and is of most benefit to those pursuing management careers in the field.

A DAY IN THE LIFE

Underwriters work at desks in offices. Since the majority of them work for insurance companies, the offices are usually pleasant and comfortable. Insurance underwriting is typically a forty-hour-a-week job, although overtime is occasionally required.

There may be some travel demands, depending on the area of specialization. For example, underwriters assessing the risk for construction projects

**HELP WANTED
UNDERWRITER**

Appraise and choose for company which risks to insure. Base decisions on data prepared by actuaries, and facts supplied by people applying for coverage. Take into account medical histories and other factors which might affect a policy premium. Study the risks and liabilities involved in running a business and determine the amount of coverage a company, law firm, or medical practice requires. Need to enjoy detail-oriented work. Good judgment, analytical ability, and decision-making abilities a must. Salary Range: $25,000–$61,000.

may need to go on-site to evaluate all of the relevant factors in determining a policy's premiums.

JOB GROWTH

There are over 105,000 underwriters in the United States, the majority of whom work for insurance companies. The largest number (approximately 40,000) are employed as underwriters for property and liability policies. The next largest speciality, life insurance, employs 14,000 insurance company underwriters. Other underwriters working for insurance companies specialize in medical service plans and health benefits, and in pension funds.

Underwriters also work for independent insurance agencies, banks, mortgage companies, and real estate firms. Those working for independent agencies do not represent one particular insurance company. Instead, part of their job is to decide which insurance company best serves the needs of the agency and the client.

Employment prospects for underwriters are expected to grow by 24 percent through 2005, amounting to about 17,000 positions. More jobs will come from the need to replace underwriters who have retired, transferred to other jobs, or left the field entirely. There will be some growth, though. Larger numbers of people will be raising children, which increases the demand for life, health, and property insurance. Families that depend on two incomes will need greater amounts of insurance to protect against the loss of one income due to death or illness. Longer life expectancies will increase the need for long-term health benefits.

One factor working against growth in this field is a trend toward self-insurance. Self-insurance means that a company determines its own legitimate business-related risks and pays money into a fund dedicated to paying or disputing claims made against it.

Also, many insurance carriers are changing the nature of their business. Some are dropping lines of personal or individual insurance in favor of more lucrative commercial insurance. Underwriters who specialize in a particular area of insurance may find difficulty in transferring to another area, but transferring will still be easier than gaining entrance to the specialty as a newcomer; this is because the underwriter will already have knowledge about the systems and procedures of the industry.

Human Resources

BENEFITS MANAGER/COMPENSATION MANAGER/EMPLOYEE ASSISTANCE PROGRAM MANAGER

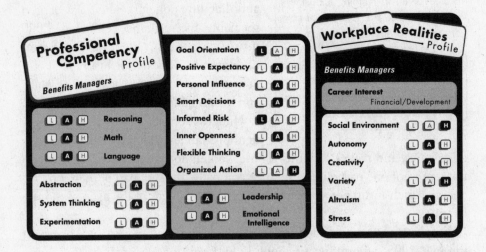

Human resources department functions are increasingly important to corporations. Some of the most demanding tasks confronting human resources departments are the management of a wide range of employee benefits and the management of a company's compensation program.

Most labor disputes have historically involved compensation or working conditions. Today, with health care costs increasing at greater than 15 percent each year, many labor disputes revolve around a company's medical benefits packages. Employees want to be fully covered, and want the coverage to extend to their family members. Employers, looking to stem the overwhelming expense of medical insurance, typically insist upon co-payment by employees. Sitting in the middle of these ongoing disputes are the benefits managers who represent management and assist the employees.

Benefits managers supervise a company's employee benefits program, the largest portions of which are usually *medical insurance*, *workmen's compensation*, and *pension plans*. Each of these fields requires separate expertise since they are all extremely complicated. For example, pension plans might include such options as profit sharing, stock ownership, or a payroll deduction that is matched by the employer and used for various investments. Managing these funds requires knowledge of the stock and bond markets and a particular attention to the current values of the investments at all times.

Workmen's comp is another area in the benefits manager's bailiwick. Workmen's compensation is payment an employee receives for a work-related disability. Often these claims are easily proved by a doctor's examination. At other times, though, claims cannot be substantiated by an examination, and they may lead to an investigation of the employee's actual condition.

Benefits managers serve as intermediaries in claim disputes between employees and the medical insurance carrier. This requires professional acumen, tact, and a knowledge of insurance practices and familiarity with the various benefits plans the company makes available to its employees. Benefits managers oversee all of these detail-oriented tasks, and many others.

Compensation managers establish a competitive pay scale for a company's employees. This is not an arbitrary task. They compare wages paid by their company with those of other companies in the industry, government minimum wage standards, and collective bargaining agreements between labor unions and other similarly situated employers.

Other factors that enter the compensation equation are a study of what a particular job involves, the job description, and evaluations regarding the job's value to the company's processes. By studying these aspects of a job and interacting with other human resource professionals such as staffing specialists, the compensation manager arrives at a relative value for the job's worth, which is then converted to a monetary figure. Pay raises and overtime compensation also undergo similar study.

All of this work is designed to accomplish two goals: to maintain the stability of the company's workforce and to maintain parity with industry compensation. Every employee wants to receive higher pay, but a pay scale not in keeping with an industry's standards means a company could be frittering away profit. When employees are paid basically the same amount as other employees in the same industry, they tend to stay with their employer, thereby reducing the costs attributed to high employee turnover. A benefits manager and a compensation manager set a company's standard for total compensation by constantly monitoring and adhering to industry standards. And with the current downward pressure on wages, competent compensation managers are in great demand, because they can make money for the company by saving money for the company.

Employee assistance program managers provide companies with similar services to benefits managers, but they also serve as more personal counselors in working with employees' individual needs. They talk informally with personnel and attend meetings of managers, supervisors, and work units to ensure effective communication among participants and to resolve human relations and work-related problems that affect employee morale and productivity. These managers provide assistance in identifying, evaluating, and solving human relations and work performance problems within a company.

Employee assistance program (EAP) managers can also handle the company's employee benefits program, notably its health insurance and pension plans. Expertise in designing and administering benefits programs continues to gain importance as employer-provided benefits account for a growing proportion of overall compensation costs, and as benefit plans increase in number and complexity. For example, pension benefits might include savings and thrift, profit sharing, and stock ownership plans, and health benefits might include long-term catastrophic illness insurance and dental insurance. Familiarity with health benefits is a top priority at present, as more firms struggle to cope with the rising cost of health care for current employees and retirees.

In addition to health insurance and pension coverage, EAP managers are involved in creating the new benefits designed to meet the needs of a changing workforce, such as parental leave, child care and elder care, long-term nursing home care insurance, employee wellness programs, and flexible benefits plans (in which employees have the option of receiving cash instead of benefits). EAP managers must keep abreast of changing federal and state regulations and legislation that may affect employee benefits.

Some EAP managers can also be known as *employee welfare managers*. They are responsible for a wide array of programs covering occupational safety and health standards and practices, health promotion and physical fitness, medical examinations and minor health treatments such as first aid, plant security, publications, food service and recreation activities, carpooling, employee suggestion systems, child care and elder care, and counseling services. They also help employees deal with emotional disorders, alcoholism, or marital, family, consumer, legal, or financial problems. Career counseling and second-career counseling for employees approaching retirement age or outplacement may also be provided.

EARNING POTENTIAL

A recent survey of all management and staff positions in the human resources field found that the median annual salary for **benefits managers** was $59,500, and for **compensation managers**, $58,200. Beginning salaries for both positions were around $47,000, and were $73,000 at the high end.

The median annual salary for **employee assistance program managers** was approximately $51,800. Beginning managers can expect to earn in the range of $40,000, while more experienced managers can earn $60,000+.

EDUCATIONAL REQUIREMENTS

Because benefits and compensation are such complex areas of human resources, anyone interested in reaching the higher levels in the profession is encouraged to study for a master's degree in the field of human resources or business administration. It is unlikely that anyone who has only a bachelor's degree will be promoted to an important managerial level in a large corporation in the future. Although **benefits manager** and **compensation manager** are specialized jobs, they both require knowledge of the broader base of human resources services as well as knowledge of federal regulations, investing, auditing, accounting, and other related fields. A master's degree serves as an excellent way to gain knowledge of several related fields while specializing in one field. For purposes of career advancement, a master's degree will prove to be important to those wishing to reach the highest management levels; today we are seeing human resources professionals sitting on the boards of major corporations, and even heading such companies, so valuable is their expertise to the overall profitability of a company.

Because of the diversity of duties and levels of responsibility, **employee assistance program managers** have educational backgrounds that vary considerably. In filling entry-level jobs, firms generally seek college graduates. Some employers prefer applicants who have majored in human resources, personnel administration or human resources management, training and development, or compensation and benefits. Depending on the school, courses leading to a career in human resources management may be found in departments of business administration, education, instructional technology, organizational development, human services, communication, or public administration, or within a separate human resources institute or department within the school.

Because an interdisciplinary background is appropriate for work in this area, a combination of courses in the social sciences, business, and behavioral sciences is useful. Some jobs may benefit from a background in engineering, science, finance, or law. Most prospective personnel specialists should take courses in compensation, recruitment, training and development, and performance appraisal, as well as courses in principles of management, organizational structure, and industrial psychology. Other relevant courses might include business administration, public administration, psychology, sociology, political science, economics, and statistics. Technological adaptedness is important for all these jobs.

For many specialized jobs in this field, previous experience is an asset; obviously, for managerial positions it is essential. Employers prefer to select entry-level workers who have gained some experience through an internship or work-study program while in school. Personnel administration and human resources development require the ability to work with individuals as well as a commitment to organizational goals. This field also demands other skills that people may develop elsewhere, such as technological literacy, highly developed communication skills, teaching, and supervising. This field offers clerical workers opportunities for advancement to professional positions, and responsible positions are sometimes filled by experienced individuals from other fields, including business, government, education, social services administration, and the military.

A DAY IN THE LIFE

Benefits managers and **compensation managers** work in the human resources offices of corporations. Most of the work they perform involves processing information, so they rarely have responsibilities that take them out of the office.

Benefits managers spend a great deal of time in an office, on the telephone with medical providers and insurance companies trying to resolve payment or coverage disputes. They also work with computers in overseeing pension plan holdings and other matters.

Compensation managers also spend most days in an office, working with financial software applications on computers. They work largely with numbers and factors (such as productivity) that are reduced to formulae.

Employee assistance program managers usually work in offices which are typically clean, comfortable, and quiet. The physical demands are modest, with a lot of time spent sitting at a desk, computer, or telephone and in meetings with management and employees.

All human resources managers work under little direct supervision, but they must work in cooperation with others. They usually work forty-hour weeks, but night or weekend hours may be necessary.

HELP WANTED
BENEFITS
MANAGER/COMPENSATION
MANAGER/EMPLOYEE
ASSISTANCE PROGRAM
MANAGER

Benefits Manager

Supervise employee benefits program. Mediate claim disputes and oversee the investigation of employee's actual physical condition for claims. Job requires professional acumen, tact, and a knowledge of insurance practices and familiarity with the company's benefits and investment plans. Salary Range: $47,000–$73,000.

Compensation Manager

Establish a competitive pay scale for employees after conducting comparative compensation studies. Salary Range: $47,000–$73,000.

Employee Assistance Program Manager

Communicate with personnel to encourage morale and productivity. Assist in identifying, evaluating, and solving human relations problems. Provide information to employees on benefits plans, and research and possibly implement new benefit plans. Salary Range: $40,000–$60,000.

JOB GROWTH

Jobs in all human resources fields are expected to grow at a rate exceeding the national average through 2005. Although true management jobs in the field are expected to decrease during that period, two areas that show the best growth within the next ten years are **benefits managers** and **compensation managers**—which, considering corporate America's desire to hold down wages and benefits, is only logical. Federal growth figures for labor relations training and human resources managers are lumped together, and show an additional 40,000 jobs through 2005.

Many human resources positions can be handled by managers or staff on a part-time or consulting basis; interviewing, hiring, firing, and outplacement determinations are no longer a full-time need for many companies. A field such as employee training can easily be outsourced to consultants working on a contract basis. Consequently, while all of these jobs will show growth, a significant portion are likely to be in the consulting industry, with companies that provide one or more of these services to traditional employers. But since **benefits** and **compensation** are particular to a specific company, they require enough work to ensure their continuing as full-time positions.

While the short-term projections for managers in general are not particularly strong due to the 1990s corporate downsizing trend, experienced **human resources managers** are expected to increase by 30 percent by 2005. There are, however, a lot of unemployed managers looking for work, so competition is stiff; current skills, education, creativity, and track record will always win the day.

One route to consider for managers who already have experience might be working as *consultants*. Someone who can manage the benefits packages or compensation determination for one company should be able to transfer those skills to other companies in the same industry. Although benefits and compensation managers will be necessary to companies, they will need to rely on outside consultants if they lose some of their support staff. Outsourcing is the trend among businesses, and someone with the skills, qualifications, and credentials to be a consultant should give thought to an option that is becoming a trend, and that one day soon may become an established career path.

Demand for **employee assistance program managers** is governed by the staffing needs of the firms where they work. A rapidly expanding business is likely to hire additional human resource professionals either as permanent employees or consultants, while a business that has experienced a merger or a reduction of its workforce will require fewer human resource professionals. Employment may also be adversely affected by corporate downsizing or restructuring. On the other hand, as human resources management becomes increasingly important to the success of an organization, some small and medium-sized businesses that do not have a human resources department will need to develop these functions as part of responsible growth. In any particular firm, the size and the job duties of the human resources staff are determined by a variety of factors, including the firm's organizational philosophy and goals, the labor intensity and skill profile of the industry, the pace of technological change, governmental regulations, collective bargaining agreements, standards of professional practice, and labor market conditions.

HUMAN RESOURCES MANAGER/HUMAN RESOURCES STAFFING SPECIALIST

Formerly known as the *personnel* department, a corporate *human resources* department is responsible for interviewing and hiring job applicants, as well as for their development, disciplining, and ultimate termination. The goal of many H/R departments is to save money for the company.

Human resources managers concern themselves not only with an applicant's qualifications, but also with such intangible qualities as personality, temperament, and how an applicant will fit in with the organization's corporate culture; ultimately a bad fit will be costly to the corporation. By hiring the right candidate for the job, human resources managers and their staff help to improve morale, productivity, and the company's competitive ability.

Professional Competency Profile
Human Resources Manager

Skill	L	A	H
Reasoning		A	
Math			H
Language		A	
Abstraction		A	
System Thinking			H
Experimentation		A	

Skill	L	A	H
Goal Orientation		A	
Positive Expectancy		A	
Personal Influence			H
Smart Decisions			H
Informed Risk			H
Inner Openness			H
Flexible Thinking		A	
Organized Action		A	
Leadership	A		
Emotional Intelligence			H

Workplace Realities Profile
Human Resources Manager

Career Interest
Development/Persuasion

Factor	L	A	H
Social Environment			H
Autonomy		A	
Creativity		A	
Variety			H
Altruism			H
Stress		A	

Human resources managers in smaller companies may also offer training programs that provide employees with a means to sharpen and improve their skills.

It's the human resources manager who usually oversees individual firings and large layoffs, which demand expertise in employment law as well as an understanding of human psychology and behavior. With many large companies continuing the trend of downsizing, one of the most pressing tasks facing human resources managers is to decide—in meetings with corporate management and department heads—how many employees will be laid off; what severance, unemployment, or outplacement benefits they will receive; and how to announce the layoffs.

A human resources manager in a large corporation oversees several departments headed by other managers. Some of these departments include *compensation and benefits*; *training and development*; and *labor relations*. (See pages 302–3; 313; 317 for these other titles.) These specialties require training in accounting principles, government regulations, insurance practices and insurance law, and proven job training methods.

Human resources management is an attractive job for many people who like to be challenged. It is one of the most demanding jobs in the corporate world, and—in a field where mistakes can cost a company millions—requires specific ongoing training.

Human resources staffing specialists are highly trained individuals who have the responsibility for the recruitment and selection of a company's workforce. Human resources staffing specialists write a job description based on their research that explains the duties, previous training, education, experience, and the particular skills and behavioral traits necessary to a job. Then they recruit and screen candidates for these positions.

Staffing specialists interview applicants and decide which ones best fit the needs of the organization. Employee turnover from poor recruitment and selection practices has always cost companies money because of lost production. In these days, when companies are operating with fewer employees, employee turnover is even more costly. Human resources staffing specialists are expected to fill jobs with applicants who will perform their job well and will stay with the organization long enough to become a financial asset. An ability to recruit and hire the right candidate is what makes the staffing specialist so valuable to an organization.

EARNING POTENTIAL

Salaries for H/R personnel vary widely depending on the size of the organization. One recent survey quoted the median annual salary for **human resources managers** as $37,000. Another survey of workplaces in 160 metropolitan areas showed a higher average salary, ranging from approximately $51,000 to as much as $105,000 for the most experienced managers.

The median annual salary for **human resources staffing specialists** is $35,200, although these salaries also varied widely. Starting salaries for those with a bachelor's degree averaged $22,900 annually, while specialists with a master's degree started at $30,500.

EDUCATIONAL REQUIREMENTS

Since H/R is now a specialized field, most staffing specialists hold college degrees in some related major, such as personnel administration or industrial and labor relations. Other applicants include general business graduates, and graduates with a combined business and liberal arts background. Writing and communication skills are essential to every human resources professional.

No applicant new to the field is hired as a human resources manager. Experience, education, and track record are the requirements necessary for managerial jobs in this field. Many people interested in the field can prepare themselves for eventual managerial jobs by completing an advanced degree program in personnel, employee training, or labor relations. An M.B.A. degree with a concentration in human resources management is also an excellent preparation for career advancement.

Employers will pay for all or part of an employee's graduate education in a field that will enhance his or her value to the company. Since experience is also a necessity for management positions, the ideal situation for those seeking H/R management positions is to work for a company while attending graduate school, thereby doubling their value to the employer.

A DAY IN THE LIFE

Human resources jobs are office jobs. Although managers and staff members may travel a great deal in order to recruit prospective employees on college campuses or at professional meetings and conventions, most of the work involves office interviews and paperwork. In large companies, **human resources managers** will probably specialize in a few areas of the profession. Managers in other departments will tend to their own specialities. In small companies, though, human resources managers are expected to be generalists and to oversee all personnel-related functions.

Human resources staffing specialists work in offices, primarily for larger employers or for staffing organizations. In fact, the staffing industry is one of the hot growth areas for human resources professionals. Most of their duties are performed in the office, although some travel may be required to determine the exact nature of a position that they must fill or to interview prospective employees.

H/R staff jobs are usually forty-hour-a-week positions. Overtime may be essential when interviewing applicants for a position that must be filled quickly.

As in many other professions, human resources managers are filling some of their subordinate positions with part-time employees—perfect for experienced H/R staff members who want more flexibility and the time to concentrate on their own developing business or family interests.

JOB GROWTH

Opportunities for **human resources managers** will continue to grow much faster than the national average for all jobs through 2005. Human resources departments have become essential to the corporate structure. Businesses will continue to rely on their human resources departments to manage most employee matters that arise, and the field will continue to grow to keep pace with the ever-increasing complexity of employment law, benefits, and management. It is also a profession which arms its practitioners with many skills useful in a volatile workplace. Growth for H/R management (including labor relations and training management) will be from about 194,000 to about 234,000 positions.

Human resources staffing specialist positions will also show higher than average growth for all jobs through 2005—and at a much faster rate than the growth for managers. Most of the new jobs will be in the private sector. Employers' concerns about productivity and work quality will fuel the need for skilled staffing specialists who can recruit, hire, and train the right candidates. However, since a large number of people are attracted to the human resources field, getting these positions will become increasingly competitive.

Official growth statistics for staffing specialists show growth from 81,250 people in 1995 to 95,446 in 2005. However, this number does not include all the H/R staffing specialists that work in the burgeoning consulting industry, which would include: employment agencies, temporary help agencies, and outplacement organizations. Consequently the real-world growth figures for professionals with staffing experience could easily be ten times the official estimates.

DIRECTOR OF TRAINING/TRAINING MANAGER/CORPORATE TRAINING SPECIALIST

All of the specialties in the personnel and human resources field are interrelated, but the smaller the company, the more often the duties of each specialized field overlap. The era of the personnel department generalist is alive in small businesses, and small businesses are where the growth is. However, in large corporations, where the current climate is one of downsizing and doing more with less, it has been replaced by an era of specialists assigned to particular tasks (who then develop a working knowledge of how their piece fits into the whole).

One vital task H/R departments are responsible for is skills training. This includes training not only for new employees, but also for experienced professionals who need to be shown new ways to perform their jobs or trained on

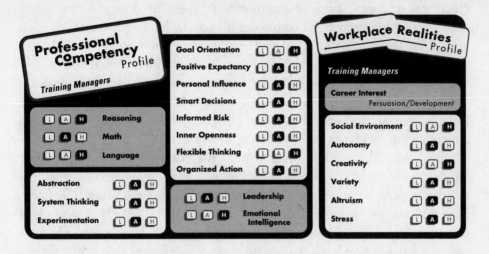

new equipment. Companies have come to realize the importance of employee training not only to avoid work-related accidents, but also to improve productivity, work quality, morale, and teamwork. However, the loyalty and general sense of inclusion that training may bring about are important, but ancillary, benefits to the training process; the real goal is educating workers to impact the bottom line: profit.

Directors of training and *training managers* develop, organize, and direct personnel training programs for their employers. They conduct orientation programs and oversee on-the-job training for new employees. They discuss employee problems with supervisors and management in order to develop training programs geared to improving employees' job skills, work methods, and safety practices.

Specific training methods vary according to a company's needs. Companies that depend on speed and accuracy, such as large shipping companies and overnight delivery companies, may train employees in various areas of the shipping process in time management. This on-the-job training process accomplishes two aims: it trains new employees in the process of unloading, sorting, packing, loading, and delivery, and it also helps to determine what phase of the operation best suits the employee.

Advanced training methods can include classroom instruction, interactive computer instruction, simulated conditions, and small workshops. During the next ten years and beyond, directors of training and training managers will be expected to integrate computer programs and computer instruction methods into their professional arsenal.

Corporate training specialists work under the supervision of the directors of training and training managers to develop and implement programs to train employees in diverse facets of a corporation's operation. Programs may range from training for newly hired employees to ongoing training for seasoned managers. Most training programs fall between these two extremes and involve direct hands-on training on the technical equipment used in the corporation's industrial processes, or the communication tools used by white-collar professionals.

Corporate training specialists are not managers, but they work in close proximity to management personnel. Management usually provides them with the anticipated goals of a training program; the specialists then devise their programs to meet the goals. A program may include prepared manuals, other handouts, testing of employees, and other practical exercises to illustrate the use of the equipment and its part in the entire production process. Training specialists also provide a link between management and labor. For example, a piece of equipment or its operation may need to be modified in order to work at its most productive level in a certain setting. Employees report their experiences with equipment to the training specialists, who can, in turn, work with management to develop the changes necessary.

EARNING POTENTIAL

A recent study found that corporate **directors of training** earned $63,100 as a median annual salary and **training managers** earned an average of $48,500. However, no one enters the field as a manager or director of training, and most starting salaries for H/R candidates with a bachelor's degree averaged $22,900, while starting salaries for those with a master's degree averaged $30,500.

The median salary for **corporate training specialists** is $39,300, starting at an average of $31,900 and reaching an average of $49,000 for experienced specialists.

Salaries in federal government jobs for training specialists are lower. In 1993, the annual starting salary for H/R applicants with a bachelor's degree was $18,300; with a master's degree, $27,800.

EDUCATIONAL REQUIREMENTS

Since no one begins his or her career as a director of training or training manager, the educational requirements to enter the field are important, but the personal qualities candidates for a management position possess are equally important. A **director of training, training manager**, or **training specialist** must be able to communicate easily and effectively. The jobs combine teaching and sales skills in presenting new information to listeners. Candidates must also have the ability to supervise and direct people of various backgrounds, and to get people to work together as a team. Creativity in developing training programs, the communication skills to sell people on new ideas, and an understanding of human nature are all qualities training professionals must possess.

The credentials a training professional needs are more specific. For an entry-level job, applicants need a bachelor's degree from a college or university. This is a field, though, where someone can enter the field or the job through a clerical or support position and work toward the degree while getting a foot on the professional ladder. Many colleges offer programs in human resources management through their business schools, and these programs are an applicant's best bet for employment in the field.

All aspiring managers in the H/R field should complete a master's degree either before beginning work, or during the first few years of employment with a company. Most employers will pay for part or all of the expense of a master's degree that benefits the company.

Training directors, managers, and specialists cannot expect their education to end after receiving a degree, though. Advances are continually being made in work methods, efficiency and safety practices, and teaching and behavioral methods. **Directors of training** and **training managers** are therefore constantly challenged to develop new skills themselves and then to share that learning with others. Furthermore, **training specialists** are responsible for remaining current in many aspects of production techniques and equipment advances. Their jobs require constant continuing education.

A DAY IN THE LIFE

Directors of training and **training managers** work in offices and corporate training centers. The amount of time spent in offices may be combined with a good amount of time in the field, conferring with employees and researching new programs and systems. There also may be some travel involved in coordinating branches and standardizing systems.

Because managers and directors spend time creating as well as implementing programs, their jobs can run more than the normal forty hours a week. Although they will schedule training sessions during the working day, the responsibility to create, run, and then report on the results of their programs is time-consuming.

Corporate training specialists also spend some time in offices and in classrooms, but they also perform the actual on-the-job training on the shop floor, demonstrating the uses of equipment, company procedures, and so forth. Typically, the hours they spend in their office are directed toward developing

> **HELP WANTED**
> **DIRECTOR OF TRAINING/TRAINING MANAGER/CORPORATE TRAINING SPECIALIST**
>
> **Director of Training/Training Manager**
> Develop, organize, and direct personnel training programs. Conduct employer orientation programs and oversee on-the-job training. Discuss employee performance problems with supervisors and management. Improve employees' job skills, work methods, and office safety practices. Salary Range: $48,500–$77,500.
>
> **Corporate Training Specialist**
> Identify training needs of employees, and develop and implement programs to train employees. Evaluate effectiveness of the programs. Also devise programs to meet corporate goals. Salary Range: $31,900–$55,500.

new programs. Since they train people on new equipment, they must also spend time becoming familiar with the equipment. The preparation and implementation of the kinds of programs corporate training specialists are responsible for will involve, more often than not, more than the standard forty hours.

JOB GROWTH

Human resources training specialists are employed in almost every industry in the country. Most H/R jobs exist in the private sector, but municipal, state, and federal government agencies account for 15 percent of H/R jobs.

The official growth figures for all training specialists are lumped together with labor relations growth predictions, which estimate a further 40,000 jobs over the next ten years. However, the computer revolution has so dramatically increased the needs for adult training and education at all levels (and in both the public and private sectors) that these jobs are generally thought to have some of the best growth potential of all jobs in the coming years.

Employment for human resources specialists is expected to grow at a higher rate than the national average during the next ten years. As a result of the complex nature of many jobs, the aging work force, and advances in technology that leave workers without the skills or knowledge to perform their jobs, employers will attempt to improve efficiency by devoting more resources to increasingly specific training programs for employees. This anticipated emphasis on training and education bodes well for people already in the H/R field as well as for people entering the field.

The only factor that could adversely affect the growth in human resources training positions is the continued downsizing that large companies are engaging in. If there are fewer employees to train, employers will need fewer trainers. However, employers will find that **directors of training** and **training**

managers actually reduce expenses as a result of raising employee productivity. And the current boom in small business will generate many more opportunities for H/R people with a broad range of human resources experience.

Consulting firms and individual consultants will be in demand by companies seeking to outsource certain functions. Since many H/R functions overlap, employers may want to eliminate some positions that can be filled by part-time employees or consultants. A good personnel trainer, specializing in one industry, might find him- or herself in greater demand as a consultant than as an employee.

Corporate training specialist is a good entry-level job for someone interested in the human resources field. Although it does not require a great deal of the specialized knowledge that has led to the expansion of human resources functions over the past two decades, it provides interested individuals a starting place from which to gain experience and additional knowledge. Furthermore, many of the program development skills one learns as a corporate training specialist are transferable to many other human resources positions, and the actual training skills are a boon to a career in any industry.

Employee training is a field that will continue to grow more important through the year 2005. But there will be stiff competition for management jobs because of the reduction of the number of management positions by big business.

LABOR RELATIONS SPECIALIST/DIVERSITY MANAGER

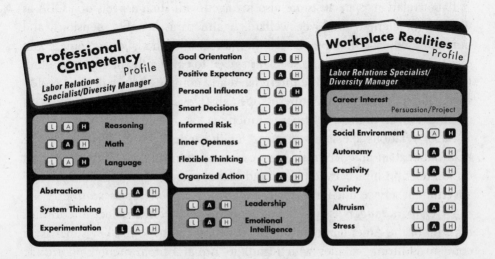

A vital area of responsibility for corporate profitability and therefore for human resources management is conflict resolution. **Labor relations specialists** and **diversity managers** seek to maintain productive lines of communication between corporate management and the workforce.

Labor relations specialists concern themselves largely with dispute resolution. Human resources is a staff function in a company: it does not produce income, so its role is to save the company money. Helping to resolve disputes before they escalate into expensive legal proceedings is an important element of a labor relations specialist's job—perhaps the most important element. The best way to avoid litigation, strikes, or labor unrest is to manage the contractual obligations of a collective bargaining agreement (CBA) properly. CBAs, the agreements between labor unions and employers, include procedural rules governing the steps employees and employers must take in order to resolve disputes. If a union member employee, for example, believes he has been passed over for a particular job despite having seniority qualifying him for the position, he must bring his grievance through the proper channels, notably the company's labor relations department. Labor relations specialists working in management positions ensure that the proceedings adequately represent the interests of both labor and management. They help to prepare information that management negotiators use in their contract talks with labor unions and employees. Once these agreements have been worked out, labor relations specialists in the H/R field implement the policies and proceedings in the agreement as they apply to employees. They also follow the appeals process, if necessary, to make certain the collective bargaining agreement is being honored.

Labor relations specialists are also involved with such aspects of a CBA as wages and salaries, employee welfare, health care, benefits, pensions, and union and management practices as they affect both the labor agreement and employees. Human resources specialists need to constantly interact with other H/R personnel because of the interrelated and complex nature of their profession. Although each area requires its specialists, every distinct area touches on all other aspects of the department's functions.

Labor relations specialists working for the federal government study the field rather than practice in it. They examine and interpret CBAs and report on the relationships between labor and management in private industry. The government service title for this job is *industrial relations representative*.

Diversity managers ensure that a company's workforce reflects the diverse makeup of the American community as delineated by law. They supervise a company's hiring policies with regard to Equal Employment Opportunity Commission (EEOC) and Affirmative Action guidelines. They also hire people within the parameters of such laws as the Americans with Disabilities Act, which protects disabled job candidates from discrimination.

Diversity managers not only hire people in accordance with these regulations, but also investigate claims and grievances filed by employees under these laws. Diversity managers are trained in the interpretation of these laws and help develop company hiring and employment practices that adhere to them. When these practices are called into question, the diversity managers expedite the first stage of the investigation process.

Hiring practices are no longer mandated only by law: they are mandated by common sense. Despite the fact that the Supreme Court has recently ruled that there will be changes in Affirmative Action programs, employers realize that highly qualified candidates for jobs come in all ages, colors, religions, and nationalities, and both sexes. Many companies do not need the federal government to investigate their employment practices because they police themselves—and assure themselves of a variety of workers who work together both productively and harmoniously.

One of the fastest-growing areas in corporate America is compliance: making certain that federal and state regulations regarding employment, job safety, environmental waste disposal, and many other areas are strictly followed. In terms of personnel compliance, diversity managers must remain current with a vast number of federal laws—laws that change constantly, such as the Supreme Court ruling on Affirmative Action. Because the government has stepped up its investigation into unfair labor practices, and because the penalties for violating these and other "compliance-mandated" regulations have increased significantly over the past few years, employers need diversity managers who can make difficult decisions, develop a close familiarity with the law, and speak out to notify a company if its practices do not conform to the law.

Not all of these functions are easy to handle. Many require someone who feels comfortable working within a large organization while still retaining his or her independence. A diversity manager's job is difficult and challenging, but it is also one of the most rewarding jobs in the very popular H/R field.

EARNING POTENTIAL

A recent survey found the median annual salary for **labor relations specialists** in private industry to be approximately $47,100, and up to $55,100 at the high end. Bachelor's degree graduates who majored in labor relations received starting salary offers averaging $36,100 a year. Labor relations supervisors earned up to $74,000.

Labor relations specialists working for the federal government who have a master's degree or doctorate and several years of work experience received an average salary of $50,400 a year in 1993.

Wages for personnel specialists, such as **diversity managers**, range near the high end of all human resources salaries, averaging $57,900, while the most experienced managers earned as much as $72,000.

EDUCATIONAL REQUIREMENTS

Human resources is now a highly specialized field that requires candidates to have a broad educational background. While many H/R managers, staff members, and job applicants hold college degrees in some related major, others are hired on the basis of their transferable skills and their educational background in a seemingly unrelated field, such as liberal arts, where communication skills are emphasized. Most newly hired candidates, though, have a human resources or business background.

Labor relations specialists need a bachelor's degree as a minimum point of entry, but a master's degree will enhance the prospects of a promising future. Prospective labor relations specialists might concentrate on college course work that includes labor law, collective bargaining, economics, the history of labor unions, and industrial psychology. Furthermore, because grievance proceedings, contract interpretation, and negotiation are fields normally associated with lawyers, labor relations specialists find that the law is a good background for a career in this field. A law degree should be considered an alternative or additional degree to the master's degree, for it enhances career advancement opportunities.

A good career step for labor relations specialists who want to enhance their credentials and expertise with a master's or law degree is to work in the field while attending graduate or law school at night. (A four-year night program is offered by a limited number of law schools: interested parties are advised to contact the admissions departments of law schools in their areas.) Large corporate employers will frequently pay for all or part of this graduate education.

Undergraduate and graduate courses in employment law are essential preparatory training for **diversity managers**, who spend much of their time interpreting federal laws. Many people find themselves gravitating to diversity management work after they have begun working for a human resources department in some other capacity.

No applicant new to the field is hired as a **human resources** or **diversity manager**. Experience and education are the requirements for true managerial jobs. But many people interested in the field can prepare themselves for eventual managerial jobs by completing an advanced degree program in personnel, employee training, or labor relations. An M.B.A. with a concentration in human resources management is also an excellent preparation for career advancement in the field.

A DAY IN THE LIFE

Labor relations specialists, like all other H/R staff members and managers, work in offices for companies or serve as consultants in the industry. Specialists who represent unions work either as salaried employees of the unions or, more likely, as consultants who represent the union's interests in negotiations and grievance proceedings. Most labor relations specialists, though, will be employed by companies.

This is work that requires close attention to details and a sense of equity. Labor relations specialists who are employees for corporations can find themselves in awkward situations if they support the resolution of a dispute that does not favor their employer.

Although many H/R jobs require a standard forty-hour week, labor relations specialists may find themselves working much longer hours during preparation periods for contract renewals. During these periods labor relations specialists generate a tremendous amount of paperwork to provide information to corporate counsel representing management interests in negotiations.

Most of the work performed by **diversity managers** involves reviewing regulations, remaining up-to-date on the state of the law, insuring the company's compliance, and preparing for grievance hearings. Diversity managers also perform some of the other functions of H/R personnel, such as interviewing and hiring candidates, but they spend more time serving as liaison between management and individual employees, or a group of employees, or a government agency.

Although diversity managers may be found in companies of all sizes, people who have made a career of studying the laws governing diversity hiring are more likely to be found in large corporations.

Although they generally work a forty-hour week, diversity managers may find themselves working much longer hours if they are preparing for a grievance hearing or studying a sweeping change in government regulations.

JOB GROWTH

As businesses continue to cut back on the number of workers they employ and concentrate on cutting costs and profits, **labor relations specialists** will find

**HELP WANTED
LABOR RELATIONS
SPECIALIST/DIVERSITY
MANAGER**

Labor Relations Specialist
Prepare for and conduct contract talks with labor unions and employees. Coordinate grievance proceedings, and help in resolving disputes. Implement corporate policies and proceedings. Salary Range: $36,100–$74,000.

Diversity Manager
Ensure diversity within the corporation as mandated by law. Investigate discrimination claims and grievances. Need to remain current with changing federal laws as they apply to diversity. Salary Range: $46,400–$72,000.

increased opportunities. Resolution of disputes will remain a key area for these specialists, as both labor and management attempt to rein in growing legal fees and litigation expenses. Private industry accounts for 85 percent of the jobs cited in the human resources field. The other 15 percent are in government jobs. In 1995 the federal government estimated 287,228 professionals were employed as personnel, training, and labor relations specialists; by 2005, we can expect over 369,000 in these jobs.

The future appears to be very good for labor relations specialists. On the one hand, the nature of work itself will be changing: fewer full-time employees will be needed to perform jobs; the relationship between labor unions and management will change; employees too will have changing responsibilities. On the other hand, some basic principles of employer-employee relations will never change. Labor relations specialists with a grounding in traditional labor practices will have to adapt—and to develop—new labor agreements, wage structuring, and work definitions. The next several years will be an exhilarating and challenging period for people in the field of labor relations.

Most jobs for **diversity managers** will remain in the private sector. Employers have growing concerns about following federal and state guidelines, especially employers whose businesses depend on government contracts. Diversity managers will continue to provide invaluable service to these companies.

Although the government constantly changes its employment laws, no one doubts that the changes will only prove to be more complex and confusing than those being replaced. Because they are trained to analyze these complex laws, diversity managers are necessary to many companies. And because they work to promote employee harmony, they also create a better atmosphere for management, labor, and productivity. This specialized field will become increasingly important as even more people immigrate to the United States and minority populations continue to contribute to society.

MANAGEMENT CONSULTANT

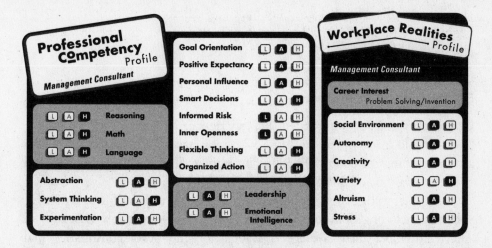

Industries and organizations need effective control over their inventories and expenses. For various reasons, a large company or organization may realize the need to reorganize its corporate structure, or may need to reevaluate its budgetary process. These are just a few of the organizational problems that *management consultants* help solve. Management consultants can also be known as *management analysts*.

The work of management consultants varies with each company for which they work. Consultants may work together in teams or independently. Once the consulting assignment starts, consultants define the nature and the extent of the problem in question. Consultants may begin analyzing data on an organization's annual revenues, employment, or general expenditures as the assignment requires. They may interview employees or observe the operations of a single organizational unit. Next, they use their expertise in management systems to develop solutions to the problem. They must take into account the nature of the business with which they are dealing, and they need to be aware of the organization's present internal structure. Once they have found an adequate solution, they formally report their findings and recommendations to the organization's representatives and may be involved in implementing solutions. Other consultants can help determine a course of action when a difficult problem arises; they also might be asked to help organizations predict and circumvent future problems.

Consultants can be solo practitioners, the heads of small consultancies, or the employees of large international consulting firms that employ thousands of consultants. Most of these firms specialize in providing consultation in a specialized area, such as human resources or information systems. Consulting services are usually provided on a contract basis. Before a consulting contract begins, the estimated cost of the project, its requirements, and the deadline are all established.

EARNING POTENTIAL

Consultants' salaries vary widely by experience, education, and employer. According to a recent survey, those who were salaried workers had median annual earnings of about $40,300. The middle 50 percent of them earned between $26,500 and $60,100 per year.

According to the Association of Management Consulting Firms (ACME), earnings including bonuses and/or profit sharing for research associates in ACME member firms average $31,300. For entry-level consultants, that number was $39,100; for management consultants, $56,300; for senior consultants, $76,700; for junior partners, $105,600; and for senior partners, $166,100.

Salaried consultants (those working as employees for consulting firms) often receive full benefits like any other corporate employee. Self-employed consultants do not experience the benefits, but can earn anywhere from $400 to $1,000 per day.

EDUCATIONAL REQUIREMENTS

While there are no standard requirements for prospective consultants, employers in the industry do prefer to hire those with an exemplary track record and an advanced degree. In addition to having a formal education, many entrants to this occupation do well by having prior experience working in industry or management or in another occupation. Business management, as well as computer and information sciences and engineering, are all solid backgrounds for consultants.

Consultants hired immediately after college graduation sometimes participate in a consulting firm's formal training programs. These programs outline company policies and procedures, as well as computer systems and software, research processes, and management principles and practices. If individuals enter at the middle level with previous experience, then they usually do not participate in such training programs. However, most consultants at different points in their career do attend conferences in order to stay aware of trends in their field.

Consultants should be confident and self-motivated. They should possess good communication and writing skills. Because they work independently, they must be able to manage time well, and they need to be creative in order to develop solutions to problems. Regardless of the scope of a project, a consultant's findings and reports affect the lives of many workers and other people, and a consultant needs to be aware of this.

Seasoned consultants are sometimes responsible for supervising entry-level workers, and all consultants are involved in seeking out new business. Workers with exceptional skills eventually move on to become partners or principals in a firm. Some, of course, open their own firms. Little capital is actually required to start one's own consulting firm, and a self-employed consultant can effectively control the costs of such a firm.

The Institute of Management Consultants (a division of the Council of Consulting Organizations) offers the designation of Certified Management Consultant (CMC) to those who pass an examination and meet minimum levels of education and experience. While not mandatory in the field, certification offers a jobseeker a competitive advantage, first from the enhanced skills and second from the accreditation.

A DAY IN THE LIFE

Management consultants usually work a forty-hour week. It is very common for consultants to work overtime in order to meet deadline demands. Although much time is spent in their own comfortable offices, consultants may spend an equal amount of time with their clients, and their surroundings will vary accordingly—sometimes in the dregs of factory facilities, other times in posh executive offices—providing the consultant with an ever-changing and diverse working atmosphere.

Self-employed consultants, of course, work their own hours and may work from home or independent office, as well as in the workplaces of their clients. Such a practice can be limiting, and independent consultants must constantly reach out to build a strong client base.

JOB GROWTH

Employment of **management consultants** is expected to increase much faster than the average for all occupations through the year 2005. Predictions of growth range from the out-of-date to the patently unreliable. However, while there are no reliable numbers, it is still possible to make some educated guesses.

**HELP WANTED
MANAGEMENT
CONSULTANT**

Collect, review, and analyze data, and then make recommendations to the organization's management. Responsible for defining problems and ultimately implementing changes. Must be able to work well alone and in teams. Exemplary track record and advanced degree preferred; business management experience a plus. Salary Range: $26,500–$166,100+.

Growth is expected in large consulting firms and in smaller firms that focus exclusively on specific areas of expertise. The official federal numbers suggest a growth from 137,000 in 1995 to 172,000 in 2005. Nevertheless, the numbers are likely to be substantially greater, because of the corporate restructuring of the last few years. As corporations shrink in size, they are outsourcing more and more functions to consulting companies, which are experiencing explosive growth as a result. Consequently, since consultants make their services available on an "as needed" basis, we can expect a similar explosive proliferation of the myriad consultant titles. Industries and government agencies will increasingly rely on consulting firms and independent consultants for their expertise in organizational operations.

There are other reasons for the rise in consulting needs. More than ever, American industry is competing globally, so industries cannot afford inefficiency and wasted resources. Management consultants help cut costs, streamline operations, and help develop marketing strategies for an organization's global future. Businesses likewise need help downsizing staff and eliminating full-time personnel. Sometimes, as these personnel leave, they are replaced by staff from consulting firms on a contractual basis. Smaller businesses that want to expand their operations now will use consultants rather than add to the permanent payroll. Also, as business technology improves, consultants are increasingly needed to help facilitate an organization's technological changes.

Competition for consulting work is expected to be keen in the private sector. The variety of consulting options makes consulting an attractive field for individuals of diverse academic and professional backgrounds.

We can expect that the shrinking budget projections for both government agencies and industries that we have been seeing in the 1990s will continue. Consulting work is one occupation that will thrive on this recent development. Most consulting work will be focused on helping industries and organizations meet their goals of shrinking or expanding their operations, while remaining competitive, in compliance with the law and without further alienating the regular workforce.

Law

ATTORNEY: BANKRUPTCY LAWYER/TAX ATTORNEY/ELDER LAW
ATTORNEY/INTELLECTUAL COPYRIGHT LAWYER/ENVIRONMENTAL
LAWYER

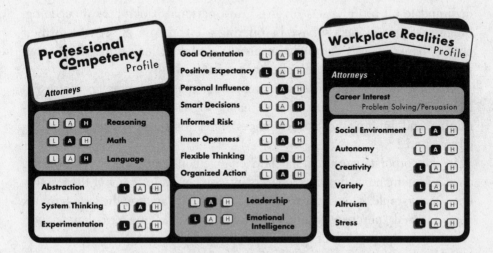

Law is a service profession, and as such, it changes according to the needs of society. Because of these society changes, new areas of law are constantly evolving to provide service to newly emerging client bases. A **lawyer/attorney** is the person who interprets and applies the letter of the law to advance his/her client's cause.

During the boom in the corporate economy during the 1980s, the hot area of law was mergers and acquisitions (M&A). Corporate attorneys at large firms worked long hours either putting together mergers between companies or trying to prevent hostile takeovers from occurring. Today, there is somewhat less M&A work for law firms, so law firms, like companies in other industries, find themselves looking for other services to provide for clients. The turbulent nature of the times we live in now means that *bankruptcy lawyers* occupy one of the fastest-growing areas of the law.

There are two related but separate fields of bankruptcy law: *commercial bankruptcy* and *personal bankruptcy. Commercial* or *corporate bankruptcy* is an involved process involving knowledge of the Uniform Commercial Code (covering commercial transactions and debtor/creditor laws), the tax code, and corporate law.

Personal bankruptcy is a growing field as people continue to lose their jobs and find themselves falling deeper into debt. The number of people failing to make their mortgage payments or credit card payments increases every month. In order to find relief from their accumulated debt, increasing numbers of people are turning to these lawyers for guidance in filing personal bankruptcy proceedings. Because the details are less complicated than those in corporate bankruptcy, an attorney does not need a large staff to help him or her identify or liquidate all of the assets involved in a personal bankruptcy proceeding. Since sole practitioners survive by offering a broad base of services to their clients, bankruptcy is definitely an area they should look into. Many small practitioners handle it for their clients on a flat-fee basis.

Tax attorneys handle matters as simple as preparing income tax returns, to advising people on the financial demands of starting a business, to determining and limiting tax consequences for a multimillion-dollar estate or corporation.

In the corporate world, the tax laws change constantly, so tax attorneys are always in demand as business advisors for companies in many of their activities—for example, when companies plan mergers (to analyze the long-term tax costs involved), purchase equipment (to determine the long-term depreciation value of the equipment), or consider public stock offerings. Many tax attorneys have developed a background in accounting, business, or finance, which gives them a deeper understanding of their clients' needs and problems.

Tax attorneys also have bright futures representing successful professionals with less sizable, but no less important, problems. Here the tax attorney's legal expertise focuses on the tax laws as they apply to you and me, rather than the corporation. Successful and prudent professionals will use a personal tax attorney to minimize the tax burden on major investments, purchases, and sales; and for estate planning that provides the maximum amount of money for their chosen beneficiaries and limits the amount paid as taxes.

There is a third general direction for attorneys interested in tax: the IRS. The Internal Revenue Service hires many tax attorneys to check tax returns of businesses and individuals, to audit returns that raise suspicion, and to prosecute tax cheats. Oftentimes tax cases are heard in a special tax court: these are proceedings held in front of a judge who is a specialist in taxation. The complex and highly technical nature of the tax field demands that a specialist hear the cases. Often IRS tax attorneys move into private practice later in their careers after developing an intimate understanding of the world of tax law and the workings of the IRS.

Elder law attorneys represent the specific legal needs of a growing elderly client base. The baby boomers who burst upon the scene after World War II are now getting old and gray and infirm. I know, I'm one of them myself.

Better health care means that these aging boomers can be expected to clutter up the sidewalks and retirement homes far longer than their forebears. Since society has never been composed of so many healthy and often wealthy "wrinklies and crumblies," this has opened up a demand for changing laws to reflect the needs of America's seniors, and for the lawyers who can interpret and refine those laws.

Many matters regarding elder law revolve around health care (how many years will people continue to be covered after they have outlived their insurance company–defined life expectancy?) and finances (retirees have prepared for their future, but how long will their money last if they live twenty years longer than they thought they would?). As the baby boomers reach old age, the call for elder law specialists will increase further, as Social Security runs out of funds to support the huge number of pensioners. This means that palsied boomers (and not too long after, you yourself) will be in greater need of representation. We will turn to elder law attorneys for help.

Intellectual copyright law is also known as *intellectual property law*, and like the three fields described above, it is a growing area of the law. Intellectual property differs from real property (real estate) in that it is generally not a three-dimensional thing that can be physically possessed. It is, rather, an idea that someone seeks to protect from theft by registering ownership (copyright). A work of art, a book, an invention, and a design for a product are examples of intellectual property, as are software or technology developments. To understand the scope and importance of this field of law consider Bill Gates, the richest man in America, whose entire personal fortune and that of his company Microsoft is founded on intellectual copyright.

Environmental lawyers are those attorneys with a specialized knowledge of environmental laws and regulations. The typical responsibilities of environmental lawyers include the performance of in-depth research into the purposes behind environmental laws and regulations, and into judicial decisions that have been applied to those laws and regulations under circumstances similar to those currently faced by the client.

Environmental law is a complex area of specialization, with the details of an environmental lawyer's job depending on his or her particular specialization and position.

Although all environmental lawyers are allowed to represent clients in court, some appear in court more frequently than others, and some specialize exclusively in *litigation*. In this legal specialty, as in others, litigators are seen to be a breed apart. Litigators need an exceptional ability to think quickly and speak with ease and authority, and must be thoroughly familiar with courtroom rules and strategy. Nevertheless, environmental litigators spend most of their time outside the courtroom conducting research, interviewing clients and witnesses, and preparing for trial.

Environmental attorneys may also specialize in other areas of the law, such as corporate and real estate transactions, giving advice on permitting and regulatory compliance issues. They may represent public interest groups, waste disposal companies, manufacturing companies, or construction firms in their dealing with the federal Environmental Protection Agency (EPA) and other state and federal agencies. They help clients prepare and file for permits and approvals for applications relating to the ability to conduct certain activities. They also represent clients' interests in administrative adjudication and during the drafting of new regulations. Environmental lawyers may also participate in writing articles and giving educational seminars on environmental law topics.

Most environmental attorneys work in private practice in the area of civil law, but *environmental criminal law* is a small but growing area. In civil law, attorneys assist in litigation, contracts, and business and real estate matters; in criminal law, attorneys defend in criminal court their clients who have been charged with criminal violations of environmental laws. Some environmental lawyers are employed full-time by a single client, and if that client is a corporation, that lawyer is known as an *in-house counsel*. The lawyer will usually advise the company about the legal questions that arise from its business activities and that may involve government regulations, contracts with other companies, or property interests. They may also supervise cases handled primarily by attorneys employed by law firms.

Many environmental attorneys work for state and federal governments. They may help develop programs, draft laws, interpret legislation, establish enforcement procedures, and argue civil and criminal cases on behalf of the government. Other attorneys work on behalf of nonprofit environmental organizations that seek to protect the environment. A very small number of environmental attorneys teach in law schools.

EARNING POTENTIAL

Salaries of experienced **attorneys** vary widely according to the size and location of the firm. The average starting salary for all private firm and business attorneys is approximately $36,600, although the most highly qualified law school graduates receive starting salaries as high as $80,000 per year. The Bureau of Labor Statistics lists lawyers' earnings by level of experience.

- Lawyers with less than a year's experience average $40,302.
- Median-level earnings are $71,200.
- The most experienced *average* a yearly income of $125,855.

Tax attorneys, especially those armed with a master's degree in taxation, earn salaries that average near the top of the reported range for all attorneys. Some senior lawyers who were partners in the nation's top law firms earned over $1 million.

EDUCATIONAL REQUIREMENTS

All aspiring lawyers must receive a bachelor's degree from a college or university before being admitted to law school. Law school involves either a three-year full-time program or, in some schools, a four-year evening program. They must also pass a state bar examination after graduating from law school. Once they pass the bar exam, lawyers are admitted to the bar of a state and can begin to pay back their loans.

Law schools offer a variety of courses during the last year-and-a-half of their programs. The first three semesters of law school usually involve required courses that give students training in the basics of law. After that students are free to take elective courses that build on the basics and introduce them to specific fields that may interest them, such as the fields discussed here: bankruptcy, tax, elder law, or intellectual property.

Many law students studying to become **tax attorneys** work during the day as accountants or auditors and pursue their studies in the evenings. A background in accounting or business benefits tax attorneys because it provides them with additional experience. This added mastery helps them to find their first law jobs. Many tax attorneys are continuing in school beyond the J.D. (doctor of jurisprudence) level to receive their master's in taxation degree. This program is not offered at all law schools and so they often must travel to another city to attend classes. But this degree is becoming increasingly important, and many law firms pay the tuition for their tax associates and give them some time off to study for exams. This program usually involves two years of class work.

A DAY IN THE LIFE

Attorneys work indoors at their offices or in the offices of their clients, in restaurants, and on golf courses. Because this profession generates so much

HELP WANTED
ATTORNEYS

Bankruptcy Lawyer
Provide guidance and expertise in filing personal bankruptcy proceedings. Knowledge of court system and bankruptcy laws essential. Salary Range: $36,500–$1,000,000+.

Tax Attorney
Prepare and check income tax returns for clients. Advise entrepreneurs on financial demands of starting a business, and limit tax consequences for multimillion-dollar estates or corporations. Analyze tax costs involved in company mergers, equipment purchase, and public stock offerings. Minimize item tax burden on major investments, purchases, and sales. Background in accounting, business or finance a plus. Salary Range: $36,500–$1,000,000+.

Elder Law Attorney
Advise the elderly and their families on financing and coverage of health care benefits. Responsible for protecting the rights of seniors. Salary Range: $36,500–$1,000,000.

Intellectual Copyright Lawyer
Arrange copyright contracts for people who wish to protect ownership of an original idea or piece of work. Must understand patent, copyright, and trademark regulations, and be willing to research previous claims. Salary Range: $36,500–$1,000,000+.

profit, these offices are often very pleasant.

In most of the specialties discussed, issues that cannot be resolved with reason and negotiation progress to the courtroom for the litigation process. Personal bankruptcy, on the other hand, remains largely an administrative procedure.

While lawyers can mint money, they put in long hours of intense concentration for the privilege. This is not a field for the uncommitted or the weak-willed.

JOB GROWTH

There are approximately 437,000 lawyers in the United States. About four-fifths of that number are in private practice for themselves or are members of law firms. The other fifth work in public service. Because of the phenomenal earning potential of the law profession, competition to get into law school is intense, and after graduation the competition for placement in the best firms is extreme. It's then, once you are truly working in your profession, that the slugfest to make partner begins. So although the profession is healthy, the number of job seekers will exceed the available positions.

The legal profession has been undergoing significant changes for the past few years, and these changes are expected to continue. Firms that had been together for many years have split up; job security, due to downsizing and aerobicizing, no longer exists. The law, like academia, is still a privileged but no longer a completely protected life.

Environmental Lawyer
Requires specialized knowledge of environmental laws and regulations. Strong focus on extensive trial research and preparation, including examination of legal precedence concerning environmental laws and regulations. Represent clients in administrative adjudication and the drafting of new regulations. Salary Range: $36,500–$1,000,000+.

The future appears the most promising for these five areas of the law: Even though the economy continues to improve, many people are suffering the results of cutbacks and layoffs, which means **bankruptcy law** will continue to grow. The elderly population will increase, so **elder law attorneys** will be in greater demand. And since technological changes and the information society will move at increasing speed, **intellectual copyright attorneys** will find themselves in a cutting-edge and very busy field. The future is bright for **environmental lawyers**; concern over the environment is not likely to abate, and even though polluted sites may all be cleaned up someday, the need to regulate manufacturing will always remain. Since tax advice is essential for corporations and individuals alike, firms will continue to hire **tax attorneys** and to pay them well. In these uncertain times for law firms, tax attorneys have better chances than most other lawyers for job continuity. The field's complexities mean attorneys from other fields cannot suddenly become tax experts overnight.

There are basically two ways for new and currently practicing attorneys to increase their competitive chances in the marketplace. One is to become an expert in one or more areas of law. This almost ensures an attorney steady employment even when a particular area, for example, mergers and acquisitions, goes through a down cycle. The other way to increase one's competitive chances is to provide niche services for people. Sole practitioners who offer a variety of services to their clients are basically niche practitioners. They represent people who cannot afford and do not really need the service provided by large law firms. During the next several years, as large law firms grow larger and small firms continue to dissolve, sole practitioners and very small firms that provide services to personal and small business, rather than large corporate clients, will be the primary alternative to large law firms. It is safe to assume that many more lawyers will practice in these settings than in big firms.

PARALEGAL

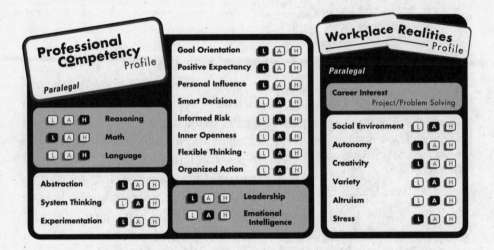

Paralegals are the staffing option of choice for many large and medium-sized law firms, and some corporations as well, all of which are striving to keep costs under control. Since not all of the work performed in a law firm must be performed by licensed attorneys, many detail-oriented tasks can be assigned to paralegals and billed to clients at lower rates than those charged by lawyers.

Law has become overwhelmed by the information explosion. Much of the research and preparation required by lawyers is proving too time-consuming for them to maintain their workload. Paralegals, working under a lawyer's supervision, perform background work, such as checking the facts of cases to make sure no important or relevant information remains undiscovered. They also spend hours in legal research, finding past cases that support or contradict a lawyer's arguments.

The sources they check include directories that cite judicial decisions by state and case number; one case inevitably leads a researcher to another and another. This task is detail-oriented and time-consuming because accuracy is everything in the legal profession, and paralegals can ultimately bear a great deal of responsibility for the accuracy of an attorney's arguments.

In addition to doing research, paralegals prepare memos and reports detailing their findings. These reports can influence the approach attorneys take to a legal argument. In the event that a case proceeds to trial, paralegals may assist in the preparation and drafting of pleadings filed with the court and may also be responsible for preparing properly annotated memos that condense pages of deposition transcripts and affidavits. Attorneys at trial need such outlines in order to find information quickly.

Paralegals work in all fields of law. Attorneys who practice in the areas of bankruptcy, corporate law, criminal law, employee benefits, patent and copyright law, and real estate rely on paralegals to help prepare drafts of contracts, mortgages, separation agreements, and trust instruments.

Paralegals are also employed by corporations, where they assist corporate attorneys in preparing employee contracts, shareholder agreements, stock option plans, and employee benefit plans. The preparation and filing of annual financial reports, the keeping of corporate minute books and resolutions, and the review of state and federal laws pertaining to the corporation's functions also fall within a corporate paralegal's job responsibilities.

Government-employed paralegals usually work for one of the public agencies. Like paralegals who work for law firms, they review legal documents, but usually for pertinence to their agency's functions. They maintain reference files, conduct research for attorneys, and help attorneys prepare for hearings.

Other paralegals are employed in community legal service projects that help the poor, the aged, and other persons who need representation but cannot afford to hire a lawyer. In some states, the law permits legal aid paralegals to represent clients at administrative hearings.

As in all occupations, some paralegals specialize. Specialties include real estate, estate planning, family law, labor law, litigation, and corporate law, and of course tax, intellectual copyright, elder law, and bankruptcy law.

Since paralegals are employed to synthesize information, computer literacy is essential because much of the information required in legal research is now available through computers linked by telephone-line modems to central repositories. Computers enable researchers to access more information in a shorter period of time. Since most lawyers in the private sector bill clients on an hourly basis, time is a necessary component of the legal profession, both for containing costs and increasing profits.

EARNING POTENTIAL

Earnings in this field vary greatly, depending on education, training, and experience. Also, the salary structure is determined in large part by the type and size of employer and the geographic location of the job. Large firms or those in metropolitan areas pay more than small firms or those in less populated regions.

According to a survey by the National Association of Legal Assistants, a paralegal's average annual salary is approximately $28,300. Starting salaries averaged $23,400, while paralegals with six to ten years of experience averaged $28,200 a year. The same survey determined that annual salaries for paralegals with eleven to fifteen years of experience averaged $29,800. In addition to a salary, many paralegals working for private law firms and corporations received an annual bonus, which averages in the range of $1,700. Employers of the majority of paralegals provided life and health insurance benefits and contributed to a retirement plan on their behalf.

Salaries for those paralegals employed by the federal government start at around $18,000 to $23,000 a year, depending on training and experience. The average annual salary for government-employed paralegals is $32,600.

EDUCATIONAL REQUIREMENTS

The backgrounds of paralegals differ as widely as the areas of law they work in. Many paralegals receive formal training from one of over 600 paralegal training programs offered by colleges, universities, law schools, and community and junior colleges. In addition to those programs, paralegal institutes have opened that teach the fundamentals of the profession. Requirements for admission to these programs vary: some require a college degree, while others may require that the applicant pass an entrance examination. Paralegal training programs include a combination of general courses on the law and legal research techniques, as well as courses that cover specialized areas of the law. Since the quality of paralegal training programs varies, one way for applicants to determine the quality of the program they apply to is to ask for information on the placement success of recent graduates.

The American Bar Association has approved 177 of the 600 programs available nationwide. Although this approval is not required by the legal profession, a graduate of an approved program may have a better chance of receiving a job offer.

Many paralegals enter the profession as a result of their on-the-job experience. Some employers promote and train skilled legal secretaries to paralegal positions. Other paralegals have previously had experience working in a particular field, such as nursing, real estate, or tax preparation.

Although paralegals need not be certified, the National Association of Legal Assistants (NALA) has established standards for voluntary certification which require various combinations of education and experience. Paralegals who meet the association's standards may take a two-day examination given each year by the Certifying Board of Legal Assistants of the NALA. Those who pass this examination are designated Certified Legal Assistant (C.L.A.), a sign of competence that may enhance employment and advancement opportunities.

HELP WANTED
PARALEGAL

Assist lawyers with their case research and preparation. Perform background checks on case facts, ensuring that no important or relevant information is left out. Conduct research into legal precedents, and prepare memos and reports detailing findings. Must be meticulous with details, thorough, accurate, and able to synthesize information. Salary Range: $18,000–$45,000.

A DAY IN THE LIFE

Paralegals work under the same general conditions as lawyers, although they rarely have private offices and leather chairs. They work at desks or in law libraries. Occasionally they are called upon to travel in order to gather information.

Paralegals employed by law firms may be asked to work long hours when the situation requires. Often, lawyers preparing for an upcoming trial, a corporate merger, or a complex real estate closing will work late into the night. The deadlines faced by lawyers may dictate a paralegal's working hours.

Corporate and government paralegals, on the other hand, generally work a forty-hour week.

Paralegals who prove their skill and ability often find themselves handling increasingly complex matters. Attorneys will delegate more varied and interesting tasks to paralegals who prove they enjoy the challenge of additional responsibility.

JOB GROWTH

Since paralegals improve the cost, efficiency, and availability of legal services, their employment prospects will continue to increase. There are over 100,000 paralegals in the United States. By the year 2005, job opportunities for paralegals are expected to have nearly doubled.

Since job opportunities will grow, many people will be attracted to the profession. Competition is expected to increase along with the new job openings. However, job prospects will still remain favorable for paralegals who received formal training in highly regarded programs.

The largest employer of paralegals will continue to be private law firms. As the population increases, the need for legal services will increase. Corporate legal departments, and real estate and insurance companies, will also hire paralegals to offset costs without decreasing services.

Following the trend in the private sector, the public sector will see an increased demand for paralegals in community legal service programs, consumer organizations, government programs, and the court system.

Media/Communications/Public Relations

Editor

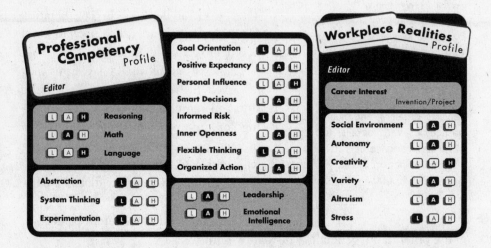

Professional Competency Profile

Editor

L A H	Reasoning
L A H	Math
L A H	Language

Abstraction   L A H
System Thinking   L A H
Experimentation   L A H

Goal Orientation   L A H
Positive Expectancy   L A H
Personal Influence   L A H
Smart Decisions   L A H
Informed Risk   L A H
Inner Openness   L A H
Flexible Thinking   L A H
Organized Action   L A H

L A H   Leadership
L A H   Emotional Intelligence

Workplace Realities Profile

Editor

Career Interest   Invention/Project

Social Environment   L A H
Autonomy   L A H
Creativity   L A H
Variety   L A H
Altruism   L A H
Stress   L A H

Editors supervise the activity of writers in dozens of fields. Editors collect, revise, annotate, and arrange written material in newspapers, magazines, trade publications, newsletters, books, audio books, radio and television broadcasts, movies, and advertisements. They operate under strict editorial deadlines. Regardless of the actual size of the organization for which they work, editors supervise some part of the writing process. Editors must always ensure that written materials meet established editorial policies of a publication, publisher, production company, or broadcast network.

Editors in newspapers or other periodicals may direct the operation of an entire publication as *editor-in-chief*, or they may act as a *managing editor, city editor, copy chief*, or editor of a special section of a publication. In smaller publications, editors will also often perform the actual reporting, photography, or layout.

A *book editor* reviews, selects, rewrites, and coordinates manuscript material to be published in book form. It is often the responsibility of book editors to analyze consumer trends and to commission, acquire, or reject a manuscript on the basis of that analysis. Book editors must often confer with authors, literary agents, and publishers in order to negotiate deals and arrange publication dates, royalties, and the number of materials to be published. The editor is also responsible for selling an author's book idea to the publishing committee, so good analytical and presentation skills play a critical role in this job.

Editors are helped by *copy editors*, who provide editorial support by check-ing manuscript material for grammatical correctness and spelling. They may also check the material for correct style, and provide research support by veri-fying facts and statistics. Assistants are often a part of the editing process, and have titles such as *assistant editor* or *editorial assistant*.

Editorial assistants summarize and report on the merits of potential titles, and respond to messages and query letters about unpublished or already pub-lished material. Finally, they provide general administrative assistance to edi-tors by answering phones, making photocopies, and performing traditional office chores.

EARNING POTENTIAL

An editor's earnings depend on the size and location of the publishing house or newspaper she or he works for. The industry averages nationwide look like this:

Publishing Houses

Entry-level Editor	$26,700
Mid-level Managing Editor	$40,000
Mid-level (nonmanaging) Editor	$35,000
Senior Managing Editor	$45,400

At the high end, in a top publishing house, a copy editor can earn as much as $49,000 and an editor-in-chief as much as $175,000.

Newspapers

Entry-level Editors	$20,000
Experienced Editors	$30,000
Senior Editors	$60,000

Highlighting the difference location can make, currently an experienced copy editor at the *Bristol* (Connecticut) *Press* earns an average of $24,200 per year while the same position with similar experience pays $47,700 at the Chicago *Sun-Times*.

EDUCATIONAL REQUIREMENTS

Positions in newspaper editing and in general editing all require a bachelor's degree, preferably with a concentration in the field of communications,

HELP WANTED
EDITOR

Collect, revise, annotate, and ar-range written material in all types of publications, broadcasts, movies, and advertisements. Confer with authors and publishers on publica-tion dates, royalties, and materials to be published. Ability to ana-lyze and foresee consumer trends helpful. Must be able to oper-ate under strict editorial deadlines. Writing proficiency essential, as well as good communication skills. Salary Range: $20,000–$175,000.

journalism, or English. Because editors work on a wide variety of material, it is often preferable for prospective editors to have a broad liberal arts background. Edi-torial positions also frequently require specialized knowledge.

Editors must be able to plan and direct many different writing assignments. They must often show tact and good judgment in the way that they choose to accept and reject written work. Good analytical as well as verbal skills and an ability to com-prehend a wide variety of written material is also important, as is an exemplary knowledge of good grammar. Strong orga-nizational skills, attention to detail, and good decision making under deadlines are all very important for editors. Editors should be familiar with the most technologically advanced forms of electronic publishing and graphics.

A DAY IN THE LIFE

Since editors always work in cooperation with both writers and other editors, their work surroundings vary. While some editors work in private offices, others may work in areas where they are surrounded by the distractions of other editors or writers. Although editors are expected to follow editorial poli-cies, they work under very little direct supervision.

The work performed by editors is primarily sedentary, involving paperwork or talking on the telephone. Their office work may occasionally be punctuated by travel assignments.

The average working week for editors is generally thirty-five to forty hours, but actual hours depend upon the kind of organization for which an editor works and the critical deadline of the moment. Morning or week-end programs or publications, for example, will require morning or weekend hours. In order to meet deadlines, editors will sometimes work overtime hours. This is especially true for editors who work for newspapers, television, or radio. And in terms of acquiring new titles, book editors often bring home various materials to read and analyze, either during the evening hours or on the weekend.

JOB GROWTH

Overall growth in the field of editorial work is expected to increase as fast as the national average for all occupations through the year 2005. Department of Labor Statistics figures predict 45,000 new positions for writers and editors over the next decade. The greatest increases in employment for salaried editors will be in the areas of newspaper, periodical, and book publishing. Hiring in nonprofit agencies is also expected to rise. As advertising and public relations agencies continue to grow, so too will the need to hire editors to work in these agencies.

Turnover in the field of editing is fairly high because experienced editors usually move on to other occupations within the publishing industry. Editing (like writing) is a laborious job, requiring careful attention to detail and long periods of intense concentration.

WRITER: COMMUNICATIONS SPECIALIST/NEWS WRITER/ COLUMNIST/TECHNICAL WRITER/ PUBLICITY WRITER/COPYWRITER

Writers belong to a broad class of individuals who communicate through the written word. Writers can work in a wide range of areas, including developing original fiction and nonfiction for books, magazines, trade journals, newspapers, company newsletters, technical reports, radio and television broadcasts, movies, and advertisements.

Because writers work in so many different subject areas, it is difficult to generalize about their typical responsibilities. Nonetheless, some aspects of the occupation are fairly constant. Writers first select a topic or are assigned one by an editor. They research the topic through a combination of personal observations, library and other research, and interviews. Occasionally, writers will change their focus as they learn more about the subject. They select and organize the material and put it into words that effectively convey the intended message to the reader. In addition to recounting the information they gather, they may analyze and interpret it. Writers frequently revise or rewrite sections, searching for the best organization of the material or just the right phrasing.

Communications specialists are journalists, reporters, and others who gather information and report their findings in stories that inform the public about local, state, national, and international events. They typically follow leads and news tips, research and review documents, travel to the scene of their story, and interview witnesses. Back at the office they prepare the material in an organized fashion, verify the facts, and write the piece.

News writers prepare news items for newspapers or news broadcasts, based on information supplied by communications specialists, reporters, or wire services. Another group of writers at news organizations are *general assignment specialists*. These people handle assigned stories for large newspapers or television stations, covering events such as an accident, a political rally, a celebrity visit, or a business merger or bankruptcy that affects local residents. *Editorial writers* write comments to stimulate or mold public opinion, in accordance with their publication's viewpoint.

Columnists analyze the news and write columns or commentaries, based on personal knowledge and subject matter expertise. Generally, columnists tend to have extensive professional writing experience.

Technical writers translate scientific and technical information for operating and maintenance manuals, catalogs, parts lists, assembly instructions, sales promotional materials, project proposals, and the like. Technical writers plan and edit technical reports and oversee the preparation of illustrations, photographs, diagrams, and charts.

Publicity writers specialize in writing in a commercial context on behalf of the organization they represent. Their goal is to influence and shape public opinions and perceptions by educating people about the person, product, or organization they represent. They prepare press releases and contact people in the media who might print or broadcast their material. Publicity writers usually work directly under *public relations professionals* (see page 346).

Copywriters write advertising copy for use in publications or broadcast media to promote the sale of goods and services. Every commercial you see on TV, every ad you read in the newspaper, was written by a copywriter.

Writers may work on a freelance basis, selling their work to publishers, public relations and advertising departments or agencies, or manufacturers.

EARNING POTENTIAL

The earnings of writers run the gamut, from subminimum wages for unknowns in the field to millions for some bestselling book or script writers. The following is a sampling of different categories of writers and how their annual earnings vary.

	Initial Earnings	High-End Earnings
News Writer	$30,000	$80,000
Columnist (per article)	$100	$7,000
Technical Writer	$26,700	$69,100
Publicity Writer	$20,000	$40,000
Copywriters	$14,500	$85,000
Communications Specialist:		
Newspapers	$21,100	$34,000
Radio	$16,000	$33,400
Television	$21,800	$69,500

Freelance writers have the most erratic incomes, since they receive compensation by the project, and must frequently work at other jobs to make ends meet, especially in the early years.

Most writers and communications specialists in the newspaper field are represented by the Newspaper Guild, a collective organization that negotiates with newspapers to establish a fixed salary scale.

EDUCATIONAL REQUIREMENTS

Writers come from all educational backgrounds; many have degrees, many don't. Technical writers often have either a degree in or knowledge of a specialized field in business, engineering, or science (which is perhaps why none of us can understand our user's manuals!).

A writer has to have an inquisitive and analytical mind, the ability to string together coherent, interesting sentences, plus the patience to sit and rewrite and rewrite and rewrite. Competence in electronic publishing, graphics, audio production techniques, and all means of disseminating the written word is becoming increasingly important.

A DAY IN THE LIFE

Writers work in a variety of environments, ranging from spartan garrets and damp basements to comfortable private offices to noise-filled newsrooms. Some work may be done via telephone or at the library. *News writers* and *magazine columnists* may have to travel in order to track down information. *Technical writers* may also travel to study their subjects.

Book writers tend to work in home offices, but extensive travel during promotion of a new book may be required. There is also the added obligation to promote books through radio and television appearances.

The physical demands on writers are modest, with a lot of time spent sitting at desks, on the telephone, or at the typewriter, computer, or word processor. Sometimes a writer sits and thinks and sometimes he just sits; writing is tough on the butt, the eyes, and the back.

Writers usually work with little supervision, but they sometimes need to work in close cooperation with others. Writers usually work far in excess of the traditional forty hours a week, but they rarely, if ever, get paid overtime. The work may be stressful, especially when trying to meet deadlines; in some positions, there are deadlines every day.

JOB GROWTH

The Department of Labor Statistics combines editors and writers in their statistics. In 1995 there were approximately 195,000 writers and editors employed, a figure they predict will increase to 237,000 by the year 2005. One-third of salaried writers work for advertising agencies, in radio and television broadcasting, in public relations firms, and on journals and newsletters published by businesses and nonprofit organizations. Some writers develop publications for government agencies or write for motion picture companies.

The overall job outlook for writers is expected to improve, but the competition will be tough. Employment of writers by newspapers, periodicals, book publishers, and nonprofit organizations should increase with a growing demand for these publications.

News writers should keep up-to-date with changing technologies in communications, such as electronic publishing and information services, audiotex, and videotex. Opportunities are likely to be better at small newspapers, weekly magazines, and small radio and television stations, although pay will be lower. Previous experience and an impressive portfolio are the passport to getting the higher-paying jobs at the more prestigious organizations.

Magazine columnists will find employment most abundant in specialty magazines such as those on sports and hobbies, and especially in those geared toward the aging baby boom generation.

Technical writers usually work for computer software firms or manufacturers of aircraft, chemicals, pharmaceuticals, and computers and other electronic equipment. The demand for technical writers should increase in response to the continuing expansion of scientific and technical information; opportunities should be particularly good because of the limited number of writers who are qualified to handle technical material.

Growth of advertising and public relations agencies will also contribute to an increase in new jobs for **copywriters**.

Locations of jobs vary widely by specialty—newspapers and professional, religious, business, technical, and trade union magazines and journals are widely dispersed across the country. Technical writing jobs are concentrated in the Northeast, Texas, and California. Positions with major book publishers, magazines, broadcasting agencies, public relations firms, and the federal government tend to be located in New York, Chicago, Los Angeles, Boston, Philadelphia, San Francisco, and Washington, D.C. Freelance writers working on articles, books, television scripts, plays, and movies are widely scattered, often working as far away from their employers as they can.

International business relations are on a fast track, and the need for writers with

Technical Writer

Translate scientific and technical information into readily understandable language. Plan and edit technical reports, and oversee the preparation of illustrations, photographs, diagrams, and charts. Salary Range: $26,700–$69,100.

Publicity Writer

Write on behalf of an organization to influence and shape public opinions and perceptions of the organization. Prepare press releases and contact people in the media who might print or broadcast the material. Salary Range: $20,000–$40,000.

Copywriter

Write advertising copy for publications or broadcast media to promote the sale of goods and services. Salary Range: $14,500–$85,000.

foreign-language expertise will undoubtedly follow. This will be particularly significant in the area of technical writing and manual writing.

Opportunities for writers should remain abundant well into the next century. While growth will not be dramatic, many new opportunities will arise as the means of communication continue to expand. Writing will continue to be a rewarding field for intelligent and motivated individuals seeking an occupation with considerable personal freedom and autonomy. It is also a profession that can be pursued on a part-time basis over the years as you work professionally in another field.

PUBLIC RELATIONS PROFESSIONAL

In the media-sensitive 1990s, the ability to influence the public's perception of an organization, individual, or event in a positive way is critical. An organization's reputation, profitability, and even its

continued existence can depend on the degree to which it is supported by its targeted public.

Public relations professionals serve as advocates for businesses, governments, universities, schools, and other organizations. They strive to build and maintain positive relationships between such organizations and the public. As managers recognize the growing importance of good public relations to their organization's success, they rely on experts in public relations for advice on strategy and policy.

PR professionals work with media in an effort to convey a desired image of the organization they represent. They prepare press releases and contact people in the media who might print or broadcast their material. Many radio or television reports, newspaper stories, and magazine articles start at the desks of PR professionals.

Public relations professionals' responsibilities may include community, consumer, and government relations; political campaigns; interest-group representation; conflict mediation; or employee and investor relations. Sometimes the subject is an organization and its policies toward its employees or its role in the community; other times, the subject might be a public issue, such as health, nutrition, energy, or the environment. PR professionals put together information that keeps the general public aware of an organization's policies, activities, and accomplishments. In turn they keep management aware of public attitudes toward their corporation.

Additional responsibilities for PR professionals might be setting up speaking engagements and preparing the speeches for company officials. They might make film, slide, or other visual presentations at meetings, school assemblies, or conventions.

Public relations professionals sometimes conduct opinion research for a company, respond to public inquiries, handle advertising or sales promotions, or support marketing efforts.

Public relations professionals are often found in government going by such titles as *press secretary*, *public affairs specialist*, and *information officer*. Public affairs specialists for government departments may keep the public informed about departmental policy, while a press secretary for a member of Congress informs constituents of the member's positions on various issues and the member's accomplishments.

As in the government, public relations professionals in some of today's corporations are sometimes called *information officers*. Since the term public relations has become synonymous with "spin doctor," government agencies and some businesses (on the advice of their PR people) are reluctant to use the title for a department responsible for disseminating serious information both in-house and to the public. "Information officer" is a neutral term that suggests greater objectivity on the part of the people responsible for corporate communications.

Whereas public relations employees tend to deal with the overall image of a company, product, or person, *information officers* are responsible for preparing and delivering press releases that explain the logic behind such profound events as corporate layoffs, the decision to purchase cheaper components from a foreign manufacturer, or the justification for closing an old plant and relocating to another area. All of these pieces of information hit the people affected hard. Information officers must explain a decision made in the company's best interest, but they must also remain aware of the decision's consequences. A more positive task information officers perform might be to announce a new breakthrough or the final result of a long-term negotiation.

Because business and trade have become global enterprises, information officers must be proficient in providing information to clients and agents in other countries who speak other languages. Communication across language barriers is always difficult, and this job is made more difficult by the fact that a foreign culture's methods and practices must be understood and respected.

Employers have found that information officers provide them with an irreplaceable service. Information officers promote the goals of a company, attempt to persuade public opinion on matters that part of the public view unfavorably, and provide data, press releases, corporate communications, and all other types of information that concerns their employer and their industry.

EARNING POTENTIAL

The median annual salary for public relations professionals is about $44,000. Starting salaries average $21,000, although graduates with a master's degree start at around $27,000. Experienced PR professionals and information officers can earn between $40,000 and $100,000. In the federal government, *public affairs specialists* average salaries of slightly more than $45,000 a year.

The salary range is naturally dependent on the size and nature of the business. Nonprofit organizations, museums, religious organizations, and advertising agencies were the lowest-paying groups, while scientific and technical organizations, manufacturers, and public utilities were the highest-paying groups.

EDUCATIONAL REQUIREMENTS

A college education combined with public relations experience, usually gained through an internship, is excellent preparation for public relations work. A public relations major should also select a subspecialty in journalism, advertising, or communications. Well over 200 colleges and approximately 100 graduate schools offer various special communications courses through their communications or journalism departments. A typical college course of study might include public relations principles and techniques, public relations management and administration, writing, visual communication, and research. Courses in advertising, journalism, business administration, political science, psychology, sociology, and creative writing are helpful, as is familiarity with computers. The Public Relations Society of America accredits public relations professionals who have at least five years of paid professional experience in the field and who pass a comprehensive six-hour examination (five hours written, one hour oral). After successfully completing the exam, PRSA members (or members of the North American Public Relations Council) with the required experience can add the credential A.P.R. to their name. While this is a voluntary accreditation, that distinction provides credibility, and may lead to higher salary potential.

To earn accreditation through PRSA, you have to pass the test once. But to maintain accreditation, you have to be recertified every three years, which means staying active in the industry and taking continuing education classes.

The International Association of Business Communicators also has a voluntary accreditation program for professionals in the communications field, including public relations professionals. Those who meet all the requirements of the program earn the designation Accredited Business Communicator. Candidates must have at least five years of experience in a communication field and pass a written and oral examination. They must also submit a portfolio of work samples demonstrating involvement in a range of communication projects and a thorough understanding of communication planning.

There are additional ways to prepare for work as a PR professional. The armed forces have lots of opportunities for PR and can provide excellent training and experience in this field. Many professional organizations, such as the Public Relations Student Society of America and the International Association of Business Communicators, provide excellent opportunities for prospective public relations workers to exchange information and to make contacts within the field. Portfolios of published articles, slide presentations, and television or radio programs are also assets in securing a position.

Critical skills and aptitudes include the ability to write and speak well, creativity, initiative, good judgment, and the ability to make decisions, solve problems, and research well.

HELP WANTED
PUBLIC RELATIONS
PROFESSIONAL

Work with media in an effort to convey the organization's desired public image. Prepare press releases, and contact those who might print or broadcast this material. Put together information that keeps the public aware of organization's policies, activities, and accomplishments, and then keep management aware of public attitudes toward the organization. Conduct opinion research, respond to public inquiries, handle advertising or sales promotions, and/or support marketing efforts. Salary Range: $21,000–$100,000.

A DAY IN THE LIFE

PR professionals work out of offices, in settings ranging from large and small companies to governmental agencies. These are generally clean and comfortable environments. The physical demands are modest, with a great deal of time spent at desks talking on the telephone or working with a computer.

PR professionals work under little direct supervision, but must work in close cooperation with others. They are primarily responsible for their own work. Although a manager will supervise a department, these departments do not consist of many people, and all of the employees are permitted a good deal of autonomy in the way they perform their job, as long as the results reflect the organization's goals and direction.

Some PR professionals work forty hours a week, but for most, unpaid overtime, night, and/or weekend hours come with the territory. Schedules can be irregular, especially when there is a deadline to meet or a speech to deliver, a meeting or community activity to attend, or a trip out of town to make. If there is an emergency or crisis, they may have to be at the job or on call around-the-clock.

Public relations professional positions are opening in all parts of the United States, but most are located in large cities like New York, Los Angeles, Chicago, and Washington, D.C., where a high number of press services, businesses, and other organizations have their main offices.

JOB GROWTH

Public relations professionals hold approximately 98,000 jobs in the United States. About two-thirds work in service industries—in management and public relations firms, educational institutions, membership organizations, hospitals, social service agencies, and advertising agencies. Others work for manufacturing and retail firms, financial institutions, government agencies, and in the entertainment field and publishing industry. Some are self-employed.

Public relations will play an increasingly important role in the next century. The next ten years will prove to be challenging and promising for public relations professionals. Employers' standards for these positions are extremely high, and the job market is competitive. Nevertheless, successful candidates will find their jobs to be stimulating, with exposure to corporate changes and growth, global interaction, and world travel that few employees in other industries can expect.

Sales and Marketing

SALES REPRESENTATIVE

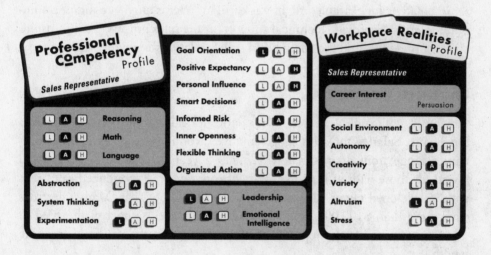

There are *sales representatives* in virtually every area of business in the world. Sales representatives sell a variety of services and products to their customers, in several different ways. Outside sales representatives for manufacturers and distributors, for example, contact prospective clients at their offices or homes. Inside sales representatives, such as real estate and insurance sales representatives, work in offices, and assist walk-in clients or those with appointments. Telemarketing sales representatives sell a firm's services or products over the telephone. They may make calls to prospective clients to sell a company's services, or arrange an appointment between the prospective client and an outside sales representative. In the new world of work, almost every salesperson conducts a portion of his or her business by telephone, making cold calls to prospective customers.

Sales reps must initially develop a list of prospective clients through research in directories, contacts with business associates, and other leads. Once they contact a prospective client, they describe how the service or product offered meets the client's needs. They must be thoroughly familiar with their company and/or product and present it in a sincere and enticing way, if they are to win the confidence and ultimately the patronage of the client. To win this confidence they must be able to determine each client's unique needs; therefore, the salesperson requires superior communication skills. This is the key talent possessed by great salespeople.

Every product and service available today is sold by a sales representative. Sometimes, technical services sales representatives operate as part of a sales team. Sales reps can also be joined by a team of experts from the company whose services the representative is selling. A data processing equipment sales representative, for example, might work with a systems engineer and/or a computer scientist to provide technical support for the sales process. Teams inspire client confidence, and they help build strong relationships with customers.

EARNING POTENTIAL

Obviously, with such a diverse field, salaries for sales professionals run across the board. Salaries for sales representatives working for Fortune 500 companies range from approximately $25,000 a year for beginners to $60,000 a year for those with at least five years of experience. Experienced sales reps with a developed client base average over $70,000 per year. Many sales reps earn more than $100,000 annually. But as with every aspect of the field of sales, the salaries of sales representatives depend upon the nation's economic health.

Sales representatives work under various commission arrangements where they improve their earnings as they sell more. Most firms pay their reps through a combination of salary and commissions that might increase a representative's base salary by 50 to 70 percent. Ultimately every salesperson, even those in positions that are salary plus commission, works on commission that's built on a percentage of the dollar value of sales—the reason being that any salary is factored into the commission structure, and any sales representative failing to meet a predetermined quota does not remain long on the payroll. Many employers offer bonuses to salespeople who exceed company quotas, and outside sales representatives usually have expense accounts to cover their travel and meals.

Successful salespeople can make significantly more money than any other profession, because they impact the bottom line so directly. Because of this, they can scale the professional heights.

EDUCATIONAL REQUIREMENTS

Educational and professional requirements for sales representatives vary and depend upon the company for which the representative works. Most employers prefer their salespeople to have college degrees, but this is not essential. Some companies ask that their salespeople have an academic background in the specific field related to the company itself. For example, companies that sell computer services and telephone systems prefer sales representatives with a background in computer science or engineering. College courses in business, economics, communications, and marketing are also helpful in the sales profession. Companies that market advertising services, for example, may seek individuals with a general college degree, an advertising or marketing degree, or a master's degree in business administration.

Sales representatives typically attend ongoing training programs throughout their careers. These programs train salespeople to answer customer objections, to close a sale, or to write a sales order.

Sales representatives need a pleasant, outgoing personality and excellent analytical, communication, and time management skills. They must always be highly motivated and exude confidence, even when they may not feel it.

A DAY IN THE LIFE

Working conditions for sales reps again depend upon the kind of sales work the rep performs. Outside sales representatives usually do a great deal of traveling and most have the flexibility to set their own schedules. Inside sales representatives and telemarketers spend their work time in offices.

Sales representatives are often assigned territorial boundaries, a specific line of services, or their own accounts, plus a responsibility to develop that and other client bases.

Sales work can be difficult and stressful. Sales reps face competition from other representatives in other companies and from fellow salespeople in their own company. Companies generally set quotas and have contests in order to encourage success in their salespeople. There is therefore often considerable pressure on sales representatives to perform at high levels by the end of each month or quarter. It's a tough but, for the tough, financially rewarding profession.

HELP WANTED
SALES REPRESENTATIVE

Sell a variety of services and products to customers in person or over the phone. Develop a list of prospective clients through research in directories, business associates, and other leads. Must be thoroughly familiar with company and product, and present it in a sincerely enticing way. Must have superior communication skills. Salary Range: $25,000–$100,000+.

JOB GROWTH

According to one survey, sales representatives hold nearly three million jobs in this country. More than half of that number sell business services, such as computer and data processing, advertising, personnel supply, and equipment rental and leasing.

Employment of sales representatives through the year 2005 is expected to grow faster than the average for all occupations. This is in response to the growth of the service industries that employ them. However, due to general corporate downsizing of the sales force in many service industries and the growing use of technologies that increase sales workers' productivity, employment of sales representatives in such areas as advertising and educational services is projected to slow. The future looks good for specialized sales representatives in the areas of *health care insurance, retail hard goods* (electronic goods, appliances, etc.), *computers, banking services*, and *franchise sales*.

Turnover is generally high in sales. Each year, many sales representatives discover that they are unable to make enough sales and leave the occupation. The successful sales representative of the future is keenly informed and in tune with her or his product and customers.

Retail Sales Associate

Retail sales associates ascertain a customer's needs and figure out a product of theirs that can fulfill those needs. They describe to the consumer the product's features or demonstrate its use, and may show similar items in a variety of colors and styles.

Retail sales associates work in almost every store and in many businesses in the United States. Grocery stores, convenience stores, department stores, and specialty shops located in malls employ millions of retail sales associates. These establishments hire every imaginable group of people, from teenagers in high school working at local drugstores to retirees working in card shops.

In some retail environments, such as stores selling personal computers and computer software, sales associates must have special knowledge of and training

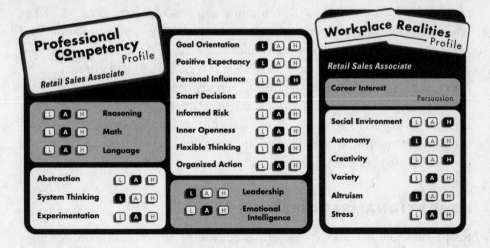

in the equipment they sell. Some computer retail stores prefer to hire sales-clerks who are college students or graduates with a background in computer science, because they have an understanding of the various products on the market, how they work, and how they compare to each other. The more intrinsic knowledge a sales associate has about the product or service being sold, the better his or her chances of winning the job and prospering in that job.

A large part of a retail sales associate's job is handling payments. All sales associates are trained in the employer's methods for filling out sales receipts, ringing up cash purchases, and processing credit card purchases. Most sales associates are charged with the responsibility for their cash drawer.

Retail sales associates must also handle customer service responsibilities, such as helping customers with returned or exchanged items and gift wrapping some items. Sales associates often make arrangements for home or business deliveries of items.

Because customers form their opinion of a store as a result of their contact with the sales force, sales associates must be neat, pleasant, and accommodating. Retail sales is a highly competitive industry, and sales associates are expected to provide whatever service a customer requires in order to satisfy the customer's needs. This emphasis on service has always been an important element of retail sales, and will become even more important as competition continues to heat up in the retail industry.

EARNING POTENTIAL

Earnings in retail vary considerably based on location and business volume of the store. Most retail sales associates working either part-time or in their first job receive the federally mandated minimum wage: as of this writing, $4.75 per hour. Compensation also varies according to the type of store and the product being sold: major appliance sales associates average $415 per week; hardware and building supply sales associates, $323 per week; department store sales associates, $255 per week; and home furnishings sales associates, $354 per week.

Retail sales associates may earn a straight salary, or salary plus commission. In sales of big-ticket items, such as cars and computers, commissions contribute substantially to income and therefore encourage sales associates to work harder to close sales on these items.

EDUCATIONAL REQUIREMENTS

Retail sales jobs do not require formal education. In fact, thousands of high school students take part-time low-level retail sales jobs every year. The qualities that employers look for in potential employees include friendliness, honesty, reliability, and patience—all characteristics that will enhance the growth of any professional career.

Most stores train employees in their own sales techniques and store policies. Large stores may hold training sessions that last several days for new sales associates. In mom-and-pop shops, the proprietor is more likely to instruct the sales associate in the daily routine.

Sales associates who sell products of only one manufacturer, such as cosmetics sales associates, often receive additional training from a sales or manufacturer's representative in the ways to position, display, and sell these products.

In the past, sales associates without college degrees might hope eventually to move up the organizational ladder in big stores. Those opportunities are largely disappearing. Most stores look for management candidates with college or graduate degrees in sales or marketing. Retail sales associates have discovered that the general nature of their duties no longer transfers to higher-level jobs. However, the "sales experience" that comes with a retail sales association position can be invaluable to the future of a professional in any profession.

A DAY IN THE LIFE

Retail sales associates work in clean and comfortable environments because retail establishments are maintained to attract customers.

Many retail sales associates work forty-hour weeks, but the working week often includes night and weekend hours—times when shopping is convenient for the majority of working customers. Many retail sales associates work part-time, either

HELP WANTED
RETAIL SALES ASSOCIATE

Determine and fulfill a customer's needs by providing a particular product. Describe a product's features and/or demonstrate its use. May show alternate colors or styles of the same or similar items. Knowledge of special equipment required in some environments. Responsible for handling payments and the cash drawer. Must be neat, pleasant, and accommodating to the customer. Salary Range: $9,880–$25,000+.

as a primary or secondary job. During peak shopping periods, such as the month between Thanksgiving and Christmas, most sales associates are expected to work longer hours to coincide with their store's late hours and increased business.

Sales associates must spend most of their working hours on their feet. Another constant factor in retail sales is contact with the public. Every retail sales associate will eventually be confronted with the difficult customer. Sales associates are expected to serve such customers with the same pleasant attitude as customers who create no problems—an expectation which can prove to be very stressful at times.

JOB GROWTH

There are over 3.5 million sales associates employed in the United States working in thousands of different settings. The largest employers of retail sales associates are department stores, clothing and accessories stores, grocery stores, and car dealerships. The Department of Labor Statistics predicts the number of retail sales associates will increase to 4.3 million by the year 2005. Many additional openings will be created every year as people leave this occupation to take other jobs.

There are always many additional jobs created during the Christmas season, and people hired on a part-time basis for the holidays often find themselves retained, on a full- or part-time basis, if they prove themselves to be good employees.

Retail sales jobs are excellent jobs for many people: high school students looking to make some expense money, people who need to supplement their income with part-time work, and people who need to gain job experience. Because there are so many different areas of retail sales, job seekers will find the work more rewarding if they are employed in a store that sells products which interest them personally, or of which they have a special knowledge, such as a bookstore, a video store, a sporting goods store, or a clothing shop. Although the earnings are limited, retail sales is a good source of employment for people just entering the job market or looking for work that provides them with a flexible schedule.

Travel Agent

Professional Competency Profile

Travel Agent

L	A	H	Reasoning
L	A	H	Math
L	A	H	Language

Abstraction	L	A	H
System Thinking	L	A	H
Experimentation	L	A	H

Goal Orientation	L	A	H	
Positive Expectancy	L	A	H	
Personal Influence	L	A	H	
Smart Decisions	L	A	H	
Informed Risk	L	A	H	
Inner Openness	L	A	H	
Flexible Thinking	L	A	H	
Organized Action	L	A	H	

L	A	H	Leadership
L	A	H	Emotional Intelligence

Workplace Realities Profile

Travel Agent

Career Interest
Persuasion/Development

Social Environment	L	A	H
Autonomy	L	A	H
Creativity	L	A	H
Variety	L	A	H
Altruism	L	A	H
Stress	L	A	H

Travel agents advise vacationing clients on what spots best suit their desires and business travelers on what accommodations best suit their schedule. They then make arrangements for transportation (by car, plane, or ship), make and confirm hotel reservations, and/or reserve rental cars. They may also plan tours and recreational events.

They can provide information on travel and weather conditions, restaurants, and tourist attractions. For international travelers, agents may provide information on customs regulations, required papers (passports, visas, and certificates of vaccination), and currency exchange rates. The job requires a great deal of personal contact.

Travel agents must be constantly aware of newly published and computer-based sources for information on departure and arrival times, travel fares, and hotel ratings and accommodations. They often recommend locations and hotels based on their personal travel experiences. Resorts, cruise lines, and hotel chains always encourage travel agents to experience their destinations firsthand.

EARNING POTENTIAL

Since a travel agent's job is largely a sales job, an agent's earnings depend greatly on his or her sales ability. An agent's experience and the size and location of the agency that employs him or her are additional factors determining income.

The annual earnings for beginning travel agents are around $12,000. This figure reflects the traditionally low commissions an inexperienced agent earns. Travel agents typically receive a minimal salary which is charged against their commissions. Most sales-related jobs require a few years during which the salesperson develops a client base and reputation. Nevertheless, figures show that the average travel agent earns in the range of $25,000 after ten years of experience. As in most sales fields, competition is intense in the travel industry.

Travel agents earn their commissions directly from the airlines, cruise lines, tour operators, and hotels they book for their clients' use. Standard commissions generally fall in the range of 10 percent. They may also charge clients a fee for their work in planning and booking a trip.

Successful travel agents receive substantial discounts on their own travel arrangements and accommodations, a perk which makes the relatively low salary a lot more attractive. This is a form of advertising for the airlines and hotels, who hope the agent will recommend their facilities to clients.

EDUCATIONAL REQUIREMENTS

Travel agents with college degrees are becoming more attractive to employers, even though there are very few college courses that relate to the profession. Courses teaching the basic elements of a travel agent's job are available in programs at community colleges and adult education facilities. Since few travel agencies are willing to train new employees in the basic skills needed for the job, interested parties should look into courses available near them.

One needed skill for travel agents is computer literacy. Since most of their work is performed on computer, travel agents simply cannot function without basic computer skills.

Employers also seek candidates with good communication and problem-solving skills. Since travel agents describe many vacation areas to interested clients, good verbal skills are a necessary attribute for the job. Knowledge of a foreign language is considered a plus for planning international travel.

Although there are no federal licensing requirements for travel agents, the state of Rhode Island requires licensing, and Ohio, Hawaii, and California require registration. In California, travel agents not approved by a corporation are required to have a license.

A DAY IN THE LIFE

Travel agents work at desks in their offices. Most of their time is spent on paperwork and computers, meeting or talking by telephone with clients, contacting

HELP WANTED
TRAVEL AGENT

Advise vacationing clients on what spots best suit their desires, and business travelers on what accommodations best suit their schedule. Make arrangements for transportation (by car, plane, or ship), make and confirm hotel reservations, and reserve rental cars. Plan tours and recreation events, provide information on travel, weather conditions, restaurants, and tourist attractions. Salary Range: $12,000–$25,000+.

airlines and hotels to make travel arrangements, and promoting group tours. They may work under a great deal of pressure during vacation seasons, when the travel, resort, and hotel seasons are at their peak. During these seasons, competition for available airline seats and room accommodations may be great. Clients tend to hold agents responsible for the success of their vacations, so the pressure to see to every detail and make sure the arrangements suit the client's specific desires is intense.

Travel agents may also travel extensively as a mixture of business and pleasure. Their job responsibilities may include promotional presentations to groups for vacation spots they have visited.

JOB GROWTH

Travel agents hold approximately 122,000 jobs in the United States, with nine out of ten employed by travel agencies. The rest work for membership agencies (such as automobile clubs that provide travel services to their members) or are self-employed.

Job opportunities for travel agents exist throughout the country. Nearly one-half are employed in suburban areas; 40 percent work in cities; and the remainder work in rural locations.

Employment in the travel-related field is expected to grow faster than the average for all jobs during the next ten years. The Department of Labor Statistics predicts the number of travel agent positions to increase by about 43,000 by the year 2005. Many new jobs will be created by the start-up of new agencies or the expansion of established ones.

Employment growth in the travel industry depends on the strength of the economy, because both a corporation's and an individual's travel plans depend on their financial stability.

FLIGHT ATTENDANT

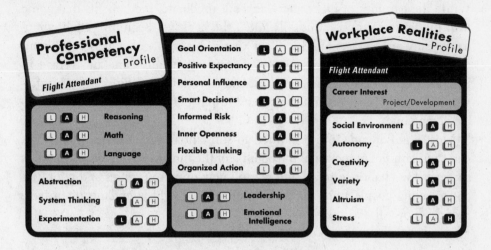

Coffee, tea or . . . Bloody Mary? **Flight attendants** are often considered glorified waiters and waitresses. However, for those of us who are aerophobic, flight attendants strive to provide a relaxed and safe atmosphere in which we can spend our final moments. Their responsibilities begin before the flight is embarked upon; after a briefing from the captain on expected flight conditions, they ready the airplane with all the amenities that will provide passengers a comfortable journey: pillows, blankets, earphones, magazines, food, and drinks. They assist passengers upon boarding with their seating and carry-on luggage storage, and answer any questions passengers may have about the flight. They advise passengers of safety regulations and emergency procedures. Once the plane is airborne, they serve beverages and meals, run films, sell duty-free goods (on international flights), and attend to passengers' special needs, which may include reassurance for nervous passengers during air turbulence, first aid in the case of an in-flight illness or injury, or assistance in deplaning in an emergency. At the end of the flight, attendants update passengers on transfer flights and assist them in exiting the aircraft. They inspect the plane for left-behind belongings, and collect blankets, pillows, and earphones.

Aside from providing passengers with service, flight attendants are considered public relations specialists for the airline. The manner with which they provide the service is the best advertisement the airline has.

EARNING POTENTIAL

While the earnings of flight attendants are moderate, the benefits that come with the territory are what usually fatten the package. Beginning flight attendants earn an average of $13,000 a year. This average increases to about $22,000 after five years' experience. Senior attendants earn an average of $38,000. Additional income can be earned working overtime and on international flights. The major airlines tend to pay better than the smaller localized companies.

Most flight attendants are entitled to substantial discounts for themselves and their families on personal travel. One of the most satisfying benefits of this career is the chance to travel and get to know numerous cities and countries and meeting people from various backgrounds. Flight attendants often have friends all over the world.

EDUCATIONAL REQUIREMENTS

Flight attendants must be at least nineteen years old, but formal educational requirements are minimal. A high school diploma or equivalent is the minimum requirement. Knowledge of foreign languages is essential for some international flights. Several years of college or experience working with the public is useful on a résumé. More important, the airlines look for candidates with an outgoing and friendly personality who can work as team players, and have a well groomed appearance, good health, excellent communication skills, poise, and the ability to stay calm in stressful situations.

Flight attendants are trained by the airline for approximately four to six weeks. The training includes company operations and procedures, emergency and first aid training, passenger relations, and, for international airlines, customs and passport procedures and regulations. Part of the training also includes working as apprentices on trial flights.

Once an attendant has completed the training program, he or she becomes a "reserve attendant" and is on call to fill in for full-time attendants during sick time or vacation leave. An attendant may remain in reserve service for a number of years before a full-time position becomes available. Seniority entitles attendants to choose their posts (or which flight routes they work on).

Flight attendants are required to attend twelve to fourteen hours of supplementary training in emergency and passenger relations annually.

HELP WANTED
FLIGHT ATTENDANT

Assist passengers with seating, luggage storage, and special needs. Advise passengers of safety regulations and emergency procedures. Serve beverages and meals, and provide first aid and assistance in an emergency. Update passengers on transfer flights, and assist them in exiting the aircraft. Requires an outgoing and friendly personality, and excellent communication skills. Salary Range: $13,000–$38,000.

A DAY IN THE LIFE

Flight attendants work unusual hours. Reserve attendants must be available at short notice—on nights, weekends, and holidays to fill in at the last minute for full-time attendants. As there are regulations as to how much time can actually be spent flying, full-time attendants generally spend about 50 percent of their working hours in the air. The remainder of their working hours are devoted to preparation, paperwork, and WAITING. The hours are irregular, and attendants spend a great deal of time on their feet and about one-third of their time away from home. The work can be stressful—especially during rough, late, or crowded flights, when conditions try passengers' tempers.

Obviously there is the risk of injury—and even the unthinkable—in this occupation.

JOB GROWTH

As many as 107,000 flight attendants are employed by U.S.-based airlines. The prospects are good for this industry, but with the Department of Labor Statistics suggesting there will be 140,000 flight attendants employed in the U.S. by 2005, the competition is expected to continue to be tough. And this is an occupation that is subject to economic turns: downsizing means less corporate travel and less disposable income for vacations.

This is a great career for young people looking to travel, and it can eventually lead to a fairly stable source of income. Some flight attendants move into administrative positions within the airline, which lets them enjoy the same benefits without having to suffer the irregular work schedule. Candidates would be well advised to get in a couple of years of college experience first—not only to increase their employability in the airlines, but also to have something to fall back on during an economic downswing, or if the lifestyle begins to take its toll.

Food Service

CHEF: EXECUTIVE OR CHIEF CHEF/ASSISTANT OR SOUS CHEF/PREP
CHEF/ INSTITUTIONAL CHEF/BREAD AND PASTRY CHEF
COOK: SHORT-ORDER COOK/FAST-FOOD COOK

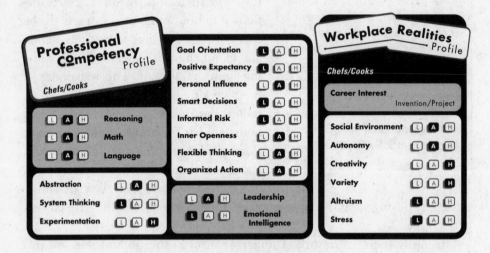

Chefs are responsible for preparing restaurant meals—or parts of meals—and are largely responsible for the reputation of any restaurant or cafeteria.

The skills and training required for being a chef in a restaurant that features a varied menu with dishes that are time-consuming, difficult to prepare, and customized to each customer's personal preferences are greater than those required of short-order or fast-food cooks, whose jobs demand more limited cooking skills and experience. Many chefs have earned praise and recognition not only for themselves, but for the restaurants, hotels, and institutions where they work, both for their skill in preparing traditional favorites and for their ability to create new dishes, flavors, and variety in their cuisine.

In large or upscale restaurants where the menus are varied and most of the food is prepared on-site start to finish, *executive* or *chief chefs* may direct the work of a specialized staff of chefs, cooks, and other kitchen workers, as well as developing menus, planning meals, estimating food requirements, and supervising or personally handling food purchasing. In some restaurants, *assistant* or *sous chefs* (underchefs) specialize in certain types of food or parts of the meal—supervising soups, entrées, side dishes, or desserts, for example.

Other kitchen workers, directed by chefs or cooks, perform tasks that require less skill or that contribute to dishes being prepared by others. Sometimes called **prep chefs**, they weigh and measure ingredients, fetch utensils, stir and strain soups and sauces, clean, peel and slice vegetables and fruits, make salads, garnish plates, and decorate pastries and desserts. They may cut or grind meat, poultry, and seafood to ready it for cooking. As part of their training to become chefs, the least skilled or least experienced kitchen workers may start their careers by cleaning work areas, washing equipment and utensils, or running dish-washing equipment. They work their way to prep chef and onward and upward, gaining sous chef experience in a number of different specialties.

Institutional chefs work in the kitchens of schools, industrial cafeterias, hospitals, and other large institutions. Unlike restaurant chefs, who prepare most individual servings to order, these chefs create a small selection of entrées, vegetables, and desserts, but in large quantities. They often are responsible for directing the work of other cooks and kitchen workers, planning meals and menus, estimating food requirements, and ordering food supplies.

Bread and pastry chefs produce baked goods for restaurants. Unlike bakers who work at large, automated industrial bakeries, pastry chefs need only supply the customers who visit their establishment. They bake smaller quantities of breads, rolls, pastries, pies, cakes, and other desserts, doing most of the work by hand.

Cooks are responsible for preparing meals in restaurants that emphasize fast service and simple cuisine that can be prepared quickly or even in advance by people with only limited cooking training or skills. Although the terms *chef* and *cook* sometimes are still used interchangeably, the term *chef* generally applies to someone with more training and more sophisticated cooking skills than cooks.

In restaurants featuring casual dining and in coffee shops that emphasize fast service, *short-order cooks* prepare meals to order, but the recipes tend to be much less sophisticated and the preparation time far shorter than in more formal restaurants (although a diner menu may actually contain more items). They grill hot dishes, prepare sandwiches, fry potatoes, or dish out portions of ready-made desserts or side-dishes prepared earlier, often working on several orders at the same time. Between busy periods, they may slice meats, cheese, or sandwich ingredients; prepare soups or stews; or clean the grill, food preparation areas, counters, and floor. In restaurants of this sort, typically one cook prepares all of the food with the help of a junior short-order cook or one or two other kitchen helpers.

Fast-food cooks learn to prepare a very limited selection of menu items, cooking and packaging food in batches and storing it in heated areas. They anticipate rapid and high-volume turnover. These jobs require relatively little training, but are fast-paced and highly repetitive, requiring excellent time management and coordination skills.

EARNING POTENTIAL

As one would expect, wages are highest in senior-level positions in the finer restaurants and hotels, where **executive chefs** may earn over $60,000 a year. According to a National Restaurant Association survey, lower-level **chefs** and **cooks** averaged between $6.00 and $8.00 an hour. **Short-order cooks** averaged just under $6.00 an hour. In fast-food restaurants, most employees earned between $4.75 and $5.30 an hour, with the median being about $4.68. **Pastry chefs** and bread bakers had median hourly earnings of $6.25, with **prep chefs** earning an average of 30 cents an hour less.

Chefs, cooks, and other kitchen workers working full-time often receive paid vacation, health benefits, and sick leave, but these benefits generally are not offered to part-time employees. Some employers provide uniforms and even free meals, but federal law allows them to deduct the cost or fair value of any meals or lodging provided, and many employers do so. This affects the cook, because if the organization declares the deduction, the cook has to declare this deducted amount as income.

EDUCATIONAL REQUIREMENTS

Many years of training and experience are required to achieve the level of skill required of a senior-level or **executive chef** in a fine restaurant. An increasing number of chefs and cooks are obtaining initial training through high school or post–high school vocational programs, which range from a few months to two years or more, and in specialized programs in two- or four-year colleges. The apprenticeship, internship, and training programs offered by professional culinary institutes, industry associations, trade unions, and the armed services are good sources of training and experience. In addition, some large hotels and restaurants run their own training programs for cooks and chefs. Those with some advanced training may get jobs as chefs without first having to work in lower-skilled kitchen jobs, and they may have an advantage when seeking jobs in restaurants or hotels where hiring standards are high.

Although the content of education and training varies widely, most courses and programs emphasize hands-on practice in preparing food, using kitchen equipment, planning menus, figuring costs, determining portion size, and purchasing food. On the more academic side, students learn such things as hotel and restaurant sanitation and public health rules, and how to figure portion size and manage costs, along with supervisory skills.

Over 550 schools nationwide offer culinary courses, 70 of which were accredited as of 1993 by the American Culinary Federation (which has been accrediting culinary programs only for a short time). Accreditation shows that a program meets standards regarding course content, facilities, and quality of instruction.

The American Culinary Federation also offers certification that formally recognizes the skills of chef or cook after the completion of a three-year course. Certification, which is based on both experience and formal training, can be at the level of cook, working chef, executive chef, or master chef.

A DAY IN THE LIFE

Chefs often work long hours, including evening, weekend, and holiday work. They may spend hours during the day developing new recipes, planning portions, and buying food and supplies before they ever begin to cook. The working conditions in restaurants vary widely. While many restaurant kitchens are large and have modern equipment, convenient work areas, and good air-conditioning, in others—even in restaurants preparing the finest food—the kitchens may be surprisingly small, hot, and cramped. Other variations in working conditions depend on the type and quantity of food being prepared, and on local laws and inspectors controlling food service operations.

Similarly, many **cooks** work long hours, including evening, weekend, and holiday work. However, in institutional settings the hours usually are more regular, with those employed in public and private schools working only during the school year. Half of all **short-order** and **fast-food cooks** and other kitchen workers work part-time, and a third of all **bakers** and **restaurant** and **institutional chefs** work part-time. In some large hotels and restaurants, kitchen workers belong to unions that bargain for better wages and benefits, the largest being the Hotel Employees and Restaurant Employees International Union and the Service Employees International Union.

In general, chefs and cooks withstand the constant pressure of working in close quarters during busy periods, standing for hours at a time, working near hot ovens and grills and around sharp utensils and machinery, and lifting heavy pots, pans, and kettles. While food preparation is not considered a dangerous line of work, cuts, burns, slips, and falls are not uncommon. The ability to work effectively as part of a team, a keen sense of taste and smell, and a high standard of personal hygiene (most states also require certificates that those working in kitchens are free from contagious diseases) are important attributes for chefs.

JOB GROWTH

Of well over three million chefs, cooks, and kitchen workers in this country, there are over half a million restaurant chefs and cooks, although many of those work in more casual restaurants where rapid preparation is valued over the ability to create haute cuisine.

Chefs are the rarity among restaurant workers: they are the people for whom restaurant work is a career, not just a temporary job. For that reason, chefs are accorded considerably better treatment, paid at a much higher level, and given greater responsibility than any other restaurant and food industry workers.

The demand for trained and experienced chefs is expected to stay strong through the turn of the century and beyond. As long as the economy remains stable, employment in restaurants is expected to grow particularly rapidly as the population ages, as people earn more disposable income, and as more women join the workforce and do less cooking at home.

Advancement opportunities are better for chefs than for many other food and beverage occupations, although many chefs get higher-paying jobs or develop more experience by changing jobs rather than being promoted. Besides culinary skills, advancement may depend on showing the ability to supervise others, plan menus and portions, purchase food, and minimize costs and waste. While some chefs gradually advance to executive chef positions or supervisory and management roles in hotels, clubs, or finer restaurants, others go into business as caterers or restaurant owners. Still others turn to teaching culinary skills in schools or programs. In the huge food service industry, a chef's training and hands-on experience will open many other doors of career opportunity.

The chef's role is ultimately a creative one, whereby many chefs develop into artists who create meals that carry their own individual identity. Successful chefs find that their talents are always in demand, and that they have a great deal of flexibility in moving within the industry. Very successful chefs may open their own restaurants, and thus win the total autonomy their artistic vision often craves.

Although the demand for **cooks** is expected to stay strong through the turn of the century and beyond, turnover in these jobs is high. The education and

HELP WANTED
CHEFS AND COOKS

Chef
Responsible for preparing restaurant meals. Create and adapt recipes, plan meals, estimate food requirements, and handle food purchasing. Direct the work of other chefs or staff. Salary Range: $12,500–$60,000+.

Prep Chef
Weigh and measure ingredients; fetch utensils; stir and strain soups and sauces; clean, peel, and slice vegetables and fruits; make salads; garnish plates; and decorate pastries and desserts. Salary Range: $12,000–$13,500.

Institutional Chef
Work in the kitchens of schools, industrial cafeterias, hospitals, and other large institutions. Responsible for directing the work of other cooks and kitchen workers, planning meals and menus, estimating food requirements, and ordering food supplies. Salary Range: $12,000–$16,500.

Cook
Prepare meals in restaurants that emphasize fast service and simple cuisine and offer foods that can be prepared in advance by people with limited cooking training or skills. Fast-paced and highly repetitive work, requiring excellent time management and coordination skills. Salary Range: $9,800–$11,000.

Bread and Pastry Chef
Prepare and supply baked goods to restaurants, institutions, and retail bakeries. Measure and mix ingredients, shape and bake dough, and add fillings and apply decorations. Salary Range: $13,000–$15,000.

training requirements for short-order and fast-food cooks is low, so these jobs allow easy entry for people without a college education and are attractive to those seeking part-time employment. But the relatively low pay, lack of advancement opportunity, and repetitive work drive many of these into other occupations or back to school.

Traditionally, many cooking positions, particularly the less-skilled roles, have been filled by those under twenty-five. This labor pool will drop during the balance of the 1990s; today the boomers are bald or graying, but their children will not enter the workforce en masse until the year 2000. Consequently, many employers will be forced to offer better wages, benefits, and training to attract and retain employees.

Opportunities for **institutional** and **cafeteria cooks** will grow less rapidly; what growth there is will focus on the health services and education sectors. While there is an effort by many institutions to improve food quality, many are contracting with large chains of institutional food service and hospitality providers rather than maintaining their own staffs. For example, the Marriott hotel chain has a division that services schools and other institutions.

Employment opportunities in the **short-order** and **fast-food** industries will always be good due to the high turnover rate in these establishments; however, the overall number of new fast-food restaurants is leveling off.

RESTAURANT OR FOOD SERVICE MANAGER

Professional Competency Profile
Restaurant/Food Service Manager

L **A** H	Reasoning	Goal Orientation	**L** A H
L **A** H	Math	Positive Expectancy	**L** A H
L **A** H	Language	Personal Influence	L **A** H
		Smart Decisions	L **A** H
		Informed Risk	L **A** H
		Inner Openness	L **A** H
		Flexible Thinking	L **A** H
		Organized Action	L A **H**

Abstraction   **L** A H
System Thinking   **L** A H
Experimentation   L **A** H

L A **H**   Leadership
L **A** H   Emotional Intelligence

Workplace Realities Profile
Restaurant/Food Service Manager

Career Interest   Project/Persuasion

Social Environment	L **A** H
Autonomy	L **A** H
Creativity	L **A** H
Variety	L **A** H
Altruism	L **A** H
Stress	**L** A H

Restaurant or food service managers oversee the food services of hotels, restaurants, and institutional dining facilities such as cafeterias in schools, hospitals, and nursing homes. They manage hotel restaurants, lounges, and banquet facilities.

Food service managers coordinate menu planning with chefs and other managers, determining costs, variety, and quality of food. They are responsible for ordering the supplies, checking the quality of the deliveries, and managing the use of the food to ensure freshness and minimum waste. They may also see to such peripheral details as ordering tableware, kitchen utensils, cleaning supplies, fixtures, and furniture, as well as overseeing the maintenance of the facility. Additionally they may have administrative responsibilities, keeping records of personnel, inventories, sales, and banking.

Food service managers hire and train the kitchen and service staff, and often supervise or even assist in meal preparation and food staff services. In larger establishments, they may be assisted by an executive chef and/or assistant managers.

Food service managers investigate customer complaints about food quality or staff service. They are at all times responsible for their establishment's compliance with health and safety standards.

EARNING POTENTIAL

The average salary for restaurant or food service managers is close to $28,000 a year. Some specific average *starting* salaries are:

Fast-Food Restaurant Manager	$24,900
Full-Menu Restaurant Manager	$30,400
Institutional Cafeteria Manager	$29,300

Earnings vary widely—from large hotel restaurants in metropolitan areas to small-town family restaurants in rural areas. For instance, one survey quoted a starting salary for food service managers in Montana at $12,900, and with experience, $17,900; another survey found a food service manager in Southern California starting as low as $10,392, but with three years' experience earning $39,490.

Many food service managers also earn bonuses which range from $1,000 to $4,000. Such bonuses are generally based on sales and performance. In addition, full-time employees receive standard benefits such as vacations and health insurance. They also usually enjoy a fringe benefit of free meals.

EDUCATIONAL REQUIREMENTS

Although it is not strictly necessary to be formally educated in food management to secure a job in the field, it is certainly an advantage in getting your foot in the door. Having said that, there has been many a determined waiter or enterprising hostess who rose through the ranks to become a food service manager.

The most secure route to a food service management position would be to seek a bachelor's degree in restaurant and food service management. There are more than 160 colleges and universities that offer four-year programs in this specialty, as well as 800 community colleges and technical institutes that offer two-year associate's degree programs. Course work in this field includes a wide variety of subjects, from meal planning, food preparation, and nutrition to business management and accounting. Many courses include lab study and internships for gaining hands-on experience.

A Food Management Professional (FMP) certification is offered by the Educational Foundation of the National Restaurant Association to those managers who complete the course and pass an exam, and who meet the work experience requirements. While this is by no means a prerequisite for gainful employment, it may give candidates a competitive edge.

Aside from the educational background, there are specific personal qualities that would maximize a person's success in this field. Self-confidence and poise, good leadership and communication skills, organization and initiative, energy and stamina, and an ability to function effectively and calmly in a stressful hive of activity are all important personal ingredients for a fulfilling career as a food service manager.

A DAY IN THE LIFE

Restaurant and food service managers work long hours, often in very hectic circumstances, and are on their feet a good percentage of the time. They commonly spend some time in offices planning and carrying out administrative responsibilities, but they also spend a good deal of time in the kitchen and on the restaurant floor, overseeing all aspects of the operation. There are times when they must pitch in and help in the kitchen with preparations or cleanup, and in the restaurant with seating, serving, and seeing to the general satisfaction of the patrons. Sometimes customers (who are, of course, always right) can test the patience of even the most diplomatic food service manager.

Managers of institutional and school cafeterias work at a much less frantic pace and spend more time on the administrative end of the business. Their hours are more conventional as well. However, both restaurant and cafeteria managers are responsible for a wide range of activities and rarely find themselves with time on their hands during work hours. It's an exciting job for people who like a constant flow of changing activities and interactions with their colleagues.

Occupational hazards in this career are minimal, although working in kitchens and around hot food can be risky. The most common complaint of food service managers is likely to be fatigue and stress.

JOB GROWTH

The government projections for food service managers are lumped together with those of lodging (hotel and motel) managers. Together there were 155,300 job openings predicted between 1992 and 2005. Well over 50 percent of these should be in the food service side, as this industry has such a strong forecast for overall growth.

The anticipated growth in population, disposable income, and leisure time, and in the number of working women with less time for cooking, have led forecasters to predict a strong future for the food service industry. Additionally, a small baby boom is filling schools and therefore cafeterias, and the aging population is increasingly being fed in institutional cafeterias throughout the country. Wherever food is served, there will be the need for food service managers.

Fast-food establishments, though leveling off in growth, still provide the most opportunities, as the turnover is high. This is an excellent starting point to gain experience for future advancement in the field.

In full-service restaurants (restaurants with sit-down table service), growth will be steady but competition will be tough, as these jobs are better-paying and more prestigious. Hotel restaurants are a good bet, as business and leisure travel will continue to grow. National chain restaurants are also a place to look for a secure future.

WAITER OR WAITRESS

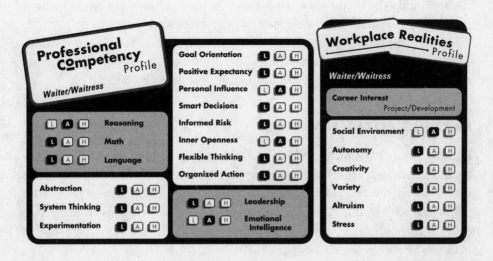

All employees are judged on the quality of their performance, but few jobs offer the immediate feedback found in the food service industry. **Waiters** and **waitresses**, for example, often see how well they did their job when they see the size of the tip (although the quality of an establishment's food is often a key ingredient in determining tip size). And this holds true for almost all waiter and waitress jobs, whether in small, informal diners or large, elegant restaurants. The service provided by the wait staff can enhance or diminish patrons' pleasure in their meal.

The fundamentals of a waiter's or waitress's job do not change greatly over time: they take customers' orders, serve food and beverages, prepare itemized checks, and often process payments for meals. How they perform these tasks does differ, though, depending on the place where they work. Waiters and waitresses in coffee shops must provide fast and efficient service to meet the needs of customers who anticipate a fast meal. In expensive restaurants that serve gourmet food, waiters and waitresses are expected to be more attentive to the patrons, serving their meals at a slower pace and providing personal service. In such establishments, waiters and waitresses are expected to be familiar with the ingredients and preparation of entrées, with wines that complement the meal, and with other suggestions to assist the diners. They may also be expected to prepare certain salads and side dishes at tableside, as a visual complement to the diner's evening out.

Although maintaining a friendly relationship with customers is necessary for waiters and waitresses, maintaining good relations with the cooks and kitchen staff is equally important. It is no secret that in every restaurant, from a coffee shop to a four-star restaurant, waiters and waitresses who treat the kitchen staff with friendliness, courtesy, and respect are more likely to have their orders prepared in a timely fashion than those who do not.

Waiters and waitresses also work in institutions, such as retirement communities, and at private, catered functions. In these situations, they usually receive a salary rather than depend primarily on tips for income.

EARNING POTENTIAL

In most instances, waiters' and waitresses' earnings depend more on tips than on the hourly wage they receive. Very few restaurant waiters and waitresses receive even the federally mandated minimum wage as a salary, because employers are given a credit for tips employees receive—as much as 50 percent of the minimum wage. Many restaurant waiters and waitresses receive between $2 and $3.00 per hour as a salary.

The median weekly earnings of waiters and waitresses employed full-time in 1992 were approximately $220 (including tips). The average range was from $180 to $300, and the top 10 percent of waiters and waitresses earned at least $380. Higher earnings result from better tips (generally between 10 percent and 20 percent of the bill), and good waiters in popular and expensive restaurants earn the most money. Of course, tips are in cash and don't always get accurately reported, so many waiters and waitresses earn more than these figures.

In many restaurants, waiters and waitresses contribute a portion of their tips to a tip pool, which is shared by busboys and the kitchen staff, employees who do not otherwise have access to tips.

Full-time waiters and waitresses in large hotels and restaurants may receive paid vacations and medical benefits, but part-time workers (by far the majority in this field) receive no benefits.

Restaurant workers in some establishments are represented by labor unions. The two principal unions for this trade are the Hotel Employees and Restaurant Employees International Union and the Service Employees International Union.

EDUCATIONAL REQUIREMENTS

There are no educational requirements governing food and beverage service jobs, although many employers prefer to hire high school graduates. Still, a customer is likely to see a high school student working in a restaurant as a busboy, and a candidate for a graduate degree waiting on tables. The position serves, for many, as a means of immediate income; it rarely serves someone as a career. The era of career waiters and waitresses who remained for years with a single restaurant and served the same customers appears to be over. The food industry for many years has been characterized by the turnover of its service staff.

Some factors pertaining to these positions are obvious but bear mentioning. Waiters and waitresses should be well-groomed and well-spoken. Because they spend all of their working hours in close contact with the public, they should have a pleasant disposition and enjoy dealing with different types of people. Occasional crises arise during the course of a shift, and a waiter or waitress should be prepared to deal with these crises calmly and effectively.

In addition, a waiter or waitress needs a good memory for faces and names; this is especially true in private clubs, where people expect to be remembered by the staff. He or she should also have a rudimentary grasp of arithmetic in order to total the bill; in many restaurants, errors on a bill are charged to the waiter or waitress who committed the error. In some restaurants, a waiter or waitress must have—or be able to fake—a passing knowledge of foreign languages in order to describe the foreign-titled entrées to patrons.

A DAY IN THE LIFE

Waiters and waitresses work on their feet. They often must carry heavy trays loaded with dishes and glassware. During busy periods they must work under stress to serve food quickly, but without giving the appearance of hurrying the customers. The only threat of occupational hazard are the burns, slips, and scrapes that are common to kitchen work.

The number of waiters and waitresses employed in a restaurant depends largely on the emphasis the restaurant places on service. In a coffee shop, a single waiter or waitress is expected to serve several different "stations" (tables or booths). In a large restaurant, a waiter or waitress will be assigned fewer stations, but he or she will be responsible for providing a greater amount of attention to the customers.

With age, the physical demands of the job become more burdensome. A waiter or waitress who spends several years carrying heavy trays on tile or carpeted concrete surfaces may suffer debilitating back and leg pain. Waiters and waitresses are cautioned to maintain conditioning and flexibility for these areas of the body.

Waiter and waitress jobs are mostly part-time jobs. Some may work forty-hour weeks, but because dining hours do not fit a convenient work schedule, many waiters and waitresses work split shifts (lunch and dinner, with a few hours off in between), or only one mealtime in a day. Because of the odd hours associated with the job, waiter and waitress positions appeal to students, homemakers, and other individuals looking to work only part-time or to supplement another income.

Although establishments that serve food to the public are monitored by boards of health, the degree of cleanliness in any restaurant depends mostly on the manager overseeing the entire operation. Nevertheless, most restaurant kitchens range from reasonably to very clean, except during busy periods, when dirty dishes, pots, and pans create a temporary mess.

JOB GROWTH

There are approximately 1.8 million waiters and waitresses employed in the food service industry, a number that is projected to increase by 637,000 by the

HELP WANTED
WAITER/WAITRESS

Take customers' orders, serve food and beverages, prepare itemized checks. Sometimes process payments for meals. Good memory and pleasant demeanor required. Must be quick on the feet, have good physical stamina, and be attentive to patrons' needs and concerns. Familiarity with the menu and how the meals are prepared required. Salary Range: $9,880–$20,000 plus tips.

year 2005. Almost two-thirds of these waiters/waitresses work in restaurants, bars, coffee shops, and other retail eating places. Many of the rest work in hotels, country clubs, and other private membership organizations.

Jobs for waiters and waitresses exist in every large city and small town, with most of the jobs found in big cities and tourist areas. Some waiters and waitresses move from a summer resort area to a winter resort area as the seasons change. Since the job's skills are transferable to almost any restaurant, good waiters and waitresses can very often find work easily.

Because they do not offer the benefits of a long-term career (pay raises, a clear path for professional advancement, increased benefits), jobs in the food service industry are subject to a high rate of turnover. Many people leave these jobs upon graduating from college or graduate school or finding full-time employment. There are almost no formal educational requirements or training necessary to enter the field.

Traditionally, restaurant service jobs have been filled by younger workers. The number of young workers is expected to shrink through the end of this century, but will start to grow after the year 2000. The benefit to younger workers during the next few years is that they can expect slightly higher wages as employers seek to attract and retain them in what has traditionally been a young person's occupation.

Since waiter and waitress jobs are not generally considered career positions, there is very little opportunity for advancement in the field. Experienced waiters and waitresses may find work at larger or better restaurants that offer the prospects of better tips, but that is more a lateral move than a career advancement.

Some large restaurant and hotel chains offer to send outstanding waiters and waitresses through their company's management training program, but these opportunities are not widespread. More frequently, a waiter or waitress who shows interest in advancing may be promoted to a position as host or hostess in a restaurant.

Support Services

RECORDS CLERK: BILLING CLERK/BOOKKEEPING CLERK/FILE CLERK/INFORMATION CLERK/ORDER CLERK/PERSONNEL CLERK

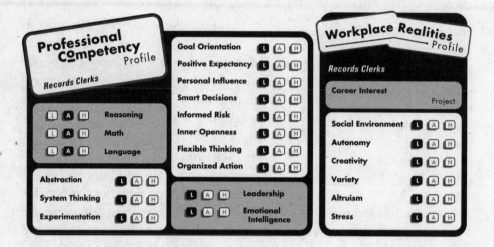

The general title of *records clerk* is an umbrella term for billing, bookkeeping, file, information, order, and personnel clerks.

Billing clerks prepare bills, keep billing records, calculate charges, and maintain the files of payments due and made for services or merchandise. They review purchase orders, bills of lading, sales tickets, hospital records, or charge slips to calculate the total amount due from a customer. Their methods of calculating charges vary depending upon the company and industry they work in.

Billing clerks who work in hospitals, for example, may be required to write letters to insurance carriers requesting detailed information on the full range of treatment a patient received in order to calculate the charges for a patient's hospital stay. On the other hand, billing clerks who compute trucking company charges for shipping various items simply may need to consult a rate book.

Bookkeeping clerks are an organization's financial record keepers. They are responsible for computing, classifying, recording, and verifying numerical data in order to develop and maintain records of the organization's financial transactions.

They may be required to compile reports to show statistics such as cash receipts and expenditures, accounts payable and receivable, and profits and losses. Bookkeepers are sometimes responsible for calculating employees'

wages, and preparing paychecks, expense reimbursements, withholding statements, Social Security forms, and other tax-related reports. They may compute, prepare, and mail monthly statements to clients or customers.

In small businesses, bookkeeping clerks are likely to handle additional
general office duties, while in larger offices, where several bookkeepers may
work in the same facility, each usually has a few specific tasks, assigned
according to seniority or specialty. They typically use computer spreadsheets
and databases to record their data.

File clerks classify, store, update, and retrieve data for all kinds of organizations, businesses, government agencies, and nonprofit institutions. In the
information age, accurate data can be thought of as the lifeblood of the organization. While most file clerks used to handle files manually, an increasing
number use computerized filing and retrieval systems. The typical responsibilities of a file clerk include reading incoming material and sorting it, and
filing correspondence, cards, invoices, receipts, and other records in alphabetical, numerical, chronological, or subject matter order. File clerks search for
and investigate information contained in files and databases, insert additional
information into file records, complete reports, keep files current, supply information from file data, and dispose of obsolete files when necessary.

In addition, file clerks may also verify the accuracy of the material to be filed,
examine microfilm and microfiche for legibility, make copies of paper and
backups of electronic documents, distribute records, and periodically review
the files to ensure that all items have been placed and sequenced properly.

Information clerks are customer-service staff employees who provide a valuable link between the services rendered by an organization and the delivery of
those services to the public. Information clerks generally work as receptionists,
interview/new accounts clerks, reservation and transportation clerks, and
hotel/motel desk clerks.

Receptionists are the people you first come in contact with upon entering
almost any business establishment. They greet everyone who walks into the
office. They answer phones, make appointments, answer questions, and often
set the tone for the entire business. If you encounter a cheerful receptionist,
your first impression of the business is usually a good one.

Interview/new accounts clerks work as intake interviewers, taking information from medical patients entering hospitals, applicants for public or private
services, and occasionally even employment applicants. They also inform
these people of any data that pertains to their treatment, services, or employment opportunities.

In the travel industry, *reservation and transportation clerks* and *hotel/motel desk
clerks* assist vacation and business travelers with directions, recommendations for

sightseeing, dining locations, and services with which travelers to a region may not be familiar.

Information clerks use computers and other pieces of office equipment to access the information they need, and then pass that information on to clients, customers, or travelers in a pleasant manner. They serve as a soothing influence to promote an organization's public image. Although their jobs are not—officially speaking—public relations positions, they are responsible for public relations in the way they deal with people. They must combine quick and efficient processing of information with direct human contact in order to relax a nervous patient, calm an angry resident complaining about service problems, or help travelers whose needs range from where to get a good meal to how to deal with an emergency.

Order clerks process orders for materials and merchandise received by mail or telephone, or in person from customers. They are also known as *order-entry clerks*, *customer service representatives*, *order processors*, and *order takers*. The largest growth among order clerks is in the area of catalog sales.

Order clerks, or customer service reps, work with telephones, calculators, and computers to process orders for merchandise, and inform customers regarding item availability and delivery dates. They may have additional responsibilities, such as checking inventory and notifying the stock control department if supply for an item falls below a certain level. They may also prepare purchase requisitions, route orders to departments for filing and processing, and follow up on orders to check delivery dates.

Order clerks compute the prices, the applicable discounts, the commissions for sales representatives, and the shipping charges for many orders. They prepare invoices and shipping documents, receive and respond to customer complaints, trace lost or delayed shipments, and solicit additional orders from the customer. They may also have to compile statistics and prepare reports on their work and the frequency with which items are ordered.

Personnel clerks compile and maintain personnel records. They record employee information, such as personal data; compensation benefits; federal, state, and local income tax data; attendance records; and performance reviews and evaluations. They update employee files to document personnel actions and to provide information for payroll and other uses. Personnel clerks record employees' termination dates and the reasons for separation from the company.

Personnel clerks review employment applications and are responsible for briefing new employees before they begin work for a company. They explain to new employees the company's various policies and rules, including safety rules. When an employee receives a promotion or decides to change his or her benefits package, personnel clerks implement the necessary changes. Personnel clerks also may administer and score aptitude tests and other instruments that measure people's interests or personality types. Increasingly, the personnel clerk position is a foot in the door of the human resources department. With effort and dedication, a person starting in this position can climb the corporate ladder.

EARNING POTENTIAL

Salaries of **records clerks** vary according to the area of the country, the size of the city, and the type and size of the employer. Although the salaries differ somewhat according to the clerk's responsibilities, full-time earnings in the field remain within a narrow range.

	Starting Salary	Median Salary	High- End Salary
Billing Clerk	$11,028	$18,400	$20,800
Bookkeeping Clerk	$12,480	$19,100	$27,040
File Clerk	$9,880	$15,700	$19,500
Information Clerk	$9,880	$16,640	$40,300
Order Clerk	$10,920	$22,200	$25,000
Personnel Clerk	$11,024	$20,300	$25,000

EDUCATIONAL REQUIREMENTS

Most **clerk** positions are entry-level jobs. Almost all employers require applicants for these positions to have a high school diploma or G.E.D. certificate. Employers may look to hire someone with an associate's degree or a bachelor's degree if they plan to train him or her in specialized areas such as employee benefits plans and tax-related reporting, but most clerk positions are open to high school graduates. Many students—from both high schools and colleges—work part-time as records clerks while they attend school.

Some records clerks will need a background, training, or aptitude in specific areas in order to perform their jobs. For instance, mathematical aptitude is important for success as a **bookkeeping clerk**. **Information clerks** must have the ability to communicate clearly with people, and this is one profession where a second language (especially Spanish) gives you a definite edge in the job market.

Computer literacy is an essential ingredient in any records clerk applicant's résumé, as well as his or her best bet for future employment. Word processing and spreadsheet programming are the two types of software programs most commonly used by clerks. Colleges offer courses in computer science that go beyond what is taught in high school.

It is helpful for **file clerks** to have received some training in office skills in high school or at a vocational institute in order to be aware of general office practices. This is especially true for file clerks who wish to advance within their company. High schools, business schools, and community colleges all offer courses that teach office skills. Most companies augment that sort of preparation with on-the-job training for new employees.

A DAY IN THE LIFE

Records clerks work in offices that range in setting from industrial sites to high-rise buildings to private homes. They typically sit at computer terminals for several hours at a stretch. Although there is no great physical demand to a clerk's job, he or she may have to stoop, bend, and reach. Also, people who spend long hours at terminals are known to suffer from headaches, eyestrain, and repetitive motion injuries to joints.

Most clerks work regular business hours. Some may work evenings and weekends, and some clerks may be hired to work on a shift basis. Clerks who work in businesses that experience seasonal busy periods, such as **retail order clerks** during the holiday season, or **information clerks** during typical vacation months, may be required to work overtime during the peak period. As is the case with many jobs today, records clerks often work part-time at their jobs, which provides them with a flexible schedule.

Information clerks are the exception. In hospitals, hotels, and the travel industry, information clerks must be available twenty-four hours a day, so they may work in shifts or find themselves working a split-shift schedule. They spend more time in one-on-one consultations with customers than on the computer terminal. Luckily they usually work in pleasant surroundings.

JOB GROWTH

There are over three and a half million **records clerks** employed in the United States, with the majority employed as **bookkeeping, accounting**, and **auditing clerks**. Records clerks are found in every industry, especially the health and business services industries.

Like many other entry-level occupations that employ millions of people and

---

HELP WANTED
CLERKS

Billing Clerk
Prepare bills, keep billing records, calculate charges. Maintain payment files. Obtain and consult records to determine total payment due from customer. Salary Range: $11,000–$20,800.

Bookkeeper
Keep financial records, and compute, classify, record, and verify the numerical data for an organization's financial transactions. Compile statistical reports to represent organization's financial status. Prepare employee paychecks and financial documents. Strong knowledge of computer spreadsheets and databases required. Salary Range: $12,480–$27,040.

File Clerk
Classify, store, update, insert, and retrieve data. Skill at computerized and hand filing systems necessary. Read and sort incoming material, and file correspondence, cards, invoices, receipts, and other records in alphabetical, numerical, chronological, or subject matter order. Verify accuracy of filed materials, examine microfilm and microfiche for legibility, make copies of documents, and distribute records. Salary Range: $9,360–$19,500.

Information Clerk/
Receptionist
Greet customers or clients, answer phones, make appointments. Cheerful and helpful manner essential. Salary Range: $9,880–$16,100.

---

require relatively little education and formal training, records clerk is a high-turnover occupation. Many people who enter the field either climb the professional ladder to other jobs and responsibilities or leave to pursue a new career. Many records clerks also find that they must move to another employer in order to receive a significant salary boost.

Because of the high turnover rate among records clerks, there will be plentiful opportunities for employment in full-time, part-time, and seasonal jobs. Even though there will be a large number of available jobs, there will not be tremendous growth in the field during the next ten years. Companies have learned to make do with fewer employees, and it is those employees with general skills who are among the most expendable.

But the job market is changing, and many people will have to hold more than one job—perhaps two or three part-time jobs. Some companies offer scaled-back health benefits to clerks who work part-time hours, making a part-time clerical job an excellent source of supplemental income. If a clerk's skills are transferable to other types of clerical functions, or if he or she possesses the skills to perform clerical duties for more than one employer, a records clerk can make a decent living. It's a good place to start a career if you didn't graduate from Harvard, and over time, it will offer increasing entrepreneurial opportunities.

Office automation has affected the future of records clerks. In many companies, computers enable one clerk to do

Interview/New Accounts Clerk
Interview new applicants or clients, and inform them of data that pertains to their treatment, services, or employment opportunities. Salary Range: $9,880–$18,200.

Order Clerk
Process orders for materials and merchandise using telephones, calculators, and computers. Check inventory and notify stock department if an item supply is low. Oversee order filing, processing, and delivery dates. Address customer complaints and trace lost shipments. Track frequency of items ordered. Salary Range: $10,920–$25,000.

Personnel Clerk
Compile and maintain all personnel records. Brief new employees on company's various policies and rules. Implement changes in benefits packages. May administer and score instruments that measure interests or report personality types. Salary Range: $11,024–$25,000.

the work previously performed by several people. Computers have replaced typewriters and adding machines, enabling people to work much faster and more efficiently. Similarly, bar codes, optical scanners, and point-of-sale terminals provide accurate data right to the central computer source, doing away with the need for people to enter the information. And large companies are centralizing all of their functions via computer, which eliminates the need to hire clerks at branch locations.

Still, the future looks good for records clerks, particularly **order clerks** and **information clerks**. Many catalog companies hire order clerks for busy-season work, which provides thousands of people with temporary jobs. And although automation has succeeded in replacing many clerical jobs, the demand for humans to deal with the public will remain strong. Many catalog companies rely on order clerks to serve as goodwill ambassadors and personalize the process of telephone ordering. However, experts believe that by the year 2005, interactive voice recognition systems will supersede the necessity for human order clerks in telephone sales. Until this technology is available to that extent, order clerks will still be very much in demand.

The largest growth area for record clerks is the health care industry. Since health care is the fastest-growing service industry in the country, and since it needs both skilled and unskilled workers to process data, job applicants are advised to investigate opportunities in hospitals, insurance companies, and doctors' offices. Banks, business, real estate services firms, and the travel and transportation agencies are also large employers of records clerks.

Although employment in the records clerk occupation will not increase greatly, it will increase steadily. There will always be clerical jobs available, but people who wish to get and hold these jobs will have to have more flexibility and skills than the clerks of the past.

Support Services

SECRETARY: EXECUTIVE SECRETARY/ADMINISTRATIVE ASSISTANT/LEGAL SECRETARY

Secretaries perform many of the necessary routine functions that allow businesses to operate efficiently. Secretaries combine administrative skills and good judgment to anticipate their bosses' needs and respond appropriately to a job's priorities. Secretaries are found in almost every business, supporting professionals at all levels. They may work for only one boss, or they may perform clerical duties for several people. They work in offices, and use computers, CD-ROMs, modems, and other office equipment to perform their duties.

Typical secretarial duties include answering phones, scheduling appointments, organizing and maintaining files, preparing preprinted forms, and keyboarding from taped dictation and notes. In addition, secretaries employed in professions that have specialized languages, such as law or medicine, must be familiar with that profession's unique terminology and procedures.

Executive secretaries and *administrative assistants* usually work for a company's top management, often delegating many clerical duties to less experienced secretaries while they attend to their bosses' specific needs. They face the demands of juggling their bosses' busy schedules, making travel arrangements, maintaining correspondence, arranging conference calls, attending board meetings, greeting clients, and supervising the clerical staff members. Administrative assistants may even assist in research projects or in preparing statistical reports; these jobs are among the highest-paying secretarial positions, so invariably they go to people with proven ability and years of experience.

The future is particularly promising for well qualified *legal secretaries*. In addition to the regular administrative responsibilities of clerical secretaries, legal secretaries assist attorneys in much of their research and preparation of legal papers. They must have a solid knowledge of legal terminology and procedures.

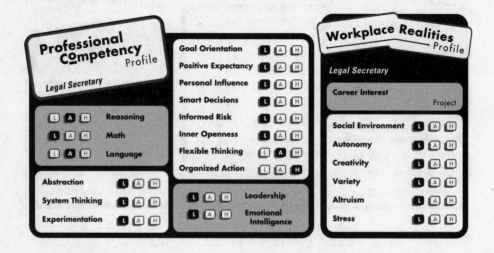

EARNING POTENTIAL

The annual average income for all secretaries is approximately $26,700. As in most occupations, salaries vary according to experience, geographic location, responsibility, and the field in which the secretary is working. A beginning secretary in a small firm in St. Louis is paid approximately $17,420, whereas an experienced secretary in a large firm in San Francisco is likely to earn in the range of $36,600. **Legal secretaries** are among the highest paid, as are **executive secretaries** and **administrative assistants**. Legal secretaries earn an average of $37,000 per year, and top-level executive secretaries earn up to $70,000. Administrative assistants earn as much as $85,000.

EDUCATIONAL REQUIREMENTS

Employers still hire secretaries with no more than a high school education, although that may not be sufficient training in terms of the skills necessary for mastering new office technology. Secretaries hoping to find jobs with quality employers will need to be technologically adapted.

High school vocational programs offer students training in the skills necessary for general secretarial positions, but applicants for secretarial positions in such areas as insurance, law, and medicine are well advised to attend a business school, a vocational-technical school, or a community or junior college that offers diverse training in all areas of administrative assistance.

Most large employers offer on-the-job training to secretarial staff. When the secretaries decide to leave their employers, they often find that the excellent skills they learned in these training programs allow them to transfer easily to another large company or a small business employer. Many small companies want to hire secretaries with big business training and experience.

A DAY IN THE LIFE

Secretaries work in offices assisting management personnel and teams of professionals. An executive secretary or administrative assistant may have a separate office located near his or her boss. In some companies, secretaries may share a common work area.

Most secretaries spend a great deal of time sitting, working at computer terminals, and answering phones. Since many of their duties involve maintaining orderly files, they use the computer to access files and enter information. They also keep hard copies of their computer entries in files.

Most secretaries employed by companies work full-time nine-to-five jobs. There are times when overtime is necessary. This is particularly true for **legal secretaries**, when there is an overload of case work or deadlines to meet before a trial.

JOB GROWTH

There are nearly 3.5 million secretaries employed in business in the United States. While the anticipated percentage increase overall for the next ten years is only nine percent, this number represents over 270,000 jobs. The highest growth potential is for **legal secretaries** (100,000 new positions) and **medical secretaries** (75,000 new positions), both of which are higher-paying jobs.

It is no secret that for many years secretarial positions were filled mainly by

HELP WANTED
SECRETARY/LEGAL SECRETARY/EXECUTIVE SECRETARY

Secretary

Perform critical support staff function for a particular individual or department. Answer phones, schedule appointments, organize and maintain files, and take dictation and notes to prepare letters or forms. Need to mix administrative skills and good judgment to anticipate boss's needs. Job requires skill with computers and other office equipment. May require familiarity with company's professional terminology and procedures. Salary Range: $17,420–$36,600.

Legal Secretary

Performs secretarial duties with specific knowledge of legal terminology and procedures. Prepares and files legal documents. Assists attorneys in research. Salary Range: $25,000–$70,000+.

Executive Secretary/Administrative Assistant

Supervise clerical staff. Maintain correspondence, and schedule meetings. Make travel arrangements for boss, attend board meetings. Greet clients. May prepare reports and may assist boss in research. Salary Range: $25,000–$85,000.

women. But once women began receiving college and graduate degrees in high numbers, they found themselves sitting in, rather than outside, the executive offices. While this advancement has provided a greater degree of fairness in hiring practices, it has left a gap in the number of semiskilled but highly intelligent people who formerly worked as secretaries. Good secretaries are in greater demand than ever before.

Secretaries work under constant pressure, their job being to reduce the pressure their bosses work under. Good secretaries provide their own job security with the transferable skills they learn. In an age when many people find themselves laid off and lacking good opportunities to find work in their specific field, it should be comforting for secretaries to know that they can use their skills in any setting, and that the demand for skilled secretaries will only grow stronger. For many people who simply do not have the opportunity to pursue a career requiring higher education, and for intelligent people with ambition and good judgment, secretarial work can be rewarding. This job also has potential because it is close to the real action of successfully running a business; more than a couple of secretaries have gone on to run their corporations, while many more use the experience as on-the-job training for their own entrepreneurial activities down the line.

Public Service

In the age of machines and computers, it's nice to know that people need people more than ever, and that there are people who find it important to make a difference with their contributions to the community. People who work in Public Service include police officers, firefighters, teachers, social workers, and a host of others. These professionals typically work for the local, state, or federal government; federal employees alone number over three million—and that is not counting the millions of aforementioned police, firefighters, and teachers. But while social workers and human service workers will be among the most sought-after professionals in the country during the next decade, not all jobs in public service have the same projections for the future.

Like every other business in the world today, the federal government is downsizing and revolutionizing its workplaces with the benefits of cutting-edge technology. With its three million workers, the fed expects to add only another 200,000 jobs over the next decade. The same trend holds true for state, county, municipal, township, and school district governments; everyone is using technology to do more with less. Yet, while the percentage growth might be small, the actual numbers of jobs will be much larger as a result of people moving on to other jobs and careers, and ultimately retiring.

With all the cutbacks that have been made in public service, government is still the biggest source of job opportunities in the country. Public service, which includes not only government jobs but also social services jobs (even those in the private sector), will employ more workers than any other industry during the next decade, just as it has in the past.

Social Services

Most social services workers are employed in government agencies that offer counseling, crisis intervention, rehabilitation, vocational training, and at-home and residential care. Some social services agencies focus on welfare relief, such as food stamps and rent assistance, or on protecting children. Others provide meals, assistance with household chores, or companionship to the elderly. Still other agencies care for recovering alcoholics and drug addicts. Job opportunities in social services will increase in proportion to the number of elderly people, children, the mentally ill, the disabled, and others who need care or assistance. On average, workers earn less money than they might in other industries. But social services is projected to be one of the fastest-growing industries.

Social services works hand in hand with government. It's one of the responsibilities of social service workers to make sure their clients don't eventually become a burden on the government. And social services' close relationship to the health care industry is a strong reason for its expansion.

INSIDER'S VIEW OF SOCIAL SERVICES

We've all heard reports that there will be an explosion of social services jobs in the coming years. Lucy Sanchez, public affairs director of the National Association of Social Workers, explains: "Managed health care and other attempts to lower the cost of health care are making changes in the way social workers practice their profession. It is making social workers more attractive and more sought-after because social workers perform therapy in the same manner as other mental health professionals, but usually charge lower fees. And because going to therapy is losing the stigma it once carried, more and more Americans are seeking counseling. Social workers provide more than half of the nation's mental health services."

In addition, Sanchez says, "Many social workers direct and are employed in employee assistance programs," and these are "now recognized by most Fortune 500 companies and other business and industry leaders as invaluable to its workforce productivity."

Sanchez continues, "Home health care is another growing field as health insurance and managed care companies attempt to find lower-cost alternatives to keeping patients in hospitals and other medical institutions. And as the population ages, there will be a need for a very large number of social workers in gerontology." She adds, "Social work research, still quite small, is just around the corner from a large growth spurt."

Sanchez concludes, "There are many social workers employed in Congress, the federal government, and state and local governments. They analyze, evaluate, recommend, and set social policy. Public social policy is a cutting-edge area as governments seek better ways and what works to address issues of welfare, child protection, foster care, health care cost containment, and mental health issues."

Education

Public service offers a respected profession, good benefits, and job security that is better than average. In particular, people who become teachers will develop a set of professional skills that can allow career segues into the private sector and to any industry within the private sector—with equally good opportunities for building an entrepreneurial career.

An automated workplace requires a new and more sophisticated worker, one who is technologically adapted and who can seamlessly weave those technological skills into an existing fabric of professional skills. This means that an educated workforce is critical to the long-term success of America. There is not a professionally worthwhile job in America that does not require at least a high school diploma, and most will require some level of college education.

This new awareness is reflected in the anticipated growth of the teaching profession, where we are expected to add a million more teaching jobs in the coming decade. The growth will be split fairly equally among primary, secondary, and high school teachers, and also teacher's aides. This predicted job growth is a conservative estimate, because recently it has been determined that Americans are having unusually large families again, which will result in 6 percent more students than previously anticipated. Additionally, more than half of today's teachers are already over forty, so there will be substantial openings as they retire, burn out, or segue their teaching skills into jobs or consulting opportunities in the private sector.

The education and training for jobs of the future begins in the schools, with the teachers, where a greater emphasis will be placed on math and the sciences. Even now, there are not enough math and science teachers to fill available openings. Bilingual and special education teachers will also see especially high demand.

Yet, despite this good news, the teaching profession will not be a lifetime stroll through the rose garden. As I prepared to write this, a Long Island school district advertised for thirty-five teachers and got a thousand applicants. Some were fresh-faced graduates, others were re-careerists coming to teaching after a career in industry or elsewhere, and still more were escaping city school jobs for the suburbs. As in every industry, the competition for good jobs in the most desirable locations will always be stiff. In the case in point, the school district was in a desirable seaside community on Long Island Sound. The chosen Thirty-Five? Those who had most effectively developed their professional mobility skills and were able to demonstrate that through the selection process.

INSIDER'S VIEW OF TEACHING

Eugene Alexander, Ed.D., secretary of the National Association of Teachers' Agencies, sees teacher starting salaries as "very good" compared to the stipends of yesteryear. A beginning teacher with a bachelor's degree may well earn in the mid-$20s to start. Of course, as we go farther into the computer age, every student will need access to computers. Alexander believes this means that all teachers will need to be computer literate, and that there will be a drive toward larger classes: "In order to pay for these things and keep taxpayers happy, we'll have to save money somewhere." That means larger classes—and higher stress—for teachers at all grade levels.

Alexander also sees colleges becoming more selective about whom they graduate, and school systems more discriminating in their selection procedures.

He also has a note of caution for the newly hired teacher. Most teachers and school districts are unionized, and this could be bad news if the demographics of a district call for cost-cutting or downsizing—which could happen even in the face of a growing national student population. The bad news for the newly hired? Union contracts typically stipulate that "the low person on the totem pole be the first to go."

In efforts to contain costs, maximize computer-age proficiencies, and compensate for union agreements that call for the preservation of older, less computer-savvy, and more expensive teachers, a number of states are now behaving more like their corporate cousins: offering buyouts to seasoned professionals in their mid-fifties. While this trend is not likely to abate in corporate America or academia, it isn't necessarily bad news, just a fact of life that must be anticipated. Given the long-term stress of teaching, and the strong need for trainers in all areas of business over the coming years, this can allow the foresighted educator to plan for a smooth and very lucrative career change later on.

TEACHING AS A GOOD CAREER SEGUE

Teaching is becoming much more appropriately rewarded, and thus is becoming more prestigious and is attracting more career changers. Encouraging this trend is an alternate teaching certification program, currently available in thirty-two states, designed to attract experienced professionals from other fields and ease their transition into the teaching profession. These programs typically require a four-year degree related to the teaching specialty the applicant wishes to pursue, and a varying number of years of professional experience. Once accepted to the certification program, would-be teachers are put through an accelerated, usually paid, teaching program. Program length varies from about three months on up.

What do you do with your teaching credentials and experience a few years down the road, when the allure of teaching somehow transmogrifies itself into a daily grind of giving the unwilling and ungrateful the tools of professional survival? As a teacher, you have a relatively easy segue into the corporate training world.

American corporations are said to train ten million people a year—and the need is seen as *five times that*! Corporate trainers teach everything from remedial reading and writing skills through executive communication and sales skills. And the jobs for corporate trainers will be growing over the next ten years as employers try to bring workers up to the speed needed in the new workplace and to help them maintain adaptedness to new professional skills as these become available or necessary. (See the job descriptions for training manager and director of training in the Human Resources section, pages 312–13.)

State and Local Government

Along with social services and public education, the public sector encompasses many other areas, including transportation, hospitals, courts, and the police and fire departments. Many of these essential services are part of state or local government. This section concludes with some of the more promising jobs in state and local government: jobs as urban and regional planners, air quality specialists, firefighters, policemen, and the like.

However, it is important to note that on the whole, in this time of government downsizing, your public service job is no longer yours for life; rather, it's yours until the budget is rewritten. The outlook for state and local government jobs is included in the following insider's view.

A CANDID CAMERA VIEW OF GOVERNMENT JOBS

Social work is clearly a growing field, but not all jobs in government are expanding at the same rate. In fact, the good and the bad news about government jobs is about evenly split.

Leonard Klein, associate director for employment of the U.S. Office of Personnel Management, offers his assessment of the stability of government jobs. He draws a parallel to other industries: certain government jobs are decreasing in number, and for reasons similar to those you'll find in the private sector. Defense is the biggest employer of blue-collar people, Klein explains, and defense budgets are being cut. Also, he says, "Blue-collar jobs are being hit because of automation, and because of the reinvention of production." Other occupations that are declining because of automation, according to Klein, are clerical jobs of all kinds: supply clerks, data processors, typists, and the like. "The culprit is automation and computers. People have their own PCs and are doing their own letter writing."

At the same time, Klein believes the types of employment opportunities that are growing nationally are also growing in government. He lists doctor, nurse, biological scientist, physical scientist, chemist, accountant, and computer programmer and systems analyst as hot jobs in government. In addition, he points to police officer, correction officer, customs official, border patroler, and immigration specialist as public service professions that are expanding.

Over the long term, Klein believes, government job stability will be good. "We're going through some downsizing, but we still hire," he stresses. He also explains that the process of finding a government job has been greatly simplified. To get job listings, you can call a job information line that's open twenty-four hours a day, seven days a week. Job opportunities are listed on a recording by occupation. The number to call is 912-757-3000.

Jobs with a Future in: Public Service

Social Services

Social Service Administrator . . . Social Worker . . . Child Welfare Social Worker . . . Family Services Social Worker . . . Mental Health Social Worker . . . Medical Social Worker . . . School Social Worker . . . Criminal Justice Social Worker . . . Human Services Worker . . . Counselor . . . School and College Counselor . . . Rehabilitation Counselor . . . Vocational or Employment Counselor . . . Mental Health Counselor . . . Marriage and Family Counselor . . . Gerontology Counselor

Education

Teacher . . . Kindergarten and Elementary School Teacher . . . Secondary School Teacher . . . Special Education Teacher . . . Bilingual Education Teacher . . . Environmental Educator . . . Teacher's Aide . . . Adult Education Teacher . . . Librarian . . . Child Care Worker

State and Local Government

Urban and Regional Planner . . . Air Quality Specialist . . . Firefighter . . . Police Officer . . . Correction Officer . . . Security Guard

ADDITIONAL OPPORTUNITIES IN THE PUBLIC SERVICE

The following Public Service jobs appear in most companies in all industries. You will find the particulars of these jobs on the noted pages:

Job Title	Industry	Page
Psychiatrist/Psychologist	Health Care	159
Biological Scientist	Biotechnology & Environmental Technology	183
Medical Scientist	Biotechnology & Environmental Technology	185
Biochemist	Biotechnology & Environmental Technology	186
Engineer	Engineering	200
Computer Software Programmer	Information Technology	214
Systems Analyst	Information Technology	213
Auditor	Financial Services	279
Accountant	Financial Services	273
Insurance Agent/Broker	Insurance	289
Chief Financial Officer	Financial Services	284
Corporate Controller	Financial Services	285
Benefits Manager	Human Resources	302
Compensation Manager	Human Resources	303
Human Resources Staffing Specialist	Human Resources	309
Director of Training	Human Resources	313
Corporate Training Specialist	Human Resources	313
Labor Relations Specialist	Human Resources	317
Diversity Manager	Human Resources	318
Management Consultant	Human Resources	323
Attorney	Law	327
Public Relations Professional	Media/Communications/PR	346
Records Clerk	Support Services	378
Secretary	Support Services	385

Social Services

SOCIAL SERVICE ADMINISTRATOR

There is a paradox at the heart of most social service programs, one created by their reliance on public funding. Every year preparation of the next year's budget causes a crisis in the offices of many social service programs because they have either exhausted their previous year's budget in less than twelve months' time, or they have failed to spend all of their allotted funds.

Professional Competency Profile
Social Service Administrator

Competency	L	A	H
Reasoning			H
Math		A	
Language			H
Abstraction	L		
System Thinking		A	
Experimentation		A	
Goal Orientation		A	
Positive Expectancy		A	
Personal Influence			H
Smart Decisions		A	
Informed Risk		A	
Inner Openness		A	
Flexible Thinking		A	
Organized Action		A	
Leadership			H
Emotional Intelligence			H

Workplace Realities Profile
Social Service Administrator

Career Interest: Project/Development

	L	A	H
Social Environment			H
Autonomy		A	
Creativity		A	
Variety		A	
Altruism		A	
Stress			H

Anyone who has worked in a government-funded program knows the dilemma these two contingencies can cause. On the one hand, programs that overspend their allocations are seen by the legislators who review the funding proposals as inefficient, disorganized, and poorly managed. Their usual punishment is a future budget cut. On the other hand, programs that fail to spend all of their funding are seen as well-run and properly managed. Their reward is a budget cut. The people who must resolve this contradiction, and who must provide for the continuing viability of any social welfare program, are the *social service administrators* (sometimes referred to as *directors*), people whose background is in social work, but whose responsibilities include financial, personnel, and project management.

Social service administrators, or *social welfare administrators*, as they are also known, work in every agency and organizational setting that provides health, counseling, and welfare services to individuals. Some of these organizations are child welfare programs, elderly assistance programs, family-oriented programs (which deal with problems from incest and abuse down to financial assistance and job-search training), health organizations, and substance abuse programs. Every community has a number of such programs that attend to the needs of people who need help but who lack the resources to obtain it from private providers.

Social service administrators are individuals with experience as social workers themselves. When they supervise their staff, they know the demands of the job they ask them to perform. Typically, social service administrators have displayed exceptional ability to organize and coordinate activities in the past, and were promoted through the ranks. Many social service programs are underfunded and understaffed, so administrators are challenged to provide the greatest amount and quality of services to the largest clientele, often relying on an inadequate budget.

In order to obtain additional funding or to preserve the continuation of their program, social service administrators find themselves adopting several different job roles. They work as public speakers, promoting their program and delivering a message concerning its importance to the community. They act as fund-raisers, making public appearances to show that their program is community-based. They work as managers, planning, overseeing budgets, and preparing and distributing reports, publicity announcements, and memos that attempt to keep their program's work in the public eye. One certain way to receive continued funding is to prove that a program serves a public that is aware and appreciative of its services. In short, a social service administrator should combine the heart of a social worker, the mind of a corporate manager, and the communication skills of a politician to protect and provide for his or her program.

EARNING POTENTIAL

Salaries for social service administrators vary dramatically from state to state, starting with Virginia where the average yearly income is $26,375, to California where the average is $95,050. The overall average is $66,350.

EDUCATIONAL REQUIREMENTS

Social service administrators customarily have a master's degree in social work and, invariably, in-depth practical experience as a social worker. Social service administrators should additionally consider taking courses in, or attending seminars on, business administration, management, finance, and human resources. Fortunately, the profession sponsors many such seminars targeted to their particular concerns.

A DAY IN THE LIFE

Because they often appear at public events in the evening, many social service administrators work much longer hours than they did as social workers. This is particularly true at budget time, when they must gather reports and statistics to prove how successfully their program performed in the previous year. Although the success rate of many social service programs is virtu-

---

HELP WANTED
SOCIAL SERVICE
ADMINISTRATOR

Oversee budget to provide the greatest amount of quality services to the largest clientele. Work with a variety of welfare programs, such as child welfare programs, elderly assistance programs, and family-oriented programs. Must act as fund-raiser, and make public appearances to show that the program is community-based. Will prepare and distribute reports, publicity announcements, and memos to keep the programs in the public eye. Salary Range: $26,375–$95,050.

---

ally impossible to prove, often a careful record of the number of clients helped, the specific monies allocated for resources, and some sense of the result of the assistance provided to clients can make a strong case for additional funding.

The working conditions for social agencies and organizations vary, but they are usually located in older buildings and in offices that are far from glamorous. The furniture is often old and scarred, the computers tend to be older models that run slowly, and other office equipment is rarely cutting edge. But no social workers enter the profession for self-aggrandizement in the hope of working in breathtaking offices. The money allocated to social service programs goes for services, not surroundings, and most social services workers and administrators are aware of this fact before they enter the profession.

JOB GROWTH

Along with the growth in social service programs throughout the country, demand for administrators to run these programs and direct the growing number of social workers will likewise increase.

Social service administrators must guard against a common complaint among managers: their reward for doing a good job at what they enjoy is a promotion that takes them out of the environment that drew them to the profession in the first place. Administrators no longer have the time to provide service to clients and experience the satisfaction of helping others directly, which they often thrive on. So in accepting a promotion to this position, they should be aware of their own strengths and preferences, to avoid accepting a position for which they are not temperamentally suited.

This is not to suggest that many social workers do not make a smooth transition from client work to supervision; many do, and flourish in their new role. The need for competent and caring administrators—who know the ins and outs of a bureaucratic process and can still relate to clients on an individual level—will always exist.

SOCIAL WORKER: CHILD WELFARE SOCIAL WORKER/FAMILY SERVICES SOCIAL WORKER/MENTAL HEALTH SOCIAL WORKER/MEDICAL SOCIAL WORKER/SCHOOL SOCIAL WORKER/CRIMINAL JUSTICE SOCIAL WORKER

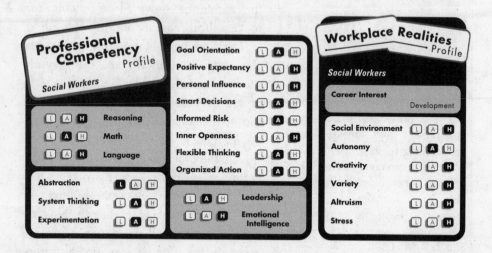

Social workers are problem solvers who provide people with workable solutions to problems that range from unemployment to serious illnesses. They are also brokers, in the sense that they connect people in need with the resources available to help them.

Most social workers provide varying levels of counseling to clients, but this type of counseling usually does not attempt to treat problems. It attempts to identify the clients' problems so he or she can be directed to a trained specialist. For example, people suffering from substance abuse, mental illness, or unexpected pregnancy need specific counseling that may require more training than the social worker possesses. In these instances the social worker will put clients in touch with psychologists, mental health specialists, and doctors who can help with treatment or information.

Social workers also perform administrative duties, such as following through with clients to be certain they pursue the counseling or treatment to which the social worker has referred them. They work directly with clients to help them with filling out necessary administrative forms and obtaining assistance from other service providers. They remain available to their clients for additional counseling and emergency intervention.

Because the field of social work is so vast, most professionals in this field specialize in a particular area. Some of the specializations are as follows.

Child welfare and family services social workers deal with family issues, such as learning and physical disabilities, adoptions, and care of abandoned, neglected, or abused children. They also deal with issues such as spousal abuse and landlord/tenant problems. They offer counseling for these problems and act as intermediaries between parties in conflict. Some social workers also specialize in *gerontology*—the study of aging and elderly people. They assist elderly people in finding affordable housing or long-term care accommodations.

Mental health social workers help mentally and emotionally impaired individuals in private and group therapy. They also train people in job skills and living skills, respond to crisis situations, and provide outreach alternatives to people who are alienated from mainstream society.

Medical social workers provide information and emotional support to medical patients and their family members. They often work in hospitals, and counsel people suffering from terminal illnesses and/or their grieving families. Medical social workers organize and run support groups that discuss people's reactions to illness. They also train family members who will care for patients when they leave the hospital or who care for patients suffering from long-term debilitating diseases, such as AIDS or Alzheimer's.

School social workers work with students who perform poorly or get into trouble. Typically, they advise students on seeking tutoring or additional counseling services, attempt to discover if and how a student's home life affects his or her school performance, help teenagers who become pregnant, and investigate the reasons behind chronic absenteeism.

Criminal justice social workers interview people accused of crimes, convicts, and parolees in order to recommend to the courts a suggested counseling component to the sentencing or parole guidelines.

EARNING POTENTIAL

A survey conducted by the National Association of Social Workers (NASW) found that annual salaries for social workers with a bachelor's degree in social work (B.S.W.) average approximately $19,200. The figure is considerably higher for social workers with a master's degree in social work (M.S.W.), where the earnings average is close to $30,000 and goes as high as $44,975. Social workers employed by the federal government earn an average salary of $41,400.

EDUCATIONAL REQUIREMENTS

As the information on salaries suggests, social workers who either have or are working toward their master's degree will earn higher salaries than those who have only a bachelor's degree. The bachelor's degree is, however, sufficient for entry into the field.

There are 297 accredited bachelor's degree programs in social work, which include courses in psychology, sociology, social welfare, and human behavior. This degree prepares students to practice as caseworkers or group workers.

There are 103 accredited master's degree programs. In addition to the course work required for a B.S.W., students are required to take classes in biology, economics, political science, social anthropology, and urban studies. M.S.W. graduates may be employed as psychiatric social workers, and will have increased professional opportunity for making client assessments, acting as a liaison between clients and psychiatrists or hospitals, and managing cases. Many social workers can use their job experience as a basis for projects or independent study for which they receive academic credit.

There are also 49 doctoral programs for people who want to pursue a teaching or research career in this field, or for those seeking the highest-level administrative posts. All supervisory, administrative, and training positions in the occupation require at least a master's degree.

The National Association of Social Workers offers two certifications: the Academy of Certified Social Workers and the Academy of Certified Baccalaureate Social Workers. Private-practice clinical social workers should be listed in the NASW Register of Clinical Social Workers or the Directory of American Board of Examiners in Clinical Social Work in order to qualify for reimbursement by medical insurance carriers for their counseling services.

Social work is a rewarding field for many who enter it, but it is also an emotionally and physically draining one. People who become social workers are usually motivated by the impact their contributions will have rather than by compensation.

A DAY IN THE LIFE

Social workers usually work a forty-hour week, though there are many part-time employees. The office settings in which they work vary according to their jobs. Some work in offices that provide services to hundreds of people; some work in schools; some, in community centers. Some social workers work in comfortable offices, while others working for poorly funded social service agencies may have less glamorous offices in old buildings needing repairs.

HELP WANTED
SOCIAL WORKERS

Social Worker
Connect people in need with the resources available to help them, and counsel clients in order to refer them to a trained specialist. Must find workable solutions to problems that range from unemployment to serious illnesses, and deal with family issues, such as learning and physical disabilities, adoption, and abandoned, neglected, or abused children. May help mentally and emotionally impaired individuals in private and group therapy. May perform some administrative duties. Salary Range: $19,200–$44,975.

Child Welfare/Family Services Social Worker
Conduct counseling for children and families in crisis. Salary Range: $19,200–$44,975.

Mental Health Social Worker
Provide therapy for mentally impaired individuals. Provide outreach alternatives to mentally impaired individuals. Salary Range: $19,200–$44,975.

Medical Social Worker
Provide medical and financial resource information as well as emotional support to medical patients and their family members. Salary Range: $19,200–$44,975.

School Social Worker
Work with students who perform poorly or get into trouble. Advise students on seeking tutoring or additional counseling services. Salary Range: $19,200–$44,975.

Criminal Justice Social Worker
Interview people accused of crimes, convicts, and parolees in order to recommend to the courts a counseling component to the sentencing or parole guidelines. Salary Range: $19,200–$44,975.

Social workers frequently work in more than one setting because their duties range widely. They spend their working hours talking and listening to people who are, for the most part, in crisis situations and in need of help. The work can be extraordinarily gratifying when positive progress is made, and painfully frustrating when clients are unresponsive. Many social workers are employed by government agencies, so there is also a lot of paperwork, red tape, and bureaucracy involved, which can send the stress barometer off the charts — for both the social worker and the hapless client.

JOB GROWTH

There are approximately 531,000 jobs in the field of social work in the United States. Approximately 40 percent of these jobs are in state, county, and municipal government agencies, in the departments of human resources, social services, child welfare, health, mental health, housing, education, and corrections.

Employment of social workers is expected to grow faster than the average for all occupations through the year 2005. It is anticipated that by then, 130,000 new positions will be filled, exclusive of jobs becoming available through employee turnover and retirement. Listed as factors in this growth are the increased number of elderly and mentally ill people in need of assistance, and a trend to attempt rehabilitation with a growing prison population.

Hospital jobs for social workers will increase over the next decade, as hospitals are required to assist in early release and discharge planning programs. Likewise, the health care field will experience a large growth in home health care, and social workers will be needed to provide their services to homebound medical patients and people suffering from disabilities.

Despite budgetary cutbacks affecting hiring practices in many state and local government services agencies, the greatest number of jobs in the social work field will continue to be in the public sector. Although there will be jobs available for clinical social workers in private sector jobs, these require greater education and offer less job security than the public sector jobs. Budgetary considerations in private agencies will lead administrators to hire human services workers (see below), who can perform some of the routine services provided by social service agencies at lower wages.

As a career choice, social work offers opportunities for people at all levels of experience. New social workers can find lower-paying jobs with agencies that will provide them with the experience they will need to advance in the field. Those with an advanced degree will find enhanced job stability and career mobility.

Human Services Worker

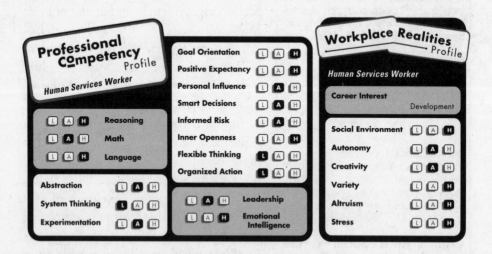

Human services refers to a variety of federal, state, and community-funded programs and agencies that provide relief services to individuals and families in need of money for basic living expenses, counseling for emotional, violent, or addictive behavior, and the staples of life, such as food and shelter. There are many programs available to people who require these services, but often the people for whom the services are designed do not know how to apply for them. Human services workers have direct contact with the people in need and assist them through the bureaucratic processes often involved in applying for federal or state assistance.

A *human services worker* can be known by many job titles: *social service technician, case management aide, social work assistant, residential counselor, alcohol or drug abuse counselor, mental health technician, child abuse worker, community outreach worker,* and *gerontology aide.* Most human services workers assist social workers or psychologists in enabling clients to apply for and receive the entitlements, services, and assistance provided for their needs by the federal government, local municipalities, or other administrative agencies.

Human services workers interview clients to determine their needs and eligibility for benefits and services. They review rent receipts and income tax returns in order to arrive at an accurate estimate of the client's income. Clients who fall below certain mandated income levels may be qualified to receive welfare benefits such as food stamps and Medicaid. Human services workers counsel clients in the steps they have to take to process the forms necessary to apply for these benefits. They may provide or arrange for transportation for their clients and, when necessary, offer emotional support to clients in dire straits or suffering from emotional problems or addictions. Part of their job is to maintain files on clients and to report periodically on their clients' progress to supervisors. The supervisors may be administrators, social workers, or psychologists.

Many human services jobs exist in community settings. For example, human services workers may transport their clients to community kitchens for meals or to adult day care centers or doctors' offices and clinics. They direct activities in group homes and halfway houses—places that provide support and supervision to individuals who are deemed partly capable of taking care of themselves, but who still need some guidance or caretaking.

Human services workers are also emergency providers. They help their clients in situations calling for crisis intervention, and may organize and manage emergency food banks or fuel delivery programs for people without food or heat. They serve as intermediaries between doctors and clients in an effort to make certain that clients understand the medical advice they receive and the consequences of ignoring the advice.

Human services workers employed in psychiatric clinics may assist clients in learning basic living skills, such as dining and bathing, and may help them to communicate better with others. In most instances, the job of a human services worker is to assist people who are, for whatever reason, not in the mainstream of society. Human services workers access the benefits that the government provides to help these people reenter the social community.

EARNING POTENTIAL

Starting salaries for entry-level professionals in this occupation range from $9,880 to $15,500 a year. Experienced human services workers average between $18,000 and $25,000, and administrative/management workers go up to $41,200.

EDUCATIONAL REQUIREMENTS

The level of formal education required for human services workers depends on the job for which they are applying. There are still jobs in this occupation that require no more than a high school diploma. However, most employers hire individuals with at least some college-level background in human services or social work.

Colleges and junior colleges throughout the country offer 390 bachelor's degree programs and 375 associate degree and other post–secondary school programs specializing in human services and mental health. These programs feature classes in psychology, sociology, crisis intervention, social work, and family dynamics. There are also a handful of master's degree programs that concentrate on human services administration.

Human services workers with a bachelor's degree in the social or behavioral sciences may quickly assume a counseling or program coordinator role as the major part of their job functions. Regardless of their educational background, though, all human services workers attend in-service programs provided by their employers to keep them aware of all the resources available to them and to their clients.

As in all positions in the social services, human services workers should be compassionate and patient, and have the confidence to deal with others' adversity in a rational manner. Unfortunately, even the most benevolent personality can burn out quickly in this emotionally draining career, and this results in a high turnover in the field. It is not uncommon for an employee in the social services field to take a break from the field to recharge.

HELP WANTED
HUMAN SERVICES WORKER

Provide relief services to individuals and families who need money for basic living expenses and/or counseling for emotional, violent, or addictive behavior. Interview and evaluate clients to determine their needs and eligibility for these benefits and services. Take clients through the process of applying for aid, maintain files on clients, and report periodically on clients' progress to supervisors. Also may direct activities in group homes and halfway houses. Help clients in situations calling for crisis intervention. May organize and manage emergency food banks or fuel delivery programs for people without food or heat. May serve as intermediary between doctors and clients. Salary Range: $9,880–$41,200.

A DAY IN THE LIFE

Human services workers perform their tasks in many different settings. Most spend at least part of their working hours in offices, clinics, or residential facilities and the rest of their time visiting clients, taking clients to service sites such as community meal kitchens, or meeting with providers in an effort to explain their clients' position. Most human services workers have a standard forty-hour work week, although some may start later in the day and finish later in the evening.

JOB GROWTH

There are approximately 189,000 human services workers employed in the United States. Employment of human services workers is evenly distributed among four major areas:

- state and local governments in public welfare agencies and in mental facilities;
- private agencies that offer services such as adult day care, crisis intervention, and counseling;
- group homes and halfway houses;
- clinics, psychiatric hospitals, and community mental health centers.

The number of jobs in this field is expected to grow so fast that employment opportunities over the next ten years will more than double current numbers. In fact, the Department of Labor Statistics lists this as the second-fastest-growing job over the next ten years, forecasting an increase of 252,000 positions.

The best job opportunities in this field will be found in job training programs, residential settings, and private social service agencies, which include services such as adult day care and meal delivery programs.

The growing need for human services workers reflects governmental efforts to provide for people who have difficulty in caring for themselves. The level of poverty in urban and rural areas continues to grow at an alarming rate, as does the number of legal and illegal immigrants who need services for themselves and their children. This country has a commitment to provide care for people in need, but many people living in poverty, suffering in abusive situations, or needing help to overcome addictions, require the assistance of professionals to enable them to find these resources and to become as independent as possible.

As the population ages, growing numbers of older Americans will be in need of human services. Furthermore, the numbers of mentally impaired, developmentally disabled, and drug- and alcohol-addicted people requiring human services are also growing. Because many federal, state, and local programs are undergoing budget cuts, social service administrators will be trying to allocate their resources as carefully as possible. This will increase the ranks of human services workers, who can perform a variety of tasks for a lower rate of pay than many highly trained (and therefore more highly paid) social workers.

This is not a career for the fainthearted, nor the empire-builder. This is a challenging career and an opportunity for a person to contribute to society while making a living.

COUNSELOR: SCHOOL AND COLLEGE COUNSELOR/REHABILITATION COUNSELOR/VOCATIONAL OR EMPLOYMENT COUNSELOR/MENTAL HEALTH COUNSELOR/MARRIAGE AND FAMILY COUNSELOR/ GERONTOLOGY COUNSELOR

The job title *counselor* applies to a diverse class of individuals who assist people with personal, family, social, educational, and career decisions, problems, and concerns. Therefore counselors must inspire respect, trust, and confidence.

A counselor's responsibilities are dependent upon the context within which he or she works. **School** and **college counselors** help students understand their abilities, interests, talents, and personality characteristics so that the student can develop realistic academic and career options. These counselors use interviews, counseling sessions, tests, or other tools to assist them in evaluating and advising students. *High school counselors* advise students on college majors, admission requirements, entrance exams, and financial aid, and on trade, technical school, and apprenticeship programs. They help students to develop job-search skills such as résumé writing and interviewing techniques.

School and college counselors are also responsible for helping students to understand and deal with their social, behavioral, and personal problems. They emphasize preventive and developmental counseling to provide students with the life skills needed to deal with problems before they occur, and to enhance personal, social, and academic growth. These counselors may provide special services, including alcohol and drug prevention programs, classes that teach students to handle conflicts without resorting to violence, and career planning and placement advice.

School counselors work with students individually, in small groups, or with entire classes. They consult and work with parents, teachers, school administrators, school psychologists, school nurses, and social workers.

Elementary school counselors do more social and personal counseling, and less vocational and academic counseling than secondary school counselors. They observe young children during classroom and play activities, and then confer with teachers and parents to evaluate a child's strengths, problems, or special needs. They also work with students to help them develop good study habits.

Rehabilitation counselors help persons dealing with the personal, social, and vocational impact of their disabilities. They evaluate the strengths and limitations of individuals, provide personal and vocational counseling, and may arrange for medical care, vocational training, and job placement. Rehabilitation counselors interview individuals with disabilities and their families, evaluate school and medical reports, and confer and plan with physicians, psychologists, occupational therapists, employers, and others. Conferring with the client, they develop and implement a rehabilitation program, which may include training to help the person become more independent and employable. They also work toward increasing the client's capacity to adjust and live independently.

Vocational or *employment counselors* help individuals make wise career decisions. They help clients explore and evaluate their education, training, work history, interests, skills, personal traits, and physical capacities, and may arrange for aptitude and achievement tests. They also work with individuals in developing job-search skills and in locating and applying for jobs.

Mental health counselors emphasize prevention, and work with individuals and groups to promote optimum mental health. They help individuals deal with addictions and substance abuse; family, parenting, and marital problems; suicidal tendencies; stress; problems with self-esteem; issues associated with aging; job and career concerns; educational decisions; and issues of mental and emotional health. Mental health counselors work closely with other mental health specialists, including psychiatrists, psychologists, clinical social workers, psychiatric nurses, and school counselors.

Some counselors specialize in a particular social issue or population group, such as *marriage and family* or *gerontological counseling*. Marriage counselors work with couples facing separation, to help them either to resolve their conflicts or to separate as amicably as possible. Gerontological counselors may provide services to elderly persons who face changing lifestyles due to health problems, as well as help their families cope with these changes.

EARNING POTENTIAL

Educational and **vocational counselors** earn a median annual salary of approximately $30,000, with the majority earning in a range between $24,000 and $41,500 a year. The higher-end jobs, which pay up to $52,000, are generally assigned to counselors with higher education degrees in the more intensive areas of **family**, **rehabilitation**, and **behavioral counseling**. (I should note here that there is no such thing as a "behavioral counselor"; that is an all-inclusive term, and refers to behavioral counseling in the different contexts of family, school, marriage, and mental health.) The average salary for **school counselors** is around $40,200, although some school counselors earn additional income working summers in the school system or in other jobs.

Self-employed counselors who have well-established practices generally have the highest earnings, as do some counselors working for private companies, such as insurance companies and private rehabilitation companies. Salaries should grow at a rate slightly better than the rate of inflation.

EDUCATIONAL REQUIREMENTS

Most counselors are master's degree graduates in a subspecialty (marriage and family, rehabilitation, etc.) within the fields of education or psychology. Courses cover such areas as human growth and development; social and cultural foundations; relationships; groups; lifestyle and career development; appraisal; research and evaluation; and professional orientation. In an accredited program, forty-eight to sixty semester hours of graduate study, including a period of supervised clinical experience in counseling, are required for a master's degree. The Council for Accreditation of Counseling and Related Educational Programs (CACREP) accredits graduate counseling programs in counselor education and in community, geronotological, mental health, school, student affairs, and marriage and family counseling.

The vast majority of states have some form of credentialing legislation for licensure, certification, or registration for practice outside schools, but the requirements vary from state to state. In some states, credentialing is mandatory, while in others, it is optional. Counselors may be certified by the National Board of Certified Counselors. As a rule, to receive this certification, a counselor must have a master's degree in counseling, two years of post–master's degree experience, and a passing grade on a written examination.

All states require **school counselors** to hold state school counseling certification. These requirements vary; some states require public school counselors to have both counseling and teaching certificates, and certain states require a master's degree in counseling and two to five years' teaching experience.

Vocational and related rehabilitation agencies generally require a master's degree in rehabilitation counseling, counseling and guidance, or counseling psychology for **rehabilitation counselor** jobs.

Mental health counselors generally have a master's degree in mental health counseling, in another area of counseling, or in psychology or social work.

A DAY IN THE LIFE

Counselors generally work in private offices in schools and other educational institutions and in mental-health facilities, reflecting the need for confidential and frank discussions with clients. These environments are typically clean, comfortable, and quiet. The physical demands are modest, with a lot of time spent sitting at desks.

HELP WANTED COUNSELORS

School and College Counselor
Help students develop realistic academic and career options. Use interviews, counseling sessions, and tests to assist in evaluating and advising students. Advise students on college majors, admission requirements, entrance exams, financial aid, and on trade, technical school, and apprenticeship programs. Help students develop job-search skills such as résumé writing and interviewing techniques. Salary Range: $17,800–$51,900.

Rehabilitation Counselor
Help clients (and their families) deal with the impact of their disabilities, and confer with them to develop and implement a rehabilitation program. Evaluate their strengths and limitations, provide personal and vocational counseling, and arrange for medical care, vocational training, and job placement. Analyze school and medical reports, and confer and plan with physicians, psychologists, occupational therapists, employers, and others. Salary Range: $17,800–$51,900.

Vocational/Employment Counselor
Help individuals with career decisions, by helping them explore and evaluate their education, training, work history, interests, skills, personal traits, and physical capacities. May arrange for aptitude and

Counselors also work in a wide variety of public and private establishments, including health care facilities; job training, career development, and vocational rehabilitation centers; social agencies; correctional institutions; and residential care facilities, such as halfway houses for criminal offenders and group homes for children, the aged, and the disabled. Counselors also work in organizations engaged in community improvement and social change, as well as drug and alcohol rehabilitation programs and state and local government agencies.

Counselors work with little direct supervision, but they must work in cooperation with others. **Rehabilitation** and **employment counselors** generally work a standard forty-hour week. Self-employed counselors and those working in mental health and community agencies often work evenings to counsel clients who work during the day. **College** career planning and placement counselors may work long and irregular hours during recruiting periods.

JOB GROWTH

There are approximately 154,000 counselors in the United States. Roughly 70 percent are school counselors at elementary schools, secondary schools, colleges, and universities.

The overall employment of counselors is expected to grow faster than the average for all occupations. Employment of **school counselors** will grow in response achievement tests. Assist clients in locating and applying for jobs, and in developing job-search skills. Salary Range: $17,800–$41,500.

Mental Health Counselor

Work with individuals and groups to promote optimum mental health. Help individuals deal with addictions and substance abuse; family, parenting, and marital problems; suicidal tendencies; stress; problems with self-esteem; issues associated with aging, job, and career concerns; educational decisions, and/or issues of mental and emotional health. Work closely with other mental health specialists. Salary Range: $17,800–$51,900.

Marriage and Family Counselor

Help couples and families resolve conflicts. Also help separating couples and their families adjust to the changing circumstances. Salary Range: $17,800–$51,900.

Gerontology Counselor

Help elderly people cope with the challenges and frustrations of their changing lifestyle. Also help the families learn to deal with the pressures of dealing with an aging family member. Salary Range: $17,800–$51,900.

to increasing enrollments and the expanded role counselors play in schools. Growth will be particularly strong in secondary schools and elementary schools where state legislation requires counselors. These counselors are increasingly becoming involved in crisis and preventive counseling, helping students deal with issues ranging from drug and alcohol abuse to death and suicide. Despite the increasing use of counselors, however, employment growth will be governed by state and federal education budgetary constraints.

Rehabilitation and **mental health counselors** should also be in strong demand. Insurance companies increasingly provide reimbursement for counseling services, and the increased demand for these services enables many counselors to move from schools and government agencies to private practice. The number of people who need rehabilitation services also will rise as advances in medical technology continue to save lives that only a few years ago would have been lost. In addition, legislation requiring equal employment rights for persons with disabilities will spur demand for counselors. Counselors not only will help individuals with disabilities with their transition into the workforce, but also will help companies in complying with the law.

With all the recent corporate downsizing, displaced workers will turn to **employment counselors** working in private job-training services to provide skill training and job-search guidance. Full-time homemakers seeking to enter or reenter the workforce and workers who want to upgrade their skills for a new or second career will also help to keep employment counselors in demand.

The increasing pressures and complexities of life will ensure a growing need for counselors of all kinds well into the next century. Whether they help students, the elderly, or individuals with mental or emotional difficulties, counselors find that theirs is a satisfying profession if they have the desire to assist others in moving their lives forward.

Education

TEACHER: KINDERGARTEN AND ELEMENTARY SCHOOL TEACHER/SECONDARY SCHOOL TEACHER/SPECIAL EDUCATION TEACHER/BILINGUAL EDUCATION TEACHER/ENVIRONMENTAL EDUCATOR*/TEACHER'S AIDE

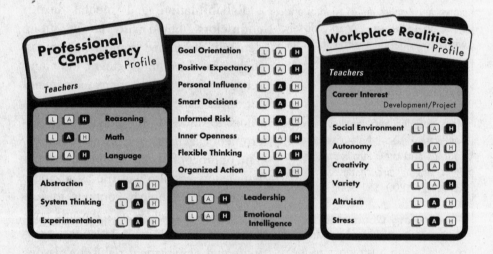

The occupation of *teacher* is as broadly varied and as difficult to generalize as any occupation in the job market. Far from being the stereotyped "by the book" schoolteacher of old movies, today's teachers differ dramatically from each other depending on their subject matter expertise, teaching methods, and type of school in which they work.

The basic responsibilities of a teacher include designing classroom presentations to meet students' needs and abilities. Teachers work with students collectively and individually, to assign lessons, give tests, hear oral presentations, and maintain classroom discipline. Teachers observe and evaluate a student's

*For this job title, see page 421. Also, for **adult education teacher**, see page 423.

performance and potential and try to assist each student in reaching that potential. Teachers' responsibilities also include assigning homework, grading papers, preparing report cards, overseeing study halls and homerooms, supervising extracurricular activities, and meeting with parents and school staff to discuss a student's academic progress or difficulties. Outside of the school, teachers may also participate in conferences and workshops.

Kindergarten and *elementary school teachers* introduce children to numbers, language, science, and social studies. They may use games, music, artwork, films, and computers to teach basic skills. Most elementary school teachers instruct students in multiple subjects, but in some schools a teacher may teach only one subject—such as music, art, reading, science, arithmetic, or physical education—to multiple classes.

Secondary school teachers help students explore more thoroughly the subjects introduced in elementary school and introduce new subjects such as foreign languages. These teachers are usually specialists in one particular area, such as English, French, mathematics, history, biology, or music. They may also teach a variety of thematically related courses. Secondary school teachers may assist students in choosing courses, colleges, and careers.

Special education teachers, who teach at all levels, instruct students with a variety of disabilities, such as visual and hearing impairments, learning disabilities, and physical disabilities. These teachers design and modify instruction to meet the students' needs. Special education teachers may also work with students who are exceptionally bright or who have limited English proficiency, but their work is more often associated with students who require remedial education or whose disabilities require special instruments and equipment in order for them to perform their classwork.

Special education teachers rely on a variety of devices to instruct, including films, slides, overhead projectors, computers, tapes, telecommunication systems, and video discs. The most valuable resources special education teachers have, though, are their patience and their ability to listen to students. Because many students with special needs do not present themselves confidently, special education teachers must be attuned to ways the students communicate. All of these qualities require experience in the classroom as well as course work and training.

Bilingual education teachers. The population of the United States has become increasingly multicultural as recent immigrants have arrived from countries all over the world. The result is a large population of recent immigrants who may not be fully—or even partly—proficient in English. Because these immigrants have tended to concentrate in specific communities—many in sections of large cities where they are able to communicate comfortably in their native tongue—the problems associated with educating them and their children have grown increasingly complex. In response to this problem, many public schools have begun to instruct students in two different languages: in English and in their native language. Bilingual education teachers are responsible for conducting these classes.

The basic responsibilities of a bilingual education teacher are approximately the same as those of any teacher, but with a specific focus on the language needs of the students. For example, some students may understand mathematics better if it is taught in Spanish. Generally, teachers design classroom presentations to meet the students' needs and abilities. Teachers work with students individually and assign lessons, give tests, hear oral presentations, and maintain classroom discipline. Teachers observe and evaluate a student's performance and potential and strive to assist the student in achieving that potential.

Bilingual teachers may teach ESL (English as a second language) classes to non-native students. These classes involve a great deal of reading, writing, and conversation in an effort to make foreign language students more comfortable with English. Many students discover that the syntax, sentence structure, verb tenses, and usage in English are vastly different from their native language. And because foreign language students are expected to read, write, and speak English with a certain degree of mastery, ESL classes are often much more significant than the foreign language classes taken by English-speaking students.

Teacher's aides, also known as *paraprofessionals* and *paraeducators*, provide instructional and clerical support for classroom teachers, allowing teachers more time for lesson planning and actual teaching. Teacher's aides assist and supervise students in the classroom, cafeteria, and schoolyard, and on field trips. They also tutor and assist children in learning class material.

The typical responsibilities of teacher's aides are difficult to categorize because aides' responsibilities vary greatly. Responsibilities may include grading tests and papers, checking homework, keeping health and attendance records, typing, filing, and duplicating materials—all matters that use up a teacher's time. Aides also may stock supplies, operate audiovisual equipment, and keep classroom equipment in order.

Certain teacher's aides work under the direction and guidance of teachers to instruct children. They work with students individually or in small groups, listening while students read, reviewing or reinforcing class work, or helping them find information for reports. They may supervise independent study or help students in vocational or work-study programs to find jobs.

Teacher's aides may confer with parents regarding the progress of students. They also provide personal attention to at-risk students whose families live in poverty, for example, or students with special needs such as those who speak English as a second language. Aides help assess a student's progress by observing a student's performance and recording relevant data.

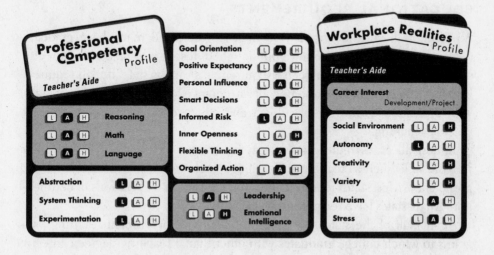

EARNING POTENTIAL

Statistics on the average salary for teachers are conflicting. A recent survey in *Career Opportunity News* reports the average starting salary for **public elementary school teachers** as $20,800 and the average high as $32,200, while the National Education Association lists the *average* salary at $34,800. Earnings vary widely based on experience, region, and academic qualifications. For instance, in Vermont the starting salary for elementary school teachers is $15,500, while the average experienced elementary school teacher in northern New Jersey earns $46,880. As a general rule, **secondary school** and **special education/bilingual teachers** earn up to 10 percent more than elementary school teachers, and **private school teachers** are generally lower-paid. The average hourly wage for **teacher's aides** involved in teaching activities is around $8.30.

Salary growth should be quite good, comfortably ahead of inflation in light of the high demand for qualified individuals. Additional income opportunities exist for teachers during the long summer break through summer school positions and private tutoring.

Most teachers belong to unions, which represent them in bargaining disputes with municipalities. Because teachers are essential to every community, and because their unions are typically strong ones, teachers' salaries have improved, and they receive good benefits.

EDUCATIONAL REQUIREMENTS

All teachers have undergraduate college degrees, and many have graduate degrees as well. All states require public school teachers to be certified in one subject or several related subjects. Requirements vary by state, but all require a bachelor's degree and completion of an approved teacher training program with a prescribed number of subject and education credits and supervised practice teaching.

Almost all states require applicants for teacher certification to be tested in basic skills such as reading and writing, teaching skills, and subject matter proficiency. Most states require continuing education for renewals of certification. Many states have reciprocity agreements.

About half of the states are experimenting with provisional teaching programs in which college graduates with other than a teaching degree can earn teaching certification through a one-year trial once they have passed the National Teachers Exam.

Most **special education teachers** will have received training in their field at the graduate level. Graduate education programs at colleges and universities across the country provide prospective teachers with in-depth exposure to the types of challenges they will face as special education teachers. In addition to being knowledgeable on the subject matter, the ability to communicate, inspire trust and confidence, and motivate students, as well as understand their educational and emotional needs, is essential for special education teachers. They should also be organized, dependable, patient, and creative.

Bilingual education teachers, in addition to the general requirements for all teachers, must be highly proficient in English as well as the other language.

Teacher's aides must have at least a high school diploma, although most have at least some college experience. Some states have established certification and training requirements for teacher's aides. Many two-year and community colleges offer associate's degree programs that prepare graduates to work as teacher's aides. Aides with teaching responsibilities usually have more training than those who do not teach. College training has become increasingly important among certain employers, and many schools require experience in working with children.

Most aides receive thorough on-the-job training. Aides should have a solid understanding of class materials and instructional methods, and must be familiar with the organization and operation of a school. Aides should also know how to operate audiovisual equipment, keep records, and prepare instructional materials. In addition, aides should enjoy working with children, be fair and patient, demonstrate initiative, follow directions, have good oral and writing skills, and be able to communicate effectively. Some aides must be able to speak a second language; others must be proficient in computer and clerical skills.

A DAY IN THE LIFE

A teacher's classroom will generally reflect the personality of the school and the teacher; some are pristine and silent, others are organized chaos. And while the teacher's personal style may prevail, the one common ingredient, the children, will always make for a stimulating and challenging atmosphere. Occasions such as field trips or outdoor classrooms may provide brief exposures to other working environments for primary and secondary school teachers. Physical demands are modest, but teachers are usually quite active, spending a lot of time standing or walking. Teachers working with physically disabled students have a more physically challenging role.

Teachers work with little supervision, but they must work in cooperation with others. When duties performed outside the classroom, such as grading tests and papers, are included, most teachers work more than forty hours a week. Teachers frequently work overtime, nights, or weekends. The work may be stressful, especially toward the end of a semester when a great deal of paperwork must be completed in a short time. **Teacher's aides** work under direct supervision of and in close cooperation with teachers. Most aides work forty-hour weeks, with occasional overtime hours.

One definite perk for teachers is that the school year runs roughly ten months, leaving teachers with a two-month break in the summer. This long break gives teachers the opportunity to pursue teaching in summer school, a completely different short-term occupation, personal interests, travel, or additional education. There are also breaks during the school year for major holidays, including a week off at Christmas and Easter. A few schools have year-round sessions, with eight weeks of classes followed by one week of vacation and a five-week midwinter break.

Many **special education teachers** also teach during the summer because students with special needs often need to take summer classes in order to catch up on course work from the previous school year or to prepare for upcoming classes.

JOB GROWTH

Of the approximately 3,225,000 teaching jobs in the United States, 1,651,000 are in elementary schools, 1,400,000 in secondary schools, and 435,000 in special education. Over 90 percent of these positions are in public schools.

The overall job outlook for teachers is expected to increase faster than the average for all occupations. Job growth will be greatest in special education, followed by secondary schools. Elementary schools will experience average growth.

Secondary and **elementary school** job growth will closely reflect the population growth. Jobs in less desirable urban and rural locations will be easier to find than those in attractive suburbs and prestigious private schools. *Mathematics* and *science specialists* will also be highly sought by schools. A possible limit on the number of new jobs could come from cuts in state spending on education, but pressure to improve education could create more jobs.

Primary school and secondary school teachers will continue to be in high demand well into the next century. The huge number of positions, combined with the turnover rate, will ensure a steady supply of openings at all levels. In addition, population growth and increased interest in better education will make this one of the best occupations for finding professional opportunity.

Special education teachers will continue to be highly sought into the next century. Special education will grow quickly in response to legislation emphasizing training and employment for individuals with disabilities, technological advances resulting in more survivors of accidents and illnesses, and growing public interest in individuals with special needs. The increasing number of students requiring special attention, combined with the relatively high turnover rate that, in part, reflects the heavy emotional demands of the position, will ensure a continuing number of openings. Many special education teachers switch to general education teaching or change careers altogether because of job stress related to excessive paperwork and inadequate administrative support. Still, this is an excellent occupation for those well-educated individuals motivated to help others.

Bilingual education teachers represent a small but growing percentage of all teachers and should continue to be in demand well into the next century. The growth of bilingual education has been relatively rapid, and as it con-

---

HELP WANTED
TEACHERS

Design classroom presentations and curriculum. Work with and lecture students, assign lessons, give tests, hear oral presentations, and maintain classroom discipline. Observe and evaluate student performance and potential. Assign homework, grade papers, prepare report cards, oversee study halls and home rooms, supervise extra-curricular activities, and meet with parents and school staff about students and school activities.

Kindergarten and Elementary School Teacher
Introduce and instruct young students in multiple subjects. Salary Range: $20,800–$46,880.

Secondary School Teacher
Help students further their knowledge of subjects introduced in elementary school, and introduce them to new subjects such as chemistry or geometry. Salary Range: $20,800–$46,880+.

Special Education Teacher
Instruct students with a variety of disabilities, and design and modify instruction accordingly. Work with students who are exceptionally bright, have limited English proficiency, or who have special requirements. Must have patience and ability to listen to students. Salary Range: $22,000–$51,500.

---

tinues to gain acceptance, the prospects are good for continued growth in the number of opportunities.

A large part of Americans' initial resistance to bilingual education is the belief that as their forefathers had to learn English when they came to America, so other immigrants should seek to assimilate themselves by learning English. This view of the world does not take into account the fact that business has created a global community that crosses all borders, and that the global community has given many countries, not just the United States, a multicultural flavor. Regardless of people's acceptance or rejection of multiculturalism, it is not only the wave of the future, but also a wave that has currently crested.

A growing area of teaching expertise is environmental studies. *Environmental educators* are being sought, from kindergarten through college levels, to raise the consciousness of America's youth about the tough decisions that must be made today to protect our world for them and their children. Environmental educators might ask students to help solve an environmental problem or to perform a laboratory experiment and discuss how its results can apply to the needs of the world around us. They may explore alternate methods of fertilization or biodegradable packaging. They may study the impact of chemicals on underwater life or conduct a community recycling awareness project with their students. In the past decade, educators have touched on this subject within science and social studies curricula.

Bilingual Education Teacher
Design classroom presentations and work with students in English and their native tongue. Observe and evaluate a student's performance and potential. Fluency in two or more languages essential. Salary Range: $22,000–$51,500+.

Teacher's Aide
Provide instructional and clerical support for classroom teachers. Assist, tutor, and supervise students in the classroom, cafeteria, school yard, and on field trips. Grade tests and papers, check homework, keep health and attendance records, and type, file, and photocopy classroom materials. Stock supplies, operate audiovisual equipment, and keep classroom equipment in order. Help teacher in assessing a student's progress. Salary Range: $9,880–$12,900.

However, the frightening decline our planet is experiencing has awakened educators to the vital nature of this subject matter, and while environmental educators may teach other subjects as well, teachers with specialized education and training in this field will find their expertise enhances their employability.

There are approximately 998,000 **teacher's aide** jobs in the United States. Roughly 80 percent of the positions are in elementary or secondary schools, with the majority of the positions assigned to the lower grades. A significant number of aides assist special education teachers in working with children with disabilities, with the remainder working in child day care centers and for religious organizations.

The overall job outlook for teacher's aides is expected to grow faster than the average for all occupations. The growth will be partly in response to the increasing number of special education classes, the restructuring of schools, and the rising number of students who speak English as a second language. Additional opportunities will arise from a high turnover rate characteristic of occupations with relatively low pay and few formal educational requirements.

As an occupation dependent on federal and state governmental expenditures, teaching has a future growth that will be sensitive to education budgets. Being a teacher's aide is ideal for individuals with modest educational backgrounds who would like to teach and work with children.

ADULT EDUCATION TEACHER

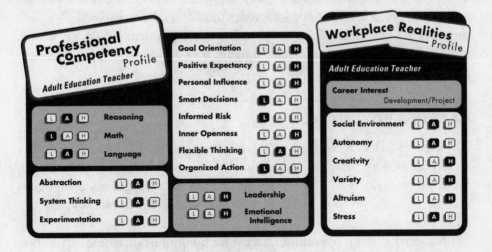

Adult education teachers instruct out-of-school youths and adults in academic and nonacademic courses in public or private schools or other organizations. Adult education teachers work in three main areas: *technical*, *adult basic*, and *adult continuing education*. Some adult education teachers instruct people who have graduated or left school for occupations that do not require a college degree, such as welders, dental hygienists, automated systems managers, X-ray technicians, farmers, and cosmetologists. Other teachers help individuals update their skills or adapt to technological advances—for example, by introducing adults to the joys of the computer keyboard and modem. Some teachers provide instruction in basic education courses for high school dropouts or others who need to upgrade their skills for inclusion in the new job market. Continuing education teachers also teach courses that students take for personal enrichment, such as cooking, dancing, writing, exercise and physical fitness, photography, and finance.

The typical responsibilities of adult education teachers include outlining a course, and lecturing in a classroom or giving students a "hands-on" experience. Increasingly, adult vocational/technical education teachers integrate academic and vocational curricula so that students may obtain a variety of skills. For example, an electronics student may be required to take courses in principles of mathematics and science in conjunction with gaining hands-on electronics skills. Teachers will demonstrate techniques, have the student apply them, and critique the student's work so that he or she can learn from the experience.

Adult education teachers who instruct in basic adult education programs may work with students who do not speak English; teach adults reading, writing, and mathematics up to the eighth-grade level; or teach adults through the twelfth-grade level in preparation for the General Educational Development (G.E.D.) examination, which offers the equivalent of a high school diploma. These teachers may refer students for counseling or job placement and may also recruit participants.

EARNING POTENTIAL

The average salary for adult education teachers who work full-time is approximately $27,000 a year, with most earning between $18,700 and $38,800 a year. Earnings vary widely by subject, academic credentials, experience, and geographic region. Part-time teachers are paid on an hourly rate and do not receive benefits.

Additional earning opportunities exist for adult education teachers as private tutors.

EDUCATIONAL REQUIREMENTS

Although training requirements vary widely by state and by field, teachers generally need work or other experience in their field and a license or certificate in those fields which one requires for full professional status. In some cases, an acceptable portfolio of work is all that is necessary—although many states require a bachelor's degree from an approved teacher training program, and some require certification.

Adult education teachers update their skills through continuing education to maintain certification. Teachers may also participate in seminars, conferences, or graduate courses in adult education, training and development, or human resources development. They also may return to work in business or industry for a limited period of time to remain up-to-date.

Besides meeting the formal educational requirements, adult education teachers should communicate and relate well with students, enjoy working with them, and be able to motivate them. In particular, adult basic education teachers must be patient, understanding, and supportive to make students comfortable, earn their trust, and help them better understand their needs and achieve their goals. This has been found to be a rewarding career by many mature workers pursuing second careers.

HELP WANTED
ADULT EDUCATION
TEACHER

Instruct out-of-school youths and adults in academic and non-academic courses in public or private schools or other organizations. Outline courses, lecture in classroom, and give students a hands-on experience. Sometimes integrate academic and vocational curricula so that students may obtain a variety of skills. May teach courses that students take for personal enrichment, such as cooking, dancing, writing, exercise and physical fitness, photography, and finance. May also teach English as a second language, or reading and writing in preparation for the G.E.D. Salary Range: $18,700–$38,800.

A DAY IN THE LIFE

Adult education teachers usually work in classrooms, which are generally pleasant, comfortable, and quiet environments. Typical employers of adult education teachers include public school systems; community and junior colleges; universities; businesses that provide formal education and training for their employees; automotive repair, bartending, business, computer, electronics, medical technology, and similar schools and institutes; dance studios; health clubs; job training centers; community organizations; labor unions; and religious organizations. In most cases physical demands are modest, but teachers are usually quite active, with a lot of time spent standing or walking.

Adult education teachers work with little supervision, but they must work in cooperation with others. When one includes their duties performed outside the classroom, such as grading tests and papers, most teachers work more than forty hours a week. Teachers frequently work overtime, nights, or weekends. Many adult education teachers work part-time. To accommodate students who may have job or family responsibilities, many courses are offered at night or on weekends, and range from two- to four-hour workshops and one-day mini-sessions to semester-long courses.

Since adult education teachers work with adult students, though, they do not encounter some of the behavioral or social problems sometimes found when teaching younger students. The adults are there by choice and are usually highly motivated—attributes that can make teaching them especially rewarding and satisfying. Nonetheless, teachers in adult basic education can deal with students at different levels of development who may lack effective study skills and self-confidence and who may require more patience and attention than other students.

JOB GROWTH

There are approximately 116,000 adult education teachers in the United States. Approximately 40 percent teach part-time, many intermittently. Many teach as a subsequent or parallel career, and often in a subject matter similar to that of their primary job. Many adult education teachers are self-employed, and just about any professional should bear this possibility in mind as he or she pursues a primary career.

The overall job outlook for adult education teachers is expected to improve faster than the average of all occupations. The growth will come as the demand for adult education programs continues to rise and participation in continuing education increases. More people are recognizing that lifelong learning is important to maintaining career stability, so there will be increasing demand by professionals for programs that help. To keep abreast of changes in their fields and advances in technology, more adults are taking courses for career advancement, skills upgrading, and personal enrichment, spurring demand for adult education teachers.

Enrollment in adult education basic programs will also increase in response to changes in immigration policies, which will require basic competency in English and civics, and greater awareness of the difficulty in finding a good job without basic academic skills. Employment growth of adult vocational technical education teachers will result from the need to train young adults for entry-level jobs, and experienced workers who want to switch fields or whose jobs have been eliminated due to changing technology or business reorganization.

Working as an adult education teacher will remain an attractive career option for those who would like to teach, and particularly for those who would like to teach part-time. However, since many adult education programs receive government funding, employment growth is susceptible to changes in government budgets.

Librarian

Librarians make information available to people who need it. They maintain a library's collections of books, periodicals, documents, audiovisuals, electronic databases, and other materials. Librarians perform a wide variety of functions, which can be categorized into three areas: user services, technical services, and administrative services.

Reference librarians and readers' advisory-service librarians, who assist

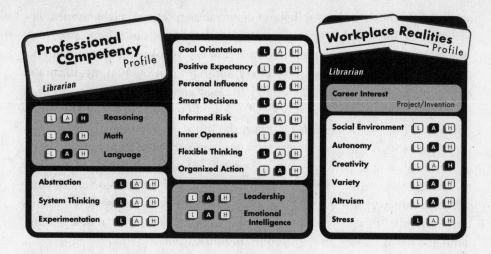

library visitors in locating the kind of information they need and in the use of reference materials and other research sources, are said to be in *user services*. They may be asked to make suggestions to help the user determine what information or services would be most helpful and expedient to his or her research or information needs.

Librarians who work in *technical services* concentrate their efforts on the acquisition and cataloguing of materials for a library's collections.

Librarians who perform *administrative services* direct the management of the library. They oversee the activities of library employees, ensure that all services within a library are functioning correctly, and help prepare and evaluate library budgets. And workers like *outreach librarians* perform duties beyond the facility to promote the library's services.

Librarians in small organizations may find that their jobs involve a lot of crossover in terms of the responsibilities.

Librarians work in different ways to organize a library's collections so that users can find information as painlessly as possible. This requires constant monitoring and updating of a library's extensive catalog. Librarians are also responsible for keeping track of current literature and of the latest published information and resources. In larger facilities, librarians may concentrate their efforts in a specific area of the library's collections. They sometimes help teachers develop text selections, and they occasionally participate in actual teaching; in some cases, librarians provide support to teachers and to after-school programs by furnishing storytelling hours for children.

Librarians are quite often employed by organizations other than a local town library. Librarians are hired by schools, colleges, universities, government agencies, medical centers, religious organizations, research laboratories, law firms, museums, and corporations. These librarians collect, catalog, and arrange specialized information resources that will be of specific interest to the organization for which they work. These librarians can offer an organization's employees suggestions on research in particular areas of study. For example, a *health sciences librarian* may order, catalog, and enable access to the information found in any dental, nursing, pharmaceutical, or veterinary library; he or she may also work for a health science association or foundation library.

Music librarians perform similar duties with materials such as musical recordings, sheet music, periodicals about music, and information about composers, conductors, and musicians. Music librarians may manage this information for public libraries, but they may also work for orchestras, movie studios, radio and television stations, museums, or foundations.

Modern library research is done with more than just card catalogs. It is now tied to electronic databases through computer terminals and to automated systems of research gathering. A librarian must make use of all of these features. In some libraries, *database librarians* are employed to plan and operate computer research systems, while information scientists may also be brought into libraries to develop successful procedures for collecting, organizing, and classifying library information.

EARNING POTENTIAL

The average salary of all librarians is $25,900, ranging from $23,800 per year in public libraries to $27,400 in school libraries. In college and university libraries, accredited librarians earn an average of $25,400 per year, and can earn upwards of $65,000 at the top level positions. Librarians trained in special fields earn an average of $27,700 a year, while those with three to five years of experience averaged $31,800, and those at a managerial level, approximately $45,200.

Federal government librarians in supervisory, nonsupervisory, and managerial positions pull down roughly $44,500 a year.

EDUCATIONAL REQUIREMENTS

To be considered for a position as librarian in most public, academic, and special libraries, a candidate must hold a bachelor's degree in library science (B.L.S.). For employment as a librarian for the federal government, a B.L.S., its educational equivalent, or equivalent experience is required. Most libraries prefer to hire an employee who has graduated from one of the sixty master's degree (M.L.S.) programs that the American Library Association recognizes as accredited programs. Most M.L.S. programs require that applicants already have a bachelor's degree in a relevant liberal arts major.

A typical graduate program takes one or two years, and includes courses in foundations of library and information science, the history of books and printing, and issues of intellectual freedom, censorship, plagiarism, and the role of information and libraries in society. Other courses provide broad examinations of user services. Students may opt to study a particular kind of library work, such as service to children or young adults, abstracting, archives, media, library administration, and library automation. A Ph.D. in library and information science will help those who wish to become college or university teachers, college administrators, or administrators in a large library system.

It is also helpful for aspiring *special librarians* to have experience and even degrees in areas of law, medicine, engineering, business, or natural or social sciences. In some special library positions, knowledge of a second language is required.

Just as public school teachers are subject to state certification in order to be hired, *public school librarians* may sometimes be required to hold a teacher's certification. Some schools require that prospective public school librarians hold a library science degree with a library media specialization, a degree in education with a similar specialty, or a degree in education media. Some states require that candidates obtain a certification as a public librarian if they wish to work for a municipal, county, or regional library system.

It is absolutely essential that librarians are computer literate—but that goes almost without saying for any job with a future in the new world of work.

A DAY IN THE LIFE

Almost all librarians work in comfortable, well-lit, and tranquil facilities. They often have a good deal of contact with the public, whether that public be students in a school library, or professionals in a corporate library. Because each user request is different, many librarians find user service both challenging and enjoyable; it is, after all, a profession for those who enjoy the challenge and reward of first gathering and then disseminating information. Librarians generally work under little direct supervision, but they are monitored from time to time for quality of performance and for quantity of tasks completed.

One-fourth of all librarians work part-time. *Public* and *college librarians* are

---

HELP WANTED
LIBRARIAN

Locate specific kinds of information and assist users with reference materials and other research sources. Acquire and catalog materials for library's collections. May direct the management of the library; responsible for overseeing the activities of library employees, library services, and budget. Help specialized groups with their reference needs. Salary Range: $23,800–$65,000.

---

sometimes required to work weekend hours, while *school librarians* have hours and schedules that mirror those of teachers. *Special librarians* in corporate libraries usually work normal business hours, but will work additional hours as business projects dictate.

One occupational hazard for librarians is that constant focus on reading materials or computer screens can create eyestrain.

JOB GROWTH

Librarians hold approximately 149,000 jobs. Most of those are in school, college, and university libraries. Others work for public or special libraries (most often run by corporations, conglomerates, or associations) or for various government libraries and facilities.

Opportunities in corporate library work reflect the growth in general business, with health care and technology leading the way. In the private sector, the outlook is best for *corporate librarians* with a background in finance, law, or science and technology.

Job prospects for public librarians vacillate with government budgetary constraints. Budgets for libraries are often the first to be cut. However, the Bureau of Labor Statistics predicts that there will be a large number of librarians retiring over the next ten years, so there will be opportunities available. Furthermore, college enrollment in library science has decreased over the last decade, making the competition for these positions less intense than in other occupations. *Database librarians* will be particularly in demand.

CHILD CARE WORKER

Professional Competency Profile
Child Care Worker

L **A** H	Reasoning
L A H	Math
L A H	Language

Abstraction	**L** A H
System Thinking	L **A** H
Experimentation	**L** A H

Goal Orientation	**L** A H
Positive Expectancy	L **A** H
Personal Influence	L **A** H
Smart Decisions	**L** A H
Informed Risk	**L** A H
Inner Openness	L A **H**
Flexible Thinking	**L** A H
Organized Action	**L** A H

L A H	Leadership
L A H	Emotional Intelligence

Workplace Realities Profile
Child Care Worker

Career Interest	Development

Social Environment	L **A** H
Autonomy	**L** A H
Creativity	L A **H**
Variety	L **A** H
Altruism	L **A** H
Stress	L **A** H

Having it all! A house with a white picket fence, a dog, two cats, three kids, a healthy marriage, and of course, a great job for you and your spouse. This calls for . . . yes, day care! Preschool! *Child care workers!* The extended family of yesteryear is now reborn in day care centers, nurseries, preschools, and family-home day care settings throughout America.

Of course it is not just the pursuit of the American dream but the necessity to make ends meet that has pushed mothers into the workforce, leaving their preschool-age children in the hands of child care workers. This trend is expected to accelerate over the next decade, promising enormous opportunity for child care workers.

Child care workers' primary responsibilities are the care of children age five and under. These workers provide for the children a safe and nurturing environment, planning activities which will stimulate them intellectually, emotionally, and physically. The preschool years are when children learn to talk, listen, share, play, socialize, and learn. Child care workers provide children with snacks and meals, tend to their grooming and toilet training needs, kiss their boo-boos, and communicate any health or emotional problems to their parents. It can be an enormously rewarding field of work for people with an affinity for the young.

EARNING POTENTIAL

The salary range for child care workers runs the gamut from minimum wage, for those just starting out in large day care facilities, to the-sky-is-the-limit for those energetic persons who can care for large numbers of children in their own homes. In general, child care workers start at around $9,500 a year, average $13,500, and earn up to an average of $23,900. Managers of day care facilities can earn in the mid to high $40s. Of course, for child care entrepreneurs, the earnings may be more than double these numbers.

EDUCATIONAL REQUIREMENTS

None! Preschool children require little academic direction. The child care worker is there to play with them . . . and anyone who has been to elementary school can do that. Still, the job does require a good deal of energy, patience, imagination, enthusiasm, and common sense to manage and care for groups of small children, and these are the traits the better day care facility will look for in an applicant. Needless to say, you also should *like* children!

Those interested in pursuing a career in child care should consider high school or college courses in child psychology, sociology, art, music, drama, and sports. Those interested in managing an agency or starting one of their own are well-advised to take business and management courses as well.

Some states are now beginning to require licensure for certain levels of child care workers. These states have varying requirements, from a high school diploma to eight hours of child care courses to be taken each year.

A DAY IN THE LIFE

Child care workers may work in their own homes, or in day care centers, nurseries, and other facilities for children. The conditions vary depending on the income bracket of the area and the children's family situation, as well as the size and profitability of the facility. Most facilities are clean and bright, and decorated with energizing kids' art.

Day care facilities schedule their hours around convenient drop-off and pick-up times for working parents—in other words, *long hours that start early*. However, unless you are a private day care worker, the hours are usually staggered in shifts to cover both morning and evening without overextending the staff.

The work can be exhausting and nerve-wracking, with all the energy and noise level, conflict, and frustration that naturally accompanies groups of small children. Child care workers spend a great deal of time on their feet—often at a swift pace. They lift and carry, tie and untie shoes, button and unbutton coats, change diapers, wipe noses and tears, wash faces and hands,

HELP WANTED
CHILD CARE WORKER

Care for children age five and under. Talk, listen, share, and play with them. Provide for them a safe and nurturing environment, and stimulate them intellectually, emotionally, socially, and physically. Provide children with snacks and meals, and tend to their grooming and toilet training needs. Communicate any health or emotional problems to their parents. Requires patience and love of children. Salary Range: $9,880–$23,900.

animate stories, and sing songs. They also spend time sitting on the floor, building with blocks, racing cars, and coloring and painting pictures. And then it's time to clean up and start all over again.

It's one of those jobs you are gonna love or hate.

Working with children can be a most rewarding occupation. Watching them grow and develop, helping them learn, and learning from them, in turn, are the simple but exquisite joys of life.

JOB GROWTH

All the talk of more disposable income for the families of America over the next decade takes into consideration that more and more women are entering the workforce, and having to leave their children in day care even sooner after childbirth. Quality care is definitely in demand and this is an area of huge potential—not only for child care workers, but for budding entrepreneurs who will develop their skills and conscientiously work toward opening their own facilities.

There are currently 260,750 child care workers (not including nursery school and preschool teachers) looking after preschoolers in this country, a figure which is expected to increase by 117,500 positions by the year 2005. More of these positions are expected to be in on-site day care facilities, which care for the children of the employees of a corporation.

Day care workers with a college degree can look forward to advancement into management positions and many open their own centers—which is where the real money can be made in this business.

State and Local Government

URBAN AND REGIONAL PLANNER

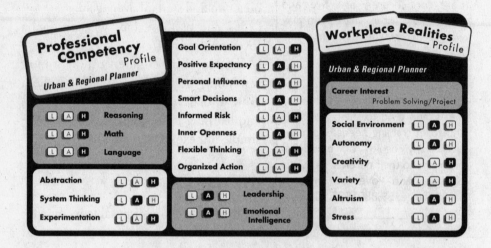

Urban and regional planning is certainly not a new concept. When seen from above, the city of Philadelphia forms a perfect grid. It has two main streets (Broad, which runs north to south, and Market, which runs east to west) that intersect at the very heart of the city: at City Hall, its center of politics, public service, and law. The city does not sprawl as it extends outward to the four points of the compass: it grows. Someone new to the city can easily find his or her way around because streets do not arbitrarily change names or numbering systems. Although this may not sound remarkable to people living in modern cities in the American South or Southwest, it is remarkable because Philadelphia, well over three hundred years old, has continued to evolve in an orderly fashion according to its founders' original plan—developed, as you may have guessed, by urban and regional planners.

Urban and regional planners take into consideration such factors as the environment, the prevailing winds, air and water pollution, the local economy, and the best way to utilize the region's natural resources or landscape for commercial purposes without sacrificing the natural beauty of the land.

But today, with an overburdened and crumbling infrastructure in most of our metropolitan areas, urban and regional planners are more concerned with remodeling older cities whose infrastructure has proved insufficient to support the vast numbers of people relying on city services. For example, no one ever envisioned that a city the size of New York would be inadequate to accommodate all of the truck and automobile traffic its streets must carry every day. Furthermore, most older cities have underground transportation and sewer systems that need repair or replacement, but it is impossible to make such repairs without shutting down busy parts of a city. Urban and regional planners attempt to improve services provided to people and, at the same time, minimize the inconvenience caused by the repair work.

Urban and regional planners first develop detailed studies that depict the proposed construction sites in their present condition, and then prepare projections of the consequences of either leaving the land or condition the way it is or making the changes. Urban and regional planners' proposals include such information as the major industry, the population density, employment and economic statistics, and the need for schools, hospitals, libraries, waste treatment centers, and other public services in an area. The point for urban and regional planners is to develop an integrated plan for a community that includes all of the factors that affect human, animal, and plant life in the region, thereby anticipating both short-term and long-term consequences. It's a job for people who are comfortable with complexity, challenge, and compromise.

EARNING POTENTIAL

Salaries in this field vary according to geographic location and size of the company, the type of employer, and the work responsibilities. The average median salary for all urban and regional planners is around $42,000. The average salary is affected by the degree of education held, as shown:

	Bachelor's Degree	Master's Degree	Ph.D.
Planner's Average Income	$39,200	$43,000	$57,000

Planners who are employed by land development firms are the highest earners, averaging $65,500. Private businesses and consulting firms also pay well, in the $58,000 range.

In federal government positions, planners average $52,400 annually. The federal government offers planners with a master's degree a starting salary of $27,800.

EDUCATIONAL REQUIREMENTS

Employers prefer to hire those applicants with advanced training in the field of urban and regional development. Most federal government jobs in this field require at least two years of graduate work or two years of experience on the job. As in every field that requires analytical work, candidates with good academic credentials will have an advantage in looking for jobs.

There are just over eighty college and university programs that offer an accredited bachelor's degree in urban and regional planning, and only ten programs offering an accredited master's degree. Consequently, competition for admission is keen. (A master's degree in landscape architecture or civil engineering is a good alternative preparation course for entry-level planning jobs.)

These programs in planning are accredited by the Planning Accreditation Board, composed of members of the American Institute of Certified Planners (AICP) and the Association of Collegiate Schools of Planning. The graduate programs are two-year programs involving studio planning sessions, workshops, and fieldwork. Most students are required to work in a planning office as interns during their graduate education. Those interested in a career as an urban and regional planner should also study relevant courses such as demographics, economics, finance, health administration, and management.

Most successful planners are certified by the AICP; certification involves passing an examination after fulfilling the prerequisites for education and fieldwork. Certified planners receive the highest pay and hold the most responsible positions in this profession.

A DAY IN THE LIFE

Urban and regional planners spend most of their time working in bright, comfortable offices that allow them to draft their designs and prepare models of their plans. They also must make frequent trips to the site where their plans are going to be developed, first to observe the conditions as they exist before the changes, and then during construction.

Most planners work a standard forty-hour week in the office, but they also must attend public meetings with civil groups to explain their plans and the impact the plans will have on the region and its citizens. They may also be required to work overtime hours when deadlines approach.

Planners work with little supervision, but must be able to work closely with others, such as civil engineers, government officials, and public interest groups. There are often heated disagreements on the environmental and community impact of certain projects, with planners right in the middle. Planners should remain circumspect, objective, confident, and diplomatic in the midst of such turmoil.

HELP WANTED
URBAN AND REGIONAL PLANNER

Determine the best way to utilize the region's natural resources or landscape. Remodel older cities to accommodate a vast number of people relying on city services. Improve public services provided to people and minimize the inconvenience caused by repair work. Develop detailed studies that depict the proposed sites before and after construction. Salary Range: $18,300–$85,000.

JOB GROWTH

The largest area of growth for urban and regional planners is in suburbs and their surrounding regions, where new construction of housing developments and shopping centers is changing the landscape dramatically. In the private sector, architectural and surveying firms, and management and public relations firms employ urban and regional planners.

There are 28,000 urban and regional planners employed in the United States, two-thirds of them employed by local government planning agencies. Employment for urban and regional planners is expected to grow by 25 percent over the next ten years, which translates into about 5,000 jobs. The fact that cities and the federal government do not have sufficient funds to tackle all of the projects that need attention is of some concern, but however difficult, budgets will have to be found, and planners will have to be hired to direct the updating of the crumbling infrastructure of our urban and suburban communities.

Most of the new jobs will open in rapidly expanding communities that have a tax base and an industrial base large enough to support new programs and development. There is also much work to be done in the cramped older cities on the East Coast, in the Midwest, and in the vast cities in the West and Southwest. In addition, regional planners are going to be needed as suburban and regional communities experience greater traffic congestion—the result of continuing construction that eliminates much of the clean air and free space that first attracted people to those communities.

Another booming area for urban and regional planners to consider is Eastern Europe. Since the breakup of the Soviet Union, many former Eastern bloc countries have asked urban and regional planners to visit and provide them with insights or proposed changes that will make their cities more livable for the inhabitants, and more commercially productive. The global economy is changing the face of the world, and almost every country will need well-trained and skilled urban and regional planners.

AIR QUALITY SPECIALIST

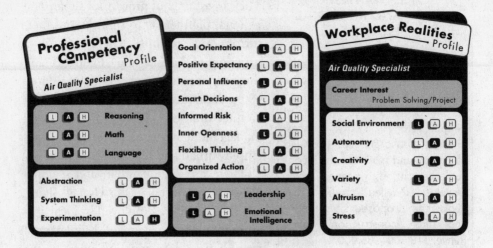

One image that defined industrial America—the country that existed in time between the end of the Depression and the dawning of the postindustrial state—was of billowing black clouds of smoke spewing forth from chimneys attached to steel mills, coal foundries, automobile plants, and factories all over the landscape. The benefit of that smoke was a burgeoning economy built on a belief in endless natural resources and the earth's ability to cleanse itself. As we now know, this belief was shortsighted. What manufacturers could not foresee was a day when the clean air their products polluted would prove to be a more valuable—and possibly more scarce—commodity than the products that came off the assembly lines.

Eventually, environmentalists and other concerned parties realized that exposure to the unregulated discharge of smoke-borne particulates and by-products posed a threat to millions of citizens. The Environmental Protection Agency has long since targeted manufacturing plants for practices that contaminate the air and create a hazard for people and wildlife. The regulation of this type of pollution, though, requires specialists who can determine the types of waste that result from manufacturing processes and who can offer guidance in alternative disposal methods.

Air quality specialists are those individuals who professionally monitor and determine the quality of the air in a number of settings, but most commonly industrial establishments. In recent years, as air pollution control and regulation have become more stringent, this position is increasingly important to corporations and other organizations.

The typical responsibilities of air quality specialists include analyzing

samples of air at industrial and other facilities to determine the amount of sus-
pended foreign particles and gauging the effectiveness of control methods.
Using technical filtering apparatus, they weigh and measure particles, such as
lead, rock, or coal dust, computing the concentration per cubic foot of air
tested. They prepare summaries of their findings for submission to the appropriate department, and also may recommend remedial measures.

Additional responsibilities of air quality specialists include conducting tests
and field investigations to obtain data for use by environmental, engineering,
and scientific researchers who are investigating sources of air pollutants and
methods of control. These chemical and physical laboratory and field tests
involve collecting samples of gases from smokestacks, engine exhaust emis-
sions, and other atmospheric pollutants, to analyze the characteristics or composition of gaseous materials.

EARNING POTENTIAL

The average annual salary for air quality specialists according to one study was
approximately $27,000. Beginning specialists received salaries that fell within
a range from $20,000 to $28,000, while more experienced specialists earned
between $25,000 and $40,000. Salaries depended on a variety of factors,
including the size and location of the city, the complexity of the job, and the
level of education. Most positions also provided employee benefits.

EDUCATIONAL REQUIREMENTS

Most positions require a four-year undergraduate degree. Some of the courses
air quality specialists take in college include environmental, physical, and biological sciences; mathematics; computer science; and communications.
Because they must be able to explain their findings accurately, air quality specialists find that communications is a valuable minor.

Some two-year programs leading to an associate's degree in environmental science technology and one-year programs leading to a certificate
are available. These programs provide a good general knowledge of air, water,
and soil pollution control as well as basic preparation for a job. Completion of such courses increases an applicant's chances for employment and
promotion.

Air quality specialists usually begin training while on the job, learning their
particular skills under the direction of a more experienced specialist. They
observe the processes and the uses of the equipment, and perform routine
tasks, such as recording meter readings and taking air samples.

A DAY IN THE LIFE

Air quality specialists work both indoors and outdoors and may be exposed to noise from machinery and some unpleasant odors. They must pay close attention to safety procedures as they may be confronted with hazardous conditions such as slippery walkways, dangerous gases, and malfunctioning equipment. The physical demands are moderate, with a good deal of stooping and reaching and some significant lifting.

Air quality specialists work with little direct supervision but must work in cooperation with others. The job can involve shift work as well as occasional overtime or weekend hours. Working under emergency conditions may be particularly stressful.

JOB GROWTH

A recent survey found that there were approximately 35,000 air quality specialists in the United States. The vast majority worked for local governments, but some worked for private testing companies and corporations. Geographically, they worked all over the country, with most jobs in larger towns and cities.

The overall employment of air quality specialists is expected to grow about as fast as the average for all occupations. New positions will come mainly from population growth and economic growth. Job turnover will also account for many openings. Although statistics show that the job growth will not be dramatic in this field over the next ten years, the jobs themselves are good ones, providing stable employment to the people who do enter the field.

Because governmental regulation of air pollution is unlikely to abate in the future, opportunities for air quality specialists will continue to be plentiful, even though the total number of positions is not large. This will present a solid career opportunity for technically minded individuals who have an interest in air pollution and the environment. Since there is no set curriculum determining entry into this field, many people may decide on it as a career after they have received on-the-job exposure to its duties. For this reason, it is a career to be considered by people with a general science background who may be looking not only to find a completely new career, but also for a new specialty/sense of direction within their existing career.

FIREFIGHTER

Professional Competency Profile

Firefighter

L A H	Reasoning
L A H	Math
L A H	Language

Abstraction	L A H
System Thinking	L A H
Experimentation	L A H

Goal Orientation	L A H
Positive Expectancy	L A H
Personal Influence	L A H
Smart Decisions	L A H
Informed Risk	L A H
Inner Openness	L A H
Flexible Thinking	L A H
Organized Action	L A H

| L A H | Leadership |
| L A H | Emotional Intelligence |

Workplace Realities Profile

Firefighter

Career Interest
Project/Development

Social Environment	L A H
Autonomy	L A H
Creativity	L A H
Variety	L A H
Altruism	L A H
Stress	L A H

Firefighters risk their lives to protect private and public property and the lives of all of us every year. Firefighters are trained in teamwork and organization. During a fire, each firefighter performs specific duties that are assigned by a crew chief as circumstances dictate. Some of these duties may be relatively safe ones, such as connecting hoses to hydrants, operating a pump, or positioning ladders. But the duties may change during the course of a fire, as firefighters substitute for tired crew members and take their turns at physically demanding jobs, such as training hoses on the fire, or steadying ladders.

Firefighters' jobs become more challenging as they assume additional responsibilities, such as working with emergency medical services, assisting natural disaster recovery teams, and working to clean up hazardous chemical spills.

Not all firefighters work in the cities and suburbs. Some serve as *fire lookouts* in the national forests. Fire lookouts observe the vast forests from their remote lookout stations and report smoke or other signs of fire to their headquarters. *Fire rangers* patrol the forests to ensure that campers and hikers are observing all fire regulations. When fires break out in forests, specially trained firefighters known as *smoke jumpers* parachute from airplanes to fight the fire from different sides in order to contain its spread and the damage it can cause.

Another duty firefighters assume is fire prevention. Most fire departments have personnel trained to inspect buildings for fire hazards and code violations. These *inspectors* review blueprints and building plans, fire doors and fire escapes, storage of hazardous materials, and sprinkler systems and fire extinguishers. Firefighters often address schoolchildren and civil organizations on the subject of fire safety.

Some firefighters work to be *fire marshals*, who investigate fires to determine their starting point, the cause behind them, and whether or not arson or other criminal activities were involved. They may also serve as expert witnesses in court proceedings.

The familiar scene of firefighters cleaning their trucks and maintaining their equipment is still acted out in every firehouse today. Between fires, firefighters must be certain that the equipment they rely on to save their lives and the lives of fire victims is in good repair. They spend a great deal of time checking and repairing their gear and equipment.

EARNING POTENTIAL

Firefighters' salaries are estimated in weekly amounts. The median weekly salary is $636. The middle 50 percent of firefighters earn between $499 and $824. The highest 10 percent earn more than $987.

Firefighters all receive medical and liability benefits. Their protective clothing is usually provided free of charge by the municipality that employs them. Many firefighters stay in the job to enjoy the early retirement packages that provide them with half pay at age fifty after they have put in twenty-five years of service.

EDUCATIONAL REQUIREMENTS

Applicants for firefighting positions must be at least eighteen years old and have a high school diploma or its equivalent. They must pass a written test, as well as physical tests that measure their strength, coordination, and agility. They must also pass a medical exam and undergo drug testing. In fact, random drug testing is a common occurrence with firefighters.

Almost all of the training required to become a fireman is supervised by a fire department. Firefighting techniques, fire prevention, hazardous material handling, and emergency medical procedures are part of the information covered in training programs.

A DAY IN THE LIFE

HELP WANTED
FIREFIGHTER

Protect private and public property from fire. Work with emergency medical services, assist natural disaster recovery teams, and clean up hazardous chemical spills. Identify fire hazards and code violations. Check and prepare gear and equipment. Ability to work with a team critical. Work involves hazardous situations. Salary Range: $12,000–$52,000.

Most firefighters work in firehouses, which have sleeping and dining areas. For starters, firefighters often work long shifts, which require them to sleep in the firehouse while they are on duty. Most firefighters work more than fifty hours per week because of their long shift assignments. In some areas firefighters work a twenty-four-hour shift and then have forty-eight hours off. There are other shift arrangements as well, but, in general, firefighters do not work a standard 9-to-5, forty-hour week.

Needless to say, the profession has many risks. Firefighters risk death by fire, smoke inhalation, toppling rubble, or collapsing buildings. Forest fires can trap firefighters in an instant, sealing off their escape routes and surrounding them completely. In 1994 a sudden updraft of superheated air from a canyon caused several smoke jumpers to be killed in a blaze. Firefighters also fight fires at chemical plants and warehouses, which expose them to the risks of poisonous chemicals and gas. They wear protective gear to fight these fires, but their risk is still very high. There are some risks associated with most jobs, but few face the everyday challenges of the firefighter.

JOB GROWTH

There are approximately 238,000 employed firefighters in the United States, 90 percent of whom work in municipal and county fire departments. The other 10 percent work primarily for the federal and state governments, and include fire rangers.

Employment for firefighters is expected to increase at an average rate compared to all other jobs through 2005. Because the job provides excitement and does not require more than a high school education, it is attractive to a large number of people. Most firefighting jobs require applicants to pass a written and physical examination, but many people pass these tests and still must wait for paid positions. The job competition in this field is keen.

The best employment opportunities in firefighting are expected to occur in smaller communities rather than large ones. Small communities that have expanding populations will need more firefighters. Large cities that have fully staffed fire departments in place will not experience more than an average need as current firefighters retire.

Despite the hazards of the job, most firefighters choose to stay in the profession and receive their pension. There is little turnover in this field, which is unusual for a job where threat to life and limb is the order of the day.

Firefighters are respected people in their community because citizens know the hazards they face and admire their courage. This sort of respect, combined with the job security associated with firefighting and the benefits of an early retirement package, weigh equally with the terrible risks firefighters take.

POLICE OFFICER

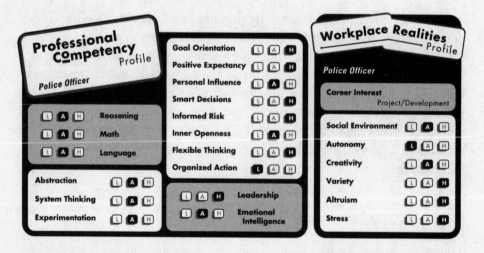

Most people have a general idea of the work *police officers* perform because they have seen police at work. Police officers prevent and investigate crimes, offer assistance at accident scenes, and direct traffic. Large city police departments usually assign police officers to one or two specific duties, such as traffic control or patrol duties, homicide or vice. Large city police departments also have special units that handle crisis situations, or patrol on horseback or motorcycle.

Suburban police departments usually require officers to handle a variety of general duties, such as automobile patrol, radio dispatch, and community relations with merchants and citizens who need to be educated about criminal problems and preventive measures. In rural areas, sheriffs and deputies enforce the law for entire counties; that means large patrol areas, and constant movement, for the officers involved.

New police recruits train on the job by starting off with patrol duties, either in a police car in some urban areas, or on foot. They are usually paired with experienced police partners who provide them with the experience necessary to anticipate, recognize, and handle developing situations.

Officers on patrol observe conditions that differ from the norm, such as open doors and windows, burned-out lights, or public hazards. All of these conditions present opportunities for crime or public danger, two occurrences police are trained to prevent or handle.

Police officers arrest perpetrators of crimes when they see them committing the crime, but *detectives* investigate crimes when no apparent perpetrator is found at the crime scene. Some police officers progress to become detectives. Detectives are police officers who have passed department tests and shown the ability to investigate criminal cases.

State police officers patrol state-controlled highways and turnpikes, and patrol rural communities that do not have their own police department. *State troopers*, as they are called, investigate the causes of accidents and monitor traffic to determine that drivers are observing the state's speed laws. State police also oversee driver's license testing. They also investigate crimes that come under their jurisdiction.

EARNING POTENTIAL

The average annual income of all police officers and detectives is approximately $32,000. This of course varies widely relative to the size and population of the area and the responsibilities and seniority of the officer.

	State Police	Local Police
Entry-level Police Officer	$22,800	$18,900
Sergeant	$30,100	$25,420
Director/Chief	$56,000	$30,240

Salaries are generally higher in densely populated urban areas, where the job demands may be significantly greater. In Chicago, officers start at $28,300 and earn up to $59,500, whereas in Memphis they start at $24,800 and earn up to $28,500.

These salary figures do not include overtime earnings, or vacation and medical benefits, which add significant value to the overall earnings figures.

EDUCATIONAL REQUIREMENTS

Police officers must apply for their positions under civil service regulations that control hiring practices for most state and local law enforcement employment. All applicants must be United States citizens and at least twenty years of age. Applicants are put through a battery of written and physical examinations that determine their fitness for the job.

Police officers must have at least a high school education, and the trend toward hiring applicants with at least some college education is growing. Because the work of police officers requires clear written and spoken communication, interaction with the public, and the ability to respond quickly in all types of situations, many police officers are encouraged to take college-level courses in psychology, English, criminal justice, and public relations. All police departments offer training programs to their new officers. This program usually includes classes in constitutional law, civil rights, state laws and local ordinances, and accident investigation.

A DAY IN THE LIFE

Most police officers in urban, suburban, and state departments are employed full-time and work a standard forty-hour week (with lots of paid overtime available). Almost all police officers, though, must work on different shifts during the course of a year. Shift assignments usually rotate on a regular basis.

Police officers spend most of their working hours out of doors in all weather conditions. In especially bad weather, police officers may have to respond to emergencies that expose them to the elements. Furthermore, because of the nature of their work, police officers place themselves at risk of injury or death. This risk often causes great stress in a police officer's family situation. It's a tough job that deserves everyone's respect.

JOB GROWTH

The approximately 1,700 state and local police departments in the United States employ over 550,000 law enforcement officers. Nearly 12 percent of this number are state police officers, and the great majority that remains work in local police departments.

The Department of Labor Statistics estimates that 100,000 new police officer positions will be added to the workforce by the year 2005. Although the demand for police services will increase, lack of municipal funding will pre-

HELP WANTED
POLICE OFFICER

Prevent and investigate crimes, arrest suspected perpetrators of crimes, and offer assistance at accident scenes. Anticipate, recognize, and handle developing situations. Ability to negotiate and handle hostile situations important. Job may involve some life-threatening situations. Salary Range: $18,900–$59,500.

vent police departments from hiring as many officers as are needed. Many exclusive residential communities will retain private security guards to provide patrol services for their areas, and a percentage of these will be moonlighting police officers.

Job security for police officers is good. Although budget cutbacks occasionally result in layoffs, police services are so important to communities that officers are among the last employees to be laid off. One way police departments avoid the need for layoffs is to offer early retirement plans. These plans permit former police officers to work at a second career while receiving pension benefits. Because police work requires good physical fitness, many police officers in their forties and fifties elect to take early retirement, which produces a healthy turnover.

As with all jobs that provide service to the public, law enforcement jobs will place increasingly greater demands on those who work in the field, because the public puts increasing emphasis on the need for protection from criminal activity. Police officers, who already work under greater than normal stress, will be subjected to even more as their ranks do not grow in direct proportion to the need for more officers.

On a more positive note, this is a secure career that offers a great opportunity for moving on to a second career at a relatively early age, and with the luxury of a pension that may pay as much as one-half of the officer's last annual salary. And because police officers are generally among the most responsible members of a community, job opportunities abound as private security guards, or as security chiefs of staff at corporations and institutions.

CORRECTION OFFICER

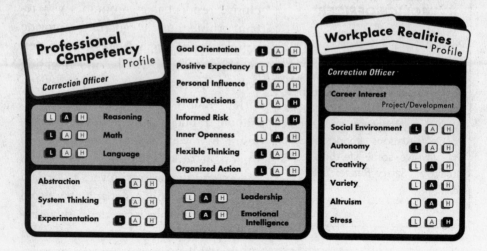

Who says crime does not pay? The frightening increase in crime in our country is a national concern. Along with changing patterns in violent crime and sentencing strategies comes a need for more facilities to house accused and convicted criminals, and professionally trained staff to supervise those facilities. The hopeful ingredient in this recipe is that an effort to provide quality supervision with an emphasis on rehabilitation is in effect.

Correction officers are employed by federal, state, and local governments to oversee prisoners in their everyday activities, observing their conduct, ensuring their safety, and helping with their rehabilitation. Their responsibilities include monitoring prisoner activities, such as work, exercise, dining, and bathing; assigning prisoners work projects and training them in new tasks; enforcing rules and regulations; settling inmate disputes; escorting prisoners from cells to visiting rooms, medical offices, and courtrooms; inspecting the penal institutions for safety hazards and escape attempts; advising prisoners of rehabilitation, vocational, and educational options; and assisting and supplementing therapists with psychological and emotional counseling.

Correction officers keep daily records and report verbally and in writing on prisoner conduct, work quality, and general well-being. They are expected to check prisoners' mail and visitors for prohibited items, and may assist in investigating crimes within the prison, or in searching for escaped prisoners.

EARNING POTENTIAL

Beginning correction officers' average annual income is around $20,500 a year. Those with five years' experience earn an average of $25,000. These salaries vary somewhat relative to the size, location, and amount of responsibility the officer carries. An entry-level correction officer in the Dakotas or in the Kentucky or Louisiana state system earns about $13,500 per year, whereas in New Jersey, he or she starts at an average of $26,000 a year. In many states, correction officers are represented by labor unions; most are provided with major medical insurance plans, and many can also get disability and life insurance at group rates. Sick leave, pension benefits, and paid vacation are standard.

Correction officers in supervisory positions earn an average of $40,000 a year.

EDUCATIONAL REQUIREMENTS

Most correction institutions require candidates to be eighteen years old, a high school graduate, and a United States citizen with no criminal record. Candidates also must meet formal standards of physical fitness. While a college degree is not essential, an associate's degree in psychology, criminology, or a related field is preferred by an increasing number of institutions, as their focus shifts from penalization to rehabilitation of inmates.

The American Correctional Association and the American Jail Association, among others, provide guidelines for training programs which all correction officers must attend. These programs teach newly hired correction officers the standards and policies of their specific institution, as well as prepare them for handling the routine situations they may face in their workday: crisis intervention; issues involving inmate rules, rights and behavior; contraband control; counseling; self-defense; and use of firearms. Formal training usually lasts several weeks, followed by on-the-job training.

Correction officers are required to complete considerable paperwork and must be able to communicate well verbally and in writing. They work under little direct supervision but must work well with others. A compassionate nature is important, especially for those correction officers who counsel inmates.

A DAY IN THE LIFE

This is not a vocation for the faint of heart or the weak in the knees. The working conditions for correction officers vary according to the facility.

**HELP WANTED
CORRECTION OFFICER**

Oversee prisoners and help with their rehabilitation. Responsibilities include: monitoring prisoner activities, work projects, and training in new tasks; enforcing rules and regulations; and escorting prisoners to medical offices and courtrooms. Advise inmates on vocational and educational options, and assist therapists in providing prisoners with psychological and emotional counseling. Salary Range: $13,000–$26,000 to start.

Working conditions for correction officers in minimum security facilities are usually clean, comfortable, safe, and relatively unstressful. However, in small, medium security municipal jails or precinct houses, conditions are less idyllic, and correction officers' responsibilities are wide-ranging and often quite stressful. Correction officers who are employed at maximum security prisons may work in noisy, crowded, poorly lit, poorly ventilated, and often dangerous conditions. Some correction officers must be armed while on duty.

In some prisons, correction officers monitor prisoner activities from a centralized control tower, using closed-circuit television and computer tracking systems. In others they walk the wards and spend a good deal of time on their feet.

This can also be an outdoor job at times. Correction officers may be stationed outdoors, supervising exercise or activity periods, or guarding the gates.

Correction officers generally work a forty-hour week, although this often includes night and weekend shifts. Some overtime may be required, and as these jobs are typically represented by unions, overtime is usually paid at prevailing rates.

JOB GROWTH

Mandatory sentencing guidelines, longer sentences, and reduced parole are all measures being taken to deter crime and decrease the crime rate. In the meantime, the government will need to build more institutions to house criminals, and this will result in the hiring of more personnel. Consequently, significant job growth is expected.

There are approximately 340,000 correction officers employed in the United States. This number is expected to increase by 20,000 per year through 2005. Most of these positions will be in the larger rural correctional institutions.

Correction facilities have been somewhat unsuccessful in recruiting qualified candidates, so there is an abundance of opportunity. And although competition will be stiff for the higher-paying supervisory positions, the layoff rate is very low. This career offers good job security for the foreseeable future.

SECURITY GUARD

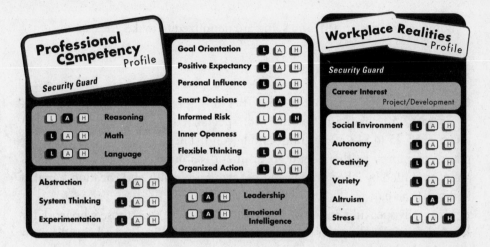

Professional Competency Profile
Security Guard

L A H	Reasoning
L A H	Math
L A H	Language

Abstraction	L A H
System Thinking	L A H
Experimentation	L A H

Goal Orientation	L A H
Positive Expectancy	L A H
Personal Influence	L A H
Smart Decisions	L A H
Informed Risk	L A H
Inner Openness	L A H
Flexible Thinking	L A H
Organized Action	L A H

L A H	Leadership
L A H	Emotional Intelligence

Workplace Realities Profile
Security Guard

Career Interest
Project/Development

Social Environment	L A H
Autonomy	L A H
Creativity	L A H
Variety	L A H
Altruism	L A H
Stress	L A H

Security guards, also known as *security officers*, are employed by a wide variety of businesses to protect properties against theft and vandalism, and to survey properties for fire or other potential hazards. They may be employed by security firms who offer services to a large number of institutions, or they may be hired directly by the business they work for as in-house guards. They are also employed at various government facilities.

In addition to property inspection and safety patrol, security guards have varying responsibilities according to their employer.

• Guards who work for commercial businesses, such as retail stores, banks, offices, and hospitals, or public buildings such as museums, generally patrol the property on foot, keenly aware of all unusual activities, and observing customers and employees, to prevent damage or theft. These guards are often undercover.

• Guards patrolling airports inspect baggage and the premises for possible arms or explosives, and check for stolen luggage.

• Guards working at government buildings, scientific laboratories, factories, and military bases are responsible for checking the identification of all persons entering the facility.

• Guards who monitor sports events, concerts, rallies, and other public events are responsible for crowd assistance and control.

• Armored car guards protect those who transport money or valuables from one location to another.

• Personal bodyguards protect celebrities or high risk individuals against an adoring or threatening public.

Some guards are armed, and some are deputized to make arrests.

EARNING POTENTIAL

Guards are usually paid by the hour. Beginning guards earn anywhere from $4.75 to $7.50 per hour. Guards with specialized training can earn in the range of $5.25 to $12.50 per hour and beyond. The average yearly income for guards employed by the federal government is around $22,000. Many guards are represented by labor unions and get standard health and vacation benefits and overtime pay.

Generally speaking, in-house guards are paid more than those who work for security firms. Earnings for privately retained personal bodyguards can be considerably higher.

EDUCATIONAL REQUIREMENTS

A security guard need not hold a college degree, or even a high school diploma, although most firms prefer they have the latter. Security agencies have licensing registration requirements for guards, which require that an applicant be at least eighteen years old, have no criminal record, and complete reading and writing tests, classroom training, and on-the-job training. The training includes public relations and property rights; emergency and first aid procedures; crisis intervention; search and seizure procedures; and other specialized procedures that may pertain to the particular job.

Good physical health, emotional stability, and mental alertness are prerequisites for most positions as a guard.

Because limited formal training is required for this occupation, it appeals to those looking for a second job or a part-time job, and especially to retired military or retired employees from elsewhere in the protective service industry looking for a second career.

A DAY IN THE LIFE

Security guards generally work a forty-hour week, although the hours may be flexible for those working at twenty-four-hour facilities where shift work is required. There may be overtime required, but for the most part this is paid.

**HELP WANTED
SECURITY GUARD**

Protect property against theft and vandalism; protect individuals from threats to their well-being. Secure money or valuables in transit. Search for arms or explosives. May be required to carry arms, work undercover, and be deputized to make arrests. Salary Range: $4.75–$14 per hour.

The working conditions for guards vary widely. Guards may work indoors, in quiet museums or noisy factories, or outdoors, in inclement weather. They may be stationed in a booth at the entrance to a facility, or they may patrol the grounds by foot, cart, or car.

In general they work alone, with little supervision. There can be stress and the risk of danger in emergency situations.

JOB GROWTH

Job prospects for security guards over the next decade are expected to be excellent. There is an intensifying need to protect political and business leaders, and the technology that is in place in private and commercial enterprises against damage, fraud, espionage, terrorism, and theft from both within and without.

Opportunities will be most abundant in contract guard agencies, where the salaries are slightly lower but where more and more companies are turning to save themselves the responsibility of hiring, training, and maintaining the personnel records on in-house guards.

The competition for in-house guard positions will become stiffer, as these positions generally offer better pay, benefits, and job security.

Selected Resources

HEALTH CARE
    Administration
    Nursing
    Physical Health
    Dentistry
    Mental Health

THE TECHNOLOGIES
    Biotechnology and Environmental Technology
    Engineering
    Information Technology

BUSINESS AND PROFESSIONAL SERVICES
    Financial Services:
        Banking
        Securities
        Accounting
        Insurance
        Financial Management
    Human Resources
    Law
    Media/Communications/Public Relations
    Sales and Marketing
    Food Service
    Support Services

PUBLIC SERVICE
    Social Services
    Education
    State and Local Government

Health Care

ADMINISTRATION

American Association of Medical
Assistants
20 North Wacker Drive, Suite 1575
Chicago, IL 60606-2903
312-899-1500

American College of Healthcare
Executives
1 North Franklin, Suite 1700
Chicago, IL 60606-3491
312-424-2800

American Health Care Association
1201 L Street NW
Washington, DC 20005
202-842-4444

American Health Information
Management Association
919 North Michigan Avenue
Chicago, IL 60611
312-787-2672

American Medical Technologists
710 Higgins Road
Park Ridge, IL 60068
708-823-5169

Healthcare Financial Management
Association
Two Westbrook Corporate Center,
Suite 700
Westchester, IL 60154
708-531-9600

National Association of Emergency
Medical Technicians

102 West Leake Street
Clinton, MS 39056
601-924-7747

Nuclear Medicine Technology
Certification Board
2970 Clairmont Road, Suite 610,
Atlanta, GA 30329-1634
404-315-1739

NURSING

American Association of Nurse
Anesthetists
222 South Prospect Avenue
Park Ridge, IL 60068-4001
708-692-7050

American Association of
Occupational Health Nurses
50 Lenox Pointe
Atlanta, GA 30324
404-262-1162
800-241-8014

American Hospital Association
1 North Franklin
Chicago, IL 60606
312-422-3000

American Nurses Association
600 Maryland Avenue SW
Suite 100 W
Washington, DC 20024-2571
202-651-7000

National Association for Home Care
519 C Street NE
Washington, DC 20002
202-547-7424
(send SASE for general information)

National Association for Practical
Nurse Education and Service
1400 Spring Street, Suite 310
Silver Spring, MD 20910
301-588-2491

National Association of Pediatric
Nurse Associates and Practitioners
1101 Kings Highway N, Suite 206
Cherry Hill, NJ 08034-1921
609-667-1773

National Federation of Licensed
Practical Nurses
1418 Aversboro Road
Garner, NC 27529-4547
919-779-0046

National League for Nursing
Communications Department
350 Hudson Street
New York, NY 10014
212-989-9393

National Rehabilitation Association
633 South Washington Street
Alexandria, VA 22314
703-836-0850

RN
Medical Economics Publishing
5 Paragon Drive
Montvale, NJ 07645-1742
201-358-7200

PHYSICAL HEALTH

Accreditation Council for Graduate
Medical Education
515 North State Street, Suite 2000
Chicago, IL 60610
312-464-4920

American Association of Colleges of
Podiatric Medicine
1350 Piccard Drive, Suite 322
Rockville, MD 20850
301-990-7400

American Association for Respiratory
Care
11030 Ables Lane
Dallas, TX 75229-4593
214-243-2272

American Board of Preventive
Medicine
9950 West Lawrence Avenue
Suite 106
Schiller Park, IL 60176
847-671-1750

American Medical Association
515 North State Street
Chicago, IL 60610
312-464-5000

American Occupational Therapy
Association
4720 Montgomery Lane
P.O. Box 31220
Bethesda, MD 20824-1220
301-652-2682

American Physical Therapy
Association
1111 North Fairfax Street

Alexandria, VA 22314
703-684-2782
800-999-2782

American Podiatric Medical
Association
9312 Old Georgetown Road
Bethesda, MD 20814-1621
301-571-9200

American Society of Radiology
Technologists
15000 Central Avenue SE
Albuquerque, NM 87123-4605
505-298-4500

Society of Diagnostic Medical
Sonographers
12770 Coit Road, Suite 508
Dallas, TX 75251
214-239-7367

DENTISTRY

American Association of Dental
Assistants
203 North LaSalle Street, Suite 1320
Chicago, IL 60601-1225
312-541-1550

American Association of Dental
Schools
1625 Massachusetts Avenue NW
Washington, DC 20036
202-667-9433

American Association of
Orthodontists
401 North Lindbergh Blvd.
Saint Louis, MO 63141-7816
314-993-1700

American Dental Association
211 East Chicago Avenue
Chicago IL 60611
312-440-2500
(for Commission on Dental
Accreditation, direct correspondence
to Suite 3400; for SELECT Program,
direct correspondence to
Department of Career Guidance,
Suite 1804)

American Dental Hygienists
Association
Division of Professional
Development
444 North Michigan Avenue
Suite 3400
Chicago, IL 60611
312-440-8900

National Association of Dental
Laboratories
555 East Braddock Road
Alexandria, VA 22305
703-683-5263

National Board for Certification in
Dental Technology
555 East Braddock Road
Alexandria, VA 22305
703-683-5263

MENTAL HEALTH

American Association for Counseling
and Development
5999 Stevenson Avenue
Alexandria, VA 22304
703-823-9800

American Association for Marriage
and Family Therapy

1133 15th Street NW, Suite 300
Washington, DC 20005
202-452-0109

American Association on Mental
Retardation
444 North Capitol Street, NW
Suite 846
Washington, DC 20001-1512
202-387-1968
800-424-3688

American Counseling Association
5999 Stevenson Avenue
Alexandria, VA 22304-3300
703-823-9800

American Psychiatric Association
1400 K Street NW
Washington, DC 20005
202-682-6000

American Psychological Association
750 First Street NE
Washington, DC 20002
202-336-5500

National Board for Certified
Counselors
3 Terrace Way, Suite D
Greensboro, NC 27403-3660
910-547-0607

The Technologies

BIOTECHNOLOGY AND ENVIRONMENTAL TECHNOLOGY

Air and Waste Management
Association
1 Gateway Center, 3rd Floor
Pittsburgh, PA 15222
412-232-3444

American Chemical Society
1155 16th Street NW
Washington, DC 20036
202-872-4600
800-227-5558

American Institute of Biological
Sciences
1444 Eye Street NW, Suite 200

Washington, DC 20005
202-628-1500

American Institute of Chemists
501 Wythe Street
Alexandria, VA 22314-1917
703-836-2090

American Institute of Physics
1 Physics Ellipse
College Park, MD 20740-3843
301-209-3100

American Society for Biochemistry
and Molecular Biology
9650 Rockville Pike
Bethesda, MD 20814-3996
301-530-7145

American Society for Microbiology
1325 Massachusetts Avenue NW
Washington, DC 20005
202-737-3600

American Society of Biological
Chemists
9650 Rockville Pike
Bethesda, MD 20814-3996
301-530-7145

American Zoo and Aquarium
Association (AZA)
Office of Membership Service
Oglebay Park
Route 88
Wheeling, WV 26003
304-242-2160

Association of American
Geographers
1710 16th Street NW
Washington, DC 20009-3198
202-234-1450

Botanical Society of America
1735 Neil Avenue
Columbus, OH 43210
614-292-3519

Center for American Archeology
P.O. Box 366
Kampsville, IL 62053
618-653-4316

Department of Energy Headquarters
Operations Division
1000 Independence Avenue SW
Room 4E-090
Washington, DC 20585

202-586-4333
(hotline for job vacancies, updated
every Friday)

Environmental Protection Agency
Recruitment Center
401 Main Street SW, Room 3634
Washington, DC 20460
202-260-2090/3308

Federation of American Societies for
Experimental Biology
9650 Rockville Pike
Bethesda, MD 20814
301-530-7000

Genetics Society of America
9650 Rockville Pike
Bethesda, MD 20814-3998
301-571-1825

Geological Society of America
P.O. Box 9140
3300 Penrose Place
Boulder, CO 80301
303-447-2020

National Accrediting Agency for
Clinical Laboratory Sciences
8410 West Bryn Mawr Avenue
Suite 670
Chicago, IL 60631
312-714-8880

National Solid Wastes Management
Association
4301 Connecticut Avenue NW
Suite 300
Washington, DC 20008
202-244-4700

Natural Resource Conservation
Service
Personnel Division
P.O. Box 2890
Washington, DC 20013
202-720-4264

ENGINEERING

American Association of Engineering
Societies
1111 19th Street NW, Suite 608
Washington, DC 20036
202-296-2237

American Chemical Society
1155 16th Street NW
Washington, DC 20036
800-227-5558
202-872-4600

American Institute of Chemical
Engineers
345 East 47th Street
New York, NY 10017
212-705-7338
800-242-4363

American Society for Engineering
Education
1818 N Street NW, Suite 600
Washington, DC 20036
202-331-3500

American Society of Civil Engineers
1801 Alexander Bell Drive
Reston, VA 20191-4400
800-548-ASCE

American Society of Mechanical
Engineers (ASME)

345 East 47th Street
New York, NY 10017
212-705-7722

Institute of Electrical and Electronics
Engineers
345 East 47th Street
New York, NY 10017
212-705-7900

Institute of Industrial Engineers
25 Technology Park
Atlanta, GA 30092-0460
770-449-0460

Society of Manufacturing Engineers
(SME)
1 SME Drive
P.O. Box 930
Dearborn, MI 48121
313-271-1500

INFORMATION
TECHNOLOGY

Access
1900 West 47th Place, Suite 215
Shawnee Mission, Kansas 66205
800-362-0681
(initial six-month nonmember listing,
$15; each additional three months,
$15; initial six-month listing for
members of the Data Processing
Management Association, $10)

AIIM Job Bank Bulletin
Association for Information and
Image Management
1100 Wayne Avenue, Suite 1100
Silver Springs, MD 20910
301-587-8202

(four-month subscription: nonmember, $100; member, $25; issued semimonthly)

ASIS Jobline
American Society for Information Science
8720 Georgia Avenue, Suite 501
Silver Spring, MD 20910-3602
301-495-0900
(free; monthly)

Association for Computing Machinery
1515 Broadway
New York, NY 10036
212-869-7440

Association for Systems Management
1433 West Bagley Road
P.O. Box 38370
Cleveland, OH 44138
216-243-6900

Computer
IEEE Computer Society
1730 Massachusetts Avenue NW
Washington, DC 20036
202-371-0101
(available to members only)

ComputerWorld
500 Old Connecticut Path
Framingham, MA 01701-9171
508-879-0700
800-343-6474
(annual subscription: U.S., $39.95; Canada, $110; issued weekly)

ComputerWorld Campus Edition
500 Old Connecticut Path

Framingham, MA 01701-9171
508-879-0700
(annual subscriptions, $5; free to students; published each October)

CU Career Connection
University of Colorado
Campus Box 133
Boulder, CO 80309-0133
303-492-4727
(two-month fee for passcode to the job hotline, $30)

Data Processing Management Association
505 Busse Highway
Park Ridge, IL 60068
708-825-8124

High Technology Careers Magazine
4701 Patrick Henry Drive, Suite 1901
Santa Clara, CA 95054
408-970-8800
(six issues per year, $29)

Institute for Certification of Computing Professionals
2200 East Devon Avenue, Suite 247
Des Plaines, IL 60018
708-299-4227

Quality Assurance Institute
7575 Philips Boulevard, Suite 350
Orlando, FL 32819
407-363-1111

Semiconductor Equipment and Materials International
805 East Middlefield Road
Mountainview, CA 94043
415-964-5111

Technical Employment News
P.O. Box 1285
Cedar Park, TX 78613
(weekly subscriptions, $55; annual

subscription $88, U.S. and Canada)
512-250-9023
800-678-9724

Business and Professional Services

FINANCIAL SERVICES

BANKING

American Bankers Association
1120 Connecticut Avenue NW
Washington, DC 20036
202-663-5000

American Institute of Banking
1213 Bakers Way
Manhattan, KS 66502
913-537-4750

Association of Master of Business
Administration Executives
AMBA Center
South Summit Place
Branford, CT 06405
203-315-5221

Banking Federation of the European
Economic Community (BFEC)
Federation Bancaire de la
Communaute Europeenne (FBCE)
c/o Umberto Burani,
10, rue Montoyer, B-1040
Brussels, Belgium
32-2-5083711 (telephone)
32-2-5112328 (fax)

Banking Law Institute (BLI)
22 West 21st Street
New York, NY 10010

212-645-7880
800-332-1105
212-675-4883 (fax)

BANKPAC
(formerly: Bankers Political Action
Committee; Banking Profession
Political Action Committee)
c/o Meg Bonitt,
American Bankers Association
1120 Connecticut Avenue NW
Washington, DC 20036
202-663-5115/5076
202-663-7544 (fax)

Electronic Banking Economics
Society (EBES)
P.O. Box 2331
New York, NY 10036
203-295-9788

European Community Banking
Federation (ECBF)
Federation Bancaire de l'Union
Europeenne (FBCE)
10, rue Montoyer, B-1040
Brussels, Belgium
32-2-5083711 (telephone)
32-2-5112328 (fax)

Savings and Community Bankers of
America
Educational Services
Center for Financial Studies

900 19th Street NW, Suite 400
Washington, DC 20006
202-857-3100

U.S. Council on International
Banking (USCIB)
1 World Trade Center, Suite 1963
New York, NY 10048
212-466-3352
212-432-0544 (fax)

Women in Banking and Finance
55 Bourne Vale
Bromley, Kent BR2 7NW, England
44-181-4623276 (telephone)

Women's World Banking—USA
8 West 40th Street
New York, NY 10018
212-768-8513
212-768-8519 (fax)

SECURITIES

Association of Securities and
Exchange Commission Alumni
(ASECA)
West Tower, Suite 812
1100 New York Avenue NW
Washington, DC 20005
202-408-7600
202-408-7614 (fax)

International Securities Market
Association—England
7 Limeharbour
London E14 9NQ, England
44-171-538-5656 (telephone)
44-171-538-4902 (fax)

National Association of Securities
Dealers (NASD)
1735 K Street NW
Washington, DC 20006-1506
202-728-8000
202-293-6260 (fax)

National Association of Securities
Professionals (NASP)
700 13th Street NW, Suite 950
Washington, DC 20005
202-434-4535
202-434-8916 (fax)

North American Securities
Administrators Association (NASAA)
1 Massachusetts Avenue NW
Suite 310
Washington, DC 20001
202-737-0900
202-783-3571 (fax)

Securities and Futures Authority
Cottons Centre, Cottons Lane
London SE1 2QB, England
44-171-378-9000 (telephone)
44-171-403-7569 (fax)

Securities Industry Association (SIA)
120 Broadway
New York, NY 10271
212-608-1500
212-608-1604 (fax)

Securities Transfer Association
(STA)
55 Exchange Place
New York, NY 10260-0001
212-748-8000

Western Pennsylvania Securities
Industry Agency
1 Oxford Centre, 40th Floor
Pittsburgh, PA 15219
412-731-7185

ACCOUNTING

Academy of Accounting Historians
(AAH)
University of Arkansas
Department of Accounting
Fayetteville, AR 72701
501-575-6125
501-575-7687 (fax)

Accounting Aid Society (AASD)
719 Griswold, Suite 2026
Detroit, MI 48226
313-961-1840
313-961-6257 (fax)
itpass@igc.apc.org (E-mail)

Affiliation of Independent
Accountants
9200 South Dadeland Boulevard,
Suite 510
Miami, FL 33156
305-670-0580
305-670-3818 (fax)

American Accounting Association
5717 Bessie Drive
Sarasota, FL 34223
941-921-7747

American Institute of Certified
Public Accountants (AICPA)
1211 Avenue of the Americas
New York, NY 10036-8775
212-596-6200

800-862-4272
212-596-6213 (fax)

American Society of Tax
Professionals
P.O. Box 1024
Sioux Falls, SD 57101
605-335-1185

American Society of Women
Accountants
1255 Lynnfield Road, Suite 257
Memphis, TN 38119
901-680-0470

American Women's Society of
Certified Public Accountants
401 North Michigan Avenue
Suite 2200
Chicago, IL 60611
312-644-6610

Associated Accounting Firms
International (AAFI)
(formerly: Association of Regional
CPA Firms)
1000 Connecticut Avenue
Suite 1006
Washington, DC 20036
202-463-7900
202-296-0741 (fax)

Associated Regional Accounting
Firms (ARAF)
3700 Crestwood Parkway, Suite 350
Duluth, GA 30136
770-279-4560
770-279-4566 (fax)

Association for Accounting
Administration (AAA)

136 South Keowee Street
Dayton, OH 45402
513-222-0030
513-222-5794 (fax)

Association of Accounting
Technicians (AAT)
154 Clerkenwell Road
London EC1R 5AD, England
44-171-8378600/8146999
(telephone)
44-171-8376970 (fax)
aatuk@pipex.com (E-mail)

Association of Government
Accountants
2200 Mount Vernon Avenue
Alexandria, VA 22301
703-684-6931

EDP Auditors Association
3701 Algonquin Road, Suite 1010
Rolling Meadows, IL 60008
708-253-1545

European Accounting Association
(EAA)
European Institute for Advanced
Studies in Management
13 Rue d'Egmont B-1050
Brussels, Belgium
32-2-5119116
32-2-5121929 (fax)
vandyck@ciasm.be (E-mail)

Foundation for Accounting
Education (FAE)
530 Fifth Avenue, 5th Floor
New York, NY 10036
212-719-8300
800-537-3635

Governmental Accounting Standards
Board (GASB)
401 Merrit 7
P.O. Box 5116
Norwalk, CT 06856-5116
203-847-0700
203-849-9714 (fax)

Information Systems Audit and
Control Association
3701 Algonquin Road, Suite 1010
Rolling Meadows, IL 60008
708-253-1545

Institute of Certified Management
Accountants (ICMA)
10 Paragon Drive
Montvale, NJ 07645
201-573-9000
800-638-4427
201-573-8438 (fax)

Institute of Internal Auditors
249 Maitland Avenue
Altamonte Springs, FL 32701-4201
407-830-7600

Institute of Management
Accountants
10 Paragon Drive
Montvale, NJ 07645
201-573-9000
201-573-9000 (fax)

InterAmerican Accounting
Association (IAA)
(formerly: InterAmerican Accounting
Conference)
275 Fountainebleau Boulevard
Suite 245

Miami, FL 33172
305-225-1991
305-225-2011 (fax)

National Association of State Boards
of Accountancy
545 Fifth Avenue
New York, NY 10168-0002
212-490-3868

National Society for Public
Accountants
1010 North Fairfax Street
Alexandria, VA 22314
703-549-6400

INSURANCE

ACFE Job Bank
Association of Certified Fraud
Examiners
716 West Avenue
Austin, TX 78701
512-478-9070
800-245-3321
(membership fee $75; send two
copies of résumé and cover letter
indicating salary requirements and
where you are willing to relocate)

Actual Training Program Directory
Society of Actuaries
475 North Martingale Road, Suite 800
Schaumburg, IL 60173-2226
708-706-3500
(free; published each January)

American Academy of Actuaries
1100 17th Street NW, 7th Floor
Washington, DC 20036
202-223-8196

American Agents & Brokers
330 North 4th Street
St. Louis, MO 63012
314-421-5445

Best's Insurance Reports,
Property/Casuality Edition
A.M. Best Company
Ambest Road
Oldwick, NJ 08858-9988
908-439-2200
(annual fee $70)

Independent Insurance Agents of
America
127 South Peyton
Alexandria, VA 22314
703-683-4422
800-962-7950 (fax)

Insurance Field Directories
Insurance Field Company
P.O. Box 948
Northbrook, IL 60065
708-498-4010
($55; published each September)

Insurance Information Institute
110 William Street
New York, NY 10038
212-669-9200

Insurance Institute of America
720 Providence Road
Malvern, PA 19355
610-644-2100

Insurance Phone Book and
Directory
US Directory Service
121 Chanlon Road

New Providence, New Jersey
07074
908-464-6800
($67.95, plus $4.75 shipping)

Life Insurance Marketing and
Research Association
P.O. Box 208
Hartford, CT 16141-0208
203-777-7000

National Association of Life
Underwriters
1922 F Street NW
Washington, DC 20006
202-332-6000

National Association of Professional
Insurance Agents
400 North Washington Street
Alexandria, VA 22314
703-836-9340

Professional Insurance Agents
400 North Washington Street
Alexandria, VA 22314
703-836-9340

Society of Actuaries
475 North Martingale Road
Suite 800
Schaumburg, IL 60173-2226
708-706-3500

FINANCIAL MANAGEMENT

American Education Finance
Association (AEFA)
5249 Cape Leyte Drive
Sarasota, FL 34242
941-349-7580

941-349-7580 (fax)
gbabigianc@aol.com (E-mail)

American Finance Association
(AFA)
Stern, 44 West 4th Street
Suite 9-190
New York, NY 10012
212-998-0370

Association of Commercial Finance
Attorneys (ACFA)
1 Corporate Center, 18th Floor
MSN 712
Hartford, CT 06103
203-520-7094
203-240-5077 (fax)

Commercial Finance Association
(CFA)
225 West 34th Street
New York, NY 10122
212-594-3490
212-564-6053

Financial Analysts Federation
P.O. Box 3726
Charlottesville, VA 22903
804-977-8977

Financial Management Association
International
College of Business
Administration
University of South Florida
Tampa, FL 33620-5500

Financial Management Service
Department of the Treasury
401 14th Street SW

Washington, DC 20227
202-874-6750

Financial Managers Society
8 South Michigan Avenue, Suite 500
Chicago, IL 60603
312-578-1300

Government Finance Officers
Association of United States and
Canada
180 North Michigan Avenue
Suite 800
Chicago, IL 60601
312-977-9700
312-977-4806 (fax)

Institute of Certified Financial
Planners
3801 East Florida Avenue, Suite 708
Denver, CO 80210
303-751-7600
303-759-0749 (fax)

Institute of Chartered Financial
Analysts
P.O. Box 3668
Charlottesville, VA 22903
804-977-6600

Institute of International Finance
(IIF)
2000 Pennsylvania Avenue NW
Suite 8500
Washington, DC 20006-1812
202-857-3600
202-775-1430 (fax)

International Association for
Financial Planning
2 Concourse Parkway, Suite 800

Atlanta, GA 30328
404-395-1605

National Association of County
Treasurers and Finance Officers
c/o National Association of Counties
440 First Street NW, 8th Floor
Washington, DC 20001
202-393-6226

National Society for Real Estate
Finance (NSREF)
2300 M Street NW, Suite 800
Washington, DC 20037
202-973-2801

New York State Consumer Finance
Association (NYSCFA)
90 South Swan Street
Albany, NY 12210
518-449-7514
518-426-0566 (fax)

New York State Government
Finance Officers Association
119 Washington Avenue
Albany, NY 12210-2204
518-465-1512
518-434-4640 (fax)

North American Economics and
Finance Association (NAEFA)
Department of Finance
Syracuse University
Syracuse, NY 13244-2130
315-443-2963
315-443-5389 (fax)

Securities Industry Association
120 Broadway

New York, NY 10271
212-608-1500

HUMAN RESOURCES

American Society for Training and
Development
1640 King Street, Box 1443
Alexandria, VA 22313
703-683-8100

Employment Management
Association
4101 Lake Boone Trail, Suite 201
Raleigh, NC 27607
919-787-6010

HR Magazine
606 North Washington Street
Alexandria, VA 22314
703-548-3440

Institute of Management Consultants
521 Fifth Avenue, 35th Floor
New York, NY 10175
212-697-8262

International Personnel
Management Association
1617 Duke Street
Alexandria, VA 22314
703-549-7100

National Training Laboratory
1240 North Pitt Street
Alexandria, VA 22314
703-548-1500

Society for Human Resource
Management

606 North Washington Street
Alexandria, VA 22314
703-548-3440

LAW

ALA Management Connections
Association of Legal Administrators
175 E. Hawthorn Parkway
Suite 325
Vernon Hills, IL 60061-1428
708-816-1212
(free; updated weekly)

American Association for Paralegal
Education
P.O. Box 40244
Overland Park, KS 66204
913-381-4458

American Bar Association
Information Services
750 North Lake Shore Drive
Chicago, IL 60611
312-988-5000
800-621-6159

CU Career Connection
University of Colorado
Campus Box 133
Boulder, CO 80309-0133
303-492-4727
(two-month fee for passcode to the
job hotline, $30)

Internships for College Students
Interested in Law, Medicine, and
Politics
Graduate Group
86 Norwood Road

West Hartford, CT 06117
203-236-5570/203-232-3100
($27.50, published annually)

National Association for Law
Placement
1666 Connecticut Avenue
Suite 328
Washington, DC 20009
202-667-1666

National Association of Legal
Assistants
1516 South Boston Avenue
Suite 200
Tulsa, OK 74119
918-587-6828

National Federation of Paralegal
Associations
P.O. Box 33108
Kansas City, MO 64114
816-941-4000

National Paralegal Association
Box 406
Solebury, PA 18963
215-297-8333

NCRA Employment Referral
Service
National Court Reporters Association
8224 Old Courthouse Road
Vienna, VA 22182
703-556-6272
(six-month registration:
nonmembers, $20; free to
members)

Paralegal Placement Network Inc.
P.O. Box 406

Solebury, PA 18963
215-297-8333
(regular fee, $10.00; Nat. Paralegal
Association members, $15)

Resume Bank
American Corporate Counsel
Association
1225 Connecticut Avenue NW
Suite 302
Washington, DC 20036
202-296-4522
(six-month registration:
nonmembers, $65; members,
$25; complete job-matching
application, and five copies of
résumé free)

MEDIA/COMMUNICATIONS/ PUBLIC RELATIONS

American Society for Health Care
Marketing and Public Relations
American Hospital Association
1 North Franklin
Chicago, IL 60606
312-422-3737

American Society of Journalists and
Authors
1501 Broadway, Suite 302
New York, NY 10036
212-997-0947

Council of Sales Promotion Agencies
750 Summer Street
Stamford, CT 06901
203-325-3911

Dow Jones Newspaper Fund
P.O. Box 300

Princeton, NJ 08543-0300
609-452-2820

Editorial Freelancers Association
71 West 23rd Street, Suite 1504
New York, NY 10010
212-929-5400

Institute for Public Relations
Research and Education (IPRRE)
University of Florida
P.O. Box 118400
Gainesville, FL 32611-8400
904-392-0280

International Advertising Association
521 Fifth Avenue, Suite 1807
New York, NY 10175
212-557-1133

Investigative Reporters & Editors
University of Missouri
26A Walter Williams Hall
Columbia, MO 65211
314-882-2042

League of Advertising Agencies
Directory
2 South End Avenue #4C
New York, NY 10280
212-945-4314

National School Public Relations
Association (NSPRA)
1501 Lee Highway, Suite 201
Arlington, VA 22209
703-528-5840

PR Newswire Job Bank
865 South Figueroa, Suite 2310
Los Angeles, CA 90017

213-626-5500
800-321-8169
(send résumé and cover letter)

P.R. Reporter
P.O. Box 6000
Exeter, NH 03833

Promotion Marketing Association of
America, Inc.
Executive Headquarters
257 Park Avenue South
11th Floor
New York, NY 10001
212-420-1100

Public Relations Consultants
Directory
American Business Directories Inc.
5711 East 86th Circle
Omaha, NE 68127
402-331-7169

Public Relations Society of
America
33 Irving Place, 3rd Floor
New York, NY 10003
212-995-2230

Public Relations Student Society of
America (PRSSA)
33 Irving Place, 3rd Floor
New York, NY 10003
212-460-1474

SMPS Employment Referral Society
for Marketing Professional Services
99 Canal Plaza, Suite 250
Alexandria, VA 22314
703-549-6117
800-292-7677

(nonmembers, $100; members, $50;
five copies résumé and SMPS
application—on file for three
months)

Society for Technical
Communication
901 North Stuart Street, Suite 904
Arlington, VA 22203
703-522-4114

Writers Guild of America
555 West 57th Street
New York, NY 10019
212-767-7800

SALES AND MARKETING

Adventure Travel Society
6551 South Revere Parkway
Suite 160
Englewood, CO 80111
303-649-9016
303-649-9017 (fax)

Air Transport Association of
America
1301 Pennsylvania Avenue NW
Suite 1100
Washington, DC 20004-7017
202-626-4000

Airline Employees Association, Intl.
Job Opportunity Program
5600 South Central Avenue
Chicago, IL 60638-3797

American Advertising Federation
Education Services Department
1101 Vermont Avenue NW
Suite 500

Washington, DC 20005
202-898-0089

American Marketing Association
250 South Wacker Drive
Suite 200
Chicago, IL 60606-5819
312-648-0536

American Society of Travel Agents
(ASTA)
1101 King Street, Suite 200
Alexandria, VA 22314
703-739-2782
703-684-8319 (fax)

American Travel Inns (ATI)
(formerly: American Travel
Association)
36 South State Street, Suite 1200
Salt Lake City, UT 84111-1416
801-521-0732
801-521-0732 (fax)

Association of Flight Attendants
1625 Massachusetts Avenue NW
Washington, DC 20036
202-328-5400

Association of Retail Travel Agents
(ARTA)
845 Sir Thomas Court, Suite 3
Harrisburg, PA 17109
717-545-9548
800-969-6069
717-545-9613 (fax)

The Convention Liaison Council
1575 Eye Street NW, Suite 1190
Washington, DC 20005
202-626-2764

Cruise Lines International
Association
500 Fifth Avenue, Suite 1407
New York, NY 10110
212-921-0066

Direct Marketing Association
1120 Avenue of the Americas
New York, NY 10036-6700
212-768-7277

Freighter Travel Club of America
3524 Harts Lake Road
Roy, WA 98580
360-458-4178

Future Aviation Professionals of
America
4959 Massachusetts Boulevard
Atlanta, GA 30337
404-997-8097
800-JET-JOBS

Greater Independent Association
of National Travel Services
(GIANTS)
2 Park Avenue, Suite 2205
New York, NY 10016
212-545-7460
800-442-6871
212-545-7428 (fax)

Independent Travel Agencies of
America Association (ITAA)
5353 North Federal Highway
Suite 300
Fort Lauderdale, FL 33308
305-772-4660
800-950-5440
305-772-5797 (fax)

Institute of Certified Travel Agents
(ICTA)
148 Linden Street
P.O. Box 812059
Wellesley, MA 02181-0012
617-237-0280
800-542-4282
617-237-3860 (fax)

International Association for Air
Travel Couriers
P.O. Box 1349
Lake Worth, FL 33460
407-582-8320
407-582-1581 (fax)

International Association of Travel
Exhibitors (IATE)
P.O. Box 2309
Gulf Shores, AL 36547
205-948-6690
205-948-6690 (fax)

International Association of Travel
Journalists (IATJ)
P.O. Box D
Hurleyville, NY 12747
914-434-1529

International Federation of Women's
Travel Organizations (IFWTO)
13901 North 73rd Street, #210B
Scottsdale, AZ 85260-3125
602-596-6640
602-596-6638 (fax)

Meeting Planners International
Informant Building, Suite 5018
1950 Stemmons Freeway
Dallas, TX 75207
214-712-7700

Retail Advertising and Marketing
Association
500 North Michigan Avenue
Suite 600
Chicago, IL 60611
312-251-7262

Sales and Marketing Executives
International
977 Statler Office Tower
Cleveland, OH 44115
216-771-6650

Sales and Marketing Management
355 Park Avenue South
New York, NY 10010
212-592-6300

Travel Industry Association of
America
1100 New York Avenue NW
Suite 450
Washington, DC 20005-3934
202-408-8422

U.S. Travel Data Center
(affiliate of the Travel Industry
Association of America)
2 Lafayette Center
1100 New York Avenue NW
Suite 450
Washington, DC 20005
202-408-1832

Yours In Travel Personnel Agency
12 West 37th Street
New York, NY 10018
212-697-7855

FOOD SERVICE

Alaska Culinary Association
P.O. Box 140396
Anchorage, AK 99514
907-265-7116

American Culinary Federation
10 San Bartola Road
P.O. Box 3466
St. Augustine, FL 32085-3466
904-824-4468

Berks Lehigh Chef's Association
2012 Redwood Avenue
Wyoming, PA 19610
610-678-1217

National Food Broker Association
2100 Reston Parkway, Suite 400
Reston, VA 22091
703-758-7790

National Restaurant Association
1200 17th Street NW
Washington, DC 20036
202-331-5900

SUPPORT SERVICES

American Society of Corporate
Secretaries
521 Fifth Avenue
New York, NY 10175-0003
212-681-2000

California Federation of Legal
Secretaries
2250 East 73rd Street, Suite 550
Tulsa, OK 74136
918-493-3540

National Association of Executive
Secretaries
900 S. Washington Street, No. G-13

Falls Church, VA 22046
703-237-8616

Public Service

SOCIAL SERVICES

ACCION International
120 Beacon Street
Somerville, MA 02143
617-492-4930

American Counseling Association
5999 Stevenson Avenue
Alexandria, VA 22304
703-823-9800
800-347-6647

American Friends Service
Committee
1501 Cherry Street
Philadelphia, PA 19102
215-241-7000

American School Counselor
Association
801 North Fairfax Street, Suite 301
Alexandria, VA 22314
703-683-2722

American Vocational Association
1410 King Street
Alexandria, VA 22314
703-683-3111
800-892-2274

Child Welfare League of America
440 First Street NW, Suite 310

Washington, DC 20001
201-638-2952

Council for Standards in Human
Service Education
Northern Essex Community College
Haverhill, MA 01830
508-374-5889

Council on Social Work Education
1600 Duke Street, Suite 300
Alexandria, VA 22314-3421
703-683-8080
(send $10 for Directory of Accredited
BSW and MSW Programs)

Educators for Social Responsibility
23 Garden Street
Cambridge, MA 02138
617-492-1764

Human Service Council
3191 Maguire Boulevard, Suite 150
Orlando, FL 32803
407-897-6465

National Association of Social Workers
750 First Street NE, Suite 700
Washington, DC 20002-4241
202-408-8600

National Center for Charitable Statistics
1828 L Street NW, Suite 1200B

Washington, DC 20036
202-223-8100

National Civic League
1445 Market Street, Suite 300
Denver, CO 80202-1728
303-571-4343

National Exchange Club Foundation
for the Prevention of Child Abuse
3050 Central Avenue
Toledo, OH 43606
419-535-3232
800-760-3413

National Network for Social Work
Managers
1316 New Hampshire Avenue NW
Suite 602
Washington, DC 20036
202-785-2814

National Organization for Human
Service Education
Fitchburg State College, Box 6257
160 Pearl Street
Fitchburg, MA 01420
508-345-2151

Save the Children Federation
54 Wilton Road
Westport, CT 06880
203-221-4000

Social Service Association
6 Station Plaza
Ridgewood, NJ 07450
201-444-2980

EDUCATION

Academy for Educational
Development (AED)

1875 Connecticut Avenue NW
Washington, DC 20009
202-884-8000
202-884-8400 (fax)
admind@aed.org (E-mail)

American Association of School
Administrators
1801 N Moore Street
Arlington, VA 22209-9988
703-528-0700

American Association of School
Librarians
50 E. Huron Street
Chicago, IL 60611
312-944-6780

American Association of University
Administrators
1012 14th Street NW, Suite 500
Washington, DC 20005
202-737-5900

American Association of University
Professors
1012 14th Street NW, Suite 500
Washington, DC 20005
202-737-5900

American Educational Studies
Association (AESA)
University of Cincinnati
Graduate Studies and Research
Cincinnati, OH 45221
513-556-2256

American Federation of Teachers
555 New Jersey Avenue NW
Washington, DC 20001
202-879-4400

American Library Association
50 East Huron Street
Chicago, IL 60611
312-944-6780

American Society for Training and
Development
1640 King Street
Alexandria, VA 22313
703-683-8100

Association for Community Based
Education (ACBE)
1805 Florida Avenue NW
Washington, DC 20009
202-462-6333
202-232-8044

Association for Educational
Communications and Technology
(AECT)
1025 Vermont Avenue NW, Suite 820
Washington, DC 20005
202-347-7834
202-347-7839 (fax)

Center for Adult Learning and
Educational Credentials (CALEC)
1 Dupont Circle NW
Washington, DC 20036
202-939-9475
202-775-8574 (fax)

College and University Personnel
Association
1233 20th Street NW, Suite 301
Washington, DC 20036-1250
202-429-0311

Council on International
Educational Exchange (CIEE)

205 East 42nd Street
New York, NY 10017
212-661-1414
212-972-3231 (fax)

Earthwatch (formerly: Educational
Expeditions International)
680 Mount Auburn Street, Box 403
Watertown, MA 02272
617-926-8200
800-776-0188
617-926-8532 (fax)
info@earthwatch.org (E-mail)

Educational Research Service (ERS)
2000 Clarendon Blvd.
Arlington, VA 22201
703-243-2100
703-243-1985 (fax)

Institute for Educational Leadership
(IEL)
1001 Connecticut Avenue NW
Suite 310
Washington, DC 20036
202-822-8405
202-872-4050 (fax)

High/Scope Educational Research
Foundation
600 North River Street
Ypsilanti, MI 48198-2898
313-485-2000
800-40-PRESS
313-485-0704 (fax)

Federal Librarians Round Table
American Library Association
Washington Office
1301 Pennsylvania Avenue NW
No. 403

Washington, DC 20004
202-608-8410

Independent Educational Services
(IES)
(formerly: Cooperative Bureau for
Teachers)
353 Nassau Street
Princeton, NJ 08540
609-921-6195
800-257-5102
609-921-0155 (fax)

Intercultural Development Research
Association (IDRA)
5835 Callaghan Road, Suite 350
San Antonio, TX 78228
210-684-8180
210-684-5389 (fax)

International Association for
Educational Assessment (IAEA)
P.O. Box 6665
Princeton, NJ 08541
609-921-9000
609-520-1093 (fax)

Madison Center for Educational
Affairs (MCEA)
455 15th Street NW, Suite 712
Washington, DC 20005
202-833-1801
202-467-0006 (fax)

National Association of Educational
Office Professionals (NAEOP)
P.O. Box 12619
Wichita, KS 67277
316-942-4822
316-942-7100 (fax)

National Association of Secondary
School Principals
1904 Association Drive

Reston, VA 22091
703-860-0200

National Association of Student
Personnel Administrators
1875 Connecticut Avenue NW
Suite 418
Washington, DC 20009
202-265-7500

National Council for Accreditation
of Teacher Education
2010 Massachusetts Avenue NW
Suite 500
Washington, DC 20036
202-466-7496

National Education Association
1201 16th Street NW
Washington, DC 20036
202-833-4000

National Council of Educational
Opportunity Associations (NCEOA)
1025 Vermont Avenue NW
Suite 1201
Washington, DC 20005
202-347-7430

National Council on the Evaluation
of Foreign Educational Credentials
c/o AACRAO
1 Dupont Circle NW, Suite 330
Washington, DC 20036
202-293-9161
202-872-8857
aacrao@umdd (E-mail)

National Rural Education
Association (NREA)
Colorado State University
230 Education Building
Fort Collins, CO 80523-1588
970-491-7022
970-491-1317 (fax)

Special Libraries Association
1700 18th Street NW
Washington, DC 20009-2508
202-234-4700
202-265-9317 (fax)

University Council for Educational
Administration (UCEA)
Pennsylvania State University
212 Rackley Bldg.
University Park, PA 16802-3200
814-863-7916/7917
814-863-7918 (fax)

STATE AND LOCAL GOVERNMENT

American Federation of State,
County, and Municipal Employees
1625 L Street NW
Washington, DC 20036
202-429-1000

American Planning Association
122 South Michigan Avenue
Suite 1600
Chicago, IL 60603
312-431-9100

Civil Service Employees Association
P.O. Box 7125
Capitol State
Albany, NY 12210
518-434-0191
800-342-4146

Council of State Governments
P.O. Box 11910
3560 Iron Works Pike
Lexington, KY 40578
606-244-8000

International City/County
Management Association
777 North Capitol Street NE
Suite 500
Washington, DC 20002
202-289-4262

International Association of Fire
Fighters
1750 New York Avenue NW
Washington, DC 20006
202-737-8484

National Association of Counties
(NACo)
440 First Street NW, 8th Floor
Washington, DC 20001
202-393-6226

National Association of Government
Communicators
669 South Washington Street
Alexandria, VA 22314
703-519-3902

National Planning Association
1424 16th Street NW
Suite 700
Washington, DC 20036
202-265-7685

New York State Professional
Firefighters Association
111 Washington Avenue
Suite 207
Albany, NY 12210
518-436-8827

State Services Organization (SSO)
444 North Capitol Street NW
Washington, DC 20001
202-624-5470

Index

ABOUT THE AUTHOR

MARTIN YATE is an internationally bestselling author and America's leading advocate for working professionals. His books include: *Knock 'Em Dead*; *Cover Letters That Knock 'Em Dead*; *Resumes That Knock 'Em Dead*; and *Beat the Odds*. His previous positions include National Director of Training for Dunhill Personnel System, Inc., and Director of Personnel for Bell Industries' Computer Memory Division.

MY TWO CENTS' WORTH

Comments, questions, or suggestions? Please complete this questionnaire and mail it to me:

Martin Yate
c/o The Ballantine Publishing Group
201 East 50th St.
New York, NY 10022

Hey Martin,
Here's how I used *CareerSmarts*.

1. Give me some additional information about the following issue.

_____

_____

2. Add a chapter on the following topic, since it would really be helpful to people like me.

_____

And, oh yeah, stick my name in the hat when you're done reading this. I deserve a shot at a free dinner for two at the restaurant of my choice as much as anyone else who fills this out.

Name: _____

Address: _____

_____

Daytime phone: _____

Evening phone: _____

Occupation: _____